Point Park College

Joseph Shuman
Journalism Collection

Given in Memory of:

Shinya Matsudaira
January 13, 1969~April 28, 1995

From:

The Matsudaira Family

Censorship in Ireland, 1939–1945

Censorship in Ireland, 1939-1945
NEUTRALITY, POLITICS AND SOCIETY

Donal Ó Drisceoil

CORK UNIVERSITY PRESS

When I paid my official call on the president, Dr Douglas Hyde, in the Phoenix Park, his secretary, Mr McDunphy, hissed in my ear, 'Don't mention the war!'

John Maffey, UK representative to Éire, 1939–1949,
Irish Times, 3 July 1962

. . . wars by definition are abnormal times. But they paint in primary colours the patterns of information dissemination and control that remain pastel-shaded in peacetime.

Michael Cockerell, Peter Hennessy and David Walker,
Sources Close to the Prime Minister
(London, 1984)

For my mother Josephine and late father Diarmuid
who began their life together in Emergency Ireland,
and for Orla and Kim

First published in 1996 by
Cork University Press
University College
Cork
Ireland

British Library Cataloguing in Publication Data
A CIP catalogue record for this book is available from
the British Library.

ISBN 1 85918 073 6 hardback
1 85918 074 4 paperback

Typeset by Tower Books of Ballincollig, Co. Cork
Printed by ColourBooks, Baldoyle, Co. Dublin

CONTENTS

ACKNOWLEDGEMENTS

I would like to acknowledge the assistance of a number of people who helped to make this work possible.

Firstly, thanks to Professor Dermot Keogh, who supervised the doctoral thesis on which the book is based, for his continuing support and encouragement. I am also grateful to Professor Joe Lee and all at the Department of History in UCC who have helped in various ways through the years.

Thanks are due to the staffs of the UCC Boole Library, the Cork City Library, the National Library of Ireland, Trinity College Library, the Archives Department, UCD and the National Archives, Dublin. I am particularly grateful to Peter Young, Victor Laing and the staff of the Military Archives in Cathal Brugha Barracks for their hospitality and co-operation during my many visits there, and to all at Cork University Press.

I am grateful to my family and friends for their support while this work was in progress, and particularly to Ethna MacManus, Carol Jones and Sharon Jones. Thanks also to Aengus Nolan for kindly sharing some of the fruits of his research in the USA with me, and to Finbarr O'Shea for his helpful comments.

Finally, I am especially indebted to my mother Josephine for her constant support and to Orla for her invaluable help at every stage.

Donal Ó Drisceoil
Cork, 1996

ILLUSTRATIONS

TERMS AND ABBREVIATIONS

Text

The Censorship	Where the term is used with an upper case 'C' it denotes the organisation which operated the emergency censorship as opposed to the system itself.
Ireland	For the sake of convenience, the constitutional term 'Ireland' (the English for Éire) is used to refer to the former Irish Free State and later Republic of Ireland. Where the need arises, terms such as 'the twenty-six counties', 'the South', etc. are used.
Dáil	The lower house of parliament
Gardaí	The Irish police
Minister	As well as its usual political usage, this term was also the official title of certain diplomatic representatives
Oireachtas	Parliament
Seanad	The upper house of parliament
Tánaiste	Deputy prime minister
Taoiseach	Prime minister

G2	Military Intelligence Files, Military Archives, Dublin
IRA	Irish Republican Army
ITGWU	Irish Transport and General Workers' Union
ITUC	Irish Trade Union Congress
LDF	Local Defence Force
LSF	Local Security Force
TD	Teachta Dála, a member of the Dáil

References

CAB	Cabinet Minutes, National Archives, Dublin
D/FA	Department of Foreign (formerly External) Affairs files, National Archives, Dublin
D/FA (Sec.)	Department of Foreign Affairs, Secretary's files, National Archives, Dublin
D/J	Department of Justice, wartime censorship files, National Archives, Dublin
D/T, S	Department of the Taoiseach, S files, National Archives, Dublin
MA	Military Archives, Dublin
NA	National Archives, Dublin
NAUSA	US National Archives, Washington DC
NLI	National Library of Ireland, Dublin
OCC	Office of the Controller of Censorship files, Military Archives, Dublin
OSS	Organisation of Strategic Services files, National Archives, Washington DC

INTRODUCTION

Britain's declaration of war on Germany on 3 September 1939 marked the beginning of what became the Second World War. In Ireland it marked the beginning of 'the Emergency'. For the next five and a half years the Irish authorities set about the task of preserving the state and keeping it out of the most bloody and widespread conflict in history. Ireland, declared a journalist who supported neutrality, 'has had more than enough history; it badly needs a rest'.[1] Amongst the measures adopted by de Valera and his Fianna Fáil government to preserve the state and its neutrality was a censorship that was more rigid and wide-ranging than that imposed in most other countries, particularly other neutrals. The explanation for its relative extremism lies partly in the particular nature of Irish wartime neutrality and partly in the nature of the Irish state, its society and political culture.

It has been persuasively argued that the state had been in a condition of permanent emergency from its foundation, against the background of civil war, in 1922.[2] The threat to the new state from the armed Republicans who refused to accept its legitimacy placed its first government, under William T. Cosgrave and Cumann na nGaedheal, on the defensive from the outset; its overriding concern was the protection of the new order against internal attack. This, allied to the adoption of the secretive British parliamentary and administrative models and the conservatism of the dominant Irish Catholic Church and rural bourgeoisie, helps to explain the emergence of a closed, introverted society 'with an even more closed system of government'.[3] Censorship became an important mechanism of control in this environment, a measure designed, in its various manifestations, to maintain the security of the state and protect the (narrowly defined) morals and culture of 'the nation'. This coincided with the growth of censorship on an international level in the interwar years. The First World War had established propaganda as a powerful political weapon, and its power in the 1920s and 1930s was increased by the utilisation of the developing mass media of film and radio. Governments feared the influence of fascist and communist propaganda on their mass electorates, while the growing predominance of Hollywood raised fears of cultural imperialism.[4]

One of the first legislative measures passed by the Irish Free State parliament was the 1923 Censorship of Films Act, which gave an official film censor the power to keep from the public films which he believed to be 'indecent, obscene or blasphemous' or 'would tend to inculcate principles contrary to public morality or would be otherwise subversive of public morality'.[5] Three years later the Wireless Telegraphy Act gave the government a monopoly over broadcasting and built-in censorship powers over the emerging popular medium of radio. In 1927 the IRA's assassination of the Vice-President of the Executive Council and Minister for Justice, Kevin O'Higgins, led to a reversion to civil-warlike emergency powers with the draconian Public Safety Act, which included a prohibition on the publication of any statement by or on behalf of 'an unlawful organisation'. In 1931 the Free State constitution was amended to make any such publication an infraction of basic law.[6]

'Obscene' publications were covered by the Customs Consolidation Act and the Obscene Publications Act, which had been inherited from the British, but during the 1920s Catholic pressure groups, together with exclusivist cultural nationalists, campaigned for increased protection against 'infidel and immoral publications'.[7] This pressure led, in 1929, to the passage of the Censorship of Publications Act, which empowered a Censorship Board to ban publications that, in its opinion, were 'in their general tendency indecent or obscene'.[8] The wide interpretation of this provision led to the banning of many of the major literary works of the twentieth century, including the books of a number of contemporary Irish writers, over the next three decades. Official censorship was backed up by unofficial censorship; writers and artists were harassed and stigmatised, while libraries and booksellers were pressurised into not stocking or removing from their shelves titles which had escaped the official net.[9]

The first decade of independence did not bode well for the development of a democratic political culture or a functioning civic culture in the new state. Political insecurity, and the conservative impulses of moral and cultural protectionism, led to a closed, overcentralised and authoritarian political system and a sense of cultural and intellectual isolation. The coming to power in 1932 of de Valera's Fianna Fáil, with its radical image and rhetoric, offered hope to some of an alteration to the status quo;[10] they were to be disappointed.

De Valera continued the tradition of closed government inherited from his predecessors[11] and also maintained their cultural censorship policy. He courted an initially hostile Catholic Church, further enshrining that Church's moral code in the law of the land. Having defeated the short-lived threat from the fascistoid Blueshirts in 1934, the leaders of the self-proclaimed 'slightly constitutional party' which had first entered the Dáil in 1927 could now 'pose as, and even become, constitutionalists, defenders of law, order and majority rule against a militaristic threat'.[12] That threat now came from the IRA, whose support de Valera had at first welcomed and to whom he made conciliatory gestures such as the release of Republican prisoners and the unbanning of the organisation with the repeal of the Public Safety Act (including its censorship provisions). These measures failed to have their desired effect, however, and de Valera was unsuccessful in his efforts to wean the IRA off the gun and carry them with him on his journey away from traditional Republicanism. The organisation was declared illegal again in 1936 and in June 1939, in reaction to the IRA's declaration of war against Britain, Fianna Fáil introduced the draconian Offences Against the State Act, with censorship powers similar to those of the old Public Safety Act.

The primary object of Fianna Fáil in power was the establishment of the sovereignty of the twenty-six county state; to this end it set about revising the 1921 Treaty out of existence. In 1932 the payment of land annuities to the British was withheld, initiating a six-year economic war between the two countries. Over the next four years the oath of allegiance and the office of the governer general were abolished and the British king was removed from the Free State constitution. The process culminated in the successful passage of de Valera's constitution in 1937[13] and the Anglo-Irish agreements on finance, trade and defence in the following year. The latter put an end to the economic war and, most importantly in terms of sovereignty, placed the 'Treaty ports' of Berehaven, Cobh and Lough Swilly under Irish control. Fianna Fáil had now succeeded, in de Valera's words, in establishing 'Irish sovereignty over the twenty-six-counties and the territorial seas'.[14] The outbreak of war in the following year was to provide the opportunity to demonstrate that sovereignty to the Irish people and the wider world.

For de Valera, and for the majority in the country, neutrality was the obvious policy for Ireland to pursue in the war for both pragmatic and symbolic reasons. In the latter regard, it was the 'means whereby the end of sovereignty might be freely expressed in the form of an independent foreign policy – a policy independent, above all, of British policy'.[15] From a pragmatic point of view, Ireland had no imperialist interests under threat, it made sense to want to avoid the horrors of war, and neutrality was the policy which divided the people least; domestic partisans came mainly in the form of those who still viewed 'England's difficulty' as 'Ireland's opportunity' and, on the other side, those who viewed Britain's war as their war also. Two decades had not yet passed since the war of independence and the civil war. Anti-British feeling was still strong and there was a real fear that if the Irish joined the war on the British side, it could provoke a German-backed IRA revolt, possibly leading to a second civil war; in this sense, as one commentator has put it, 'Neutrality came from fear of ourselves.'[16] In addition, an alliance with Britain, standing alone up to

1941, would have left the country extremely vulnerable to German air attacks of the type that devastated Belfast. An alliance with the Axis states would have had little support outside of a small group of extreme nationalists, and would have been 'strategically suicidal'.[17]

Hanspeter Neuhold has likened the task of a small country remaining neutral during war to 'the search by Ulysses for the thin line of survival between Scylla and Charybdis, since the success of neutrality depends to a high degree on factors beyond the neutral's control'.[18] Ireland was fortunate that the invasion and occupation of the state never became a strategic imperative for any of the belligerents. So long as Britain held out, Irish neutrality suited German purposes and the threat from the latter source abated once the conflict broadened and the focus shifted eastward from the second half of 1941. From 1942 'the rationale of neutrality as a security policy became less obvious'[19] as Ireland's strategic significance dwindled in the context of the broader world conflict.

The most serious danger in the first years of the war probably came from Britain, and in order that it would not feel compelled to seize its former ports (the danger of which first arose in the summer of 1940 and continued while Britain stood alone against an enemy which occupied most of western Europe), de Valera played a 'double game'.[20] This involved publicly maintaining the formality of neutrality while simultaneously ensuring that Britain 'could not acquire by conquest much more than she gained through co-operation'.[21]

This co-operation was extensive. The British were supplied with 'a constant stream of intelligence information',[22] and the Irish later obliged the Americans in a similar fashion. This information included weather reports and sensitive details about Axis shipping and submarine movements. The British were allowed the 'use of Shannon airports for largely military purposes' and to overfly Irish airspace in specified areas; as the war progressed Allied pilots and aircraft which came down on Irish territory were repatriated while Germans continued to be interned; there was compliance with British military requirements and visits by military and naval attachés to ensure that British interests were being safeguarded; there was close co-operation and liaison between the military authorities North and South, and plans for British help in the event of a German invasion. There were also shared arrangements in shipping and co-operation in the joint purchasing of commodities, a situation which gave the British extensive control over Irish supplies. No restrictions were placed on the departure of thousands of Irish people to fight in the British forces and work in a British war economy which continued to be fed with Irish agricultural produce.[23] 'We could not do more if we were in the war', commented the secretary of the Department of External Affairs.[24] The British and American military authorities, particularly their intelligence branches, declared themselves fully satisfied on a number of occasions with the Irish contribution to the Allied war effort, and the feeling grew in these quarters that Ireland's benevolent neutrality was preferable to its becoming an official belligerent with the demands in relation to defence and supplies which this would entail; British and American political and press attitudes towards Irish neutrality should be viewed against this background.

It was fortunate for the maintenance of Irish neutrality that British and American requirements at the operational level could be satisfied without provoking German retaliation. Furthermore, the state's geographical location – out of the path of advancing war machines – made it the luckiest of the European neutrals, while partition, advanced as a justification for neutrality, was also a major factor in its survival. The existence of Northern Ireland gave the Allies a crucial foothold on the island, allowing the British a base from which to defend their north-western ports and trans-atlantic convoys and the Americans an ideal headquarters for their operations in Europe.

Neuhold has identified two major contributions which a neutral can make to the viability of its status. One is to take suffecent defensive measures to convince a would-be aggressor that the costs of invading and occupying its territory (in terms of troop numbers, casualties, war materials, time and political prestige) would exceed the benefits.[25] This Ireland failed to do, mounting a defence effort which was not 'remotely comparable to that of the other successful democratic neutrals'.[26] While the poet Patrick Kavanagh was being a little unkind when he remarked that the defence forces would be 'hard put to defend a field of potatoes against an invasion of crows',[27] it is highly probable that the 'entrance and occupation price'[28] incurred by any aggressor against Ireland would have been extremely low.

The second major contribution is for a state to 'enhance its reliability and prevent interference by powers tempted to fish in troubled political waters'.[29] Here the Irish were more successful, and more practised, since the maintenance of domestic stability was one of the state's priorities since its foundation. A state of emergency was declared, empowering the government to legislate by decree and expanding the role of the state in society and the economy to an extraordinary degree. The military intelligence branch of the army, G2, 'had a far broader remit and were far less constrained by law, custom, by civil government or by rival institutions than the British or American wartime security agencies'.[30] Very little occurred in wartime Ireland without its knowledge – politicians, public servants, political activists of all persuasions, aliens, Allied and Axis diplomats, journalists – none escaped the attention of G2. The government introduced internment, military tribunals and the death penalty, and dealt severely with the internal security threat posed by the IRA; it set out to ensure that no belligerent would have 'any due cause, and proper cause, of complaint',[31] any opportunity, excuse or justification for questioning or violating Irish neutrality. The need for public impartiality and popular unity was emphasised and any disturbance in the state's political, or socio-economic waters was kept to a minimum or, at least, well hidden.

A central weapon in the state's arsenal, one that became 'neutrality's backbone',[32] was the emergency censorship. The powers of wartime censorship were contained in the Emergency Powers Act, which was introduced on the outbreak of war. It was both a security and a political censorship which became a central player in de Valera's 'double game', and covered the press, publications of all kinds, film, and postal, telegraphic and telephonic communications. On the one level, it operated as an internal security mechanism in the traditional sense, giving the authorities an important informative and preventative weapon in the maintenance of political, military and economic security, supplementing the intelligence work of G2 (which carried out its own covert censorship activities). At the same time it was central to the public presentation of impartiality by denying belligerents 'due cause' or domestic partisans any excuse or encouragement to create trouble for the state or its policy; the aim was to 'keep the temperature down',[33] both internally and between Ireland and the belligerents. A linked objective was the maintenance of the unity of the population by the suppression of anything which might prove divisive or present a threat to public order. War news was 'neutralised' (including the suppression of reports of the concentration camps); newsreels were banned; children's games were seized; the expression of opinions on the war, neutrality and much else of vital importance, in both public media and private communications, was disallowed.

Neutrality, which could not be defended militarily, was put forward as being the only policy compatible with the security of the state; thus, the political censorship of opinion was defined as a security mechanism, essential for the survival of the state and, hence, justified in all its excesses. Political censorship has been defined as 'Political conditioning by negative propaganda, preventing the promotion of alternative ideas to those projected as the basis of the authority, legitimacy and policies of the government'.[34] This was precisely the political role performed by the emergency censorship, in relation to both neutrality and the more general policies of the government. While all of the wartime censorships functioned as security mechanisms against internal and external threats, what most set the Irish system apart was its insistence on a 'truly neutral outlook'[35] among the people. Neutrals like Switzerland and Sweden had not abdicated their responsibilities in the area of defence as Ireland had and they did not, despite their more precarious geostrategic locations, regard the neutralisation of domestic opinion – the creation of a 'moral neutrality' – as either necessary or desirable.

The irony, of course, was that Ireland's policy, while presented as impeccably impartial, was, in reality, extremely benevolent towards the Allies, to an extent that went beyond the normal tendency of neutrals to be 'neutral for the power that threatened them most'.[36] The partiality shown by the extensive co-operation with the Allies, the 'asymmetrical nature' of military preparations and expectations, the lack of 'due diligence' with regard to defence, the permitted contribution by the state's citizens to the British war effort – all of these have led to the conclusion that Ireland was not a neutral in the generally accepted sense of the term and that it would be more accurate to describe it simply as a non-belligerent.[37] Although the policy that was pursued was pragmatic and justifiable in terms of *raison d'état*, the government did not wish to have it exposed in its true form and an image more fitting to prevailing popular expectations and Fianna Fáil rhetoric was presented. The neutrality that came to dominate public perception was an illusion of strict impartiality and moral superiority, the crowning glory of independence, untainted by the hidden realities, particularly the close links with the 'old enemy'. The censorship was a crucial player in this area.

The continuation of pre-war political, economic, social and cultural themes and priorities in a world convulsed by total and terrible war, and Ireland's determined disengagement from that war, has resulted in 'the Emergency' being characterised in tragicomic terms. It has been seen as the ultimate symbol of the isolationism of the Irish state ('Plato's cave'),[38] an 'unreal', 'absurd' and 'bizarre'[39] episode, the very term 'Emergency' steeped in bathos.[40] With the benefit of hindsight, such characterisations have some validity. The censorship did contribute to the creation of what, in retrospect, can appear to be an unreal sense of priorities. Its story is sometimes tragedy, sometimes farce, interesting in itself but also important as a window of enquiry into the nature of wartime Ireland. The purpose of this book is to detail and critically analyse the censorship; to place its policies and actions in context; to locate it in the political culture and emotional climate of the Ireland of those years; and to explain its actions with reference to the policy priorities of those who controlled it and broader international developments. The recent release of official files relating to the censorship, and the Emergency in general, have made this first history of this important topic possible. The author draws his own conclusions from the evidence presented, but that evidence also stands alone; it is open to the reader to interpret and apply it as he or she sees fit.

Notes and References

1   M.J. MacManus, 'Eire and the World Crisis', *Horizon*, Vol. V, No. 25, January 1942, p. 19.
2   Dermot Keogh, 'Ireland and "Emergency" Culture, Between Civil War and Normalcy, 1922–1961', Dermot Keogh (ed.), *Ireland: A Journal of History and Society*, Vol. 1, No. 1: 'Irish Democracy and the Right to Freedom of Information', 1995, pp. 4–43.
3   ibid., p. 11.

4   K.R.M. Short, 'Preface', in K.R.M. Short (ed.), *Film and Radio Propaganda in World War II* (London and Canberra, 1983), pp. 1–11; Philip M. Taylor, 'Propaganda in International Politics, 1919–39', in Short, *Film and Radio Propaganda*, pp. 18–42; Nicholas Pronay, 'Introduction', in Nicholas Pronay and D.W. Spring (eds.), *Propaganda, Politics and Film, 1918–45* (London, 1982), pp. 4–19.
5   Censorship of Films Act 1923 (Government Publications, Stationery Office).
6   Kieran Woodman, *Media Control in Ireland, 1923–1983* (Southern Illinois, 1985), p. 17.
7   Terence Brown, *Ireland: A Social and Cultural History, 1922–1985* (London, 1985), p. 69, quoting the Catholic Truth Society of Ireland.
8   Censorship of Publications Act 1929 (Government Publications, Stationery Office).
9   Julia Carlson (ed.), *Banned in Ireland: Censorship and the Irish Writer* (London, 1990), p. 11.
10   Among them was the writer Seán O'Faoláin (see Brown, *Ireland*, p. 155).
11   Keogh, 'Ireland and "Emergency" Culture', p. 11.
12   J.J. Lee, *Ireland 1912–1985: Politics and Society* (Cambridge, 1989), p. 180.
13   It was also the culmination of a process of incorporating Catholic teaching into law.
14   Ronan Fanning, *Independent Ireland* (Dublin, 1983), p. 120.
15   Ronan Fanning, 'Irish Neutrality – An Historical Review', *Irish Studies in International Affairs*, Vol. 1, No. 3, 1982, p. 30.
16   Garret Fitzgerald, 'Neutrality came from fear of ourselves, not Germany', *Irish Times*, 6 May 1995.
17   Patrick Keatinge, *A Place Among the Nations: Issues of Irish Foreign Policy* (Dublin, 1978), p. 91.
18   Hanspeter Neuhold, 'Permanent Neutrality in Contemporary International Relations: A Comparative Perspective', *Irish Studies in International Affairs*, Vol. 1, No. 3, 1982, p. 26.
19   Keatinge, *A Place Among the Nations*, p. 91.
20   Lee, *Ireland*, p. 244.
21   ibid.
22   NA, D/FA (Sec.) A 3, memo by Joseph Walshe, 'Help given by the Irish government in relation to the actual waging of war', 24 May 1941.
23   ibid.; Fanning, *Independent Ireland*, pp. 124–5, Viscount Cranborne list for the British War Cabinet.
24   NA, D/FA (Sec.) A 3, handwritten addendum to Walshe memo, 24 May 1941.
25   Neuhold, 'Permanent Neutrality', p. 26.
26   Lee, *Ireland*, p. 236. Lee argues that it was this economising on defence which allowed the Irish public finances to remain relatively unscathed by the war. For details of Irish defensive shortcomings see, for example, Lee, *Ireland*, pp. 234–6; Dermot Keogh, *Twentieth-Century Ireland: Nation and State* (Dublin, 1994), pp. 108–9; assorted articles in *An Cosantóir*, Emergency special issue, September 1989 and *The Irish Sword*, 'The Emergency 1939–45', Vol. XIX, Nos. 75 and 76, 1993–4.
27   John Ryan, *Remembering How We Stood: Bohemian Dublin at the Mid-Century* (New York, 1975), p. 7.
28   Neuhold, 'Permanent Neutrality' p. 26.
29   ibid.
30   Eunan O'Halpin, 'Army, Politics and Society in Independent Ireland, 1923–1945' in T.G. Fraser and Keith Jeffery (eds.), *Men, Women and War* (Dublin, 1993), p. 159.
31   Maurice Moynihan (ed.), *Speeches and Statements by Eamon de Valera, 1917–73* (Dublin, 1980), pp. 417–8.
32   Robert Fisk, *In Time of War: Ireland, Ulster and the Price of Neutrality, 1939–45* (London, 1985), p. 162.

33 Frank Aiken, Minister for the Co-ordination of Defensive Measures, *Seanad Debates*, Vol. 24, cols. 2614–5, 4 December 1940.
34 Nicholas Pronay, 'The Political Censorship of Films in Britain Between the Wars', in Pronay and Spring (eds.), *Propaganda, Politics and Film*, pp. 99–100.
35 NA, D/FA, 214/66, letter to Joseph Walshe on press censorship in Switzerland, 8 February 1943.
36 Lee, *Ireland*, p. 244.
37 Trevor C. Salmon, *Unneutral Ireland: An Ambivalent and Unique Security Policy* (Oxford, 1989), pp. 152–4.
38 F.S.L. Lyons, *Ireland Since the Famine* (London, 1973), pp. 557–8.
39 Kevin Myers, 'An Irishman's Diary', *Irish Times*, 13 April 1995 and 9 May 1995.
40 Fintan O'Toole, 'Our second World War finally comes to an end', *Irish Times*, 10 February 1995.

1.
FOUNDATIONS

PLANNING, ESTABLISHMENT AND GENERAL ORGANISATION

Following the establishment of the Irish Free State in 1922 the British authorities were concerned about how the new situation would affect the existing British wartime censorship scheme. The terms of the Treaty, including continuing British control over the ports of Lough Swilly, Berehaven and Cobh, meant that Ireland remained an intrinsic part of the British security and defence system and would be part of any future war in which Britain might be involved. In 1924 the British presented the Irish government with a set of written proposals covering the censorship of radio and cable stations in the event of war, and in 1925 a subcommittee of the Executive Council (the Free State cabinet) was appointed to deal with the question. It obtained memoranda from various government departments on the issue and, although it did not pursue the matter further, the secretary of the Committee of Imperial Defence was formally told that the British proposals had been agreed to in principle.[1] The British raised the issue again in 1928, and were informed that an Irish scheme of censorship would be prepared. In 1931 the Executive Council appointed the first interdepartmental committee on censorship in time of war. It held twelve meetings in that year but did not complete its work or make a report.[2]

In the summer of 1935 the British began an examination of the question of censorship in wartime, and by October, against the background of the Italian invasion of Ethiopia and the possibility of an Anglo-Italian war, had extended this into the initial stages of the planning for a ministry of information.[3] In Ireland in that same month of October 1935 the Fianna Fáil Minister for Defence, Frank Aiken, appointed the second interdepartmental committee on censorship 'to prepare and submit proposals for the operation of censorship in time of war'.[4] The committee held its preliminary meeting on 21 November 1935[5] and went on to hold twenty-eight meetings before submitting its report, which was approved by the cabinet on 13 September 1938.[6] By this stage the context had been fundamentally altered by the return of the Treaty ports in the previous April, which established the basis for Irish neutrality in the war that would begin a year later.

The committee, lacking practical experience and any autonomous Irish precedents on which to base its work, relied on a study of British regulations, schemes and reports, and took the approach of adapting and amending these to suit Irish conditions where appropriate. The draft scheme and the instructions and handbooks for censors were thus all largely based on British precedents and experience.[7]

The recommended scheme provided for a controller of censorship, who would be a senior military officer, to control and co-ordinate a cable/radio division and a postal division, each under a chief censor. Press censorship would function separately, operated by a press bureau under a director subject to the control of the Minister for Justice. The report recommended that suitable key personnel be selected and trained for censorship duty in peacetime and that a controller of censorship be designated immediately. It would be the latter's task to complete in detail and revise where necessary the outlined scheme and instructions, and to organise a skeleton censorship organisation in line with the recommendations and subject to changes in the communications system and to any general plan which emerged based on the position of the state in time of war.[8]

The report formed the basis of two conferences presided over by the Taoiseach, Éamon de Valera, on 28 October and 11 November 1938, at which arrangements were made for planning the organisation of a censorship service.[9] It was decided that a member of the committee, Thomas J. Coyne, who was a principal officer in the Department of Justice, should undertake responsibility for the planning. He was to devote all of his time to the task for the next six months. While engaged in this work Coyne remained nominally responsible for his Department of Justice duties but was regarded as seconded to the Department of Defence. He was thus responsible to the Minister for Defence, Frank Aiken, a relationship repeated during the Emergency when they became controller of censorship and Minister for the Co-ordination of Defensive Measures respectively. In planning the organisation, recommending persons for key positions and preparing or completing regulations and instructions, Coyne was to maintain consultation with Colonel Liam Archer of G2 (Military Intelligence) and with Frank Gallagher, deputy director of Radio Éireann and former editor of the *Irish Press*, who had been asked by de Valera to regard himself as press censor designate.[10]

Coyne's six months of work resulted in a set of proposals which, having been agreed to by G2,[11] was submitted by the Department of Defence to the Department of Finance in April 1939. The proposals dealt with the administrative structure envisaged and recommended that the persons who would hold key positions should be designated without delay. The

Department of Finance costed the proposals and in June 1939 furnished a list of senior civil servants whom it felt would be suitable for appointment as key personnel.[12]

The senior posts provided for in Coyne's scheme were: controller of postal and telegraph censorship, chief postal censor, chief telegraph censor, three deputy chief censors, and six censors. Coyne himself was earmarked for the position of controller, Jack Purcell as chief postal censor and E. Cussen as chief telegraph censor. On 22 August 1939 the government made an order for the release of the earmarked personnel for censorship duty if and when required. Meanwhile, those who would form the core of the Censorship organisation underwent preliminary consultations and training.[13]

While the interdepartmental committee report had envisaged a Censorship centred on the military, the plans with which the government were now working were civil service based, with the military in an advisory and consultative role. The entire Censorship staff was to be drawn from the existing personnel of the civil service. While a certain number would, of necessity, be post office staff, the majority were to be transferred or loaned to the Department of Defence from other government departments whose normal activities would have to be suspended or curtailed in an emergency, such as the Land Commission, the Office of Public Works, the Department of Local Government and the Gaeltacht Services Division of the Department of Lands.[14]

In the meantime, however, a covert censorship had already begun under the direction of the military. Shortly after the transfer of the Treaty ports to Irish control in April 1938, the government was warned by the British authorities that German espionage activities had extended to Ireland. In response to this situation a Defence Security Intelligence Service was established under the auspices of G2 in the autumn of 1938.[15] In May 1939 a new section in the Post Office Investigation Branch was established for the purposes of postal supervision. A system was put in place whereby the Minister for Justice would issue warrants to G2 for postal supervision on request. (Up to this point, postal warrants were only issued 'on the written request of the Commissioner, Garda Síochána, that it is necessary for the prevention or detection of crime'.)[16] This system remained in place until the end of the war in Europe in 1945, and was operated alongside and in conjunction with the 'open' emergency postal censorship.

The training of officers for all branches of the 'open' censorship had not long been underway when Germany invaded Poland on 1 September 1939. On that day the cabinet decided upon the appointment of Joseph Connolly, chairman of the Commissioners of Public Works, as controller of censorship, Thomas J. Coyne as assistant controller, and Michael Knightly, editor of the Dáil Debates, as chief press censor.[17] Their appointments were publicly announced on 4 September, by which time Ireland's neutral status had been endorsed by the Dáil and Seanad and a state of national emergency declared; all stages of the Emergency Powers Bill were rushed through and the resultant Emergency Powers Act gave the government dictatorial powers 'for securing the public safety and preservation of the State in time of war',[18] including the legal right to make emergency orders which would 'authorise and provide for the censorship' of communications.[19] The emergency censorship was thus legally born, with the Emergency Powers Act providing the foundation upon which a censorship code was built up by means of a series of emergency orders.

The organisation which came into being was built loosely around the skeleton created in peacetime, but it did differ in a number of ways from the original plans. The controller, for example, was a civil servant and not a military officer, while his control extended to press as well as postal and telegraph censorship. It is not clear when the idea of a separate press bureau under the Minister for Justice had been abandoned, but at least until 4 August 1939 the plans being circulated within government dealt with an organisation under a controller of postal and telegraph censorship. In any case, by 1 September the government had, as noted, decided upon the appointment of a controller, assistant controller and chief press censor. This was followed by the appointment of the chief postal and telegraph censors and other senior officers.

Frank Aiken, who as Minister for the Co-ordination of Defensive Measures (1939–45) had responsibility for the wartime censorship.

On 8 September Frank Aiken was replaced by Oscar Traynor at Defence and became the wartime Minister for the Co-ordination of Defensive Measures. It was under this *ad hoc* ministry that the Censorship operated (though for the purposes of establishment and accountancy it was a branch of the Department of Defence).[20] De Valera's choice of one of his most senior ministers and close associates for this position (effectively minister for censorship) illustrates the importance he attached to it. Aiken was dogged, rigid and unyielding – 'determined not to let anything past his gimlet eye'.[21] One contemporary believed that Aiken's 'incapacity to be intimidated' made him an ideal choice;[22] others were not so sure. Frederick Boland of the Department of External Affairs commented later that 'Unfortunately, good judgement was not Frank Aiken's long suit',[23] while his Anglophobic reputation led many, such as the American minister David Gray and *Irish Times* editor Bertie Smyllie, to regard him as hopelessly biased against the Allies. Aiken performed his wartime role with customary zeal, firm in the belief that a watertight censorship was essential to the maintenance of neutrality. As well as making policy decisions and being the public face of the Censorship, the minister played an active role in its day-to-day activities, issuing directions and intervening in all areas of the organisation.

Directly under Aiken in the hierarchy of power was Joseph Connolly, his old friend and fellow Ulster man, who acted as controller of censorship for the first two years. Besides the office of the controller, which co-ordinated the organisation, there were three executive divisions, each under a chief censor, dealing with postal, telegraph and press censorship respectively. Film censorship was carried out by the existing official film censor, in consultation with the Emergency organisation where relevant. The sole broadcasting station, Radio Éireann, was controlled and operated by the state and thus was able to censor itself, again in consultation with the Censorship. Nothing, however, was done to stop those people with radios from receiving the Allied and Axis propaganda which filled the wartime airwaves. Consideration had been given by the interdepartmental committee to the possibility of confiscating wireless sets, but it was decided that, apart altogether from the practical difficulties, the disadvantages of allowing people retain these sets (the reception of belligerent propaganda) were outweighed by the advantages of broadcasting as a means of keeping in touch with the public, especially in times of special emergency.[24] Jamming the signals was likewise regarded as impractical, besides which the government's primary concern was not the reception of belligerent propaganda *per se*, but that no Irish controlled media should become, or be regarded as, channels for its dissemination.

The controller's office was located at Upper Yard, Dublin Castle. From here the whole organisation was co-ordinated, supervised and controlled. While decisions of censorship policy were a matter for Aiken and the government, the controller considered and prescribed the methods by which policy could best be implemented, prepared the necessary orders and issued the necessary instructions to the staff. He kept under review the law as it affected censorship and submitted proposals for new legislation where and when it was deemed necessary.[25]

The assistant controller assisted the controller in general administration and took his place in his absence. He operated the information division, which was responsible for the collection, collation and distribution of any information intercepted by the Censorship of interest to the various departments concerned. He also directed the attention of the staff to specific matters on which information was required or to which special attention was to be paid. It was the assistant controller who prepared the 'Black' and 'White' lists in connection with the postal and telegraph censorship and maintained contact in this regard, and in general, with G2.[26]

Joe Connolly remained as controller for two years before returning to his post as chairman of the Commissioners of Public Works. He was succeeded as controller by Coyne on 15 September 1941;[27] the post of assistant controller then effectively ceased to exist and Coyne carried out the duties of both posts until the end of the Emergency. (On Coyne's accession to the top position, chief postal censor, Jack Purcell, nominally became assistant controller. Effectively, however, this amounted to no more than his filling in for Coyne during his absences.)

Connolly was a former senator and had been Minister for Posts and Telegraphs and for Lands respectively in de Valera's first two cabinets; his ministerial career ended with the abolition of the Free State senate in 1936 whereupon he was appointed chairman of the Commissioners of Public Works. He was, in his time as controller, the subject of much criticism from opposition politicians and newspaper people. He was depicted as lacking the necessary objectivity, discretion, tact and judgement for such a position (criticism similar to that levelled at Aiken). Connolly's appointment is interesting as Coyne would have seemed the obvious candidate; he had served on the interdepartmental committee and had been responsible for planning the organisation and operation of the censorship. He had been earmarked for the position and was still controller designate as late as 4 August 1939.[28] The plans did not include the position of assistant controller and it is possible that it was created specifically to enable Coyne to play a central role while at the same time allowing the Fianna Fáil man Connolly be the figurehead of the organisation. This argument is strengthened when one sees the dominant role Coyne played even when he was nominally assistant, and by the effective dissolution of the latter post on Coyne's accession to the position of controller.

Coyne was an extremely able and well-liked man. A brother of the well-known Jesuit, Father Edward Coyne, he had served in the RAF in the First World War, after which he took up legal studies and was called to the bar in 1922. After serving as private secretary to the Minister for Home Affairs,

Kevin O'Higgins, he was appointed to the permanent civil service on the staff of the Department of Justice in 1925; seconded to External Affairs, he served under Charles Bewley in Rome and in Geneva as assistant to the permanent delegate to the League of Nations. Coyne was recalled to the Department of Justice in 1934 where he served as a principal officer until 1939. During that time he was centrally involved in drafting the emergency legislation which was introduced at the outbreak of war, and more particularly, as mentioned earlier, in planning the emergency censorship.[29]

Coyne was certainly more popular in newspaper circles than his predecessor as controller; Smyllie, editor of the *Irish Times*, attributed to him 'one of the shrewdest and subtlest brains in this beloved country of ours'.[30] His appointment as controller was received more in hope than in confidence, however; as the *Irish Times* pointed out in an editorial which was 'Stopped by the Censor' at the time of his promotion:

> the Controller of Censorship, for all his dictatorial powers, merely is an instrument of Government policy. So long as Mr de Valera and his Ministers believe in the principle of a political censorship, the choice between one Controller and another is a choice between Tweedledum and Tweedledee.[31]

The entire staff of the Censorship, numbering over two hundred in all, were civil service personnel, as planned. Most were loaned to the Department of Defence without being replaced, although thirty-eight new entrants to the civil service were taken on specifically for the Censorship. These were clerical officers, attached to the Postal Censorship. The bulk of the staff were engaged in the postal division where large numbers were required because of the volume of correspondence which had to be examined. Women were extensively employed here, mostly as examiners or supervising examiners, but, except as typists, were hardly represented at all in any other branch of the organisation. This reflected a general situation whereby the sexism of Irish society, institutionalised in de Valera's 1937 constitution and by rules such as the marriage bar, excluded women from positions of power in public life. The Postal Censorship staff was centralised in Dublin, close to the central sorting office, and the division was headed by Jack Purcell, chief postal censor, who had been an assistant principal in the Department of Posts and Telegraphs.[32]

The Press Censorship was headed by chief press censor, Michael Knightly, a 1916 and war of independence veteran who had been a journalist with the *Irish Independent* before being appointed editor of the Dáil Debates in 1922. His branch was also located in Dublin, in the Upper Yard of the Castle along with the office of the controller. In the case of the Telegraph Censorship it was necessary, given its nature, to install small technical staffs at the various points where messages were received and transmitted. The chief telegraph censor, E. Cussen, who had been a principal officer in the

Thomas J. (Tommy) Coyne, a civil servant who was the leading figure in the Censorship organisation. He was assistant controller from 1939 to 1941 and controller of censorship from 1941 to 1945.

Department of Posts and Telegraphs, was based in Dublin, through which most messages were routed. The staffs of the Press and Telegraph Censorships were relatively small in comparison to the postal division and would have been even smaller but for the necessity of having relays of staff to work shifts to cover the long hours of working.[33]

LEGISLATION

The Emergency Powers Act 1939 provided the legal foundation for the emergency censorship. It authorised the government, by means of emergency orders, to do what it deemed 'necessary or expedient for securing the public safety or the preservation of the State, or for the maintenance of public order, or for the provision and control of supplies and sevices essential to the life of the community'. It was specifically authorised to provide for 'the censorship, restriction, control, or partial or complete suspension of communication'; the preservation and safeguarding of the secrecy of official documents and information; the prohibiting of the publication or spreading of subversive statements and propaganda; and 'the control and censorship of newspapers and periodicals'.[34] The Act also authorised the government to amend existing legislation for emergency purposes, which allowed it amend the existing Censorship of Films Acts to extend the powers of the film censor.[35] (The emergency legislation with regard to film censorship is treated in Chapter Two.)

The constitutional guarantee of 'the right of the citizens to express freely their convictions and opinions' is qualified by the provision that the 'organs of public opinion . . . shall not be used to undermine public order or morality or the authority of the State'. The constitution also states that the 'publication or utterance of blasphemous, seditious, or indecent matter is an offence which shall be punishable in accordance with law'.[36] This qualified guarantee of free expression prevented the imposition of a general censorship in 'normal' times, but not 'in time of war or armed rebellion'. At the same time as the passage of the Emergency Powers Act (3 September 1939), the Dáil amended this Article to extend the definition of 'in time of war' to include 'a time when there is taking place an armed conflict in which the State is not a participant but in respect of which each of the Houses of the Oireachtas shall have resolved that, arising out of such armed conflict, a national emergency exists affecting the vital interests of the State'.[37] The fundamental right to free expression was thus denied, and a court challenge precluded, by a parliamentary majority declaring a 'national emergency'.[38]

Postal and Telegraph Censorship Legislation

Under the Irish constitution of 1937 the inviolability of posts is not guaranteed as it is in other constitutions like that of Switzerland, while the right to free expression, as mentioned, was nullified 'in time of war'. Under municipal law the quasi-inviolability of the posts was secured by the Post Office Act of 1908. Under the terms of that Act the expression 'postal packet' also applied to telegrams, thus extending the same degree of inviolability applied to posts to cable and radio messages and 'foreign' and 'inland' telegrams. (In post office terminology, inland also applies to postal packets sent to and from the UK.) While the provision in this Act for a Secretary of State to order the examination of specific postal packets under warrant was considered sufficient for the imposition of a wartime postal and telegraph censorship in Britain, the interdepartmental committee concluded that such power, as vested in the Minister for Justice, was too limited for the required purposes in Ireland. Given that no impediments existed in international law, the imposition of a general censorship of posts and telegraphs could not be challenged legally.[39] The covert censorship of letters undertaken by G2 under warrant from the Minister for Justice was operated under the aforementioned 1908 Post Office Act.

The specific powers for a postal and telegraph censorship were contained in Part 4 of the Emergency Powers Order 1939, Articles 17 to 27 inclusive. These authorised control over posts, private and public telegrams, and telephone communications; the conveyance of informative articles on the person of travellers; cable and wireless communications; signalling; and carrier pigeons.[40]

A number of implementing orders were made by Aiken to give full effect to the provisions of the articles. These were:

Emergency Powers (Censorship of Postal Packets) Order 1939, which covered the censorship of postal packets (including telegrams) exchanged with places outside the state.

Emergency Powers (Censorship of Postal Packets) (No. 1) Order 1939, which covered the censorship of internal telegrams.

Emergency Powers (Restriction on the Conveyance of Informative Articles) Order 1939, which was made in December 1939 to close a gap in the censorship which allowed people to carry documents in and out of the state without examination or question. It enabled the authorities to interrogate and, if necessary, search travellers entering or leaving the state with a view to preventing censorship evasions. The powers contained in the order were not availed of to any great extent and were useful more as a deterrent.[41]

Emergency Powers (Telegraph Cable Companies) Order 1939, which authorised entry to the stations and works of the Western Union Telegraph Company, Valentia, Co. Kerry and the Commercial Cable Company, Waterville, Co. Kerry, and to control and censor telegraphic communication therein.[42] These powers were not fully utilised and the 'censorship' was restricted to the provision of watching staff to prevent overt irregularities and to ensure that all terminal traffic (i.e. that originating in and destined for places within the state) was circulated for censorship through the central telegraph office in Dublin.

The reasons for the absence of a censorship at these stations were twofold: firstly, these stations transmitted messages by 'boosting' or 'relaying' them as they passed through them. It was considered pointless to try and obtain the expensive special apparatus needed to slip off a duplicate of these messages in transit as they would be unintelligible without a mechanical unscrambler and a knowledge of the codes and cyphers used in almost all wartime traffic. Secondly, the British authorities would almost certainly have lifted the cables and closed down the stations at the first sign of interference by the Irish authorities. Thus, in the case of the cable companies, it was a case of surveillance rather than censorship.[43]

Emergency Powers (Wireless Telegraphy Apparatus) Order 1939, which revoked the fifty-two current licences for experimental transmitting stations held under the Wireless Telegraphy Act on the outbreak of war; all transmitting apparatuses held by the licensees were seized under this emergency order and taken into the custody of the chief telegraph censor.[44]

While Article 19 of the Emergency Powers Order enabled a minister to make an order prohibiting or restricting telephone communications, no statutory telephone censorship was in fact imposed. Between 1940 and the end of the Emergency the supervision of telephone conversations was exercised by the Post Office for G2, and although the question of the legal position was raised by G2 at the time, 'it was decided to ignore it'.[45]

The legal power and authority for the implementation of a complete censorship of posts and telegraphs was contained in the provisions of the Emergency Powers Act and the Emergency Powers Order. The fact that the censorship which was implemented was partial and limited (though 'adequate and suitable' according to Coyne) was a consequence of administrative, financial and political factors and not of a lack of legal authority.

Press Censorship Legislation

There were four implementing emergency orders made with respect to press censorship between September 1939 and February 1942.

Emergency Powers (No. 5) Order 1939: This order was made on 13 September 1939 and replaced the provisions with regard to press censorship contained in Article 51 (2) of the Emergency Powers Order 1939. That article had empowered a minister to make provision by order for preventing or restricting the publication of matters 'as to which he is satisfied' that the publication or the unrestricted publication thereof would or might be prejudicial directly or indirectly to the public safety or the preservation of the state. It was realised immediately that these provisions did not 'meet the needs of the problem' of press censorship; the requirement of a ministerial order in every case would have made the business of censorship too cumbersome and slow, and it was felt that the Censorship should be able to issue *ad hoc* directions to the press. Furthermore, the general order made no provision for the control of newspapers published outside the state (described as 'extern' papers).[46]

The EP (No. 5) O 1939 addressed these shortcomings and defined how the press censorship would operate. It gave 'authorised persons' (a minister, the controller, the assistant controller and the chief press censor) the power to issue directions to 'newspapers' (including journals, magazines and other periodical publications) prohibiting, permanently or for a specified period, the publication of any specified matter or any particular class or classes of matter. They could, further, prohibit publication of the newspaper unless it was submitted for censorship and passed, or prohibit the publication of any specified matter, or class or classes of matter, unless they were, likewise, submitted and passed. A newspaper was not allowed to give any indication that such directions had been issued to it. Directions could be given in writing, verbally, by telegraph or telephone. (The directions also applied to posters and placards produced in connection with newspapers.) The order also gave authorised persons the power to prohibit the importation of any specified 'extern' newspaper and to direct the seizure by the Gardaí of same.[47]

When this order was being prepared the question of taking similar powers of seizure with regard to newspapers published within the state was considered. It was felt, however, that the power to issue directions and to require submission before publication would provide sufficient control, as internal newspapers operated within the jurisdiction of the state and could be made amenable to the law. Experience was soon to show, however, that 'extremely dangerous' matter could be published while a reasonable doubt existed as to whether it contravened the censorship directions. The *Irish Workers' Weekly* ignored a direction to submit its entire issue and continued to offend while the case was in the hands of the chief state solicitor. The *Leader* carried a piece which 'grievously offended governments and peoples of foreign states'; it had not been submitted and was stopped at the wholesale distributors. The publishers subsequently withdrew the issue on the threat that a prosecution would follow, but they could have 'published and be damned'; the authorities had no power to stop them. Neither had they power to deal with objectionable matter in books, leaflets and other printed matter. In July 1940 the Censorship sought the power to direct the seizure of any printed matter, irrespective of where it was published. 'The Government may feel that this is a very wide power to vest in an administrative authority', wrote the controller, 'but it appears to be warranted by the exigence of the present situation.'[48]

Emergency Powers (No. 36) Order 1940: This order was made on 12 July 1940 and gave the Censorship the additional powers which it had felt were necessary. It gave authorised persons (as for EP (No. 5) O 1939) the power to direct the seizure, by Gardaí, of any document containing matter, the circulation or exhibition of which 'would be prejudicial to the public safety or the preservation of the State or the maintenance of public order'.[49] The direction alone was sufficient authority for the Gardaí to make such seizures.[50]

Emergency Powers (No. 67) Order 1941: This order was made on 28 January 1941. It sought to fill the gap in the censorship through which journalists, particularly visiting correspondents, could send abroad uncensored press messages. Its object was to deter this practice by making it a criminal offence to send out of the state, by any means, any message intended for publication

> relating to any event arising out of or connected with the war or internal public order which happened or is alleged to have happened in or over the State or its territorial waters, or relating to any actual or alleged attack on the State or to the supply of commodities in the State, without first submitting such message to an authorised person and having it passed.[51]

Experience brought to light a number of defects in these three orders. The principal defects, as identified by the Censorship, were as follows:

> (1) that in the case of directions to the press there is no provision for postal service which is, in practice, the only feasible method as well as the one which has actually been employed up to date although there is no authority for it,
>
> (2) that the powers of the Censor do not extend to pamphlets, etc. but are restricted to newspapers i.e. periodical publications,
>
> (3) that claims for compensation in respect of the seizure and disposal of documents by or on behalf of the Censorship are not expressly ruled out as they ought to be,
>
> (4) that the power to seize documents, etc. in certain circumstances is not as effective as it might be through lack of ancillary powers to enter and search suspected premises,
>
> (5) that lack of power to seize is limited to documents and does not extend to other articles of propaganda, e.g., effigies of Hitler etc. or the V badges which are being prominently displayed by shops and have been the subject of repeated complaints,
>
> (6) that the Emergency Powers (No. 6) Order, 1941, has proved ineffective to control the transmission of press messages outside the State and that further and better powers are required for this purpose.[52]

A new order was drafted with the object of remedying these defects and providing 'the further and better powers which experience has shown to be necessary'.[53]

Emergency Powers (No. 151) Order 1942: This order was made on 17 February 1942, revoking and replacing the previous orders. It addressed the perceived defects contained in these orders while embracing, in amended form, their principal provisions. The new provisions extended the powers of censorship to printed matter of all kinds, notably pamphlets, leaflets and casual publications. Printers and publishers could now be prohibited from printing any specified matter or classes of matter and could be required to submit matter for censorship before printing or publication. The powers of seizure were retained and extended to offensive articles of propaganda which were not documents. A publication could not be seized if a printer or publisher had submitted it for censorship and obtained permission to print or publish it. Finally, new restrictions were imposed on the transmission of uncensored press messages out of the state. No message could now be sent out without the permission of the Censorship, except those which dealt exclusively with sporting or social events.[54]

It was claimed at the time of its making that this order would be 'adequate to enable censorship of the press to be made effective in any future emergency'.[55] Some months after the ending of the war, however, in a review of the emergency censorship, Coyne identified a number of short-comings which he believed would need to be addressed in planning for any future censorship.[56] Two of the minor defects identified by the controller concerned definition. Article 3 authorised the prohibition of the importation of 'any specified publication' except under licence. A publication was defined in Article 2 as 'any issue of a newspaper'; Coyne suggested that because, in practice, it was likely to be found necessary to exclude not just 'any' but *all* issues of a newspaper, a new form of words should be found. Article 4, which authorised the seizure of propagandist documents, emblems, effigies, etc., was aimed at propaganda *tout court* – not particular articles but all things of that class. The wording, however, precluded an omnibus direction for the seizure of all documents of a class, e.g. anti-German propaganda, wherever and whenever they might be found. Article 8 applied the operative provisions of press censorship to printers, i.e. the giving of directions to printers as to newspapers. This provision was ineffective as printers differed from newspapers in two important respects. In the first place, the names and addresses of newspapers were well-known or easily accessible, while it was 'impossible at any given time to know who is a printer and who is not'. Secondly, it was even more difficult to know what a particular printer was printing or planning to print. To overcome these problems, Coyne suggested a registration or licensing of printers and the power to issue directions to printers generally by means of public advertisement or in *Iris Oifigiúil*. Article 9, which sought to control the transmission of press messages abroad, was 'largely a futility'. The gap in the postal and telegraph censorship allowed virtually free communication with the North and thus with Britain; there were no restrictions on cross-channel correspondents entering and leaving the country, while there was no frontier control checking the entry of US and other foreign correspondents from the North. Furthermore, the authorities never knew how many foreign press people were in the country, who they were and what they were writing. As a partial remedy Coyne again suggested some type of registration system, as well as the exclusion of correspondents who had 'given offence' and the penalisation of their employers.

The principal weaknesses of the order, from the point of view of the Censorship, were carried over from the original press censorship Order (No. 5, 1939); they were twofold: firstly, no effective means of enforcement were provided for and, secondly, the powers granted to the Censorship were wholly negative.

With regard to enforcement, the Emergency Powers Act 1939, prescribed – for offending newspapers – fines and imprisonment, and provided the courts with the power to direct the forfeiture of any goods or chattels by means of which the offence was committed. Coyne viewed court proceedings and such penalties as inappropriate and ineffective mechanisms for dealing with press offences. In the first place there was the slowness and uncertainty of court proceedings; he felt that fines and imprisonment were not a sufficient deterrent, while there could be no certainty about how the court would exercise its discretion with regard to the forfeiture of printing presses. Moreover, the taking of a newspaper to court was fraught with complications; 'Don't prosecute a paper is the first rule of statecraft'. Besides the fact that no amount of proceedings could undo the damage perceived to have been caused by some 'indiscreet or malicious disclosure', the possibility existed that a newspaper could actively invite prosecution for the sake of the *réclame*. A lengthy hearing would provide valuable advertising and a good chance of acquittal on a technicality. The newspaper could count on public support and invoke, as well as the principle of press freedom, the danger posed to all those employed in the production and distribution of the newspaper.

Coyne remained convinced that in any future emergency, effective powers of enforcement of directions would be needed. These would take the form of powers of entry, search and seizure on newspaper premises; the power to suppress by executive act a newspaper which persistently offends; and the power to seize the printing machinery of a suppressed newspaper.

The other principal weakness in the existing legislation, from the point of view of the Censorship, concerned the negative nature of its powers. The authorities could prohibit but not require the publication of matter and were powerless to interfere with presentation, except indirectly. By methods of selection, emphasis and typography newspapers could give a particular 'slant' to stories that were in themselves unobjectionable to the Censorship. The latter attempted to deal with such practices by means of 'requests' to the newspapers to conform with its wishes with regard to the manner and form of handling the news. Newspapers justifiably challenged the censors' right to interfere with news handling and regularly sought to have such 'requests' put in writing so that they could be used to expose the Censorship at a later date. The 'requests' were never put in writing as the newspapers were correct in believing them to have no force in law. The Censorship dealt with matters of layout and wording by altering proofs and indicating the changes which would render them unobjectionable. Newspapers usually conformed as the relevant item or issue could otherwise be prohibited from publication. Fortunately for the censors they never had to prohibit the publication of a newspaper because of a refusal to make changes in form; Coyne himself admitted that it was doubtful whether 'public opinion' (not to mention the courts) would have approved of such a step.

In December 1940 Coyne informally consulted the legal adviser in the Office of the Attorney General, Philip O'Donoghue, on this issue. He confirmed that the existing legislation did not confer the power to direct newspapers to publish certain matter or to present it in a certain way. He indicated that a new order would be needed, if such positive powers were to be taken, along the lines adopted by the Australian authorities. He warned, however, of the dangers inherent in adopting such powers[57] and it was these political considerations, as well as the sufficient effectiveness of the Censorship's 'indirect methods', which precluded such a change in the law. The first consideration was that such a new order would need to be stringently enforced and, in the words of O'Donoghue, 'That would probably mean the closing down of some or all of the daily papers from time to time'[58] – a situation the authorities were anxious to avoid. Secondly, and more importantly, the adoption of positive powers would have had the effect of transforming 'a mere censorship' into complete control,[59] in terms of the matter published and its presentation. This would have had the effect of making the authorities seem responsible for everything that appeared in the press, making the newspapers 'Government publications in essence'.[60] This would have been highly undesirable in both the international and the national contexts. The government did not wish to supply belligerents with ammunition to fire at Ireland's neutrality by taking direct responsibility for any unneutral utterances or campaigns in the press. Internally, such control would have had a negative effect on public morale, the sustenance of which was partially dependent on the 'necessary illusion' that the press was free and independent; this was particularly true in time of war. These concerns applied more to the question of content than to that of layout; Coyne believed that the Censorship could have been more effective and less open to charges of abuse had its powers in this regard been specific rather than indirect and ill-defined. (This probably resulted from sloppy drafting rather than political considerations.) He recommended that the positive powers which should be taken in a future emergency be restricted to those with regard to news presentation, including the power to insist on the publication of source.

Another concern of the controller's was the secrecy of the Censorship's actions. While newspapers had been prevented from giving any hint that the censor had been at work, in practice this prohibition was ineffective, as for example when newspapers went to press with no leading article – leaving nobody in any doubt as to the reason. A proprietor, editor or journalist could disclose to a third party the details of the Censorship's actions; most of the revelations about the Irish Censorship in the foreign press were based on such information. It was for this reason that the directions, in contrast to, for example, the British defence notices, were mostly framed in general terms, requiring the submission of specified matter or classes of matter without any indication of how it would be treated. This safeguard was, of course, imperfect as 'ill-disposed' newspapers could disclose how the Censorship had acted towards the various matters and classes of matter concerned. Parliament was a popular arena for the revelation of the censor's actions but Coyne accepted that legal limitations could not be placed on such disclosures; instead, he recommended the establishment of a *modus operandi* between government and parliament to ensure that parliamentary privilege would not be used to evade or nullify the censorship. In terms of legislation, he recommended a 'prohibition on the disclosure of censorship directions to unauthorised persons'.

The Swiss equivalent of the Emergency Powers Act – the Federal Decree of 30 August 1939, which included the powers of censorship – declared as its aim 'the maintenance of neutrality'. Ireland, unlike Switzerland, never formally declared its neutrality and the Emergency Powers Act did not refer specifically to it; the Irish authorities, however, regarded the Act as referring to neutrality 'in fact' if not in name.[61] A number of the emergency orders made under the Act were included in the wartime book *Neutrality Laws, Regulations and Treaties*, edited by Deak and Jessup. The editors noted, however, that 'With respect to several other emergency orders, it is impossible to ascertain – since the word "neutrality" is carefully avoided – whether they are measures aimed primarily at the preservation of neutrality or the protection of internal order against disturbances from causes independent of the state of war'. Interestingly, among the examples mentioned in this regard is EP (No. 5) O 1939, which related to press censorship.[62] As we shall see, the censorship powers were multifunctional while the fact that neutrality was not specifically mentioned did not impede their implementation in this regard.[63]

NOTES AND REFERENCES

1   NA, D/J, Report of the Interdepartmental Committee on Censorship, 1938. See also, memos on 'Censorship in Time of War' (MA, G2/P/21560).

2   NA, D/J, Committee Report on Censorship 1938.

3   Michael Balfour, *Propaganda in War, 1939–1945: Organisations, Policies and Publics in Britain and Germany* (London, 1979), p. 53; James C. Robertson, *The British Board of Film Censors: Film Censorship in Britain, 1896–1950* (London, 1985), p. 109.

4   NA, D/T, S 8202, 'Censorship in wartime – establishment of interdepartmental committee, 1935'. The committee was chaired by Maurice Moynihan, secretary of the Department of the Taoiseach. The joint secretaries were Dan Bryan, G2 (Military Intelligence), and originally E.C. Powell and later J.G. Buckmaster of the Department of Defence. The other members were Seán Murphy, Department of External Affairs; Philip O'Donoghue, Department of the Attorney General; Thomas J. Coyne, Department of Justice; E. Cussen, Department of Posts and Telegraphs; and Colonel Liam Archer, director of G2 (Military Intelligence).

5   ibid.

6   NA, D/J, Committee Report on Censorship 1938; NA, D/T, S 10829, 'Censorship in Wartime – Interdepartmental Committee'.

7   NA, D/J, Committee Report on Censorship 1938.

8   ibid.

9   Present at the first conference on 28 October, besides de Valera, were Paddy Ruttledge, Minister for Justice, Thomas J. Coyne of the Department of Justice, and Maurice Moynihan, secretary of the Department of the Taoiseach. De Valera, Moynihan and Coyne attended the second conference on 11 November together with Stephen Roche, secretary of the Department of Justice; General MacMahon, secretary of the Department of Defence; Liam Archer, director of G2, and Hogan of the Department of the Taoiseach.

10 NA, D/T, S 11306, memoranda on censorship in time of emergency.

11 MA, G2/X/0042, 'Censorship Regulations and Reports', Archer to Secretary, Department of Defence, 6 February 1939.

12 NA, D/T, S 11306, Finance memorandum, 'Staffing of Censorship to be established in time of war', 15 June 1939.

13 ibid.; Defence memorandum, 'The appointment of "key" personnel for postal and telegraph censorship', 4 August 1939; extract from Cabinet Minutes, 22 August 1939; MA, OCC 1/11, 'Censorship Organisation – Staffing', November 1939.

14 NA, D/T, S 11306, Finance memorandum, 15 June 1939.

15 NA, D/FA (Sec.) A8(1), Bryan to Aiken, 21 June 1945 and Bryan memo on Defence Security Intelligence, June 1945. This was an important development as it marked the re-entry of Military Intelligence into the area of political security and intelligence work, which had been the sole responsibility of the Gardaí since 1926. (See Eunan O'Halpin, 'Army, Politics and Society in Independent Ireland, 1923–1945' in T.G. Fraser and Keith Jeffery (eds.), *Men, Women and War* (Dublin, 1993), pp. 161–9.)

16 ibid. (The officer in charge of this special section was sent to London to gain first-hand knowledge of how a similar section was operated by the British.)

17 NA, CAB 2/2, Cabinet Minutes, 1 September 1939.

18 *Dáil Debates*, Vol. 77, *Seanad Debates*, Vol. 23 (2 September 1939, 3 September 1939).

19 Emergency Powers Act 1939 (Government Publications, Stationery Office, 1939).

20 MA, OCC 1/15, Notes for Minister on Estimates, 1940–1 (February, 1940).

21 Dermot Keogh, *Twentieth-Century Ireland: Nation and State* (Dublin, 1994), p. 124.

22 C.S. Andrews, *Man of No Property: An Autobiography* (Vol. Two) (Dublin and Cork, 1982), pp. 123–4.

23 Quoted in Keogh, *Twentieth-Century Ireland*, p. 124.

24 NA, D/J, Committee Report on Censorship 1938.

25 MA, OCC 1/15, Notes for Minister on Estimates, 1940–41 (February 1940); OCC 1/11, 'Censorship Organisation – Staffing', November 1939; NA, D/T, S 11445/8, 'Security Measures in time of Emergency', Departmental Reports: Co-ordination of Defensive Measures. (This consists of an extensive memorandum by Coyne on 'action to be taken by the Government and by the different government departments concerned for the establishment of Censorship in time of war or emergency'. Sent to the Department of the Taoiseach by the Department of Defence, 6 September 1945.)

26 ibid.

27 NA, D/T, S 11306, various memoranda regarding censorship.

28 ibid., Department of Defence memorandum, 4 August 1939.

29 Biographical details of T.J. Coyne, supplied by the Department of Justice; 'An Irishman's Diary', *Irish Times*, 19 May 1945.

30 'An Irishman's Diary', *Irish Times*, 19 May 1945.

31 MA, OCC 7/58, *Irish Times* censored proofs, 16 September 1941.

32 MA, OCC 1/11, 'Censorship Organisation – Staffing', November 1939; OCC 1/15, Notes for Minister on Estimates, 1940–41 (February, 1940).

33 ibid.

34 It was subsequently realised that this form of words was restrictive as it specified 'newspapers and periodicals'. What was required, and later taken, was the power to censor publications of all kinds – books, pamphlets, leaflets, etc.

35 Emergency Powers Act 1939 (Government Publications, Stationery Office, 1939).

36 *Bunreacht na hÉireann* (1937), Article 40. 6. 1° (i). The Censorship of Publications Act 1929, the Censorship of Films Acts 1923 and 1930, and the Offences Against the State Act 1939 (censorship provisions) were rendered constitutional by this qualifying proviso.

37 ibid., Article 28. 3. 3°.

38   The state of emergency declared on 3 September 1939 remained in place until September 1976 when an alternative resolution with the same effect was passed (redefining the emergency as arising out of 'the armed conflict now taking place in Northern Ireland'). The emergency was not finally lifted until February 1995, in response to the IRA and loyalist paramilitary ceasefires declared in the autumn of 1994. The inconsistency of the constitution in simultaneously conceding and denying fundamental rights is discussed by Desmond M. Clarke, 'Emergency Legislation, Fundamental Rights and Article 28. 3. 3° of the Irish Constitution', *The Irish Jurist*, Vol. 12, Part 2, 1977, pp. 217–33.

39   NA, D/T, S 11445/8, Coyne memo on censorship, September 1945.

40   Some other provisions of a penal character were contained in the Emergency Powers Order (EPO) which were aids to the censorship. These included Articles 28 and 29 of Part 1, dealing with the safeguarding of information and restrictions on photography; and Article 57 of Part 8 which made specific provision for the control of lighthouses and buoys. A number of emergency directions were issued which related to island wireless stations, lighthouse and beacon stations, lifeboat wireless stations, wireless telegraphy schools, airport wireless stations and newspaper private wires. These were imposed by administrative action under the general powers of Part 4 of the EPO 1939 and no subsidiary statutory powers were issued (MA, OCC 5/43, memoranda on the cessation of censorship, revocation of Orders, etc., May 1945).

41   MA, OCC 5/14, Archer to Coyne, 27 September 1939 and various correspondence and memos, November–December 1939; NA, D/T, S 11445/8, Coyne memo on censorship, September 1945.

42   MA, OCC 5/13, Emergency Powers (Telegraph Cable Companies) Order 1939 – direction made by Aiken thereunder.

43   NA, D/T, S 11445/8, Coyne memo on censorship, September 1945.

44   MA, OCC 5/43, memoranda on the cessation of censorship, revocation of Orders, etc.

45   NA, D/FA (Sec.) A8(1), 'Security Intelligence', Dan Bryan (G2) to Aiken, 25 May 1945.

46   MA, OCC 1/15, Censorship memo on EP (No. 5) O 1939.

47   Emergency Powers (No. 5) Order 1939 (Government Publications, Stationery Office, 1939).

48   MA, OCC 5/19, Connolly memo, 3 July 1940.

49   'Document' included newspapers, journals, magazines or other periodicals; photographs, cartoons and other pictorial representations; books, pamphlets, leaflets or circulars and 'any other document of whatsoever kind', whether or not it was intended for publication, distribution or sale.

50   Emergency Powers (No. 36) Order 1940 (Government Publications, Stationery Office, 1940); MA, OCC 5/19, 'Proposed order relating to the seizure of newspapers and other periodicals'.

51   Emergency Powers (No. 67) Order 1941 (Government Publications, Stationery Office, 1941); MA, OCC 5/22, Censorship statement sent to the Government Information Bureau for broadcast and distribution to the press.

52   MA, OCC 5/27, Censorship memo, 'Proposed Draft Order for the purpose of consolidating the existing Orders with respect to the censorship of the press, etc.', January 1942.

53   MA, OCC 5/27, Coyne to Brady, 31 October 1941.

54   Emergency Powers (No. 151) Order 1942 (Government Publications, Stationery Office, 1942); MA, OCC 5/27, memo, 18 February 1942.

55   MA, OCC 5/27, memo, November 1941.

56   NA, D/T, S 11445/8, Coyne memo on censorship, September 1945. All further references to shortcomings in EP (No. 151) O 1942 and recommendations for the future come from this source.

57　MA, OCC 5/25, Philip O'Donoghue to Coyne, 20 December 1940.

58　ibid.

59　ibid.

60　ibid.

61　NA, D/FA 214/66, letter to Walshe regarding press censorship in Switzerland, 15 February 1943.

62　NA, D/T, S 11306, Department of External Affairs memorandum for de Valera on press censorship of election speeches, 15 February 1943.

63　It did create difficulties in other areas, however. For example, in the order which provided for the internment of members of the belligerent forces (EP (No. 170) O 1942) the draftsperson worked in the words 'having regard to the international obligations of the State'. This phrase was, however, probably redundant (as would have been shown had it been tested by the courts) having regard to the terms of the enabling Act (NA, D/FA 214/66, letter to Walshe, 8 February 1943).

2.
'NEUTRAL AT THE PICTURES'

'Mr de Valera insists that Irishmen shall be neutral in thought, word
and deed – and also neutral at the pictures.'

'De Valera's Land of Silence',
Daily Mail, 15 January 1942

FILM CENSORSHIP

The 1930s saw film reach the height of its power as a source of entertainment, information and influence. It had, in the interwar period, developed
into the first truly mass medium and governments across the world were
not slow to realise that it was a 'singularly powerful medium for propaganda'.[1] The onset of war saw the propaganda potential of film, based on
its mass accessibility and inherent persuasiveness, exploited to the full by
all sides. Features, documentaries and especially newsreels were all utilised
by the belligerents to convey to their own publics, and those of their allies
and the neutrals, their views of the world in general and the war in particular. This situation posed obvious problems for an Irish government intent
on minimising the public's exposure to belligerent propaganda. The primary
source for the latter was Britain; Ireland was part of the UK distribution
network and a virtual monopoly was enjoyed by British and American films.
Cinema in Ireland, no less than elsewhere, had achieved mass popularity
in the 1930s.[2] Its 'danger' had been recognised early by the authorities, and
the imposition of a censorship based on 'moral' grounds was one of the
first legislative actions of the new state; the onset of war brought new
cinematic dangers and the government reacted by extending the powers of
the film censor to enable him to 'neutralise' the product of the film industry
before it reached Irish screens.

Under the Censorship of Films Acts 1923 and 1930 (the latter authorised
the censorship of 'talkies'), a film could only be rejected on the grounds

that it was 'indecent or subversive of public morality'. These Acts were amended by Article 52 of the Emergency Powers Order 1939 to give the censor the power to reject a film if he was of the opinion that its exhibition would be 'prejudicial to the maintenance of law and order or to the preservation of the State or would be likely to lead to a breach of the peace or to cause offence to the people of a friendly foreign nation'. Subsequent to the making of the Emergency Powers Order the Carlton Cinema in Dublin screened *The Spy in Black* (1939), a British spy thriller, directed by Michael Powell, which was based on German spy activities in Scotland during the First World War. The official film censor, James Montgomery, had passed the film for exhibition prior to the making of the order on 3 September; he was now of the opinion that it was offensive to Germans and that if it had been presented to him for censorship under the new conditions he would have cut it severely. He contacted the proprietors who, although not legally compelled to do so, agreed to allow him to cut the film.[3] In order to regularise the censor's action in this case, and as it had come to notice that film renters and distributors were contemplating the reissue and re-release of a number of old films which might now be 'undesirable', the Emergency Powers (No. 6) Order 1939 was made on 26 September; this allowed the censor to revoke certificates which had been granted to films prior to 3 September.[4]

In the meantime there had been a certain amount of confusion and interdepartmental wrangling about the issue of responsibility for emergency film censorship and the precise role of the emergency censorship organisation in the process. When the emergency legislation with regard to film was being drafted the article which extended the powers of the official film censor was inserted on the initiative of the Department of Justice, within which the film censor operated. The legislation also gave the Minister for Justice the power to hear appeals, or appoint someone to hear appeals, on behalf of films rejected on emergency grounds. Coyne believed that there was much to recommend the use of the ordinary, peacetime film censorship organisation, which had the confidence of the industry and the public, as the executive agency of the emergency censorship. He added the proviso, however, that it was only a suitable arrangement if the censor and Minister for Justice were prepared to act on the advice of the Minister for the Co-ordination of Defensive Measures or the controller of censorship. The law as it stood lay the sole discretion with the official censor who could not legally be compelled to exercise such discretion in accordance with the directions of a minister or even of the government. Similarly, the Minister for Justice could, theoretically, ignore the advice of Aiken or his representatives.[5]

On 15 September Coyne and Connolly paid a visit to the film censor's office to discuss with Montgomery the future line of policy with regard to the certification of films and to identify the 'general classes of film and film matter that would in the present emergency be objectionable and should not be passed by the Censor'. Connolly outlined his list of objectionable films and film matter thus:

> 1. All films dealing with war preparations, parades, troop movements, naval and aircraft movements, Defence preparations, pictures of shelters, sandbagging, etc.
>
> 2. All references for or against any of the countries involved as belligerents either in regard to war propaganda or propaganda for or against peoples – their mode of living, culture, etc.
>
> 3. All films dealing with Imperial, Colonial or Dominion activities which tend to glorify the Empire or British rule – White man's burden – spreading the benefits of white (British) civilisation – Kiplingesque – Gunga Din – Bengal Lancer – Four Feathers type of stuff.
>
> 4. All news films – Pathé Gazette – Movietone etc. must be free from war news or anything of a propagandist or partisan nature.
>
> 5. References such as 'Our King and Country' – 'This Little Island of Ours' (meaning Great Britain). 'We' (meaning the British people) - 'Our troops' and the like must be eliminated.

In the course of the visit the controller and his assistant viewed three newsreels which had been submitted for censorship. Connolly 'instructed' (his own word) Montgomery to eliminate a section which featured Chamberlain and British officials, and dealt with air raid precautions and general protective measures from a purely British point of view.[6]

The Department of Justice immediately made clear that it was not in agreement with some of Connolly's views; the controller responded by telling Aiken that the question of responsibility for emergency film censorship needed to be resolved without delay. He described as undesirable the anomalous position whereby the Emergency Censorship prohibited the press from publishing certain types of matter 'while at the same time equally offensive or worse matter is allowed go through in the form of newsreels or provocative propagandist films'.[7] In Britain, in the early stages of the war, an arrangement had been devised whereby the Board of Film Censors continued to have nominal responsibility for war censorship but acted on the advice of a panel of attached representatives from the three defence departments as part of the controlled division of the Ministry of Information. Coyne felt that a similar system could operate in Ireland, but that if this was not possible to arrange, then a new emergency order would need to be made relieving the Minister for Justice and the official film censor of any responsibility in the matter of emergency censorship and giving the 'final word' in this area to the Minister for the Co-ordination of Defensive Measures.[8]

Aiken met with Gerald Boland, Minister for Justice, to discuss the issue and on 20 September 1939 informed Connolly that 'it had been decided that all matters affecting the censorship of films were now in the hands of the Department of Justice and that for the future the Controller of Censorship would have no responsibility for anything in connection with the censorship of films'.[9] This remained the position until July 1942 when a new order was made giving a minister the power to direct the censor to reject a film on emergency grounds or to suspend any certificate granted by him. The provision of an appeal to the Minister for Justice in the case of such films was withdrawn and replaced by an unofficial appeal to Aiken. This system, added to the ministerial power to direct the film censor, brought emergency film censorship, for the first time, directly under the control of the emergency censorship organisation. It had fulfilled a consultative role up to this, while Coyne was often appointed by the Minister for Justice to hear appeals on behalf of films rejected on emergency grounds. In general, though, the film censorship operated firmly within the parameters set by the Emergency Censorship and in line with the philosophy of 'neutral entertainment'.

Montgomery's first Emergency task was to circulate the renters of newsreels, informing them that:

> In order to avoid demonstrations prejudicial to the maintenance of law and order, or the creation of scenes likely to lead to a breach of the peace, films showing pictures of rulers, statesmen, warriors and flags of the belligerents must not be shown.
>
> In order to avoid offence to the peoples of friendly foreign nations, war news must not be accompanied by titles or commentary of a propaganda nature.[10]

This ruled out most newsreels, which gradually came to be dominated by war news/propaganda. The American magazine *Look* estimated that four-fifths of all newsreel footage released in the US from 1942 to 1946 was devoted to some aspect of the war.[11] This preoccupation had begun earlier in Britain where 'newsreels bore the brunt of the propaganda war'; this was partly because well-produced newsreels, like modern television news bulletins, could give an illusion of completeness (whereby what had not been included did not appear to be missing), and partly because cinema was 'so completely controllable by the authorities and unverifiable by the audience'.[12]

The strict demands of Irish censorship forced the British newsreel companies to produce special, 'neutralised' editions for the Irish market; they presented to Irish viewers a radically different world to that shown to their British counterparts, a world into which the tribulations of their near neighbours and the war in Europe did not impinge. In mid-May 1940, for example, in a week which saw the arrival of the Dutch government as refugees in London and the bombing of Rotterdam and Canterbury, Gaumont British News, the largest circulation newsreel in Ireland and the UK, featured in its Irish edition: the New York World Fair; US polo stars playing for charity; the Feria Fete in Seville; a carnival in Zurich; the opening of the baseball season in the US; torrential floods and storms in America; and the pope proclaiming a saint in Rome.[13] A week later on 23 May, at the height of the battle for France, this is how the news for the previous three days, produced in both cases by Gaumont, appeared on British and Irish screens:[14]

Ireland	*Britain*
1. Italian royalty received by Pope Pius.	1. The Navy on guard in the north.
2. Australian boat race.	2. The fleet at Alexandria.
3. Sultan of Morocco at the Mouland Festival.	3. War zone special:
4. Madame Chiang Kai Shek inspects air-raid damage at Chunking.	Belgian towns attacked.
	Bombed hospitals.
	BEF tank blows up bridges.
	Refugees hide from machine guns.
5. Kentucky Derby.	Belgian Army on the road.
6. Dublin Great Spring Show at Ballsbridge.	Parachute troops prisoners guarded.
	German wounded and prisoners arriving in England.

Despite prior 'neutralisation' by the producers, such newsreels were still subjected to censorship by the Irish authorities; in February 1942 the *Daily Telegraph* reported on cuts made in a number of Irish editions, including scenes of children feeding elephants in London Zoo and old women playing bowls – both groups carried gas masks thus potentially evoking sympathy with the British![15]

In May 1943 the special newsreels were discontinued due to a raw film stock shortage in England. This prompted Martin Quigley, an OSS (the forerunner of the CIA) agent who operated in Ireland posing as a representative of the Motion Picture Producers and Distributors of America, to contact the latter with the suggestion that a newsreel edited in the US for export had a better chance of acceptance in Ireland than the regular British newsreels which were rejected by the censor. He suggested that several issues of United Newsreel should be sent over for a 'censorship test' and if the results were satisfactory a service should be established for the rest of the war. Quigley ended his telegram by stressing that it was 'important this neutral country should have newsreel'.[16] United Newsreel was a US government propaganda newsreel produced by a corporation established in 1942 by the five major newsreel firms in association with the film division of the Office of War Information. It was distributed in sixteen languages in friendly, neutral and 'doubtful' countries as well as behind enemy lines.[17] The strict demands of Irish censorship, however, were to doom this experiment to failure.[18]

The principal problem with newsreels was that audiences, internationally, tended to express openly their approval or disapproval at what appeared on the screen. In Ireland in the 1930s militant republicans disrupted screenings on a number of occasions, such as in December 1934 when a Dublin cinema showed a newsreel featuring a British royal wedding.[19] Aiken believed that 'if a newsreel is shown in which one belligerent or the other is prominent, somebody may start to "booh" and somebody may start to cheer, and we do not want that sort of competition to start'.[20] However, in neutral Portugal British and American newsreels were a prominent feature of nearly all cinema performances during the war. Prior to each screening, a notice appeared on the screen calling on the audience to make no demonstration; this injunction was, apparently, generally obeyed by the 'mixed' audiences.[21]

While engaged in his Emergency work, the censor simultaneously continued to carry out his duty of protecting the fragile faith and morals of Irish cinema patrons. Probably his most famous victim in the first year of the Emergency was *Gone with the Wind* (1939), the epic romance which packed English cinemas for the duration of the war. The cuts which he demanded from the renters, including a scene which featured the birth of a child, were so severe that the film was withdrawn by them.[22] (Many of the films which were banned outright were treated as such 'on account of obnoxious details which, were they deleted, would simply leave the film in such a state of emasculation that it would be almost meaningless'.[23]) Montgomery retired in October 1940 and was replaced, on 1 November, by Dr Richard Hayes.[24] ('We had films before our eyes, now we have a Hayes', commented *Dublin Opinion* on his appointment.[25]) The new censor's yardstick was straightforward: 'There is a simple moral code and there are principles on which civilisation and family life are based. Any ignoring of these or any defiance of them in a picture bans it straightaway as far as I am concerned'.[26] He frowned particularly on 'lascivious dances' in American musicals and on all forms of 'Anglicisation' and 'Americanisation'. He was very careful not to allow 'any light or frivolous treatment of marriage to appear on the screen'; abortion and birth-control were forbidden subjects, though 'illegitimacy' and divorce were permissible provided they were presented in a suitably unfavourable light. On one occasion Hayes obliged a distributor to change the title of a film from *I Want a Divorce* to *The Tragedy of Divorce*.[27]

In an interview published in *The Bell* in November 1941 the 'Genial Censor' (as the article described him) was asked for his opinion on 'the crack-down on all war pictures, news-reels and the like'. He responded that 'a full ninety-per-cent of the films we get from England and America these days have more than their fair share of propaganda, even the non-war films. And it's the devil's own job cutting it out'.[28] The devil's own job perhaps but Hayes proved himself to be very adept at it and Coyne need have had no fears about the censor's ability to 'neutralise' the films brought before him. He banned Charlie Chaplin's *The Great Dictator* (1940), a 'satirical masterpiece'[29] featuring Jack Oakie as Benzino Napoloni and Chaplin as Adenoid Hynkel,

A scene from Charlie Chaplin's *The Great Dictator* (1940) which was banned in Ireland during the war. The film censor believed that 'If that film had been shown in this country it would have meant riots and bloodshed.'

dictator of Tamania, a burlesque of Hitler.[30] Hayes was not impressed, declaring it 'blatant and vulgar propaganda from beginning to end. About as vulgar as Gilray's cartoons of Napoleon . . . If that film had been shown in this country it would have meant riots and bloodshed'. When asked whether the same argument applied to the showing of newsreels, he was in no doubt: 'We simply couldn't risk these things with the sort of mixed audiences you get in this country. And, well, you know the Irishman's propensity for – shall we say? – argument'.[31]

The censor viewed on average two full-length pictures every day, plus trailers and re-shows of films in their new 'cut' versions.[32] In June 1943 Martin Quigley, the American spy who operated in Ireland under the cover of a film representative, spent a week in the censor's office, watching him work and attempting to 'learn the principles and the specific application of the censorship to particular scenes'. Hayes told him that at the start of the war de Valera had sent the following suggestions for cuts in films: '1. All prominent personalities of the belligerent nations, 2. All flags of the belligerents and 3. All national anthems of the belligerents'. The British flag was usually cut (as was the case since the establishment of the Free State) but the American flag was usually left alone, as it was unlikely to cause any disturbance in a cinema. This fear of disturbance, explained Quigley in a letter to his company in New York, was the reason why the political censorship was so strict. 'I am told that in country theatres especially, certain elements in the audience are inclined to start a disturbance if given the slightest opportunity. This applies, of course, chiefly to anything which might seem pro-British.' Also cut were words like 'Quisling', the names of Hitler, Mussolini or any other Axis leader, and expressions like 'Huns', 'Jerries' and 'Japs'. Even the word 'Nazi' was not acceptable, as the official position of the German legation was that the use of the word outside Germany had an adverse connotation. The V-sign was disallowed as were the words 'Pearl Harbour' because 'the attack on Pearl Harbour was of a treacherous nature, so any reference to it is unfriendly to Japan'![33]

American films generally received kinder treatment than British ones, according to Quigley; one manager told him that in one of his pictures a scene of RAF fliers and Chinese fliers was cut while one of US airmen was left in. This is backed up by journalist Cobbet Wilkes's observation in the *Spectator* in July 1943 that he had 'occasionally seen films in Dublin showing the American forces, but never the British forces'.[34] A few Pacific newsreels had been shown but it was not permitted to identify which side was which. A telegram in March 1945 from United Artists to Quigley tells of the rage of an American producer at cuts made to his film. These included quotations from Abraham Lincoln, the Statue of Liberty and the 'Star Spangled Banner', as well as various scenes from home-front America such as dialogue on trains and welcomes for returning 'heroes'. He was particularly upset as he had 'not only expended millions of dollars on this picture but

[had] taken infinite care to present [a] picture of [the] American home front which would be acceptable in every Allied and neutral country throughout the world'.[35]

In March 1942 the Kinematograph Renters Society wrote to the Irish high commissioner in London, John Dulanty, complaining about the increasing number of bannings and cuts.[36] Ireland was considered part of the UK distribution network[37] and represented only 2 per cent of the total UK revenue. Given the proportionately higher operating costs, allied to the continuing difficulties with censorship (on both 'moral' and 'emergency' grounds) the distributors warned that they would soon have to consider whether the 'economic data line' had not been reached. They suggested that the situation had deteriorated since Hayes had replaced Montgomery and that unless the interpretation of the censor could be made 'a little more elastic' the distributors would be left with no other course than the closure of their offices in Dublin.[38] This threat was repeated in the following June when leading members of the British film trade visited Dublin.[39]

Neither this threat, nor a similar one from an American trade representative (Quigley) in the following year, was carried out. This was a matter of some relief for the Irish film trade and also for the government which cashed in on the popularity of cinema by exacting a flat rate of import tax from each film.[40] Nevertheless, the trade in Ireland continued to encounter difficulties in its efforts to maintain its business and provide the population with its most popular form of entertainment.

Following the Soviet entry into the war on the Allied side in June 1941 Soviet films were allowed into Britain, and from late 1941 a steady stream of Soviet features, documentaries and short films were screened in Britain.[41] There was a natural overflow into Ireland, and in June 1942 Hayes passed two such films, *A Day in the Life of Soviet Russia* and *Russian Salad*, for exhibition. The attention of Aiken was subsequently drawn to them (by Hempel, the German diplomatic representative, according to David Gray, the US minister[42]) and having viewed the films he formed the opinion that their exhibition would be prejudicial to the interests of the state. As no provision existed for the revocation of a certificate in such circumstances, a draft of a new order dealing with emergency film censorship was prepared. The opportunity was taken to institute a number of other changes also, and on 24 July the Emergency Powers (No. 196) Order 1942 was made.[43]

This new order gave a minister the power to direct the official censor to reject any film or suspend any certificate granted by him and empowered the latter to revoke any certificate granted by him prior to the making of the order. It also abolished the provision of an appeal to the Minister for Justice and the Appeal Board and provided for no official alternative. Since the commencement of the Emergency there had been twenty appeals made to the Minister for Justice against decisions of the official censor, and the minister, acting on the advice of the controller of censorship, had reversed the censor's decision in whole or in part in eight cases.[44] In recognition of the fact that this indicated the need for an appeals system, an administrative arrangement was devised whereby Aiken, or a member of his staff, would act as an informal, unofficial, 'nevertheless decisive appeal board'.[45] (These provisions related only to films rejected on 'emergency' grounds.)

When Aiken met representatives of the Kinematograph Renters Society (Irish Advisory Committee) – which represented 95 per cent of the renting business – to discuss the new order in September 1942, he made it clear that the more they appealed decisions to him, the less likely they were to succeed. They proceeded to argue for relaxation in the rigidity of restrictions on newsreels and features, many of which could have been made acceptable by some judicious treatment rather than being rejected in full for the sake of a small cut or the deletion of some commentary.[46]

Aiken's exercise of his new powers in September of the following year caused further consternation in the trade and led Martin Quigley to threaten the withdrawal of American films from the Irish market, an action which would have crippled the industry in the state. *A Yank in the RAF* (1941) featured Betty Grable and cast Tyrone Power as an initially uncommitted American who converts to the Allied cause.[47] The film, which had been cut by Hayes, had been on show to packed houses in the Savoy cinema in Dublin for a week when Aiken directed that it be withdrawn. This action caused the Theatre and Cinemas Association (representing film exhibitors) to seek a meeting with the minister. When they met him at the beginning of October 1943, they explained that the number of 'first-run' films available to them was severely restricted and that the withdrawal of a film like *A Yank in the RAF* represented a serious inroad into their supplies and deprived them of the sense of security which was essential in their business. The minimum requirement of the seven 'first-run' houses was 350 films per year (fifty per cinema) and given that there were only 200 to 250 'first-run' films available to them per year (and the fact that Dublin cinema-goers were lukewarm about 'subsequent-run' films) the minister was urged to understand their precarious position.

Aiken, while expressing sympathy with their position, said he believed they had had 'a fairly good deal'. He quoted figures from the official censor which showed that of the 252 films submitted during the last twelve months for which figures were available, only twenty-nine had been rejected and eighty-eight cut. Kirkham, representing the provincial cinemas, pointed out that such figures gave a false impression because the trade exercised a sort of pre-censorship and refrained from submitting a very large number of films which they themselves regarded as undesirable or unlikely to be passed by the censor. (There was a good deal of self-censorship on the part of the London and Dublin offices of the distributors, since the censor had to be paid regardless of the fate of the film.)

Aiken told the delegation that he would go as far as he could to meet their position but would not go so far as as to impair the whole position in relation to national unity or acquiesce in the exhibition of films which would be likely to occasion demonstrations in the theatres and cinemas. When it was pointed out to him that there had been no demonstrations in the Savoy during the showing of *A Yank in the RAF* though thousands had seen it (according to the US minister, David Gray, up to 38,000), Aiken referred to the 'resentment and dissatisfaction' people felt when they went home at the exhibition of this type of film![48]

A delegation, including Irish Transport and General Workers' Union (ITGWU) officials, representing cinema operatives met Aiken at the end of October 1943. When they informed him that Martin Quigley had told them, after the withdrawal of *A Yank in the RAF*, that if current censorship policy continued there was a danger that no more American films would be sent to Ireland, the minister reacted angrily. He railed against Quigley, saying that he resented his threat to starve the Irish cinema industry unless 'we agreed to let foreigners dictate our policy' and that it was in line with the British opium war against the Chinese. He would be 'glad to discuss our policy with Irishmen', but resented 'interference from any outsider'. Over the next two months the American minister, David Gray, sought to secure compensation for Twentieth-Century Fox for the losses incurred by the withdrawal of *A Yank in the RAF*; the film industry, claimed Gray, was at the mercy of 'the unpredictable mental processes' of the minister. Compensation was, not surprisingly, refused and Coyne concluded the correspondence on the matter by telling Gray that 'for barefaced audacity I know of no parallel for such a claim in the history of international relations'.[49]

When the operatives asked if it had been the German minister who had secured the banning, Aiken told them that he had taken action against the film because of letters he had received from 'Old IRA men' who objected to its exhibition. He told them that Hempel was much too wise to interfere in Ireland's internal affairs and had never done so. 'Our policy in censorship is not directed to please foreigners or to prevent their ill-will, but for the purpose of keeping our own people together to resist attack from abroad.'[50]

Despite Aiken's claims to the contrary there were numerous occasions throughout the period when action was taken in response to complaints from the representatives of foreign governments in Dublin. In February 1941, for example, following a complaint from the Swiss legation, a section of dialogue in *Too Many Girls* then showing in the Capitol Cinema in Dublin (in which a man relates that his daughter was expelled from Switzerland for running her speedboat into a pontoon on which the Swiss president was delivering a speech on safety), was removed because it was 'disrespectful to the President of the Swiss Confederation'.[51] *Sundown* was passed with extensive cuts in February 1942; however, after complaints from the Italian minister,

Vincenzo Berardis, that the film insulted the dignity of the Italian army, Hayes re-viewed it and duly cut the parts to which objection had been taken.[52] In 1944 Hayes, in conjunction with Aiken, severely cut *For Whom the Bell Tolls* so that 'nothing derogatory to General Franco or Spain' remained, following representations from the Spanish minister.[53]

The virtual monopoly enjoyed by British and American films meant that even after severe censorship sensitive Germans could still be offended. In a letter to his family in September 1941 a German interned in the Curragh wrote that 'the [cinema] programmes offered here are extremely mediocre, if they are not expressly biased i.e. anti-German, espionage and trash . . . In one case the film was such that I kicked up a row . . . and the visiting of cinemas has been forbidden for some time'.[54] (Internees were allowed to visit cinemas in nearby towns.[55])

American films also dominated the market in neutral Sweden[56] and were popular in Switzerland until the cessation of American imports in September 1943; British films like *Mrs Miniver* and *In Which we Serve*, both banned in Ireland, continued to be screened, while German features and newsreels were shown at all cinemas.[57] The German film industry, however, produced too little to maintain any cinema fully, and theatres in Portugal stopped screening its product altogether because, otherwise, British and American films would have been denied to them. All the best-known films were screened there and were not seriously interfered with.[58] Pictures with only the most vague or general war reference continued to suffer in Ireland, however, and film companies continued to have cause for complaint.

In January 1942 Warner Brothers sought an explanation through the Irish legation in Washington for the banning of *Sergeant York* (1941) in the previous month; the film had a First World War setting and was described by the Department of External Affairs as 'violent anti-German propaganda'.[59] Later in the war the same company complained that of thirteen films which they had submitted for censorship in 1943, only six had been passed. Aiken attributed this to their policy of making 'very virulent war propaganda films'.[60]

In the early months of 1944 Columbia Pictures were 'amazed' at the action of the censor in demanding the withdrawal of the song 'When the Lights Go On Again' from their short film *Community Songs No. 61*. This was an innocuous song which looked forward to the end of the war and contained no references to either side in the conflict. When their local manager in Dublin lodged an appeal with Aiken, Columbia suffered 'further astonishment' when the minister not only upheld the censor's decision but ordered the deletion of a further song, 'Bless 'em All'. The company pointed out that both songs were widely known in Ireland, and that 'Bless 'em All' had been sung by an audience of Irish soldiers at a recent sponsored performance held at the Theatre Royal, Dublin. A few months later the censor rejected another of their films, *Bell-Bottom George*, starring slapstick comedian George Formby; the film was pure farce but had the misfortune of having a story with a background involving German spies.[61] (Another Formby film became the subject of a boycott in Limerick because of the comedian's 'joke' that 'while the Japs are yellow outside, the Irish are yellow inside'.[62])

As well as censoring the exhibition of newsreels and documentaries within the state, the authorities endeavoured to keep control over the footage shot within Ireland for use in such films. Given that film shot here had to be exported for processing, usually to London, it was possible to control this traffic under the Emergency Powers (Conveyance of Informative Articles) Order 1939.[63] Such film could only be dispatched abroad by a named company, and if the Censorship was satisfied with the content, having seen either the developed positive or the dupe sheets accompanying the undeveloped negative, an 'Export Authorised by the Censorship' stamp was given.[64] The problem remained, of course, that in the case of newsreels, the juxtaposition of pictures, and of commentary with pictures (montage), was the crucial element; the successfully exported footage could be used in a particular way, or accompanied by a particular commentary, which would make the entire product totally unacceptable from the point of view of the Irish censorship authorities.[65] Their concern in this, as in all areas of censorship, was that the 'correct' image of neutral Ireland should be properly presented both to the Irish people and to the outside world.

British newsreels in the first two years of the war tended to portray Ireland as a plucky little neutral ready to defend herself against German aggression. Until 1941, when the Treaty ports had become critically important in terms of the Battle of the Atlantic, Ireland's policy was represented as wise and sensible, and in general the newsreels were patronising rather than hostile in relation to neutrality. The tone started to change in 1941, however, as shipping losses began to bite and British government impatience with Irish neutrality began to percolate through the communications media. Ireland was now accused of 'sitting on the fence' and newsreel scripts became increasingly hostile and offensive. Particularly damaging was a ten-minute Paramount news film, *Ireland – The Plain Issue*, made in early 1942. The film 'sounded – and looked – as if it was intended to prepare the British public for an Allied invasion of Éire'. The commentary presented de Valera as 'a dictator' and the Irish as 'peasants', sharing their cottages with pigs ('and, we might add, his pig with his cross-channel neighbour'). It ridiculed the Irish army, made sectarian swipes at Catholics and contrasted the South with Northern Ireland which was '100% in the war' as well as being economically stronger and more enterprising. According to Robert Fisk, the film propagated the idea that 'the Irish were unclean, weak, idle and cowardly, that their religion was demeaning and their political motives naive and selfish. The script's cynical – almost racial – abuse had something in common with the propaganda of the Nazis; it was both provocative and deeply disturbing'.[66]

In February 1942 John Dulanty, the Irish high commissioner in London, drew the attention of the apostolic delegate and Cardinal Hinsley, Catholic archbishop of Westminster, to the insults made against Catholics in the film; he also protested to the Ministry of Information.[67] In a letter to the *Irish Independent* (which was 'Held by the Censor') the chairman of Craobh na hAiséirighe, an ultra-nationalist Catholic group, called for a ban on all Paramount pictures (following the example of Spain, Italy and France in similar circumstances) and on the conduct of any business in Ireland by the company. The Catholic *Standard*, however, expressed the hope that the film would be shown in Ireland, as it would be effective in illustrating 'the dangers of the present cultural stranglehold held by foreign and antagonistic producers and distributors of films'. Paramount originally defended the film and said it would not withdraw it as it gave the 'full facts'; Ireland was defended by the British navy and ought to give facilities to it.[68] They subsequently backtracked and withdrew the film with apologies; they claimed that it had only been released because the chairman and managing director had been away in the US, and that those responsible for the film had been censured.[69] Nothing as crassly offensive appeared again, although newsreels continued to criticise Irish neutrality and to perpetuate the image of Dublin as a centre of German espionage.

Two months after the *Plain Issue* débâcle Paramount sought permission to produce another newsreel on Ireland, this time on lines approved beforehand with the authorities. Frank Gallagher of the Government Information Bureau told the Department of External Affairs that he believed it would be excellent if the government had any control over the accompanying commentary. 'Without that, and it would be unlikely that they would permit us a political censorship, the project is dangerous and would represent us as being on one side in the war.'[70] A year later, however, full advantage was taken when another company sought permission to film in Ireland.

In March 1943 the 'March of Time' requested permission to send a crew to film footage for an issue on *The Irish Question*. The 'March of Time' was 'a radically different kind of newsreel' which had been introduced by Time, Inc. in 1935. It was less a newsreel than a documentary film in which (after 1938) only one subject was dealt with in every twenty-minute issue.[71] In 1936 the company had made one of the first filmed documentary overviews of Ireland.[72] When the request to film was made in 1943, Coyne, although wary, saw the potential for 'selling our story in the world market'. He suggested to Aiken that 'it might be politic to take the big-hearted Arthur line' and waive the right to censor on the spot, provided the film-makers undertook to submit the film to Leo McCauley, the Irish consul-general in New York (where the film was to be developed and processed). They would then have to make such deletions as he required and withdraw the film altogether if it was considered 'wholly objectionable'.[73]

It was agreed with the company that the shots should be restricted to approved scenes and subjects and that McCauley in New York would see the completed film, including commentary, before it was released for exhibition; he could then veto any objectionable matter.

The 'March of Time' team filmed in Ireland from 16 September to 6 December 1943. They were accompanied for the duration by Major Guilfoyle of G2 who viewed the shots that were taken. The only one he considered objectionable featured a scene at a dance in the Gresham Hotel (on the night of the Red Cross Chase at Leopardstown racecourse) showing waiters carrying four bottles of champagne to guests. This scene of decadence was duly deleted. The rest of the film featured familiar scenes of farming, schoolchildren, air raid precaution exercises, film queues, the All-Ireland final and so on. The authorities, having vetted the footage, saw that the hostility or otherwise of the film would lay in the commentary. Frank Gallagher feared that the scenes featuring the export of cattle to Britain, the UK permit office, the award of VCs to Irishmen and the Press and Postal Censorship could be presented in such a way as to show Ireland and its neutrality in an unfavourable light. He was also afraid that the 'film queues, shops, dances etc. may be used to imply that we are junketing while the rest of the world is dying'.[74] (In contrast, and interestingly with regard to official priorities, no concern was expressed about scenes such as those of barefoot children entering rural schools.)

Coyne, on the other hand, looked on the positive side and saw the propaganda potential of the documentary. He made some interesting and revealing observations on the censorship of the film in a letter to the Department of External Affairs, designed to help McCauley in his task as censor. The controller guessed that the producers' approach would be along either of two lines, namely: that Ireland had embraced a 'cowardly neutrality' which helped the 'powers of darkness'; or that Irish neutrality was a mere pretence and that Ireland was in a *de facto* alliance with the Allies. Coyne told Boland that 'if we have to choose between being depicted as the Fighting Irish or the Irish Yaps I am all in favour of the old 69th'. He saw no harm in references to the fact that Irish neutrality had not prevented many Irishmen achieving distinction in the war and would not have been inclined to dissuade them if the 'March of Time' people saw fit to add that 'it had yet to be shown that there were any Irishmen fighting for the Japanese'![75]

In the case of exports to Britain, Coyne believed that they should make a virtue of necessity and 'claim credit for a friendly humanitarianism', stressing the role Ireland could play in the relief of postwar Europe. He saw no harm in allowing the Press Censorship to be presented as the strictest in the world provided the consul resisted any suggestion of 'ostrichism or of pro-German or anti-British or American bias'. The controller concluded by pointing out that almost all of the war and foreign news carried by the Irish papers was supplied by American and British news agencies; 'how I would like to hear the commentator say this and how much misrepresentation would be dispelled thereby'.[76]

The Irish Question was released in Britain on 12 June 1944 and was shown across the Allied and neutral world. The *Irish Press* reported that the commentary told of Ireland's 'passionate regard for the independence she has so lately won after centuries of oppression and want' and emphasised that 'Ireland is irrevocably committed to neutrality as a national policy'.[77] Coyne cannot have been too happy, however, with the stereotypically patronising approach of the commentary when it came to explaining Irish neutrality: 'Ireland's unhappy history under British rule was an important factor in Éire's decision to remain neutral, a decision which the freedom-loving nations of the world found difficult to comprehend. But those who would understand this proud and sensitive people today and in the future should look, not to logic, but to the poetry of the Irish'.[78]

The only real alternative to the mainstream American and British fare was offered by the Irish Film Society (IFS), with its programme of non-English language and classical films, as well as the occasional 'quality' recent British and American release. Film societies everywhere have traditionally provided a refuge from the interfering hands of censors, and the IFS films were not subject to censorship under the Censorship of Films Acts, as amended in 1939, because the showings were not technically 'in public'. Nevertheless, towards the end of 1943, the society began to encounter problems with the emergency censorship as its artistic agenda came into conflict with the demands of 'neutral entertainment'.

At the close of the 1942–3 season the IFS screened Michael Powell's *49th Parallel* (1941),[79] the first major classic British film of the war period and the first explicitly propagandist war film that the society had shown. The film had been partly financed by the British Ministry of Information and dealt with the story of a crew of a wrecked German submarine on the run in Canada. It was made as part of the effort to counter isolationism in North America and attempted to depict the 'moral superiority of the quietly decent Englishman and his Allies' in contrast to the fanatical Nazis; it features the classic line delivered by Leslie Howard – 'That's for Thomas Mann, and that's for me' – as he pummels one of the Germans who have destroyed his paintings and books.[80] Following protests from a few members it was decided not to show any more 'controversial' films[81] but, unfortunately for the IFS, Frank Aiken and his censors had a slightly different view of what was, and was not, 'controversial'.

In October 1943 the society screened the Soviet film *Russian Salad*. It was a musical short which was enthusiastically received by society members in the Olympia, Dublin and in a number of other IFS centres, including Cork and Limerick. The film had been given a certificate by the official censor for general release in June 1942, but, as we have seen, the certificate was suspended by Aiken's direction on 29 July. The film's distributors, Irish Photo Play Ltd, had been compensated for the losses they had incurred and given the option of distributing the film, which was held in custody of the Department of Defence, if the ban was lifted subsequently. On reading press notices given to the IFS screening of *Russian Salad* the company requested a meeting with Aiken. They had also seen that another Soviet film, *Suvorov* (1941), which they had planned to bring in, was also shown by the IFS in November and they wondered what the present position was in relation to those films.[82] Aiken met representatives of Irish Photo Play on Christmas Eve 1943 and told them that there had been no change with regard to propaganda films; their public exhibition was still prohibited and he proposed to 'get after' the Irish Film Society.[83]

At the beginning of February 1944 Jack Purcell, deputising for Coyne, held a meeting with Liam O'Laoghaire, honorary secretary and one of the founding members of the society. Purcell informed him that 'for the present, at any rate', the controller did not propose to pursue the question of compelling the society to submit its films for censorship to the official censor, but that he was interested in its programmes and would like to be made aware of what it proposed to show.[84] In fact the Censorship had no legal authority to compel the IFS to submit its films to the censor as its powers extended only to films exhibited 'in public'. IFS screenings were open only to members and were thus technically 'private'. Yet the society voluntarily co-operated with the Censorship and acceded to its requests. As Coyne later explained to Aiken, 'it was really the threat to take further and better powers if necessary which induced them to meet our point of view'.[85]

When shown the list of upcoming films for 1944 Coyne expressed concern about *We from Kronstadt* (1935) and sought more information about it. O'Laoghaire explained that the film dealt with the defence of Petrograd in the Russian civil war in 1919. 'It was selected for the Society's programme last year mainly on the basis of reviews of two Catholic critics: Mr Arthur Vesseld's review in the 1936–37 volume of *Sight and Sound* . . . [and] Mr Graham Greene's review in the book *Footnotes to the Film*.' O'Laoghaire also recalled that the film was given a favourable review in the *Catholic Herald* in 1936. 'It will thus be seen that its subject matter is not contemporary and that its effect cannot be reasonably expected to be subversive or objectionable.' The Catholic credentials of these reviewers convinced Coyne that the film was 'all right', and although the screening went ahead Aiken, obdurate as ever, was still not happy, noting 'the great difference between films displaying the Soviet defence of an "ism" and other types'.[86]

When authorising the screening of *We From Kronstadt* Coyne warned O'Laoghaire that the Censorship was not inclined to allow newspaper publicity for this or others of its films. (On 12 February 1944 the press censors were instructed that 'all notices or reviews of films by the Irish Film Society are to be prohibited in future'.[87]) The reason, he explained, was to prevent 'tendentious' press comments on the political situation in the country of a film's origin. O'Laoghaire accepted this, saying that the society would be glad to be saved from it if the effect of such publicity was likely to lead to restriction of its activities.[88]

The society's magazine, *Scannán*, was of course subject to press censorship. In February 1944 an article by 'our first American member', Martin Quigley (the US agent), entitled 'Hollywood at War' was stopped by the press censor. In the course of the piece, Quigley bemoaned the banning and cutting of Hollywood war films and the absence of newsreels in Ireland. He reminded the Irish film critic and patron that, in judging Hollywood's output, they were 'in the position of a spectator who has seen most of the worst and little or nothing of the best scenes in the play'.[89]

There was no American film, good or bad, in the 1943–4 season of the IFS. The programme featured films from Germany, France, England, Sweden, Holland and the Soviet Union. O'Laoghaire, in a note to Coyne, wrote of the difficulties 'in trying to preserve a balance' in its programmes. The society had, he explained, 'deliberately avoided spurious publicity in selecting films which would help to foster international hatreds though many of the war films were of such high technical interest that it might reasonably be expected to include them'.[90] The programme for the 1944–5 season featured a number of films with war-related themes. Coyne sent the programme to Aiken, asking him to 'note that these people are agreed, according to the foreword by Mr Owen Sheehy-Skeffington, that no good war picture should be turned down simply because it was tendentious'. In a scribbled response Aiken reiterated his position in relation to the IFS: 'I would not allow them to show pictures which the commercial cinemas would be anxious to show and which they are prevented from showing by the emergency powers . . . Neither would I allow atrocity stuff on the grounds of its artistic merit'.[91]

The film censor was consulted and, of the films on the programme which had been previously submitted to him for censorship, the only cut made was the deletion of a reference to Hitler in two reels of *His Girl Friday* (1939). More information was sought from the IFS on a number of the other films, especially *Les Otages* (1939) which Coyne considered 'doubtful'. This was a French satirical drama which was set at the time of the 1914–18 war and dealt with the taking of five hostages in a French village by German invaders. Having read a review of the film in the *Monthly Film Bulletin* of August 1939 Purcell, the assistant controller, in a note to Aiken, surmised that 'it may well be that the invading German forces are shown in anything but a favourable light'. This was despite the fact that the review specifically stated that 'the invading Germans are depicted as natural human beings, and the war is not introduced for propaganda purposes'. Yet Aiken, trusting his official's ill-founded suspicions and never having seen the film, directed that the showing of *Les Otages* be stopped.[92]

Peter Sherry of the IFS appealed to Aiken, through Coyne, for the repeal of the ban, pointing to the artistic and non-propagandist nature of the film and reiterating some general points about the 'private' nature of the showing, the international balance of the society's programme and the absence of any disturbances at any of its screenings since the beginning of the war.[93]

In rejecting the appeal Aiken failed to address any of the specific points made by Sherry. His reply was in the most general terms and provides us with an interesting summary of Aiken's narrow philosophy of 'neutral entertainment':

> While I fully appreciate the point of view of your Society I would point out that as a nation we have had, since the beginning of the war, to forego certain pleasures and conveniences, not because we hadn't a right to them, but because the exercise of that right might have been misunderstood to the detriment of our unity and ability to defend ourselves, or our relations with other peoples. I feel we will have to postpone the pleasure of seeing *Les Otages* until the war is over.[94]

Storm in a Teacup (a somewhat appropriate title, given the circumstances) with Rex Harrison and Vivienne Leigh was considered less likely to stir up passions and insult 'other peoples' and was thus allowed as a replacement for the French film.[95]

Millions Like Us, partly financed by the British Ministry of Information and directed by Frank Launder and Sidney Gilliat, was released in 1943. It was notable as the only British commercial feature of the war period which addressed the issue of the employment of women in factories.[96] When the IFS applied to show it in October 1944 Coyne's immediate suspicion was that it was 'pure and unadulterated propaganda of the stiff upper lip, keep a straight bat and don't rock the boat type'. He subsequently learned that the film had already been rejected for public exhibition on emergency grounds and, his suspicions confirmed, informed Sherry that, in his opinion, the film should not be shown. He concluded by repeating the position of the Censorship with regard to the IFS: 'I do not think that your Society should seek to show films which the commercial cinemas have been prevented from showing on these special grounds'.[97]

The problematic issue of 'private screenings' was encountered on a number of other occasions throughout the period, but the incidents were never so serious or numerous as to force the authorities to change the law. Such screenings were either stopped (through threat or where the importation of the film could be prohibited), ignored, denied publicity or glossed over.

In December 1941 a Corkman serving with the Royal Artillery in Britain requested permission to bring home with him on leave the film *Target for Tonight* (1941), or portions of it, to show to some of his friends in private.[98] This film, financed by the Ministry of Information, was one of the few 'documentaries' which was popular in Britain, principally because, at the time of the blitz, it showed 'the power to strike back' by wildly exaggerating the success of RAF raids on Germany.[99] The film had no chance of securing a certificate for public exhibition in Ireland, but it had been seen in the country earlier in the year – at a private showing in a Dublin cinema organised by the UK representative, John Maffey – having been imported in the British diplomatic bag. The Department of External Affairs had discovered this only after the event and was determined that another showing should be prohibited, if possible. Given that a film was an 'informative article' under Article 18G of the Emergency Powers Order 1939, the importation of the film was prohibited under the Emergency Powers (Restrictions on Conveyance of Informative Articles) Order 1939.[100]

Once such films were in the country it was not legally possible to prohibit their exhibition 'in private'. In the early months of 1945 a number of large private showings (attendance was by invitation) of US war features and newsreels were held in Dublin cinemas, usually on Sunday mornings.[101] A number of war films distributed by the American legation and the office of the UK representative were shown in various halls and schools under the auspices of the Voluntary Defence Services in late 1944 and early 1945. Aiken explained in the Dáil that these films were exhibited and viewed for their technical interest and 'cannot be said to have had a propagandist effect on their members'. He pointed out that such private showings were not subject to censorship and that he did not propose to take steps to amend the EPO 'unless the situation regarding the exhibition of such films required it'.[102]

That situation did not arise and four months after Aiken made that statement, on Friday, 11 May 1945, the emergency restrictions were lifted. By the following Sunday the war had arrived on Irish screens. The offensive was led by the US Army Air Force in the 'Thrill-roaring! Sky-soaring!' *Winged Victory*.[103] This was followed later in the week by the 'March of Time's *The Unknown Battle* (which again featured the USAAF) and their *Report on Italy* – both banned during the war.[104] The following week saw the arrival of Pathé Gazette's *Liberation of Stalingrad*[105] and Cecil B. de Mille's epic of Java, 1942, *The Story of Dr Wassell*.[106] The *Irish Times* cinema correspondent welcomed the films, commenting that: 'After so many years of lukewarm commentary and neutralised drama it is a great relief to see films that are publicly and shamelessly belligerent'.[107] Forty such films arrived in Dublin for submission to the censor in the week ending Saturday, 26 May and the censor already had a list of about one hundred awaiting review.[108]

Some war-starved film-goers had travelled north of the border during the Emergency to see features and newsreels banned in the South,[109] but for most the war had just begun and their demand seemed insatiable. Cinema booking lists were considerably altered and for the next three to four months films of a 'Technicolor musical variety' had to take a back seat to war films of varying quality. There was keen competition between rival exhibitors for critically acclaimed productions like *Desert Victory* (already shown 'privately' in Dublin), *49th Parallel*, *Mrs Miniver*, *Casablanca* and Noel Coward's *In Which We Serve*, the most successful British film of the war years.[110] Newsreel pictures of Buchenwald and Belsen filled theatres 'with a sudden chill', but some remained to be convinced; disapproving letters appeared in provincial newspapers following the screening of these newsreels, one writer in Kilkenny claiming that it was 'all propaganda' and that the British had used starving Indians to impersonate the Belsen inmates.[111]

It was now becoming clear to the more sensible sections of the cinema-going public how unnecessary most of the bannings and cuts had been. Coyne himself, after the war, wondered whether the powers of film censorship provided for by the EPO were not so wide that, in particular instances, 'the authorities may [have been] made to look ridiculous if challenged as to why a particular film was rejected'. Here Coyne was making reference to instances where the exhibition of a particular film was deemed to be 'undesirable', but could not be shown to be prejudicial to the public safety or the preservation of the state. He pointed to the fact that film censorship was not specifically mentioned in the Emergency Powers Act as the possible reason why the form of words used in the Act was used in the order, i.e. to ensure that it (the order) could not be challenged as *ultra vires*. To overcome this problem in any future emergency Coyne suggested that there should be a specific provision for the censorship of films (and stage plays) in the principal Emergency Act, as part of the inclusion of censorship in all its forms amongst the primary purposes of the Act.[112]

The fear of 'ridicule and contempt' had been expressed before by Coyne in relation to film censorship; but given the strictness and effectiveness of the overall censorship, the authorities were rarely seen to be as ridiculous as they often were. The bannings of Chaplin's and Formby's films, for example, could themselves have provided the raw material for cinematic comedy and farce. But if it was comedy, it was distinctly black. The arrogance which accompanies such extensive and extraordinary powers allowed Aiken to ban films which neither he nor any of his officials had actually seen. The absence of disturbances at the week-long screenings of *A Yank in the RAF* and at the exhibitions of 'unneutral' films by the IFS, as well as at the avalanche of war films which packed the cinemas after the lifting of the censorship, would seem to suggest that 'the Irishman's propensity for – shall we say? – argument' was not necessarily always on the verge of realisation.

While the Press Censorship, as we shall see, sought to ensure that war coverage in Irish newspapers was as objective, balanced and propaganda-free as possible, the film censorship was aimed at eliminating war coverage completely. The reasons for the stricter application in the case of film relate to a number of intrinsic features of the medium which made it so attractive for the propagandist, and dangerous for the censor. Of primary importance was its mass popularity, which far outstripped every other medium, and its accessibility: its ability to appeal across economic and social divides, to attract audiences from all classes and social groupings irrespective of levels of literacy or education. Linked to this was its immediacy and primarily visual appeal, so that it acted more on the emotions than on the intellect. This was an even more important factor when linked to the fact that cinema appealed to an individual as part of a crowd, so the cinema-goer was susceptible not only to his or her own emotions, but also to those of the crowd as in the case of a football match or a mass rally.[113] Aiken had a firm grasp on the difference between cinema and the press; he pointed out that war coverage in the press was 'in cold print, and if a man gets a newspaper in the morning he will not start either cheering or booing the paper'.[114]

The lack of legal authority in certain areas did not impede the 'neutralisation' of films, as we have seen in the treatment of the Irish Film Society. The acceptance of such treatment by the IFS, and of the excessive interference in their affairs by the cinema trade and the film-going public, is explicable by reference to the historical context. Specifically, there was the general consensus about the necessity for neutrality and by extension the emergency censorship (the creation of which was aided, in no small way, by the censorship itself). More generally, cultural censorship had by this stage firmly established itself in the new state. Film had preceded literature as the first victim of censorship and cuts and bans had become as much a part of the Irish cinematic experience as opening credits and musical scores. The emergency political censorship was as easily accommodated by the prevailing censorship mentality as were its mechanics by the prevailing film censorship machinery.

Theatre Censorship

Irish theatre was never subject to prior censorship; the Theatres Act of 1843, which made all plays in Britain subject to prior scrutiny, never applied in Ireland. When the subject of censorship arose in the 1920s, and film and publications fell victim to its grip, official censorship of the theatre was not debated.[115] No provision for the censorship of stage plays[116] was made in the emergency legislation either, but a theatre censorship did operate, albeit in an indirect and unofficial fashion.

In October 1939 the issue was raised when the typescript of a sketch which was to be staged at the Theatre Royal in Dublin was submitted to the Censorship. It contained characterisations of Hitler and Chamberlain (as well as of Al Capone and 'Éire') and was considered likely to provoke objections from the German and British representatives. The author was told that it could not be passed. This incident focused attention on the issue of objectionable stage representations, caricatures of statespeople and so on; a particular source of concern was visiting British comedians, the contents

of whose acts tended to fall some way short of the demands of neutral entertainment. A warning was issued by the Department of Justice to the
managers of theatres and music halls, pointing out that all objectionable
references to heads of foreign states or any matter which might cause conflict with Ireland's position of neutrality were to be rigidly excluded from
performances. Failure to do this, warned the department, could lead to the
suspension or withdrawal by the government of the licences under which
the theatres operated.[117]

In November 1940 the Gate Theatre staged *Roly Poly*, a Lennox Robinson play which was a modernisation of *Boule de Suif*, a Maupassant short
story set against the background of the Franco-Prussian war; the story
involved a French prostitute and an unsympathetically portrayed German
soldier. When the play provoked protests from the German and French
(Vichy) ministers, the producers were approached by the Department of
Justice and 'reminded' of the equivocal position of the Gate under the 1745
Act relating to the licensing of theatres. The play was 'voluntarily' withdrawn,
under protest, on 21 November. An 'unofficial' Government Information
Bureau statement was released to the press which suggested that the
authorities had requested the withdrawal of the play on 'moral grounds'.
Bertie Smyllie, editor of the *Irish Times*, correctly pointed out that this was
'baloney' and refused to print the statement; his report instead referred to
the real reason for the withdrawal, i.e. 'offence to other nationalities'. (This
item was stopped by the censor, as were all similar pieces, in line with a
general instruction issued to the press censors to prohibit all references to
Roly Poly and the controversy surrounding its withdrawal.[118])

Shortly after the withdrawal of the Lennox Robinson play, Micheál Mac
Liammóir of the Gate wrote to the writer Frank O'Connor suggesting that
the time was not right for him to produce the latter's latest play *The Statue's
Daughter*, which dealt with the implications of a rumour that a national
hero, in whose honour an Irish town was raising a statue, had fathered a
child out of wedlock. Mac Liammóir had not anticipated the response to
the Robinson play by the 'national Hoover-the-carpet movement', but was
now certain that O'Connor's play would cause more than a 'minor stink';
he told O'Connor that while raising a stink would have pleased him, he
would not risk anything that could close his theatre or hasten a general censorship of the theatre in Ireland.[119]

Occasionally the controller of censorship was approached, usually informally and often through public representatives, for an opinion as to how
the authorities would view the production of a particular play. In October
1944 the author of a work entitled *Sometime Never* submitted the typescript
to Coyne seeking an official ruling. The theme of the play was a civil war
between the North and the South of Ireland leading to an air bombardment of Southern towns by Northern aircraft. In a letter to Aiken on the
subject Coyne wrote that the play was so bad it would probably be a

'complete flop' and do little harm. He pointed out, however, that 'such a theme is not a suitable subject for stage representation at the present time and that a better play on the same subject might provoke a violent, emotional reaction in the audiences by which it was seen'. Coyne went on to say that the Department of Justice had enquired whether Aiken would be willing to move the government to take the necessary powers by way of an Emergency Powers Order to prevent the production of plays of this kind.

Aiken was indeed prepared to initiate such legislation but Coyne was of the opinion that, if the author was informed that the play was considered undesirable and not in the public interest by the government, with the implied threat that powers would be taken to prevent its production, he would abandon the whole project. Coyne was right, and though the author was 'at a loss to understand what difficulty or damage the production of a play on such a very improbable subject could possibly cause to the State', he accepted 'the suppression of it as a natural expression of the general philosophy of Government in this country'.[120]

Another production that fell victim to the government's 'general philosophy' was *The Refugee*, which was staged in the Peacock Theatre, Dublin in April 1943. The hero of the play was a Jewish refugee from German persecution in Austria and it contained several references to the treatment of prisoners in German concentration camps. In March, Hempel, the German minister, had contacted the government complaining about it. He had received an anonymous letter which claimed that the play, by a Jewish author, contained 'a good deal of open and unconcealed propaganda against German treatment of the Jews'. The Minister for Justice, Gerald Boland, believed that, with the omission of these references and some other minor changes, the play could be staged without objection. Aiken agreed and arranged for Coyne to discuss the necessary changes with the author. The latter, presumably believing that he had no choice, agreed to Coyne's suggested amendments and in the eventual production the Austrian Jewish hero had become simply a refugee from Hungary while the references to concentration camps were left out completely. Special Branch detectives viewed the opening performance and were happy that there was nothing contained in it to which exception might be taken 'on political or international grounds'.[121]

We have seen how the criteria used in the censorship of films were applied to the censorship of stage plays, regardless of the lack of legal authority in this regard. In his recommendations for censorship in any future emergency Coyne stressed the need for the power to control the production of stage plays and theatrical representations of all kinds.[122] He was clearly conscious of the fact that the failure to impose censorship restrictions on the production of plays was an oversight on the part of the authorities, given the breadth and severity of censorship in all other areas of communication and entertainment.

Dr Richard Hayes, the 'Genial Censor', evidently believed that different criteria applied when it came to censoring theatre as opposed to film. As well as operating as official film censor Hayes served as a director of the Abbey, the national theatre, and on his appointment as censor offered his resignation to the Abbey because of the possible conflict of interests. His fellow directors refused his offer and on further reflection Hayes himself concluded that 'the two positions weren't analogous at all. The Abbey audiences are 100 per cent adult and the cinema audiences may conceivably be as much as 80 per cent children'.[123] One suspects, however, given the mass popularity of cinema as opposed to theatre, that class rather than age may have been the determining factor in Hayes's differentiation. Nevertheless, his remarks unwittingly touch upon a core issue at the heart of censorship, i.e., in simple terms, the assumption on the part of those who censor that the members of a cinema audience, like small children, cannot be trusted to make their own decisions – an attitude articulated bluntly by one of Hayes's successors, Dermot Breen (who was film censor in the 1970s), when he declared that 'I interpret a film through what I would like my children . . . to see'.[124]

NOTES AND REFERENCES

1   Nicholas Pronay, 'Introduction' in Nicholas Pronay and D.W. Spring (eds.), *Propaganda, Politics and Film, 1918–45* (London, 1982), p. 16.
2   During the war the twenty-six counties alone boasted 157 cinemas, while fourteen different exhibitors brought films on tour around the small towns and villages where no permanent film theatre existed. Dublin, with a population of half a million, had forty-nine cinemas, seven of which were 'first-run' houses; within five minutes walk of Nelson's Pillar there were enough cinemas to seat 20,000 people. There were 106 centres where there was one cinema and 54 in which there were two. Cork had ten, Limerick seven, Waterford and Dundalk four each, and Galway, Athlone and Mitchelstown had three. (NA, D/J, R 25, Stopped and deleted proofs: *Sunday Independent*, 13 November 1943; *Daily Mail*, 15 January 1942.)
3   NA, D/T, S 11450, Department of Justice memo, 21 September 1939.
4   ibid.; MA, OCC 5/5, Emergency Powers (No. 6) Order 1939.
5   MA, OCC 5/5, Coyne memo, 16 September 1939.
6   NA, D/J, 'Memoranda on Film Censorship', Connolly memo and Connolly to Aiken, 15 September 1939. In point no. 3, Connolly was referring to a series of jingoistic British (and some American) features of the 1930s which projected the pro-imperialist ethos of the Commonwealth onto Irish screens. In response to violent reactions on the part of radical republicans, cuts were made to a number of such films in the 1930s, including the American-produced Indian Raj feature, *The Lives of a Bengal Lancer* (1935), referred to by Connolly (Kevin Rockett, Luke Gibbons and John Hill, *Cinema and Ireland* (London and Sydney, 1987), p. 53; James C. Robertson, *The British Board of Film Censors: Film Censorship in Britain, 1896–1950* (London, 1985), p. 90).
7   NA D/J, Connolly to Aiken, 15 September 1939.
8   MA, OCC 5/5, Coyne memo, 16 September 1939.

9   NA, D/J, 'Memoranda on Film Censorship', Connolly, 20 September 1939.
10 MA, OCC 5/5, Montgomery to Renters of Newsreels, September 1939.
11 Raymond Fielding, *The American Newsreel, 1911–1967* (Oklahoma, 1972), p. 289.
12 Nicholas Pronay, 'The News Media at War', in Pronay and Spring (eds.), *Propaganda, Politics and Film*, p. 202.
13 ibid., p. 202, from Visnews Library, Gaumont British Issues, MS. Catalogue. GM 665.
14 ibid., p. 207.
15 NA, D/J, 'Instructions to Press Censorship Staff', article from *Daily Telegraph*, February 1942.
16 NA, D/FA (Sec.) A 9(2), Quigley to Carl Milkenen, 31 May 1943.
17 Fielding, *American Newsreel*, pp. 289–91.
18 Quigley himself had been involved in the production of United Newsreel when he worked in the Office of War Information. When he volunteered for secret intelligence work in 1942, his resignation from the film division was arranged and he was provided with authentic commercial cover by the Motion Picture Producers and Distributors of America. He successfully kept his real role secret from the Germans and Japanese, the British, the US minister in Ireland, and even, apparently, from Irish Military Intelligence; 'his cover was perfect', Dan Bryan, the head of G2, admitted years later, 'we did not know he was OSS'. (Martin S. Quigley, *Peace Without Hiroshima: Secret Action at the Vatican in the Spring of 1945* (Maryland, 1991), pp. 12–18).
19 Rockett et al., *Cinema and Ireland*, pp. 53–5.
20 *Seanad Debates*, Vol. 25, col. 369, 30 January 1941.
21 MA, OCC 7/1, Department of External Affairs (DEA) to Coyne, 15 February 1944.
22 *The Bell*, Vol. 3, No. 2, November 1941, p. 111.
23 ibid., p. 112.
24 NA, D/T, S 12093, 'Censorship of Films – Appointment of Official Censor'.
25 *Dublin Opinion*, November 1940, p. 343.
26 *The Bell*, Vol. 3, No. 2, p. 108.
27 ibid., p. 113.
28 ibid., p. 109.
29 Philip M. Taylor, 'Propaganda in International Politics 1919–1939', in K.R.M. Short (ed.), *Film and Radio Propaganda in World War II* (London and Canberra, 1983), p. 18.
30 John Wakeman (ed.), *World Film Directors, Vol. One, 1890–1945* (New York, 1987), p. 883. Wakeman points out that this burlesque reflected general American opinion in 1940 which saw Hitler as a maniacal clown. An anti-Nazi film such as this would also have been banned in pre-war Britain; the declaration of war, however, dispensed with the need for such cinematic appeasement (Philip M. Taylor, 'Introduction: Film, the Historian and the Second World War', in Philip M. Taylor (ed.), *Britain and the Cinema in the Second World War* (London, 1988), p. 9).
31 *The Bell*, Vol. 3, No. 2, p. 109. In an interview in 1947 Hayes showed that political film censorship had not ended with the war: 'anything advocating Communism', he stated, 'or presenting it in an unduly favourable light gets the knife'. (Quoted in John Gerrard, 'Irish Censorship and Fighting for a Cleaner Cinema', *Sight and Sound*, Vol. 18, No. 70, Summer 1949, p. 82.)
32 *The Bell*, Vol. 3, No. 2, p. 107.
33 NA, D/FA (Sec.) A 9(2), Quigley to Carl Milkenen, 6 June 1943.
34 MA, OCC 2/132, *The Spectator*, 2 July 1943.
35 D/FA (Sec.) A 9(2), United Artists to Quigley, 8 March 1945. The only cut on 'moral' grounds which had come to Quigley's attention during his week with Hayes was the entire Vera Zorina Black Magic ballet solo in the Paramount picture *Star Spangled Rhythm*. Quigley was surprised at this cut, obviously unaware of the particular danger

which 'lascivious' dances posed to the moral fibre of Irish society (Quigley to Milkenen, 6 June 1943).

36   NA, D/FA 323/203, KRS to Dulanty, 30 March 1942.
37   Brian McIllroy, *Irish Cinema: An Illustrated History* (Dublin, 1988), p. 34.
38   NA, D/FA 323/203, KRS to Dulanty, 30 March 1942.
39   ibid., *Daily Mail*, 7 April 1942; *Irish Independent*, June 1942; DEA note, June 1942; *Daily Film Renter*, 24 June 1942.
40   McIllroy, *Irish Cinema*, p. 38.
41   Robertson, *British Board of Film Censors*, p. 120.
42   F.D. Roosevelt Library, New York, David Gray Papers, 'Ireland' – 'Censorship in Eire', undated (probably 1942).
43   MA, OCC 5/40, 'Suspension of cert. granted by the Official Censor'.
44   MA, OCC 5/39, 'Censorship of Films' memo, July 1942.
45   NA, D/FA (Sec.) A 9(2), Quigley to Carl Milkenen, 6 June 1943.
46   MA, OCC 5/39, minutes of Aiken's meeting with KRS, 18 September 1942.
47   K.R.M. Short, 'Cinematic Support for Anglo-American Détente, 1939-1943', in Taylor (ed.), *Britain and the Cinema*, p. 129.
48   MA, OCC 5/39, minutes of Aiken's meeting with the Theatre and Cinemas Association, October 1943. Short suggests that the power of example of the Yank's conversion '(perhaps linked with flyers in the RAF having a chance with Betty Grable) led to the film being banned in the Irish Republic' (Short in Taylor (ed.), *Britain and the Cinema*, p. 142).
49   NA, D/J 1/41, Gray to de Valera, 5 October 1943 and 29 November 1943; de Valera to Gray, 25 October 1943; Coyne to Gray, 13 December 1943.
50   MA, OCC 5/39, minutes of Aiken's meeting with cinema operatives, 30 October 1943.
51   NA, D/FA 216/303, Benzinger to DEA, 22 February 1941, Joseph Walshe (Sec., DEA) to Benzinger, February 1941.
52   ibid., DEA note, 5 June 1942.
53   ibid., Boland memo, 7 June 1944.
54   MA, OCC 3/47, letter extract, 10 September 1941.
55   NA, D/J R24, *Standard* (deletion), 14 September 1943.
56   MA, OCC 2/108, *Swedish News*, July 1942.
57   MA, OCC 7/1, DEA to Coyne, 15 February 1944.
58   *Daily Express*, 10 February 1941.
59   NA, D/FA 216/303, DEA to Washington Legation, 9 January 1942. The film had been 'mutilated beyond all recognition' by the censor and Coyne insisted to the Department of Justice that it be rejected *in toto* rather than have the whole institution of censorship exposed to 'ridicule and contempt' (MA, OCC 7/48, Coyne to the Department of Justice, 30 December 1941).
60   MA, OCC 5/39, minutes of Aiken's meeting with cinema operatives, 30 October 1943.
61   NA, D/FA 323/203, Columbia Pictures Corporation Ltd to High Commissioner's Office, undated and 10 March 1944.
62   Joseph T. Carroll, 'A Tale of Old Ireland', *Irish Times*, 13 August 1993.
63   The money which the government received from this processing traffic helps to explain its failure to implement George Fleischmann's plans for a processing laboratory in Ireland (McIllroy, *Irish Cinema*, p. 38). Fleischmann, who became a central figure in Ireland's film industry, was a German internee there during the war.
64   MA, OCC 7/36, 'Export of Cine-films for processing in Ireland'.
65   Pronay in Pronay and Spring (eds.), *Propaganda, Politics and Film*, p. 196.
66   Robert Fisk, *In Time of War: Ireland, Ulster and the Price of Neutrality, 1939-45* (London, 1985), pp. 390-6.
67   NA, D/J, Press Censorship Monthly Reports, February 1942.

68   NA, D/FA 323/203, *Irish Independent*, 'Held', 11 February 1942; D/J, Press Censorship Monthly Reports, February 1942.
69   NA, D/FA, 323/203, correspondence, March 1942.
70   NA, D/FA 323/203, Frank Gallagher to DEA, May 1942.
71   Fielding, *American Newsreel*, p. 231.
72   Rockett et al., *Cinema and Ireland*, p. 73.
73   MA, OCC 7/54, Coyne to Aiken, 29 March 1943.
74   ibid., Gallagher to Censorship, December 1943.
75   ibid., Coyne to Boland, 31 December 1943.
76   ibid.
77   NA, D/J R 26, 'US Government's note, press material in connection therewith which was censored'.
78   Rockett et al., *Cinema and Ireland*, p. 74.
79   *Irish Times*, 14 May 1945.
80   Wakeman (ed.), *World Film Directors*, p. 884; Robert Murphy, 'The British Film Industry: Audiences and Producers', in Taylor (ed.), *Britain and the Cinema*, p. 37.
81   *Irish Times*, 14 May 1945.
82   MA, OCC 7/55, 'Irish Film Society'.
83   ibid., Report on Aiken's meeting with IPP, 24 December 1943.
84   ibid., Purcell memo, 2 February 1944.
85   MA, OCC 5/38, Coyne to Aiken, January 1945.
86   MA, OCC 7/55, 'Notes on Russian Films shown by the IFS' (by Liam O'Laoghaire), 3 February 1944; Coyne to Aiken, 9 February 1944; Aiken note on latter.
87   NA, D/J, 'Instructions to Press Censorship Staff', 12 February 1944.
88   MA, OCC 7/55, Coyne to Aiken, 9 February 1944. A review of *We from Kronstadt* was subsequently stopped for the *Irish Times*, although a disparaging criticism of the film appeared in the *Catholic Standard* in the same week (*Irish Times*, 14 May 1945).
89   MA, OCC 7/55, O'Laoghaire to Coyne, 1 February 1944.
90   ibid., O'Laoghaire's 'Notes', 3 February 1944.
91   ibid., Coyne to Aiken, 26 September 1944.
92   ibid., Purcell to Aiken, October 1944; Aiken note on same.
93   ibid., Sherry to Coyne/Aiken, 17 October 1944.
94   ibid., Aiken to Sherry, 19 October 1944.
95   ibid., Coyne to Aiken, 30 October 1944.
96   Clive Coultass, 'British Feature Films and the Second World War', *Journal of Contemporary History*, Vol. 19, 1984, p. 16; Sue Harper, 'The Representation of Women in British Feature Films, 1939–45', in Taylor (ed.), *Britain and the Cinema*, p. 173.
97   MA, OCC 7/55, Coyne to Aiken, 17 October 1944; Coyne to Sherry, 20 October 1944.
98   MA, OCC 7/49, 'Refusal to Grant Licence for Importation of *Target for Tonight*', December 1941.
99   Eric Rhode, *A History of the Cinema from its Origins to 1970* (London, 1970), p. 370.
100 MA, OCC 7/49, 'Refusal to Grant Licence for Importation of *Target for Tonight*', December 1941.
101 NA, D/FA (Sec.) A 8(1), Dan Bryan (G2) to Joseph Walshe (Sec., DEA), 11 April 1945.
102 *Dáil Debates*, Vol. 95, cols. 1497–8, 24 January 1945.
103 *Irish Times*, 14 May 1945.
104 ibid., 17 May 1945 and 18 May 1945.
105 ibid., 19 May 1945.
106 ibid., 21 May 1945.

107   ibid.
108   ibid., 25 May 1945.
109   McIllroy, *Irish Cinema*, p. 35.
110   *Irish Times*, 24 June 1945.
111   ibid., 14 December 1978, letter from Hubert Butler recalling Irish reactions at the end of the war.
112   NA, D/T, S 11445/8, Coyne memo on censorship, September 1945.
113   For a discussion of these issues, see, for example, Richard Taylor, *Film Propaganda: Soviet Russia and Nazi Germany* (London, 1979), pp. 29-31, and Pronay, 'Introduction' in Pronay and Spring (eds.), *Propaganda, Politics and Film*, p. 14.
114   *Seanad Debates*, Vol. 25, col. 369, 30 January 1941.
115   Julia Carlson (ed.), *Banned in Ireland: Censorship and the Irish Writer* (London, 1990), p. 3.
116   This term is used to describe intended theatrical productions; books containing plays came under the purview of the press censorship.
117   MA, OCC 7/24, Connolly to Aiken, 18 October 1939; Department of Justice to Censorship, 30 October 1939.
118   NA, D/T, S 11445/8, Coyne memo on censorship, September 1945; D/J R 37, 'Seán Piondar'; D/J, No. 3, *Irish Times*; D/J, 'Instructions to Press Censorship Staff', 21 November 1940.
119   James Matthews, *Voices: A Life of Frank O'Connor* (Dublin, 1983), pp. 171, 185-6. Mac Liammóir believed that it was the 'sex-cum-religion obsession' of the authorities ('the Hoodlums') which led to the withdrawal of *Roly Poly*, and not the complaints of Hempel, who 'protested nearly everything anyway'.
120   MA, OCC 2/141, correspondence and memos regarding *Sometime Never*, by T.A.W. Purefoy, October-November 1944.
121   NA, D/FA 216/303, correspondence and memos regarding *The Refugee*, April 1943.
122   NA, D/T, S 11445/8, Coyne memo on censorship, September 1945.
123   *The Bell*, Vol. 3, No. 2, November 1941, p. 111.
124   David Collins quoting a speech by Dermot Breen to the Cork Rotary Club in Patrick Smyth and Ellen Hazelkorn (eds.), *Let in the Light: Censorship, Secrecy and Democracy* (Dingle, 1993), p. 142. The classification of films according to suitability for certain age groups was not generally carried out until the 1960s.

3.
POSTAL AND TELEGRAPH CENSORSHIP

The emergency postal and telegraph censorship, combined with the covert surveillance activities carried out by and on behalf of G2 (Military Intelligence), totally undermined the existence of private communications in wartime Ireland.

The general objects of the censorship as a whole were twofold: firstly, to stop all communications and publications which were considered prejudicial to the interests of the state, in terms of security and relations with other states; and, secondly, to collect information of value to 'the national cause' from the communications and publications covered by the censorship.[1] The preventative aspect was obviously uppermost in the censorship of film, and was the predominant object of the press branch also. With posts and telegraphs, however, the preventative and informative aspects were of roughly equal importance. After the war Coyne argued that the collection, collation and distribution of information obtained was 'perhaps the most important work of the censorship'. He contended that it was just as important, for example, to trace the activities of 'hostile persons' or to detect breaches of emergency orders as it was to prevent disclosure of information directly prejudicial to the security of the state; and no less important to obtain economic or political information of value than it was to stop it leaving the country.[2]

The 'national interests' which the Censorship sought to protect can be broadly subdivided into defence, political (internal and external) and economic interests. In all of these areas it sought to prevent disclosure of information that affected the particular interest involved and sent on to the relevant branch of the state that information gleaned which could contribute to their efforts.

Defence interests: The 'negative' objective in this area was the prevention of the disclosure and circulation, deliberate and inadvertent, of information relating to the defence of the state. This included references to defence policy, the defence forces and defensive measures generally. Special care was taken to prevent the revelation of details such as the location, movements, numbers, equipment, etc., of the army, Local Defence Force (LDF), air corps and navy; matter relating to fortifications, mining of harbours, bridges, roads, etc.; maps, plans, photographs and other representations of defence works, harbours, ports etc.; information regarding military forces outside the state; and espionage.[3]

Information relating to members of the defence forces – indiscreet letters, complaints about conditions, evidence of service offences and evasions of duty, etc. – was sent to the adjutant general.[4] The information forwarded to G2 (Military Intelligence) covered a wide range of security and political concerns; the document showing the headings under which information derived from the censorship was collated and summarised for military intelligence purposes is reproduced in full in Appendix 2.

Political interests: This covered both external and internal political interests. In relation to external affairs the aim of the censorship was 'to prevent the circulation of statements or information which might prejudice or adversely affect national policy or prestige, or relations with other states and to bring to notice persons suspected of contravening laws and regulations designed more particularly to ensure political security'.[5] G2 (see Appendix 2) and the Department of External Affairs were the chief recipients of information in this area. The Department of External Affairs was interested in matters which related to diplomacy, was considered prejudicial to relations with foreign states or, generally, had any bearing on foreign affairs or Ireland's international position.[6] Particular attention was paid to comments on neutrality, especially those made by influential persons or in newspapers published outside the state. Information was gathered (and its disclosure prevented) on opinions on Irish political and diplomatic relations and appointments, visits by Irish residents abroad in suspicious circumstances, visits to Ireland by serving members of the British forces, and so on.[7]

In terms of the internal political situation the Censorship was expected to prevent the circulation of propaganda and matter which might have a negative effect on civilian morale, encourage violence, cause disaffection or impede civil government. It was also expected to help prevent sabotage and bring to notice people suspected of having contravened emergency laws.[8] Information pertaining to internal politics was sent to the Department of Justice or the Garda Special Branch, as well as to G2. It embraced all matters affecting internal state security and 'the preservation of good order',[9] with particular emphasis on the activities of 'subversive elements and illegal organisations', internees and aliens resident in the state, public opinion on defensive measures,[10] information disclosing treason, offences against the state and other 'serious crimes'.[11]

Economic interests: The task of the Censorship in relation to economic security was to 'prevent the disclosure and circulation of matter prejudicial to national commercial and financial interests'; to check profiteering and speculation in controlled commodities, and to bring to notice suspected tax evaders and others suspected of contravening various economic and financial regulations.[12]

Information relating to economic affairs was sent to a number of relevant departments. The wartime Department of Supplies, for example, was kept informed on all matters pertaining to the maintenance of essential supplies and services, for example evidence disclosing evasions of orders affecting supplies. The Department of Industry and Commerce was supplied with information regarding activities which were likely to affect the economic situation, and general information regarding economic affairs and international economic conditions. Similar information pertaining to agricultural matters was sent to the Department of Agriculture while matters disclosing breaches of Customs and Excise laws and regulations were passed on to the Revenue Commissioners. Information affecting more particularly the financial security of the state was forwarded to the Department of Finance. This included matters such as investments abroad of Irish residents, possession of Irish investments by foreigners, the transfer of securities, currency exchange, and so on.[13]

The issue of the use made of information obtained through censorship was 'a sore subject' and was the basis of a memo prepared by the Censorship for Aiken prior to the Estimates debate in the Oireachtas in February 1940. The memo declared it 'the right and duty of the Government to avail of the information obtained in the public interest. This in fact is what the Censorship is for.' It argued that the state was entitled to use any information which it could obtain for 'the common good', whether this information related to criminal offences or otherwise. It pointed out that the secrecy of the post is not expressly recognised by the constitution and that the imposition of censorship

> . . . is the very negation of secrecy. Censorship and secrecy are incompatible – the one excludes the other – and as the object of censorship is to enable the authorities to know what is going on it is foolish to expect them not to use this information – in the interests of the State of course – when they obtain it.[14]

POSTAL CENSORSHIP

The Postal Censorship was housed in a converted warehouse at 11–17 Exchequer Street, Dublin, close to the central sorting office.[15] It was by far the largest division of the organisation, employing roughly 75 per cent of all the Censorship personnel. (At its highest, the staff of the Censorship as a whole, including examiners, administrative staff, sorters, etc. never exceeded 200 and for most of the period numbered approximately 160.[16]) Despite its relative size the branch was far too small to operate anything but a partial censorship of the post, the volume of which was little short of 100 million separate packets a year.[17] This problem of smallness, as Coyne pointed out, is always an administrative problem in Ireland:

> The Irish Civil Servant has rarely any opportunity of becoming a real expert in any particular branch of administration but must needs be a jack of all trades or, to put it more flatteringly, a virtuoso of uncommon versatility. Between the Irish postal censor and, say, the British postal censor there was the same sort of difference as you might expect to find in an assistant in a country shop and an employee of a big department store.[18]

There were almost ten thousand people employed in postal censorship in Britain during the war,[19] which, even when the larger volume of traffic is taken into account, highlights the aptness of Coyne's analogy. Despite its small size, however, some degree of specialisation was achieved and by the careful and selective application of limited resources quite an efficient censorship operation was achieved.

When the letters arrived each day from the sorting office nearby they were first concentrated on a staff of four sorters loaned from the post office. They opened the letters, examined them and set aside for special treatment those addressed to persons whose names appeared on the 'Black', 'White' and 'Watching' lists. (The Black List consisted of those under suspicion and whose correspondence was required by G2 or by the various sections of the Censorship itself. The White List consisted of those whose correspondence was exempted from censorship, e.g. heads of state, heads of diplomatic missions. The Watching List consisted of those whose correspondence was observed temporarily in order to confirm or allay suspicions.) These letters were then handed to the chief postal censor or his deputy for appropriate treatment. The remainder, or as much as could be examined, were then distributed by the sorters to the supervisors of the relevant sections which were to examine them. The supervisors divided the letters among the fifteen to twenty examiners under her or his control, usually one hundred letters per examiner per day. Letters of an objectionable or possibly objectionable nature were brought to the notice of the supervisor. Those which required further examinations, alterations, deletions or other treatment were submitted to the assistant censor, the more important being passed further up the hierarchy to the deputy chief or chief censor.[20]

First among the requisites of a good examiner, according to Coyne, was 'a good national outlook, next honesty, then reticence and the ability to hold one's tongue, thereafter common sense and a good memory and, finally, though perhaps it should have come first, good health and, in particular, good eyesight'.[21] Because of the confidential nature of the work all of those employed in the Postal Censorship were investigated by G2 and the Gardaí in order to ensure their reliability. It was found necessary on a number of occasions to dispense with the services of examiners who were discovered to be associating with IRA suspects or who were suspected of being in financial trouble (because of the large amounts of money passing through their hands). Those whose reliability was considered doubtful were transferred from the Postal Censorship, while problems were also encountered because some departments had taken the opportunity to off-load their least efficient officers for postal censorship duty.[22]

The popular perception of the postal censor was, in Coyne's words, of 'a person pursuing a debased calling . . . a sort of natural-born Paul Pry who takes a perverse pleasure in poking his nose into [other people's] private affairs'.[23] Although it was officially denied, a number of examiners found it very difficult to 'hold their tongues'. All staff employed in the Censorship were advised, upon engagement, of the terms of the Official Secrets Act and were required to sign a declaration undertaking not to divulge any information relating to their work to an unauthorised person.[24] The confidential nature of their work was impressed upon them by Colonel Liam Archer of G2 at the outset and the message was repeated at regular intervals. In a confidential letter to Purcell, the chief postal censor, in October 1939, the controller informed him that he thought it necessary to 're-warn the girls that comments are current indicating that they are talking outside about what passes through their hands in their work. It may be necessary to point out that any such breach of trust will be treated with the utmost seriousness and may result in the dismissal of the officer involved'.[25] There was a continuation of complaints that officers were making the contents of letters the subject of conversation among their friends, but no definite evidence was forthcoming.

As well as 'loose tongues', light fingers presented a problem and in 1944 theft on a 'fairly considerable scale' occurred within the Postal Censorship. A thief of 'uncommon skill' stole large amounts of money, usually in the form of postal orders, from letters to which she had access during her work as an examiner. This woman, apparently, dressed 'above her means', gambled at cards, greyhounds and horses, and generally lived 'in a manner not at all commensurate with her official emoluments'. After numerous complaints from those out of pocket as a result of her activities, she was found out by post office investigating officers who 'set her up' in time-honoured fashion. The case led to an internal enquiry which resulted in changes being made to the examination and supervision system making such theft more difficult; it was, however, not possible to make the system itself watertight given the nature of the work and the shortage of staff.[26]

POSTAL CENSORSHIP OFFICE.
(As imagined by our Grangegorman Correspondent.)

Cartoon from *Dublin Opinion,* 'The National Humorous Journal of Ireland', October 1939.

Another problem was the 'grossly indecent' nature of some letters which 'outraged' the young female examiners who came across them. This difficulty was addressed by placing the names and addresses of offending correspondents on the Watching List and their letters were subsequently diverted from the examiners by the sorters. In order to save female examiners embarrassment by having to admit knowledge of an indecent letter, they were authorised to submit any such letter in a sealed envelope to the chief postal censor, without any indication of who had submitted it. Purcell suggested that the complete solution to this problem, in any future emergency, was to employ only elderly male officers to examine obscene correspondence![27]

Far from causing outrage and embarrassment, however, the majority of letters served only to bore, achieving levels of banality, according to Coyne, which had to be seen to be believed. 'If history is the record of the crimes, miseries and follies of mankind', he wrote, 'then the Censor is in daily contact with the raw materials of history.'[28]

The majority of examiners were concentrated in the general section, which examined correspondence in the English language. It contained subsections that examined air mail, letters to and from newspaper and news agency offices and so on. This section also diverted letters to the other appropriate sections which were: registered correspondence, trade, financial, parcels and news, establishment (which dealt mainly with public enquiries and matters relating to the duties of civil servants), and foreign languages. The latter was the most specialised section of the Postal Censorship. In the allocation of personnel, a number of officers were chosen on the basis of their knowledge of French, German, Italian and Spanish. These full-time censors were supplemented by others who gave part-time attendance when required and were competent to deal with correspondence in other languages, such as those from Scandinavian and East European countries.

The activities of the foreign languages section were principally focused on correspondence with the continent of Europe. Because of the small volume and its concentration on the same group of examiners, they were in a position to watch all the letters exchanged between the same addresses in Ireland and in Europe, thus ensuring a constant watch on the channels of communication between persons in Ireland and their correspondents on the continent. This close censorship – 'the ideal censorship' – enabled an accurate record to be kept of everybody in Ireland who was corresponding with Europe and their contacts there. (Correspondence written in English exchanged with the continent was also examined in this section in order that this close watch could be maintained.) 'This record was invaluable', according to the chief postal censor, 'and it was essential that it should be maintained because of the fairly large number of political refugees who have found asylum here.'[29]

A 100 per cent censorship was applied to correspondence to and from the continent of Europe for the entire duration of the Emergency. The small foreign languages section was able to carry this out because of the small volume of traffic involved (about fifty letters outward per day) – the result of the serious disruption to the continental postal system occasioned by the war. All correspondence by air, outwards and inwards, irrespective of origin or destination, was fully censored. This was deemed necessary as air mail was considered the most likely channel for information considered dangerous to the state, given the heavy delays in long-distance surface mail transit. There was full censorship also of mail exchanged with Palestine. This, according to Purcell, was because it enabled 'control to be exercised over the activities of Jewish émigrés who had been allowed into this country and a watch to be maintained on the bodies associated with international Jewry'. The tiny amount of correspondence exchanged with South America and Japan was also fully censored.[30]

Internal post, including that exchanged with Northern Ireland, was not subjected to general censorship and, initially, nor was that exchanged with Britain. In May 1940, however, with the Germans overrunning the Low Countries and heading for France, the British began a test-check of letters exchanged between the two countries that, according to the office of the UK representative, revealed 'a very considerable leakage of information, which cannot be permitted'. They decided to initiate a censorship of mails from Britain to Ireland (South *and* North) and an examination of mails to Britain from the island of Ireland. In June the Irish government followed suit, announcing the introduction of censorship between Ireland and Britain. This decision presented the Postal Censorship with enormous logistical difficulties. The existing staff were already fully occupied in dealing with the approximately thirteen thousand items in total exchanged daily with the rest of the world.[31] A full censorship of the letters traffic alone exchanged with Britain would have required over a tenfold increase in the number of examiners. The unavailability of suitable personnel in such numbers and the expense involved immediately ruled out any possibility of a comprehensive response to the British move. The only possible line of action open to the Irish government was to introduce a very limited, selective censorship of mails exchanged with Britain. This amounted initially to the examination of approximately 10 per cent of the daily traffic, i.e. approximately ten thousand postal packets.[32] (Co-operation was maintained between the Irish and British Censorships, with each keeping the other up to date with their respective instructions to censors, policy changes, etc.[33])

These early spot-checks and random 'raids' on cross-channel mail revealed 'a certain state of alarm attributable to the recent surprise mobilisation of the LSF [Local Security Force]' and a hostile and critical attitude to conditions in Ireland on the part of wealthy English people 'taking peaceful shelter within our country'. As a result, several such people were visited by the Gardaí and warned. Besides such 'Anglophiles' ridiculing Irish ability to resist invasion,[34] general military and defence details (troop mobilisation, parachute landings, etc.) were being revealed in the correspondence of 'the less educated classes'.[35] Given the nature of the information gleaned from these early spot-checks it was decided to reduce considerably the censorship of post exchanged with America in order to release staff to deal with the added burden of cross-channel mail.[36]

Censorship of cross-channel mail never exceeded 12 per cent in total,[37] but its examination was arranged in such a way as to give the most effective results. All letters to and from most districts were censored on a rotation basis (usually a five-day rotation), thus ensuring that the posts to and from most areas came under control at some stage. Mail despatched from Dublin to London, EC was always censored in order to control correspondence with Fleet Street. Similarly, mail from Dublin to Manchester was always examined because of the location in the latter city of the offices of the Irish editions of a number of English newspapers. Bristol mail was censored in the interests of the Department of Supplies, given that the British supply departments were located there. Full control was applied to other mails at various times, for example all the correspondence posted at Foynes by passengers travelling by the emergency air services.[38]

From August 1940 reports began appearing sporadically in the British and Irish press which suggested that the British were considering the introduction of censorship of correspondence exchanged between Northern Ireland and the South. This possibility would have presented the Irish government with severe difficulties if they were to respond in kind, given the huge volume of cross-border postal traffic. In August 1941 the government decided that any examination could not exceed 5 per cent, 'not to start', in Aiken's words, 'until the other side fires the first shot'.[39] The 'first shot' was never officially fired, and in October 1941, in reply to a parliamentary question from an Ulster Unionist MP, the British government stated that, having given the matter close attention, the decision had been taken to adopt 'other methods'. These methods were assumed by the Irish authorities to be spot-checking combined with the warrant system; Connolly told Aiken that he was in 'no doubt whatever that a secret censorship of letters to certain addresses has been in operation not only since the war began, but for a long time before it'.[40] (As early as 1925, a G2 memo stated that secret censorship was 'extensively practiced' in the Six Counties; practically all correspondence from the North to the South was passed to Belfast GPO periodically for examination, and the correspondence of suspect persons was constantly examined.[41]) The Northern authorities also examined all documents in the possession of travellers who were crossing the border.[42]

The Southern Irish authorities never initiated an open censorship of mails exchanged with Northern Ireland, but, in common with the North, a secret censorship of such post was carried out by G2 under the warrant system. In late 1943 the authorities in the South began to take measures to counter the high level of desertions from the Irish to the British army which had been occurring since the outbreak of the war. An arrangement was put in place whereby correspondence for soldiers which originated outside the state could be intercepted in the Postal Censorship and examined by G2. The main object was to record and frustrate the recruitment efforts of the Combined British Recruiting Centre in Belfast and to this end a special check of mails addressed to that location was undertaken. The early results were declared to have been 'entirely satisfactory' and a marked drop in desertions was recorded.[43]

Internal post did not come under the purview of the emergency censorship legislation, but G2 operated, for the duration of the Emergency and for a period before, a covert censorship which was carried out under warrant from the Minister for Justice.[44] This surveillance was carried out by a specially established section of the Post Office Investigation Branch.[45] When asked in the Dáil whether a special staff had been established in the Postal Censorship for the collection of information from internal correspondence, the Minister for Justice replied that he 'would not like to answer that'.[46]

In the first month of the Censorship a number of instructions were issued to the public through press notices and broadcast announcements. People were asked to keep their letters brief, legible and on one side of the page; to write their name and address on the cover of each postal packet; to use Irish and English as much as possible, and where another language was used to indicate that language on the cover. There were no restrictions on any particular classes of mails or on any destinations; the only absolute restriction was that code, cypher and invisible ink were not to be used. Correspondents who ignored this restriction had their letters detained and were liable for prosecution under the Emergency Powers Order 1939.[47] The public was also informed that envelopes should not contain lining paper or blank sheets; such packets were acknowledged as probably being intended for philatelists, but the contents were destroyed and replaced as a precaution.[48]

Despite warnings people continued to write letters of exceptional lengths; it was not unusual for the Censorship to receive letters of seventeen and eighteen pages in length, and in one case an examiner was faced with a missive of forty-five pages. The censors were generally lenient in relation to overlengthy letters, but where offenders persisted they had their letters returned with the request to be more brief. The other instruction most frequently ignored was that relating to the sender's name and address appearing on the back of each envelope.[49]

With the introduction of the censorship of cross-channel mail the opportunity was taken to reiterate these points to the public and to add a number of others based on the experience gained in the first ten months of censorship. As the theatre of war became less distant from Irish shores there was an increasing tendency on the part of letter-writers to discuss matters of national defence, economic dependence on Britain, the financial position of the state, landings of German parachutists and other such related matters. This resulted in a reminder to the public, in the press and on Radio Éireann,

> . . . that they must refrain from writing on matters which would or might affect the security of the State directly or indirectly. Failure to do so may amount to a criminal offence. For these reasons therefore postal communications should be confined strictly to private or business matters, as even the exchange of rumours or idle gossip may involve the writer in serious consequences.[50]

The principal culprits were the so-called 'West British' who, according to Coyne, were responsible for a 'steady stream of vilification of Ireland' in their letters to Britain.[51] These people, according to Purcell, the chief postal censor, were 'essentially British. They had never heard of 1916 or 1921 or, if they had, had made up their minds that the events of those years were regrettable lapses, the result of waywardness, to be quietly forgotten by persons of good taste. They saw everything through British spectacles . . . and lamented the fact that Ireland was "missing out" on "this great crusade for civilisation"'.[52] In October 1940 a draft order was prepared dealing with the dissemination of rumours. It sought to prevent 'the spreading of scare stories; the outraging of national sentiment at home and the slandering of this country in communications going abroad; and mischievous or defeatist statements in regard to our neutrality'. The purpose of the order was to make an example of 'certain notorious and highly placed offenders' by prosecuting them on the basis of statements made by them in their letters and gathered in the course of censorship.[53] That such measures were being contemplated was an illustration of the high state of anxiety which was prevalent in the country around this time, fuelled by the proximity of the war and the fear of invasion.

The methods employed in the treatment of letters which contained objectionable matter were threefold: firstly, a postal packet could be detained or 'stopped' and, if it was considered necessary or desirable, destroyed; secondly, letters were returned to senders accompanied by a warning or an instruction for them to be rewritten in accordance with the rules of the Censorship if the sender wished it to be forwarded; the third method employed was that of deletion. In the early stages, deletions were made by obliterating the offending sections with obliterating fluids or by scratching out with a pen or knife. This method was quickly found to be time-consuming and ineffective; the 'obliterated' words could often be read after a simple chemical treatment or sometimes by just holding the letter up to the light.[54] Even more ineffective was an unapproved method used by one officer by which he covered objectionable passages with strips of adhesive brown tape.[55] From November–December 1939 the method preferred in most cases was the excision of offending sections with a knife or scissors. 'If people must write stupid things', wrote Purcell to Coyne, 'they must, I think, put up with the annoyance caused them if their letters are mutilated.'[56] Those who continued to write on both sides of a page and had their letters thus mutilated were, of course, doubly annoyed.

Delays in delivery were inevitable but were, according to the Censorship, attributable more to the disruption of the international postal system and censorship in other countries than to the activities of the Irish censors.[57] Between January 1940 and December 1944, 288 complaints from the public were received by the Postal Censorship, relating to delays in delivery, mutilation of contents, crossing out of contents and so on. Given that approximately 20 million postal packets were examined in this period, this seems an incredible record. After the lifting of the censorship Purcell recorded his surprise at the fact that there was no widespread resistance to or protest against the examination of letters.[58] The vast majority of people seemed to have accepted postal censorship as a 'necessary evil' and acquiesced in what was, after all, a gross intrusion upon their privacy and a violation of their rights. A memorandum outlining the necessity for censorship as seen by the authorities was sent out to about twenty of 'those persons whose complaints show that they feel they have just cause for complaint and that they do not appreciate the need for certain censorship restrictions'.[59] In answer to the questions 'why was my correspondence opened?' and 'of what am I suspected?' the memo reassured 'persons of integrity' that they should not have felt slurred or imagined that they were under suspicion if their mail had been opened. The censorship, they were told, applied to 'everybody' and the names and addresses of well-known or 'respected' people could be used as a cover by those wishing to evade it.[60]

While theoretically the censorship applied equally to everybody, special treatment was given to those on the Black List, while others enjoyed immunity. General exemption was officially restricted to communications in the service of a foreign government and communications in the service of or on behalf of the Irish state (save in exceptional circumstances). Official correspondence between diplomatic or consular missions and their governments, and the private correspondence of diplomatic officers or consuls *de carriére* was exempted provided that the postal packets were accompanied by a signed certification that the correspondence was official or, in the case of individuals, an external endorsement with the diplomat's recognised signature and the name of his mission. While officially exempt, G2 kept all such correspondence under close surveillance and occasionally interfered with its transmission, on the basis that 'the immunity enjoyed ... by letters of this kind is a matter of courtesy, not of right'.[61] In relation to a number of letters from Henning Thomsen (Hempel's second in command at the German legation and, unlike Hempel, a Nazi) to his family in Germany, G2 consulted External Affairs as to whether the letters should be forwarded. In one instance in March 1944, during the 'American Note' affair, Dan Bryan, in consulting Joseph Walshe, secretary of the Department of External Affairs, about forwarding a letter containing 'indiscreet references to current events', reminded him that Thomsen's last letter 'had to be lost'.[62]

In the early days of the censorship a number of complaints were made by the representatives of foreign governments that private correspondence to and from the missions was being censored. The Department of External Affairs apologised and claimed that this was due to 'inadvertence' on the part of the Censorship. For the Axis missions the main problem was that all direct communications were passed through Britain, so that, even if their communications were exempt from Irish censorship, they would come under the notice of the British censor. Thus, in the early part of the war both the German and Italian governments requested the Irish government to allow official correspondence for their ministers in Dublin to be transmitted in the Irish diplomatic bag. The requests were refused because such an arrangement would 'present too many difficulties and objections'; in fact, the routing of Axis communications through Britain was done as part of the co-operative security arrangements between the two countries. (The Department of External Affairs did agree to forward occasional letters from Hempel and his wife to their families in Germany.[63])

The diplomatic bag was used to deliver private correspondence to and from Irish persons living in Europe, through the Irish legations. From April 1941 External Affairs submitted private letters delivered in the 'bag' to the Censorship, requesting that, as well as censoring the letters in the normal way, the Censorship would detain additional letters contained within the envelopes and intended for re-posting from Ireland to Britain and Northern Ireland, and delete references to the channel through which the letters were transmitted.[64] In March 1942 the Washington legation let it be known that the US State Department had prohibited the use of diplomatic bags for the forwarding of private correspondence, thus ending the use by Irish ministers of the diplomatic bag for this purpose.[65]

Unofficial exemptions were also granted. For example, letters abroad from Catholic bishops, priests, abbots and nuns were sent by arrangement to the Censorship from where they were forwarded 'with the utmost dispatch and uncensored'. Most of the letters were to Rome and were sent in the diplomatic bag, though the 'religious correspondents' were warned that letters to other destinations were always liable to be censored by the British *en route* through London. This service was also availed of by Northern clerics, for example the Bishop of Dromore, Co. Down. Connolly signed his letters to the bishops 'Your Lordship's most obedient servant' and in return for his 'favours' was showered with many blessings.[66]

From the beginning of the war the Department of External Affairs allowed the Loreto nuns to exchange letters with their convent in Madrid through the Irish diplomatic bag.[67] The Irish diplomatic 'postman' in Madrid, Leopold Kerney, although officially immune from censorship, had his own correspondence censored from 1941. This was at the instigation of G2 who took on board the suspicions of British Intelligence about the Irish envoy. The British had kept him under surveillance since his contacts with the German agent Helmut Clissmann during negotiations about the release/'escape' of Frank Ryan in 1940 and mistakenly assumed him to have pro-Axis leanings. Kerney had been acting as a conduit for forwarding letters to Irish nationals on the continent, originally at the behest of the Department of External Affairs, which sent him correspondence from Frank Ryan's sister to be forwarded to the prisoner in 1939 and 1940. In March 1941 G2 discovered that Clissmann's wife (who was Irish) had had letters from her father in Ireland forwarded from Denmark under cover by Kerney. From then on Kerney's correspondence was examined under a warrant issued by the Minister for Justice under the Post Office Act of 1908.[68] While this censorship was not carried out under emergency legislation it was done by the emergency Postal Censorship, in conjunction with G2 and External Affairs. In May 1941 Kerney was told that the transmission of private letters in 'the bag' was to be confined to personal letters from himself and his shorthand typist and those from the mother provincial of the Loreto convent.[69] In June 1942 Walshe instructed Kerney not to transmit letters for others either through the ordinary post or in the diplomatic bag. 'This practice', Walshe told him, 'has caused considerable embarrassment with the neighbour in relation to security matters.'[70]

Kerney was aware that his correspondence was being examined, humorously writing at the end of one letter: 'However, please keep this to yourself; I am sure that the Censor who opens this letter in the usual manner, will be equally discreet.'[71] His wife wrote to their son in December 1942 stating that it was 'mortifying to think that the Irish Censorship doubts the good faith of its Minister in Spain', and in the same month Kerney protested to the Censorship, saying that 'this attitude on your part contrasts with that of the Spanish, and even the English, Censorship authorities who are always courteous enough to leave my correspondence unviolated'.[72] Given the British interest in Kerney it was hardly the case that 'the Sassanach' trusted him more than some of his own 'countrymen', as he believed.[73]

The Censorship sent Kerney's letters on to G2 for copying and a selection was then sent on to Walshe and Boland at External Affairs for their information or an opinion on appropriate treatment. Suspicion of Kerney increased following his 'indiscreet' meeting with Nazi *coup d'état* specialist, Edmund Veesenmayer in Madrid in August 1942. With the Germans still expectant of victory in the east, Veesenmayer was turning his thoughts towards England and a possible role for Ireland in German plans.

Fortunately, the high level of intelligence co-operation between the British and Irish prevented any serious misunderstanding about Irish intentions from arising.[74] Kerney, however, continued to be watched and in January 1943 Dan Bryan, the head of G2, wrote to Walshe in relation to a letter from Kerney addressed to his daughter which had arrived in the diplomatic bag from Madrid. It proved conclusively to Bryan that the minister had 'contact with Frank Ryan, direct or indirect, which has not been reported to you [Walshe]'. The use of his daughter 'as a covering address' was regarded by Bryan as a new element 'which looks like subterfuge'. Bryan's obviously deep suspicions about Kerney are further illustrated by his questioning whether the warning to the daughter not to mention the matter to her mother was intended really to 'prevent us obtaining information through the medium of censorship of his action . . .'.[75] In the following month the minister was brought back to Dublin and before returning to Madrid was subjected to a 'serious' talk from de Valera about the need for extreme care and prudence in security matters, particularly in view of the prospect of a second front being opened.[76]

Because of the economic importance of the Irish Hospitals Sweepstake special arrangements were made in relation to the postal correspondence of its operators, Hospitals Trust, Ltd. A Censorship staff was employed in their premises at Ballsbridge who made a selective check of Sweepstake matter being dispatched to addresses in Britain and Northern Ireland, while a staff of members of the trust worked in the premises of the Postal Censorship, sealing selected Sweepstake correspondence to foreign addresses after examination by censors. Up until at least December 1939 the trust also supplied the Censorship with blank envelopes and postage stamps for the purpose of reconstituting correspondence from the public which contained Sweepstake tickets, receipts, etc. and had been opened by the Censorship in the ordinary course of selective examination. The fact that a branch of the Irish government was colluding in the evasion of the International Postal Convention, which prohibited the sending of such material to countries where lotteries were illegal, was thus hidden.[77] In late 1944, with the outcome of the war beyond doubt, exemption was granted, on recommendation from de Valera, to the post of the United Nations Relief and Rehabilitation Administration.[78] Finally, in terms of special treatment, permission was given to personnel of the American air companies stationed at Foynes to convey their private post with the companies' business mail. It was inspected first by an officer of G2.

Having examined the objects, organisation, workings and scope of the Postal Censorship, I now propose to examine briefly a range of specific instances and cases in which it was utilised, both as an informative and preventative mechanism.

An early example of the use made of information obtained in the censorship, involves the case of Werner Unland, a German agent who had arrived in Ireland from England about a fortnight before the outbreak of war. In the first month of censorship, observation of continental mail brought his presence in the country to notice; subsequent control of his correspondence disclosed his activities and indicated his contacts outside the country. One of his letters, which was written on 'very unusual note paper', later provided a valuable clue to the authorities when a scrap of identical note paper was found in the possession of Gunther Schütz, alias Hans Marschner, a more famous German spy who parachuted into Co. Wexford in March 1941. Schütz had written to Unland prior to his arrival, unaware that Unland's post (like all of that exchanged with the continent) was being watched. Unland also seemed unaware of this and regularly wrote to the continent. He was also kept under surveillance by G2, ironically by the very man who had 'kept an eye' on Frank Aiken during the civil war. When a piece of the same unique stationery was found on Schütz as Unland had been using in his letters, G2 would have been convinced, according to Carrolle Carter, that he was an emissary from the Reich. Both Unland and Schütz were subsequently interned.[79]

The censors were quite proud of their role in this episode, and boasted of their achievement after the war. An episode less worthy of boast involved the case of a Dutch woman who applied for a visa to work in Ireland in early 1940. She had already obtained an employment permit from the Department of Industry and Commerce in order to take up a teaching post. However Colonel Liam Archer of G2 intervened, communicating to the Department of Justice that her presence in the country would be 'undesirable' and the granting of a visa should be reconsidered. The objection was based not on any evidence that this woman was likely to subvert the state or operate on behalf of any of the belligerents in undermining Irish neutrality, but solely on the fact that the contents of letters she had been exchanging with an Irishman were considered obscene. The Postal Censorship had been opening their correspondence and its intimate and frank nature had seemingly embarrassed some sensitive examiners. The man was interviewed by the Gardaí and a prosecution based on the supposed obscenity of some of the letters was considered but not proceeded with, apparently because of the minister's reluctance to have a case based on information obtained through the censorship. The Censorhip stopped delivering the couple's letters and the Department of Justice cancelled the authorisation for the grant of a visa to the woman.[80]

Most foreign nationals resident in Ireland had their correspondence monitored by the Censorship, and actions were taken by the Department of Justice on the basis of information gleaned in this way. Dr Kappeller, an Austrian refugee, had been sending items for broadcast in Germany to the pro-Allied French Radiodiffusion Nationale. In April 1940 the Department of Justice asked the Irish Co-ordinating Committee for Refugees to make clear to Kappeller that since he was afforded refuge in a neutral country he was expected to refrain from engaging in any form of propaganda or public discussion of international affairs. Others who expressed opinions were similarly gagged; Kurt Werner, a German national resident in Ireland who wanted to become a foreign correspondent for certain Swiss newspapers, was prohibited, by an order made under the Aliens Order 1939, from publishing in any newspaper or magazine or corresponding with any publication. Another German, Dr Hennig, who wrote articles for Catholic newspapers in England, had some 'anti-Axis' references in one of his articles withdrawn by the Censorship and was warned by the aliens officer to refrain from such references in future and to contain himself to liturgical matters.[81]

The correspondence of those other guests of the nation, the belligerent internees at the Curragh, were for the first two years of the war censored by a military censor at the camp. In October 1941 a batch of letters from German internees came to Purcell's attention. They had been censored by the Curragh censor but still contained objectionable matter. Arrangements were made so that from 1942 onwards, the censorship of internees' letters was carried out jointly by the military and civilian censors.[82] Full censorship was applied to this correspondence, as well as to that to and from civilian internees at home and abroad. The letters sent by German internees in the Curragh proved 'a constant source of worry' and while they were generally dealt with more expeditiously than normal mails, complaints were often made by the German internees, through the German minister, to the Department of External Affairs about delays in delivery. Internees' correspondence stood on 'firmer ground' than that of ordinary correspondence on account of the provision made for it in Red Cross conventions. Boland, assistant secretary at External Affairs, believed that 'if we did hold up these letters and our right to do so was subsequently questioned, we would not have a very strong case, I think'.[83]

From October 1940 letters from Ireland to prisoners of war abroad (usually Irish people serving in the British forces who had been taken prisoner) were no longer forwarded with deletions; sufficiently objectionable missives were detained or destroyed while less objectionable ones were returned to the sender to be rewritten. Many of these letters were the result of the Irish Red Cross 'allotment' of PoWs to Irish people for the purpose of letter-writing. The acceptability of allowing this practice in view of Irish neutrality was questioned by Purcell, but the system continued to operate and in February 1943 the Department of External Affairs recommended the waiving of postal charges for all PoW correspondence, in line with the terms of the International Convention on the Treatment of PoWs, 1929 (which Ireland had signed but not ratified). The Censorship raised no objection but made clear that it reserved the right to examine anything the Irish Red Cross was sending out.[84] By 1945 about five thousand letters to PoWs were being received each month by the Censorship, most of which were forwarded, with only a handful being detained or returned for rewriting.[85]

The propaganda activities of Irish citizens were the subject of close scrutiny by the Postal Censorship, working closely with G2 and the Department of External Affairs. One such citizen was Liam D. Walsh, a former G2 officer, adjutant of Blueshirt leader Eoin O'Duffy, and employee of the Italian legation.[86] He was in contact with prominent officers of the 'Fichte Bund', a quasi-official German propaganda organisation and was regarded by the Germans as a potential contact man for spies (at least two, Walter Simon and Gunther Schütz, who came to Ireland had Walsh's name as a contact).[87] In the early months of the war, examination of his correspondence revealed a series of propagandist articles which he was sending to Germany. In December 1939 he offered Oskar Pfaus, an Abwehr (German Intelligence Service) agent dispatched to Ireland to make contact with the IRA, a series of articles for a 'modest remuneration', which would compensate him for 'the employment he had lost here in consequence, as alleged, of his friendly attitude towards Germany'. The Department of External Affairs believed that to 'knowingly allow him to use our postal services' would amount to co-operation with his activities, and his future correspondence was duly detained by the Postal Censorship.[88] Walsh was a member of the Irish Fascist group, the People's National Party and later a co-founder of an organisation called the Irish Friends of Germany, which he had tried to merge with the IRA before being interned in the Curragh camp 'for subversive activities'.[89]

Giorgio Favilla, a naturalised Irish citizen of Italian origin, published a news-sheet *L'Italia Libera*, on behalf of the Dublin subsection of the Italian Anti-Fascist Federation. In September 1944 six copies of the news-sheet were intercepted in the post *en route* to the *News Review* in London, three Italian newspapers and two Italian government ministers. The issue included an attack on Berardis, the Italian minister in Ireland, who was described as being 'as much a Fascist now as he was before August, 1943', when he changed his allegiance in order to keep his position. Walshe (External Affairs), whose own anti-fascist credentials were questionable, expressed the hope that Favilla would be interned while Coyne saw his case as 'a concrete illustration of the sort of embarrassment that might arise (perhaps in a more serious form in another case) from the naturalisation of political refugees'. His case was investigated and the Department of Justice decided that his actions were not sufficiently serious to justify the revocation of his naturalisation. He was, however, directed to submit his publication to the Press Censorship, while another copy was stopped in the post in October 1944.[90]

In February 1941 copies of *Bulletin de Nouvelles*, a propaganda bulletin circulated in Ireland by the Belgian legation, was sent to the Censorship by the post office. The Belgian bulletin was objected to on the basis of its recruitment efforts for the Belgian forces abroad, and it was arranged that future copies should be sent by the post office to the Censorship for examination.[91] Propagandist and other 'objectionable' publications and materials were regularly intercepted coming through the post from abroad and also at the ports by Customs officials. In July 1940 Customs officers intercepted parcels of propaganda leaflets issued by the British Ministry of Information (MOI) *en route* to Woolworths stores throughout the country. The leaflets were sent to the Censorship and detained, and Woolworths were instructed not to distribute any that had reached them.[92] A complaint was made to the British authorities through the Irish high commissioner in London, who was assured by the MOI that the parcels had been sent in error and that there would be no recurrence.[93]

The MOI erred again in September 1941, sending quantities of V (for Victory) badges to Woolworths. These were either detained or the stores which had received them were told to return them. Many consignments of these badges and emblems were detained in the Postal Censorship towards the end of 1941, as Aiken initiated an offensive against the V campaign. It was regarded as offering 'endless opportunities to certain of our citizens to show what good Britishers they are' and as having 'mischief-making possibilities'. The minister directed that 'every effort' be made to intercept and detain mails containing these emblems, which nevertheless continued to be imported and displayed in shops in large numbers.[94] In August 1941 a number of letters were returned to a journalist in Youghal, Co. Cork for rewriting. His 'crime', according to Coyne, was to have scrawled the V sign all over the back of his copy; he was informed that the 'use of hieroglyphs or other forms of cabalistic script' was not allowed![95]

The powers of postal censorship were also used to intercept books which were considered objectionable. In April 1941 bulk consignments of *The Persecution of the Catholic Church in German-Occupied Poland* were returned to London. Joseph Walshe thought that this 'very dirty book' brought 'the Pope, the Church and its Ministers into hatred and contempt' and would do 'much real moral harm' in this country. The Censorship saw it as a threat to friendly relations with other states, holding up, as it did, the rulers and institutions of other countries to 'hatred, ridicule and contempt'.[96]

Leaflets and letters appealing for contributions to such as the British and Allied Comforts and Victims of War Fund were intercepted and detained;[97] Aiken also wanted financial contributions themselves, from persons in Ireland to such as the British Spitfire Fund, to be stopped. Coyne (who had served in the RAF in the First World War) questioned whether it was necessary to take 'such a strict view of our neutrality' and whether there was anything that could be done about it given the existing financial arrangements between the two countries and the limited scope of the Censorship.[98]

Nevertheless, details of contributions to the various war funds and appeals were kept, and schedules giving these details formed part of the Monthly Reports of the Postal Censorship. In November–December 1940 the Gardaí were given details of those groups and individuals involved in organised fund-raising for the British war effort. Consideration was given to the question of whether they were in violation of the Emergency Powers (No. 54) Order 1940, and the restrictions imposed by this order (relating to movement of money) were made known to the fund-raisers. A number were visited by the Gardaí (some were highly indignant and attributed the visits to the intervention of the German minister, Hempel) and in December 1940 the Postal Censorship reported that there was 'reason to believe' that organised efforts of this kind would be less evident in the future.[99]

In relation to economic matters the Postal Censorship did much work of an informative and preventative nature. Close co-operation was maintained between the financial section and the Department of Finance; numerous infringements of Emergency finance orders were discovered, leading to approximately one hundred prosecutions of offenders. Postal Censorship officers were occasionally called upon to give evidence in these cases.[100] At the same time as the censorship of cross-channel mail was introduced (June 1940), the US Treasury announced a prohibition on the sending of securities and evidences thereof to the US; this placed an added burden on the hard-pressed staff as an extensive search was undertaken for letters to the US containing remittances, etc.[101] The Censorship was also able to supply the Department of Finance with details that would otherwise have been very difficult or impossible to obtain, like the dollar holdings of Irish residents, which in the aggregate, amounted to a 'very considerable sum'.[102]

Much useful information was gathered regarding commodities in short supply, the difficulties encountered by importers in their efforts to obtain shipping for goods, etc.[103] The examination of letters in the trade section revealed schemes for defrauding the Revenue in the importation of various goods, manipulation of prices of commodities such as petrol, and so on.[104] Occasionally, at the request of the Department of Supplies, intensive censorship was applied to all the correspondence to and from certain companies in the state, e.g. tobacco and petrol companies.[105] In July 1942, Supplies requested the detention of letters containing ration books and the sending of these books to that department. This was to prevent contraventions of a 1942 emergency rationing order which stated that 'No person shall assign, give in exchange, pledge or otherwise dispose of any ration documents'. In August Aiken gave authorisation for letters containing ration books, odd coupons from ration books or references to a contemplated misuse of the writer's or addressee's book to be withdrawn from transit and forwarded to Supplies.[106]

Finally, a close watch was kept on the commercial correspondence of the large number of 'aliens', 'mostly Jews', who had taken up residence and established businesses in Ireland just before or at the beginning of the war. These were mainly related to the importation of goods, although a number used Ireland as a refuge from which to operate businesses abroad. Close co-operation was maintained between those who examined commercial correspondence and the G2 officers who were in daily attendance.[107]

TELEGRAPH CENSORSHIP

In comparison to the postal division, the Telegraph Censorship was operated by a small staff, which never exceeded twenty-five persons in total. Censorship control was centred on Cussen, the chief telegraph censor, who shared an office in the General Post Office (GPO) in Dublin with a censor and a shorthand typist. The rest of the staff was divided between Cork post office, Valentia and Waterville cable stations and Valentia and Malin Head radio stations. Almost all the actual censorship was done in the central telegraph office in Dublin, through which terminal traffic was routed for administrative reasons. Two assistant censors were installed in Cork as it was the only centre outside Dublin with direct cross-channel communications circuits; they kept check on press telegrams which did not pass through Dublin (principally those exchanged between Britain and the *Cork Examiner*) and censored a few local messages (though all doubtful telegrams were referred to Dublin). The personnel installed at the cable and radio stations operated as watching staff rather than as censors.[108]

The Telegraph Censorship covered the public telegraph service (inland and foreign) which included landline, cable and radio; public telephone services; wireless services under the Wireless Telegraphy Act; and special (non-public) services such as wireless stations, telegraphy schools and newspaper private wires. These non-public services were a potential source of unauthorised communications and were dealt with by a variety of legal and administrative means.[109] Directions to masters of ships registered in the state were issued to regulate the use of ships' wireless transmitting stations. Foreign ships arriving in Irish ports were visited by military, post office and customs officials who removed essential components from transmitting apparatuses to secure against irregular transmissions. Similar action was taken against Royal National Lifeboat Institution (RNLI) lifeboats, while the stations at certain lighthouses and lightkeepers' dwellings were allowed to remain open for urgent messages on the lighthouse and lifesaving services. The post office island wireless stations, which were used to communicate with the mainland, were issued with special instructions by the chief telegraph censor warning against irregular transmission, and were supervised by local Gardaí. Similar instructions were issued to the three wireless telegraphy schools (two in Dublin and one in Cork) which trained wireless operators and operated under licences issued under the Wireless Telegraphy Act and permits issued under the Emergency Powers (Wireless Telegraphy Apparatus) Order 1939.[110]

All amateur transmitting licences were withdrawn on 1 September 1939 and the apparatuses were seized by the Gardaí under the above-mentioned emergency order. However, a number of 'pirate' stations continued to operate, and the observation of listeners' report cards in the Postal Censorship led to a number of Garda raids.[111] One station in Rathmines, Dublin was being operated by the IRA. It was raided by Gardaí on 29 December 1939, the apparatus was seized and four men, including Jack McNeela (who was in charge of publicity for the IRA and also produced its clandestine paper *War News*) and Jack Plunkett, were arrested. They were originally charged with broadcasting without a licence under the Wireless Telegraphy Act and without a permit under the Emergency Powers (Wireless Telegraphy Apparatus) Order. This charge was adjourned when they came before the Special Criminal Court on 1 March 1940, because Cussen, the chief telegraph censor, was ill and was unable to attend to give evidence;[112] the defendants were convicted on a charge of 'conspiracy to usurp a function of Government'. McNeela (who was sentenced to two years) and Plunkett (eighteen months) were on hunger strike at the time of their appearance in court and McNeela died as a result on 19 April 1940, after which that particular phase of IRA hunger strikes was abandoned.[113]

The transmitter had been used by the IRA to communicate with Berlin; arms and supplies had been requested but the Germans seemed more interested in urging the IRA to come to terms with de Valera and all that resulted was mutual confusion. The main use made of this and other transmitters was for the dissemination of internal propaganda to give 'an impression of strength on the part of the IRA which it did not really possess'.[114] In February 1940, Ernst Weber-Drohl, the former 'Atlas the Strong', arrived off the Irish coast in a U-Boat with a bulky radio transmitter to replace the one seized in Rathmines. Unfortunately for him, a strong wind overturned his dinghy and the transmitter was lost; however, he managed to hand over money and code-words for the lost transmitter to an IRA contact before being picked up by the authorities.[115]

In December 1943, the Germans, seeking information on Allied plans for a second front, parachuted two Irishmen with radio transmitters into Co. Clare; they were captured and interned within hours of landing. This episode, however, sealed the fate of the transmitter which the German minister had been using to communicate with Berlin. G2 had traced signals first identified by the British in 1940 to the German legation, but, possibly because the Germans were still in the ascendant in the war, did not take any action to shut it down. G2 tried and failed to break the codes but monitored them continually and, following a period of strain between G2 and MI5 in 1941 over the transmitter, the British and Irish security authorities co-operated on the interception of the signals. The value of the meteorological information transmitted by Hempel has probably been overestimated (the Germans were receiving ample meteorological reports from their aircraft in the Atlantic), yet the erroneous attribution of responsibility for the escape of two German warships down the English Channel in February 1942 to weather reports sent from the transmitter gave the Irish authorities the opportunity to insist to Hempel that the transmissions should cease. In late December 1943 the transmitter was finally handed over to G2, and was placed in a bank vault, thus effectively cutting the legation off from Germany.[116] Dr Richard Hayes, director of the National Library (not to be confused with the other Richard Hayes, the film censor), did cryptographic work for G2, successfully breaking the ciphers used by Abwehr agents in Ireland; this material was supplied to the British security authorities, with whom he closely collaborated.[117]

There was no direct censorship control of newspaper private telegraph wires which carried news agency and general press messages into newspaper offices, but outward messages were restricted to service messages or those related to the business of the newspaper (these were the conditions of rental from the post office). The newspapers were warned that the wires would be withdrawn in the event of any unauthorised use. No newspaper would have risked such a situation (as an American journalist employed by Associated Press discovered in August 1940 when he sought to 'tie up' with one of these wires), especially as telephones could be used just as easily to evade the censorship if they so desired.[118]

The coast wireless stations at Valentia, Co. Kerry and Malin Head, Co. Donegal were still owned by the British postal administration but were operated by the Irish Department of Posts and Telegraphs on an agency basis. The stations were engaged almost exclusively with communications with ships. An emergency order was made in 1939 giving the government full control over the sending and receiving of such messages (as allowed under the Wireless Telegraphy Act) but it was not relied upon and 'censors' were installed at the stations without any legal formality.[119]

At the beginning of the war three censors were installed at each station to observe the radio traffic. However, they had little to do and the staff was soon reduced to two at each station. The principal reason for the low volume of traffic was the deletion of the stations from the list of stations distributing British admiralty war warnings and instructions to British merchant ships from early 1940. They were no longer classified as 'British' stations for working purposes and British ships communicated directly with stations in Britain, yet the situation remained complicated. Admiralty messages in code to and from ships occasionally passed through the stations, and it was not known whether these were war or merchant ships. Distress calls which were picked up were re-broadcast to British stations, though the stations were instructed not to re-broadcast those which disclosed details of belligerent activity unless clear distress to merchant ships was involved. Daily logs of distress and SOS calls, and messages relating to war actions, were sent, through the chief telegraph censor, to the office of the controller of censorship and to G2. The daily log of distress calls continued to be sent to the inspector of wireless telegraphy in London, as in pre-war days.[120] The Malin Head station transmitted signals by telegraph to Scotland giving information about submarine activities while direction-finding facilities at Malin Head were used by British ships and aircraft; similar direction-finding facilities were installed at Valentia in response to a British request and were fully operational from October 1944. In February 1945 the British requested permission to establish a mobile and temporary radar post at Malin Head due to the ineffectiveness of Northern Irish and Scottish posts because of the dampening of signals by the Donegal Mountains.[121]

There were two cable stations in operation in the state at the outbreak of war: the Western Union Telegraph Company station at Valentia and the Commercial Cable Company station at Waterville, Co. Kerry. They operated as relay stations for transatlantic cables, which carried messages to and from London and Dublin; they neither accepted nor delivered terminal telegrams. Before the war the British had suggested diverting such traffic to Liverpool or London for censorship,[122] and in July 1940, worried about the security of their transatlantic cable communications, the British again considered disconnecting the cables and connecting them directly to Britain. The companies gave their consent and the Irish government saw no basis for objection on political or practical grounds, as the plans allowed for one cable to continue through Valentia. In the event of this being cut, an alternative arrangement involving radio-telegraph communications with a company in the US was arranged for Irish government traffic, which in an emergency could be extended to deal with urgent public traffic.[123] The proposals were, however, abandoned in October 1940, and although the cables were not cut, a certain number were diverted to Britain.[124]

The duty of the three 'censors' installed at each station was entirely nominal; they served only to maintain a semblance of control as neither company was Irish and did not normally operate under post office control. In March 1940 the staffs were reduced to one censor at each station and in December 1943 it was decided that even those two officials were surplus to requirements. Experience had shown that the local superintendents and staff of the companies were fully trustworthy and could be relied upon to ensure that there would be no irregularities and that the censorship regulations would be observed. The principle of control could equally be maintained via the direct wires between the Telegraph Censorship in Dublin and the two stations, while the presence of military guards at both ensured against the entry of unauthorised persons. In early 1944 the total scrambling of all messages between North America and Britain made even the observation of these messages impossible.[125]

In May 1944, prior to the Allied landings in Normandy, the controller of censorship, Coyne, the chief telegraph censor, Cussen and Major Guilfoyle of G2 made an inspection tour of the cable and wireless stations (including Radio Éireann Athlone broadcasting station and the Shannon Airport wireless stations) and declared themselves satisfied that all staffs were trustworthy and that no unauthorised communications or security leaks would occur through any of these stations.[126]

Although the government possessed the power to censor telephone communications under the Emergency Powers Order 1939 no statutory, general telephone censorship was, in fact, imposed. A telephone observation room was opened in Dublin Castle in August 1941 and a staff of four observers and a superintendent operated a partial supervision of cross-channel and cross-border telephone communications.[127] A proper supervision of the thirty-one trunk circuits between the state and Britain and Northern Ireland would have required a staff of at least one hundred; nevertheless, according to Coyne, 'valuable results were secured' by the tiny staff involved.[128] At the same time as they imposed postal censorship on cross-channel post (May–June 1940), the British authorities established, without public announcement, a censorship control on all trunk telephone circuits between Britain and the whole of Ireland with facilities for cutting off any call immediately. In response to a request from the British in July 1941, telephone calls across the border during or after air raids were restricted to a list of numbers supplied by the British.[129] The power conferred by the EPO, while never invoked to introduce a general telephone censorship, was used in specific circumstances. For example, the Irish correspondent of the *Daily Mail* twice had his telephone disconnected by ministerial order because of alleged evasions of press censorship regulations. All the correspondents of overseas newspapers had their conversations listened into, but because they were aware of the fact, they were extra careful. The Emergency Powers (No. 67) Order 1941 made it an offence to send a press message out of the state by telephone (or by any other means) without first submitting it for censorship.[130] Despite this, and assurances given, many correspondents of the external press continued to make use of the telephone to evade the censorship (see Chapter 5).

From 1940 the post office operated a surveillance of telephone calls for G2 (as mentioned earlier, the problem of the legality of this surveillance was overcome by simply ignoring the question). Nobody appeared to be exempt from this surveillance, including all of the diplomatic missions. When the post office refused to continue this service after the lifting of the general censorship restrictions in May 1945, Dan Bryan of G2 argued vigorously for its retention, on whatever legal pretext that could be established. In a letter to Aiken, now reinstated as Minister for Defence, he stated that he 'never regarded this service as a section of the Censorship . . . I can only reiterate that I regard telephone supervision as essential to a security machine and, in practice, it has proved itself, in a number of cases, the most valuable portion of the supervision which has been exercised in the Post Office for a number of years'.[131]

Press telegrams were occasionally stopped by the Telegraph Censorship but were generally passed on to the Press Censorship before delivery as new arrangements placed the onus on the newspapers to submit any censorable matter in a press telegram received by them.[132] In May 1940 Coyne wrote to Walshe at External Affairs regarding violations of the censorship by visiting newspaper correspondents who either telephoned their messages to London or waited until they returned to London to dispatch them. Aiken viewed the situation very seriously and wondered if the Department of External Affairs could make representation to London with a view to improving the situation; he even suggested that it could be intimated to the British that if the situation continued, the Irish authorities would be forced to hold up traffic on the transatlantic cables.[133]

With regard to the public telegraph system, the censorship extended to all telegrams which originated in or were destined for places within the state, but was not applicable to transit traffic, i.e. messages originating in and destined for places outside the state. Any attempt to interfere with such messages would have resulted in them being diverted. There was a 100 per cent censorship check on outward and inward telegrams but not on all those exchanged within the state, though these were observed and treated in the same manner as external messages if they were found to be in any way objectionable.[134] Copies were kept in the GPO of all inward foreign cables and telegrams, while copies of all telegraphic messages originating in the state were kept at the office of origin.[135]

The Telegraph Censorship played a similar dual role to the postal division in terms of information and prevention, although the speed by which messages could be transmitted made the telegraph section more important in terms of prevention. The general rules, restrictions and exemptions, and the treatment of correspondence generally, were along the same lines.

Telegrams had to be written in English or Irish; code and cypher was prohibited; registered abbreviated addresses were prohibited; and each telegram had to bear the surname of the sender at the bottom of the text. In practice a degree of flexibility was applied in relation to some of these general rules. In the case of codes the general prohibition was relaxed, as in the case of posts, to allow the use of specified, recognised commercial codes.[136] Such coded telegrams were accepted from February 1940.[137] Consular and diplomatic representatives were allowed send messages in other languages while incoming telegrams in 'foreign' languages were delivered after translation had shown them to be harmless. The options open to the Irish Censorship were always limited by the fact that almost all telegrams from Ireland passed through Britain and the British would only put through messages in languages allowed by them (English and French at first, and at different times for certain periods, Portugese, Spanish and Italian). The Irish authorities refused to officially allow other languages, realising that they would be put in an embarrassing position if there was a demand to allow German (prohibited by the British) to be used. In practice, the policy was to allow any languages which were permitted by the British where it was shown that serious inconvenience would otherwise be caused.[138] The Irish Sweepstakes operators, the Hospitals Trust, were permitted to use French and Spanish, provided a translation was given with the telegram.[139]

There was no relaxation of the rules applying to abbreviated addresses and the sender's name, however, as the instructions issued to telegraph censors pointed out that 'The identity of the sender and addressee is one of the most important, if not the most important, point in censorship'. They were told that an objectionable telegram could easily be disguised as an innocent communication of a personal or commercial character, while 'its real character may only be disclosed by information as to the sender or addressee or both'.[140] The bona fides of those exchanging correspondence (telegrams and letters) were thus a very important factor in determining its treatment.

Telegrams in the service of the Irish government were exempt from censorship, save in exceptional cases where 'serious consequences' could result from transmission and where it was possible to communicate with the sender immediately with a view to altering the wording. Such 'irregular' telegrams were subsequently brought to the notice of the department or official concerned.[141] Telegrams from diplomatic missions to their governments were also exempt, provided certain procedures were followed. Such telegrams had to be handed in at the General Post Office, bearing certification of their diplomatic character. These telegrams were then given priority transmission from Dublin and were forwarded with a covering service message indicating their official status.[142] (An additional exemption was granted in July 1940 to telegrams, including those in code and cypher, from the British permit office in Dublin to the British passport office in London.[143]) While the telegrams of diplomatic representatives were not interfered with, they were observed and noted by G2, which made their contents available to the Department of External Affairs for its information.[144]

A 'Black List' was prepared and regularly updated of persons suspected of being 'seditiously disposed'. Telegrams to and from such persons were stopped and sent to the chief telegraph censor for disposal, while a record was kept of their correspondents as 'persons coming under a similar suspicion'.[145] Among the individuals treated with suspicion was the socialist and republican Peadar O'Donnell. During an outbreak of diphtheria in Dublin in January 1940 his telegram to New Jersey enquiring whether a young American boy who was staying with him and his family had been inoculated was treated as suspicious and a sharp eye kept out for the reply.[146]

Business telegrams to or from well-established businesses were usually passed with little delay once they obviously related to legitimate business affairs. Business messages to or from persons whose credentials were not known or well established, to or from addresses not known as places of business or temporary addresses like hotels from where many commercial travellers operated, and those relating to business matters which neither of the correspondents were known to be interested in, were all treated with suspicion, held and investigated.[147] Such an approach relied on good local knowledge of firms and individuals and was only possible by means of close co-operation with the Gardaí and G2.

The bona fides of senders and addressees of 'private' telegrams were not as easily established as in the case of business messages and all private telegrams sent in to or out of the state were carefully scrutinised. If a censor had any doubts about either correspondent, he/she was not to hesitate in stopping messages of a personal nature along the lines of 'Congratulations', 'Many Happy Returns', or, in particular, those mentioning a figure, for example 'Best Wishes on 21st Anniversary'. Special care was to be taken over messages purporting to relate to illnesses, deaths and funerals 'which may be sent to appeal to a tender hearted censor. From the national point of view', the instructions pointed out, 'it is obviously better that a number of innocent persons should have such telegrams stopped than that one dangerous telegram should get through'. (Apparently, it was because the British cable censor at Valentia was 'caught napping' in 1916 that the New York newspapers were able to report the rising in their Easter Monday editions. The news was conveyed by an innocent-looking message from supposed relatives of an Irish emigrant saying that 'Tom' had been operated on successfully that day.[148]) Finally, because 'spies are frequently in want of money', telegrams remitting money, messages from Ireland seeking money and telegraphic money orders were all carefully dealt with.[149]

Telegrams which fell foul of the censorship were treated in a variety of ways. In cases where a telegram was clearly 'objectionable', either on the basis of the text or of the parties involved, it was usually stopped (unless the Gardaí or G2, for example, considered alternative treatment to be more useful for their purposes). In such cases the sender and addressee were not, as a rule, informed of the fate of the message. In doubtful but not definitely suspect cases, the telegram was held pending an explanation from one or other party and released if the explanation proved satisfactory. Care was taken in such cases not to divulge the particulars of the message to the addressee, as this would fulfil its original purpose. Often an explanation of the text was sought from the office of origin, from which particulars of the sender were often requested also. When telegrams were stopped solely on the basis of non-compliance with the formal Censorship rules, for example in relation to codes, addresses or names, the sender was usually afforded the opportunity of correcting the error.[150]

In cases of doubt, where the degree of suspicion was not such as to justify stoppage, telegrams could be deliberately held up in the Censorship before transmission. Often, objectionable words and phrases, e.g. 'IRA men', were deleted and the message then forwarded. In such cases the correspondents were not informed that deletions had been made and the number of words shown in the preamble was altered to correspond with the number resulting from the deletion.[151] Another method suggested to censors was to paraphrase a text; for example, 'Congratulations Birthday best love' could be altered to 'Best wishes anniversary greetings'. It was made clear that such action should only be taken when the meaning which the telegram purported to convey was clear and the change in the phraseology did not affect the substance.[152] This method was rarely used as coded messages usually depend less on the precise words than on the general meaning.

The subject of the hunger strikes by IRA prisoners throughout the Emergency and other references to that organisation were a frequent target for the Telegraph Censorship. In a telegram to New York in relation to a hunger striker in November 1939 the word 'dying' was deleted but the fact that the prisoner was in a 'serious condition' was allowed. In a telegram from the 'Officers and men of the West Cork Battalion' to a convalescing hunger striker in a Dublin nursing home, the Censorship allowed the 'Heartiest Congratulations on a smashing victory' but deleted the details of the senders. As in the press, the letters 'IRA' were never allowed to appear, as when the *Daily Worker* in New York sent a message to Seán Murray asking to be kept informed about the 'protest movement against hanging IRA men' and the last six letters were deleted (after consultation with the Department of Justice!).[153] In November 1944, telegrams signed by fifteen prominent Kerrymen, including Cormac Breathnach, TD and Senator Donnchadh Ó hEaluighte of Fianna Fáil, were sent to local authority bodies in Kerry seeking support in the campaign for the reprieve of Charles Kerins, a Kerry IRA man under sentence of death; the telegrams were stopped.[154]

As in the Postal Censorship, the messages and contacts of foreign nationals resident in the state were closely watched and details of these were kept. A telegram from one such, a German national, in which he referred to his manager as 'Führer' and signed his telegram (referring to the late arrival of a ship) 'Robbintrip', was 'considered undesirable' and stopped.[155] Considered undesirable also were messages of loyalty from Irish associations such as the British Legion and the Old Comrades Association to the British king and other 'eminent English personages'. Such messages were very frequently sent (usually after functions marking the king's birthday, at Christmas, etc.) and had, according to Aiken, 'got us into trouble' in 1940; all telegrams bearing such greetings were stopped from 1941 onwards.[156]

In terms of providing information, telegrams relating to political, military and economic matters, as well as to individuals, were steadily supplied through the information division to the various departments concerned. In

January 1942 the Department of Supplies had a number of 'bootleggers' and racketeers, dealing in flour and other commodities, investigated by the Gardaí on the grounds of information gleaned from a series of inland telegrams. Coyne pointed out to Supplies that it would be preferable if the source of the information were not disclosed in any legal actions because if it were, in even one case which became public, no further information would be obtained from telegrams.[157] In July 1942 a shipping company was threatened with deprivation of shipping space for the importation of goods from the US on the basis of plans to evade regulations which were revealed in a telegram.[158]

CONCLUSION

Anglo-Irish wartime co-operation in the area of intelligence, and security generally, meant that the Irish postal and telegraph censorship, as well as being a national security measure, was also a part of the wider Allied security network. The 'constant stream of intelligence information'[159] supplied to the British, and later to the Americans, obviously included information gathered in the censorship, while that which was prevented was denied, in effect, only to the Germans. Furthermore, the Irish made sure that all German and Italian official communications were routed through British channels, thus ensuring that they were subject to British control. Broadcasts from the German legation transmitter were monitored in co-operation with the British and it was eventually seized; at the same time, the British were allowed to operate two 'secret' transmitters from the office of the UK representative as well as a private line to London and Belfast. The Irish authorities even allowed the British to set up an apparatus which resulted in the decreased efficiency of the Irish broadcasting system to prevent it being used by German bombers as a guide to British objectives,[160] while the Irish operated direction-finding equipment at its coastal wireless stations for the benefit of Allied aircraft.

The effectiveness of the postal and telegraph censorship as a security measure was limited by the fact that it was far from complete and there were substantial gaps through which uncensored communications could be sent and received. The existence of the border made the control of communications very difficult; there was, for example, no general censorship of mails exchanged with the North and thus no Southern Irish control over correspondence sent to or from Britain via this route. (This was a problem only when Irish and British security interests were in potential conflict, particularly in 1940–1.) There was little more than a nominal control at the land frontiers, ports or airfields while the powers contained in the Restriction on the Conveyance of Informative Articles emergency order were little used and acted more as a deterrent. Indeed, it was the deterrence factor which was generally relied upon to compensate for the lack of actual control. There was, as seen in Chapter 1, no legal impediment to the enforcement of a complete censorship, but a closure or even a substantial narrowing of the 'censorship gap' would have necessitated a full and effective frontier control, as well as a complete censorship of all mails. The political will simply did not exist to channel scarce resources to this end – a problem replicated in the approach to Irish defence generally.

Yet, Ireland did manage to prevent itself from becoming the mythical centre of espionage so beloved of the British press, and in this the Postal and Telegraph Censorship did play its part, in support of the wide-ranging intelligence and surveillance activities of G2. As we have seen, even representatives of the Irish government abroad were not above suspicion and censorship. The state passed its most important security 'examination' by not becoming a source of leaked information for the Germans in the critical period leading up to D-Day; the British helped, of course, by virtually cutting Ireland off from the outside world in the lead-up to the landings.

On the home front, the postal and telegraph censorship made probably its most direct contribution to the 'national cause' in the form of the information it supplied to the departments of Supplies and Finance. Politically, it provided the state with a welcome addition to its arsenal for the surveillance and repression of undesirable political activists and groups – republican, socialist and fascist. It was also used to silence those, like the 'West British', whose opinions were as unwelcome in private as they were in public.

The emergency censorship, in conjunction with the covert surveillance operated by and for G2, meant that private communications ceased to exist in wartime Ireland. While such control can always be justified in security terms by those who operate it, it represented, in democratic terms, a flagrant violation of the civil liberties of a large number of people. Yet, the postal and telegraph censorship never became a subject of political controversy, a situation partially attributable to the secrecy of G2's activities, but also to the fact that the rights of the press are always championed far more vigorously than the rights of the individual; the censorship of the press, by its very nature, became a far more public, political and contentious issue and it is to that important aspect of the wartime censorship that we next turn our attention.

NOTES AND REFERENCES

1 MA, OCC 1/15, Note on staff position, February 1940; NA, D/T, S 11445/8, Coyne memo on censorship, September 1945.
2 NA, D/T, S 11445/8, Coyne memo.
3 NA, D/J, Postal Censorship: 'Organisation and Administration', Appendix K.
4 ibid., Appendix I; D/T, S 11445/8, Coyne memo, September 1945.
5 NA, D/T, S 11445/8, 'Instructions for Censors'.
6 ibid., 'Distribution of Information' (Appendix A).
7 NA, D/J, Postal Censorship: 'Organisation and Administration', Appendix K.
8 NA, D/T, S 11445/8, 'Instructions for Censors'.
9 ibid., Appendix A.
10 NA, D/J, Postal Censorship: 'Organisation and Administration', Appendix K.
11 NA, D/T, S 11445/8, Appendix A.
12 ibid., 'Instructions for Censors'.
13 ibid., Appendix A.
14 MA, OCC 1/15, 'Censorship Service – Estimates: Note on the use of information obtained in Censorship', February 1940.
15 NA, D/J, Postal Censorship: 'Organisation and Administration'; D/J, Postal Censorship Monthly Reports, September 1939.
16 ibid.; MA, OCC 1/15, 'Note on Staff Position', February 1940.
17 NA, D/J, 'Controller's Correspondence', text of a speech on the Censorship given by Coyne after the war, undated.
18 NA, D/T, S 11445/8, Coyne memo on censorship, September 1945.
19 NA, D/J, Postal Censorship: 'Organisation and Administration'.
20 ibid.
21 NA, D/T, S 11445/8, Coyne memo on censorship, September 1945.
22 NA, D/J, Postal Censorship: 'Organisation and Administration'.
23 NA, D/J, 'Controller's Correspondence', Coyne speech, undated.
24 NA, D/T, S 11445/8, Coyne memo on censorship, September 1945.
25 NA, D/J, Postal Censorship Monthly Reports, September, 1939; MA, OCC 3/9, Connolly to Purcell, 25 October 1939.
26 NA, D/J, Postal Censorship: 'Organisation and Administration', Appendix O.
27 ibid., 'General Observations', Chief Postal Censor.
28 NA, D/J, 'Controller's Correspondence', Coyne speech, undated.
29 NA, D/J, Postal Censorship: 'Organisation and Administration'.
30 ibid.; NA, D/J, Postal Censorship Monthly Reports, general.
31 NA, D/J, Postal Censorship: 'Organisation and Administration', Appendix G.
32 NA, D/FA (Sec) A 9 (1), Purcell to Connolly, 12 July 1940.
33 NA, D/FA (Sec.) A 11, 'British Censorship Regulations'.
34 MA, OCC 3/22, Connolly to Aiken, 5 July 1940.
35 NA, D/J, Postal Censorship Monthly Reports, August 1940.
36 MA, OCC 3/22, Coyne to Aiken, 5 June 1940.
37 NA, D/T, S 11445/8, Coyne memo on censorship, September 1945.
38 NA, D/J, Postal Censorship Monthly Reports, general; NA, D/J, Postal Censorship: 'Organisation and Administration'.
39 ibid., Aiken to Censorship, 21 August 1941.
40 ibid., Connolly to Aiken, 12 July 1941.
41 MA, G2/P/21560, 'Organisation – Censorship', memo on 'Censorship in time of war', 9 March 1925.
42 MA, G2/X/0042, *Belfast Telegraph* cutting, 16 October 1941.
43 NA, D/FA (Sec.) P 81, G2 memo on recruitment to the British forces, 14 October

1943 and Bryan minute, 12 January 1944; NA, D/J, Postal Censorship Monthly Reports, December 1943.

44 Under questioning in the Dáil in November 1939 the Minister for Justice admitted that 'a few extra' warrants had recently been issued (*Dáil Debates*, Vol. 77, col. 933, 8 November 1939).

45 D/FA (Sec.) A 8(1), 'Defence, Security, Intelligence', Bryan memo, June 1945.

46 *Dáil Debates*, Vol. 77, col. 933, 8 November 1939.

47 MA, OCC 7/2, Government Information Bureau announcements with regard to Censorship.

48 MA, OCC 7/19, letters, etc. forwarded from the Postal Censorship to the OCC.

49 MA, OCC 1/15, memo on Postal Censorship, February 1940.

50 MA, OCC 3/22, 'Announcement on the Censorship of Cross-Channel Mails', 22 June 1940.

51 MA, OCC 5/20, Draft Order, October 1940; Coyne to Attorney General's office, 16 February 1940.

52 NA, D/J, Postal Censorship: 'Organisation and Administration', 'Attitude of the Public to Postal Censorship'.

53 MA, OCC 5/20, Coyne to Attorney General's office, 16 February 1940.

54 MA, OCC 3/26, Coyne to Purcell, 27 June 1940, Purcell to Coyne, 23 July 1940.

55 NA, D/J, Postal Censorship: 'Organisation and Administration'.

56 MA, OCC 3/26, Purcell to Coyne, 23 July 1940.

57 MA, OCC 7/2, Statement by Connolly, 5 October 1939.

58 NA, D/J, Postal Censorship: 'Organisation and Administration', 'Attitude of the Public to Postal Censorship'.

59 MA, OCC 1/15, Postal Censorship memo, February 1940.

60 ibid., 'Postal Censorship Memorandum', 1940.

61 NA, D/FA (Sec.) A 62, 'German Legation Staff', Guilfoyle (G2) to Walshe, 11 June 1943.

62 ibid., Bryan to Walshe, 27 March 1944.

63 NA, D/FA (Sec.) P 24, request from German Foreign Office, 25 September 1939, request from Italians, 18 April 1941.

64 NA, D/FA, 233/37A, DEA to Censorship, April 1941.

65 NA, D/T, S 14804, Walshe to Maurice Moynihan (D/T), 12 March 1942, regarding a cablegram received from the Washington Legation.

66 NA, D/J, Postal Censorship: 'Bishops', etc. Letters'.

67 NA, D/FA (Sec.) A 9(1), Walshe to Censorship, 25 April 1941.

68 Dermot Keogh, *Ireland and Europe 1919–1948* (Dublin, 1988), p. 166.

69 NA, D/FA (Sec.) A 8, Walshe to Archer, 10 May 1941.

70 NA, D/FA (Sec.) P 71, Walshe to Kerney, 13 June 1942.

71 Keogh, *Ireland and Europe 1919–1948*, p. 167.

72 NA, D/FA (Sec.) P 71, Kerney to Censorship, 5 December 1942.

73 ibid.

74 Keogh, *Ireland and Europe 1919–1948*, pp. 167–70.

75 NA, D/FA (Sec.) P 71, Bryan to Walshe, 7 January 1943.

76 Tim Pat Coogan, *De Valera: Long Fellow, Long Shadow* (London, 1993), p. 618.

77 MA, OCC 6/3, Purcell to Coyne, 12 December 1939.

78 NA, D/FA, 364/1, 'UNRRA Request for Exemption from Censorship'.

79 NA, D/T, S 11445/8, Coyne memo on censorship, September 1945; NA, D/J, Postal Censorship: 'Organisation and Administration', 'Organisation'; Carrolle J. Carter, *The Shamrock and the Swastika: German Espionage in Ireland in World War II* (California, 1977), pp. 200–22; Enno Stephan, *Spies in Ireland* (London, 1965) pp. 184–92. Stephan writes that Unland was a former agent who had the misfortune to engage in a harmless exchange of correspondence with Schütz.

80 MA, OCC 7/31, 'Information Regarding Aliens'.
81 ibid.
82 MA, OCC 3/47, 'Censorship of Correspondence of Military Internees', internal Censorship correspondence and correspondence with G2, November–December 1941.
83 MA, OCC 3/47, Boland to Purcell, 21 November 1941.
84 MA, OCC 3/16, 'Correspondence for PoWs interned abroad – Regulations regarding', January 1940 to April 1943.
85 NA, D/J, Postal Censorship Monthly Reports, 1945.
86 Ironically, Walshe was the author of a 1925 G2 memo on censorship in time of war (Eunan O'Halpin, 'Aspects of Intelligence', *The Irish Sword*, Vol. XIX, Nos. 75 and 76, 1993–4, p. 59).
87 Carter, *Shamrock and Swastika*, p. 102; NA, D/FA (Sec.) A 8, Archer to Walshe, 29 August 1940.
88 MA, OCC 7/28, DEA to Censorship, 18 December 1939; Connolly to Aiken, 20 December 1939.
89 Carter, *Shamrock and Swastika*, p. 252; Robert Fisk, *In Time of War: Ireland, Ulster and the Price of Neutrality, 1939–45* (London, 1985), pp. 434–5.
90 MA, OCC 2/142, correspondence regarding *L'Italia Libera*, September–November 1944.
91 MA, OCC 3/38, DEA to Censorship, February 1941.
92 MA, OCC 3/24, 'Action Regarding American Publications Observed in the Postal Censorship'; MA, OCC 3/27, 'Action Regarding MOI Propaganda Leaflets'.
93 NA, D/FA (Sec.) 9(1), July 1940.
94 MA, OCC 7/47, 'V Campaign', Aiken direction, 29 September 1941.
95 NA, D/J, No. 197, 'Miscellaneous Correspondence', 11 August 1941.
96 NA, D/FA (Sec.) A 9(1), Censorship to Walshe, 10 April 1941, Walshe to Censorship, 16 April 1941.
97 MA, OCC 3/30, Coyne to Purcell, 19 September 1940.
98 MA, OCC 3/29, Coyne to Aiken, 2 September 1940.
99 NA, D/J, Postal Censorship Monthly Reports, November–December 1940.
100 NA, D/J, Postal Censorship: 'Organisation and Administration'.
101 MA, OCC 3/22, Connolly to Aiken, 12 July 1941.
102 NA, D/J, Postal Censorship: 'Organisation and Administration', 'Financial Section'.
103 ibid., 'Trade Section'.
104 ibid.
105 ibid.
106 MA, OCC 7/50, correspondence, January–July 1942.
107 NA, D/J, Postal Censorship Monthly Reports, November–December 1939.
108 MA, OCC 1/11, 'Censorship Organisation: Staffing', November 1939; MA, OCC 1/15, Note on staff position, February 1940; D/T, S 11445/8, Coyne memo on censorship, September 1945.
109 MA, OCC 5/43, 'Telegraph Censorship: Report by Chief Telegraph Censor on statutory and administrative action necessary for cessation of censorship', 9 May 1945.
110 NA, D/J, Telegraph Censorship Monthly Reports, general; D/T, S 11445/8, Coyne memo on censorship, September 1945.
111 NA, D/J, Telegraph Censorship Monthly Reports, December 1939.
112 ibid., January–February 1940.
113 Tim Pat Coogan, *The IRA* (London, 1971), p. 183.
114 ibid., p. 274; J. Bowyer Bell, *The Secret Army: The IRA, 1916–1979* (Dublin, 1979), p. 170.
115 Coogan, *The IRA*, p. 278; Fisk, *In Time of War*, pp. 137–8.

116   Eunan O'Halpin, 'Intelligence and Security in Ireland, 1922–45', *Intelligence and National Security*, Vol. 5, No. 1, January 1990, pp. 69–71; NA, D/FA (Sec.) A 25, 'Radio Transmitter in the German Legation'.

117   O'Halpin, 'Intelligence and Security', p. 71.

118   MA, OCC 4/27, 'Control of Newspaper Private Wires', August–November 1940; NA, D/J, Telegraph Censorship Monthly Reports, September 1939 and May 1940.

119   NA, D/T, S 11445/8, Coyne memo on censorship, September 1945.

120   NA, D/J, Telegraph Censorship Monthly Reports, general; D/FA (Sec.) A 30, 'Telegraph Censorship – Malin Head and Valentia Coast Wireless Stations', Report by Chief Telegraph Censor, 8 August 1940; T. Ryle Dwyer, *Strained Relations: Ireland at Peace and the USA at War, 1941–45* (Dublin, 1988), p. 153.

121   NA, D/FA (Sec.) A 30, 'Telegraph Censorship', general.

122   NA, D/J, Report of the Interdepartmental Committee on Censorship, 1938.

123   NA, D/FA (Sec.) P 9, 'Proposed disconnection of Trans-Atlantic cables from Waterville and Valentia, July 1940'.

124   ibid.; NA, D/J, Telegraph Censorship Monthly Reports, July–December 1940.

125   NA, D/J, 'Cable and Wireless Stations Inspection, 1944'.

126   ibid.

127   NA, D/J, Telegraph Censorship Monthly Reports, August 1941.

128   MA, OCC 5/43, 'Telegraph Censorship: Report by Chief Telegraph Censor on statutory and administrative action necessary for cessation of censorship', 9 May 1945; NA, D/T, S 11445/8, Coyne memo on censorship, September 1945.

129   NA, D/FA (Sec.) A 11, 'British Censorship Regulations', Office of the UK Representative to Boland, July 1941.

130   MA, OCC 5/22, EP (No. 67) O 1941, memo regarding.

131   NA, D/FA (Sec.) A 8(1), 'Security Intelligence', Bryan to Aiken, 25 May 1945.

132   MA, OCC 4/17, 'Press Messages'.

133   NA, D/FA (Sec.) A 9(1), Coyne to Walshe, 24 May 1940.

134   MA, OCC 5/43, report by Cussen, 9 May 1945; OCC 7/22, memo on the Censorship, 17 October 1939.

135   MA, G2/X/0042, 'Censorship Regulations and Reports', 'Cable and Telegraph Traffic', 21 October 1939.

136   MA, OCC 4/10, 'Proposal to permit use of foreign texts in certain telegrams'.

137   NA, D/J, Telegraph Censorship Monthly Reports, January–April 1940.

138   MA, OCC 4/10, 'Proposal to permit use of foreign texts in certain telegrams'.

139   MA, OCC 4/8, Hospitals Trust, Ltd request for permission to use French and Spanish in texts of cablegrams sent abroad in connection with Sweep Draw, October 1939.

140   NA, D/T, S 11445/8, Coyne memo on censorship, September 1945.

141   ibid.

142   NA, D/FA 233/44, Boland to Diplomatic and Consular corps, 5 September 1939.

143   ibid., 6 July 1940.

144   See, for example, NA, D/FA (Sec.) A 8, A 8(1), A 9(1), A 9(2). Besides reading cables and post and listening in on telephone calls, the authorities had an Irish clerk working in the US legation who 'regularly rifled their files' (Carter interview with Richard Hayes, Carolle J. Carter, 'Ireland: America's Neutral Ally, 1939–41', *Éire-Ireland*, 2, 1977, p. 7).

145   MA, OCC 4/23, Cussen to Coyne, 'Treatment of Doubtful Telegrams', 19 December 1939 and 'Instructions for Telegraph Censors – Suspect Telegrams'.

146   MA, OCC 7/8, 'Telegraph Censorship: messages forwarded for information', 24 January 1940.

147   MA, OCC 4/23, Cussen to Coyne, 24 January 1940.

148   NA, D/J, 'Controller's Correspondence', text of a speech on the Censorship given by Coyne after the war, undated.
149   MA, OCC 4/23, Cussen to Coyne, 24 January 1940.
150   NA, D/T, S 11445/8, Coyne memo on censorship, September 1945.
151   ibid.
152   MA, OCC 4/23, Cussen to Coyne, 24 January 1940.
153   MA, OCC 7/8, 'Telegraph Censorship: messages forwarded for information', 12 February 1940.
154   *Dáil Debates*, Vol. 95, cols. 1408-9, 30 November 1944.
155   MA, OCC 7/8, Telegraph Censorship: messages forwarded for information', 28 November 1939.
156   NA, D/FA (Sec.) A 9(1), various examples; MA, OCC 4/33, 'Messages of Loyalty from Irish Associations to the King and other eminent English Personages'.
157   MA, OCC 7/50, Coyne to Supplies, 7 February 1942.
158   ibid., July 1942.
159   NA, D/FA (Sec.) A 3, 'Help given by the Irish government to the British in relation to the actual waging of war' (Walshe memo, 24 May 1941).
160   ibid.

4.
'DON'T MENTION THE WAR!'
THE PRESS CENSORSHIP

On Sunday, 3 September 1939, the day that Britain declared war on Germany, the editors of Ireland's daily newspapers were summoned to Government Buildings and addressed by the controller of censorship, Joseph Connolly. As a press censorship had not yet been put in place, he asked the editors to avoid giving publicity to matters which would tend to 'impair neutrality', and for the next two weeks the newspapers operated a voluntary censorship on these lines.[1] On 14 September, with its staff now in place, the Press Censorship contacted the various government departments seeking particulars of news and information the publication of which, from their point of view, was considered undesirable.[2] The replies contributed to a general forecast of those matters which it was considered would be of concern to the state and, on that basis, a set of general directions to the papers was drawn up and sent out on 17 September, accompanied by the enabling order, Emergency Powers (No. 5) Order 1939. Censorable matters, items in relation to which the press was prohibited from publishing without authorisation, were listed under the following eight headings: defence forces; foreign air, naval or military forces; safeguarding neutrality; weather reports; commercial shipping and aircraft; supplies; financial; civil service.[3] (These directions are reproduced in full in Appendix 3.)

On 19 September the editors of the five Dublin dailies, the *Sunday Independent* and the Dublin editor of the *Cork Examiner* met with Connolly, Thomas Coyne, the assistant controller, Michael Knightly, chief press censor and two of the press censors for a 'frank exchange of views' about censorship policy. The Censorship officials opened the meeting by stressing the advantages of neutrality, the fact that it was supported by the vast majority of the people and the importance of the press 'keeping in step' and not publishing anything that might endanger that policy. Connolly identified the main threat to neutrality as coming from those sections of the population who held 'extreme' points of view; these he referred to, rather confusingly, as the 'Right' and the 'Left'. The former were those, 'who are by training and inheritance inclined to lean towards a strong British bias'. The left, in contrast, were 'those who advocated that England's difficulty is Ireland's opportunity'. The controller argued that publicity for the views of one extreme would invite the other to 'an extreme method of expression, and possibly action, which might do serious damage to the peace and order of this country'.[4]

While the conference was conducted in a generally friendly manner, there was a natural antagonism on the part of the editors and irritation at the restrictions imposed on them. Particular resentment was expressed at the restrictions which were to be placed on expressions of opinion on the merits and defects of the belligerents and the conflicting policies involved, most vociferously by Bertie Smyllie of the *Irish Times*. Connolly had anticipated, in a letter to de Valera on the morning of the meeting, that most of the difficulty in this regard would come from the 'pro-British' *Irish Times*;[5] he now pointed out to Smyllie that his paper represented but a fraction of opinion in Ireland, and that its expression could be 'fuel' to certain 'disturbing elements'. When Smyllie remarked that comment for and against the belligerents was allowed in US publications, the controller replied that there was no parallel because of Ireland's 'propinquity to one of the chief belligerents'; this, and the country's 'recent history' made it all the more important to avoid such comments. 'Am I to say that there is nothing to choose between both sides?' asked Smyllie; Connolly's reply was unequivocal: 'As regards the war, yes.'[6]

As the newspapers began to submit proofs the authorities were alerted to specific matters, publicity in relation to which they wanted to control; these, allied to specific requests from government departments, were the basis of thirty-one *ad hoc* directions which were issued to the press between September 1939 and August 1941. In that month, a comprehensive set of directions was issued, divided into fifty-five sections, listing all censorable matter in one document and revoking and replacing all the existing directions. (See Appendix 3.) Between then and the cessation of censorship in May 1945, an additional eighteen directions were issued.

The staff of the Press Censorship numbered nine in all, in addition to the chief press censor, Knightly, and Coyne. The office was open from 9.30 a.m. until 3.00 a.m. on weekdays and from 3.30 p.m. on Sundays.[7] The censors worked a shift system, rotating night and day duties, which created some difficulties with regard to uniformity of treatment. Knightly took up permanent night duty in January 1941, partly for this reason, while both he and Coyne had telephones installed in their bedrooms for consultation purposes; Aiken also made himself available for this purpose. (Dan Bryan of G2 had the misfortune of having a home telephone, unlike his superior Liam Archer, and claimed that he was 'plagued with night-time calls' from press censors in the early period of the war.[8])

During the war a notice hung in the office of the censorship in Washington

RYLE, T.

FOR CENSOR

BREAD QUEUES IN DUBLIN

Distribution of bread in Dublin yesterday caused many complaints by people who were unable to obtain adequate supplies for the week-end. Large queues formed outside shops, and in one case the number counted was 500. One woman stated that all the bread she could secure was one loaf for a family of eight children. In another case a woman got one loaf for herself, husband, and five children.

A "Sunday Independent" representative who endeavoured to obtain a supply where he is registered could only secure one small pan loaf and one loaf to provide for the week-end. This ration has to be divided among seven adults. A number of women called on Ald. Byrne, T.D., and urged him to press for the immediate issue of ration cards.

G. WALKER

FOR CENSOR

JAPAN'S RELATIONS WITH VATICAN

Berne, Saturday.—In accordance with its principle of absolute neutrality the Holy See, says the Rome correspondent of "Die Tat," is avoiding expressing any opinion about "the Russian problem." With regard to Japan having a Diplomatic Representative at the Holy See, however (the correspondent says) Vatican circles explain that this would "merely legalise the already existing situation," as the Vatican already has been apostolic delegation at Tokyo.—Reuter.

An example of a proof which was 'stopped by the censor', submitted by the *Sunday Independent,* 14 March 1942.

headed 'A Censor Needs', followed by these nine points: 'the eye of a hawk, the memory of an elephant, the nose of a bloodhound, the heart of a lion, the vigilance of an owl, the voice of a dove, the sagacity of Solomon, the patience of Job, and the imperturbability of the Sphinx'. 'Qualities such as these', commented Coyne, 'are not always, or, indeed, usually found in the ranks of the Civil Service . . .'. (In defence of his profession, however, he remarked that they were not to be found anywhere else either!)[9] The absence of these qualities, and many others, not least an unfamiliarity with newspaper work (and, as Smyllie once added, a sense of humour), was the subject of numerous complaints by the papers, especially the *Irish Times*. A major cause of the problems was the desire on the part of the civil servant censors to err on the side of caution, to 'play safe' and to abide by Connolly's maxim: 'in case of any doubt, cut it out'.[10]

Matter submitted by the papers was either stopped in its entirety; passed in full; passed subject to specified deletions or alterations being made; or held, subject to consultation, confirmation of authenticity, the release of an official statement or the availability of further evidence, until after a relevant event, or until the story no longer had news value. When papers failed to submit matter which came under the purview of the directions, explanations were sought and reprimands and warnings were given. Repeated or serious offences resulted in the imposition of the most drastic administrative penalty available – an order to submit each issue in full for censorship before publication. The initiation of criminal proceedings against a number of publications and individuals for failing to comply with censorship requirements was considered on a number of occasions but was not undertaken.

Policy with regard to specific matters was usually formed on the basis of requests from the various government departments. Thus, the Department of External Affairs was closely involved in devising censorship policy in relation to news and views with an international dimension, while the departments of Justice, Finance, Supplies, Industry and Commerce, Agriculture and the Revenue Commissioners were the main determinants of policy with regard to 'domestic' affairs. The concerns of the military intelligence branch, G2, were wide-ranging, and it assigned a special officer to liaise with the civil servants who operated the press censorship. Relations between the two organisations were not always good and there were a number of clashes concerning G2's responsibility and authority. Following the publication of an item on a crashed belligerent plane in June 1942, Captain McCall, the military liaison officer, told the Censorship to consult G2 about such matters in the future. In reply Knightly told the officer that 'you can safely leave it to us to decide the matter in conformity with the general policy of the Government, after consultation where necessary with the Department of External Affairs'.[11] A year later, after the military liaison officer had complained about the passing of a story which he believed brought the army into disrepute, Coyne told McCall that he was regarded as the voice of 'a rival authority to which we may or may not be prepared to lend an ear but to which we are not prepared to lend our unfettered discretion and our independent judgement'.[12]

In the early months of the censorship a number of difficulties arose in relation to statements issued by the Government Information Bureau. The incidents were minor, yet they highlighted the need for a co-operative arrangement to be developed and at the end of November 1939 it was agreed that copies of all orders and directions concerning censorship be supplied to the bureau and that all statements issued by the latter be sent immediately to the Censorship. Where grounds existed for censoring such statements, in exceptional cases, it was agreed that an effort would be made to discuss the point at issue with the Government Information Bureau or with the department concerned, or at least to delay publication until such a discussion had taken place.[13]

The Censorship had no formal control over Radio Éireann news broadcasts and lack of co-operation in the early days of the Emergency led to some 'most embarrassing' incidents, whereby the radio news carried stories stopped for the press. An informal arrangement was put in place to rectify the situation. Censorship orders and directions were sent to the radio news room, the news editor consulted the Censorship about doubtful matters, and news bulletins were read to Frank Gallagher of the Government Information Bureau, who maintained close contact with the Censorship, before broadcast. This arrangement worked well until July 1941 and only three or four announcements were broadcast which the Censorship would have stopped. On the late news of 24 July 1941, however, a report was carried of comments made by Labour leader William Norton and fellow Labour TD Richard Corish wherein they advocated non-observance of the law if the Trade Union Bill was passed (see Chapter 6, page 253). The papers had been prohibited from publishing the remarks but Radio Éireann had received no communication about it. De Valera was so disquieted by the episode that he directed that steps be taken to extend the jurisdiction of the Censorship to the broadcasting station. Following consultation between Aiken, Connolly and Gallagher a new system was put into operation; doubtful items were now read over the telephone directly to the Press Censorship which had the responsibility to pass or stop any item thus submitted. Press censors were directed to stop any matter about which they were doubtful, even in cases where further enquiry or consultation led to the matter being passed for publication in the press. This system did not work as well as intended and on 13 May 1943 three items were broadcast which had been prohibited publication in the press. Coyne admitted that this had occurred due to 'an unfortunate lack of liaison between ourselves and the broadcasting people' and a new system was introduced whereby the Censorship saw the full text of news bulletins before they were broadcast; inconsistency in the treatment given to press and broadcast matter was thus eliminated.[14]

Irish radio, it should be noted, had not yet become a regular or major source of news. It was estimated that 52 per cent of households in large towns and cities and only 13 per cent in small towns and rural areas possessed a set. The number of licences held peaked in 1941 but declined thereafter, principally because of the difficulty of securing replacement batteries. Radio Éireann broadcast for only six to seven hours per day and had only three news bulletins on weekdays and two on Sundays. It had no news services of its own and effectively pirated its international news, principally from the BBC and Vatican Radio. It had no proper local news service either, so bulletins were dominated by international news in the form of 'a wearying series of claims and counter-claims', presented thus in order to preserve neutral balance.[15] Seán Ó Faoláin wrote in *The Bell* of Radio Éireann news listeners having to sit through long descriptions of events such as the annual pilgrimage to Croagh Patrick before hearing a few sentences about the war in Europe.[16] Popular annoyance at the paucity of 'real news' was reflected in the pages of *Dublin Opinion*, which, in July 1940, long before the Censorship took full control of news broadcasts, published the following poem by 'Lucius Flood':

> 'This is the end of the news . . .' This is the end of the what!
> News? with the half of it jargon, the half of it stone cold rot!
> You wait for it up to midnight, and what do you think you'll have?
> A paraphrase of the hokum the mid-day papers gave.
> The biggest war that ever was, and all that they've got to say
> Is the jumble of junk which follows 'Tonight's Communiqué'!
> Jargon, jargon, jargon, dull as a slab of cheese,
> And over the whole damn system, the curse of officialese.
> Stuff that should sound like a trumpet is neither cold nor warm,
> They couch the call to battle in the words of a Government Form.
> This is the stuff that murders the heart and the soul of man
> '. . . To a prepared position . . .' '. . . proceeding according to
>   plan . . .'
> I will go over to Fagan's and get me a can of booze,
> For at least *one* man in Europe, this is the end of the 'News'![17]

Besides the news, unscripted programmes of all kinds were cut to a minimum, weather forecasts were banned and even sports commentators had to forego any mention of weather conditions. In October 1940 all three home transmitters (Athlone, Dublin and Cork) were synchronised and worked on the one wavelength, as a security precaution against raiding aircraft using the stations for direction finding. (This was part of the secret security co-operative arrangement made with the British.) Internal security was also a consideration and a Garda presence was maintained at Radio Éireann; a detective was also sent to guard microphones at outside broadcasts in case undesirable elements seized a rare opportunity to air their views. The guard was doubled in 1940 following an incident at a live broadcast from a Gaelic

League *céilidh* at the Mansion House when an IRA supporter grabbed a microphone and made an unauthorised statement before being cut off. An incident during another live transmission provided one of the best remembered stories of Irish broadcasting during the war. 'Question Time', the station's most popular programme, toured the country for its Sunday night broadcasts. In October 1942 in a show from Belfast the question-master Joe Linnane asked a competitor, 'Who is the world's best-known teller of fairytales?' Instead of Hans Christian Andersen, he received the reply 'Winston Churchill', upon which the mostly nationalist audience burst into laughter and cheers. All reports of the incident were stopped by the Censorship, formal representations were made from Belfast and it was 'a long time before a team from Radio Éireann crossed the border again'.[18]

The objective of the Press Censorship, in the most general terms, was, according to Coyne, 'to prevent the publication of matter which would endanger security, directly or indirectly . . .'.[19] While it did play a role in protecting military information, Ireland's military defence was hopelessly inadequate and was no guarantee of the security of the state. Security, rather, came to be seen as depending on a number of other factors, primarily the maintenance of 'neutrality', or, more accurately, on the maintenance of a public picture of impartiality, which would give the belligerents no excuse for an attack on the state and give partisans within the country no excuse for creating division and disunity. As the government regarded neutrality as the only policy that was 'compatible with the security of the State' news or views which challenged that policy, called it into question, or could be construed as provocative were a threat to security and were thus censorable. In this way, political censorship became security censorship and thus more easily justifiable in all its excesses. 'Public disorder' presented danger from within, and thus from without, and censorship was part of a repressive arsenal utilised by the state to contain what was usually the by-product of extraparliamentary political activity. The maintenance of 'essential supplies and services' and the protection of the state's financial position were seen as the final major plank in the security of the state and, to the extent that the state was capable of controlling them, the Censorship played its part.

What must be kept in mind is that the 'neutrality' which the Censorship set out to protect was essentially an illusion, one, indeed, which the Censorship itself helped to create and sustain. Irish policy during the war was partial and it was a function of the Censorship to hide that fact behind a deceptive screen. Bertie Smyllie, editor of the *Irish Times*, was accurate in his description of censorship-enforced 'newspaper neutrality' as a 'sham';[20] it was, nevertheless, a vital part of 'the double game'[21] in which de Valera was involved in this period. Its role in this game – in papering over the gap between illusion and objective reality – is well illustrated by reference to the subject of the first written direction to the press, and one dear to Irish hearts: the weather.

Because of the military value of meteorological information, current weather reports and weather forecasts were totally prohibited for the duration of the Emergency. References to or photographs illustrating past weather conditions were usually held until ten days after the day to which they related.[22] This ban resulted, for example, in sports reports being carried with no mention of the weather[23] and meant that the great freeze-up of 1943–4, which brought 'a whole Swiss winter sports atmosphere to the country', could not be recorded in picture or word;[24] among the photographs banned was one of the Minister for Posts and Telegraphs, P.J. Little, skating on a frozen pond in Herbert Park, Dublin.[25] A thick fog in Dublin which lasted for a number of days led to a series of drownings in the city's canals; the accidents were reported, but the cause could not be stated, a situation which led to some confusion among readers outside the capital.[26] Such consequences led to irritation and ridicule but for the Censorship the weather ban was 'a matter to which we and others attach a great deal of importance'.[27] The seriousness with which they viewed their task led to the stopping in September 1939 of an article in which the writer wondered whether he could be arrested for saying 'it looks like rain' or for carrying an umbrella![28] Policy remained unchanged right to the end; as late as January 1945 an advertisement in the *Cork Examiner* for tailored trousers for skating was stopped and in the following month a passing reference to frost in a supplementary Dáil question on fuel distribution was deleted from press reports.[29]

While the Irish public and the Germans had to forego the benefit of Irish weather forecasts and reports, the Irish Meteorological Service, as part of the range of co-operative measures agreed with the British, were supplying the latter with weather reports and full meteorological data from the very beginning.[30] The Irish were thus being publicly impartial and correct in ensuring that their media were not a source of military information for either side while simultaneously secretly pursuing the benevolent neutrality which sought to ensure that 'the British could not acquire by conquest much more than she gained through cooperation'.[31]

The press censorship aided the British/Allied war effort in many other ways. For example, it made sure that British interests were not compromised by the 'unauthorised' disclosure in the Irish press of those details of air raids on Britain and Northern Ireland which were kept out of the British press. (The British authorities supplied their Irish counterparts with their instructions to censors on air raids in order that the Irish regulations could be brought into line with the British ones.[32]) Similarly, Irish papers were not allowed to report British shipping losses until the British had done so themselves.[33] Although Ireland was effectively sealed off by the British in the run-up to the Normandy landings, the Press Censorship ensured that any information which could in any way have been helpful to the Germans, such as a report from Wexford just prior to the event that a British convoy had been sighted sailing south, was kept out of the Irish press.[34] The success of this aspect of the Censorship is illustrated by the fact that it was precisely such information which agents of the Third Reich dispatched to Ireland sought to supply to Germany through radio transmitters (weather reports, the impact of air raids, and convoy movements).[35]

Reports on belligerent plane crashes were limited to the official government statement, if such was made, while later in the war reports of crash landings on Irish territory by British and American planes, the survivors of which were not interned but escorted across the border, were suppressed. Forty-five airmen were officially interned for a time but 228 others were quietly permitted to leave the country.[36] (The government justified this policy to the German minister by drawing a distinction between 'operational' and 'non-operational' flights, between planes being used 'in action' [German] and those used for 'training or testing' [Allied].[37]) All but eleven of the Allied internees were freed on 18 October 1943, and these were secretly released following the Normandy landings in June 1944. The survivors of the sixteen German planes which came down on Irish territory were interned for the duration, while information extracted from the wreckages was handed over to the British. The only reason any Allied airmen were interned was to preserve the illusion of fairness, to present, in the words of the UK representative, John Maffey, 'a shop window exhibit of neutrality'.[38] The role of the Censorship was to hide what Ireland's 'neutrality shop' really contained and to prevent it from being misrepresented.

All matter connected with the Irish defence forces and defensive measures, and anything, such as geographical information, which could be useful to hostile forces was denied publicity. Matter which was regarded as prejudicial to recruitment or might have caused disaffection in the defence forces, such as mention of poor conditions or pay, was strictly prohibited. So also was matter which could be said to bring ridicule on the defence forces or was critical of defence measures for the civilian population such as air raid precautions and evacuation arrangements. When the fear of invasion gripped the country in a real sense in the summer of 1940, the Censorship was busy stopping comments which ranged from the advocacy of conscription to suggestions that Ireland like Denmark should cut its losses in the event of invasion and offer only token resistance. During this period the government established a National Defence Conference, a purely advisory body containing three representatives each from Fianna Fáil and Fine Gael and two from Labour. Only official statements relating to the conference were permitted to be published, while all criticisms of the appointment of regional commissioners, who were to conduct administration in the event of an invasion, were stopped.[39] In general, 'the defence effort contributed more to maintaining internal morale than to providing a serious deterrent',[40] and it was in this regard that the Censorship was most effective.

As well as internal morale, internal security was a major issue for the government. States are always concerned about internal subversion, of course, but this task was given added urgency during the Emergency because of the threat which the IRA and the strand of thought it represented posed to de Valera's wartime policy. This threat manifested itself in a number of ways. In the early years of the war especially, there was the danger of a possible fifth-column IRA–Nazi link-up and the fear that this could be used by the British as an excuse for violating Irish neutrality. There was also the threat which militant Republicans posed to public order and the potentially divisive effect of their activities on the much-vaunted 'unity of the people', which the government regarded as essential for the maintenance of neutrality. Censorship was one of the repressive measures utilised to deal with this threat; it was similarly used to deny publicity to protests, demonstrations, strikes and agitations which arose from the socio-economic inequality which pertained and would have stained the official picture and had a divisive effect on 'national unity'. (These issues are treated in detail in Chapter 6.)

Despite the rhetoric of self-sufficiency, Ireland was as unprepared for war and as dependent on Britain in relation to supplies as it was in defence. This left the country extremely vulnerable and at the start of 1941 the British began to apply a punitive economic squeeze in the form of a policy of 'silent sanctions';[41] their aim was to keep Ireland's economy 'going on a minimum basis' and to remind the Irish that 'they owed their survival to Britain but had refused to pull their weight and must expect to pay some price in personal comfort'.[42] Luckily, Ireland was practically self-sufficient in food. Compulsory tillage orders were introduced to maximise food supply and a fuel drive was undertaken, involving a massive increase in turf production and exploitation of Ireland's meagre coal reserves, in an attempt to make up for the scarcity in the usual coal supply from Britain. Rationing and price controls were introduced for most consumer items and in March 1941 Irish Shipping was established in order to give Ireland belatedly its own supplies medium.

Once the British squeeze began, the work of the Censorship in the economic area increased dramatically. Effectively, only official announcements with regard to shortages and rationing were permitted. There was a 'shutdown' on the publication of any matter which the Censorship considered could have the effect of discouraging farmers from 'growing the wheat that the nation requires',[43] including any discussion on the contentiously low price which the government had decided to pay farmers. Similarly, publicity was denied to anything which might have had an adverse effect on turf cutting,[44] while steps were taken to ensure that nothing was published with regard to the local production of coal or the manufacture of peat briquettes because 'undue references might cause difficulties in obtaining coal supplies' from elsewhere.[45] Tourism remained a concern, and in October 1940 the Censorship stopped the story of a massive fish-kill which had occurred in the Blackwater river as a result of pollution from the Mallow sugar beet factory. The news was suppressed because it could 'seriously prejudice the future reputation of the river and discourage the many visiting anglers with whom it has been so popular'.[46]

In May 1941 the Censorship closed down on advertisements in the press seeking to buy or offering for sale rationed goods like tea and petrol. In October 1941 a new Control of Prices Order made it illegal to seek to buy or to offer for sale goods above the maximum set price. As the list of rationed and maximum-priced items lengthened to include most consumer items from abrasives to wireless batteries the censorship net widened to include them. The object was to prevent 'auctions' via the press in these goods and to scupper the efforts of speculators and racketeers.[47] The Censorship was also used as an information mechanism. For example, the revenue commissioners were suspicious when advertisements appeared with a box number, and the aid of the Censorship was sought in procuring the names of the advertisers; they were particularly suspicious of advertisers from the western seaboard and the border areas, who, in the former case would have been suspected of dealing in goods washed ashore and in the latter, of smuggling high duty items like spirits and cigarettes across the border.[48]

The Censorship was used to hide the extent of the continuing close economic links with the UK. In October 1941, for example, the press censors were instructed to stop all references to shipping and trade between Ireland and Britain, and in the following month there was a close-down on criticisms of the export of Irish agricultural produce to Britain.[49] When the Irish felt the need to respond in kind to British economic pressure, however, their trump card was to withhold supplies of beer! In early 1942 the British Minister of Food learned that Ireland was suspending the export of beer; he minuted that 'The effect of this on the output of essential works in Belfast and other places will I fear be serious.' (Northern Ireland received 80 per cent of its beer supplies from the South.) A deal was concluded whereby exports were resumed in return for twenty thousand tons of wheat, much to the annoyance of the American minister, Gray, who complained to the British that it represented an exchange of 'a vital necessity for what Americans regard at the best as a luxury and at worst as a poison'.[50] Reports and speculation on this and other such dealings were totally prohibited from the press.

Publicity about the purchase of ships by the Irish government and about ships which carried cargo to Ireland was severely restricted while reports on attacks on Irish ships were generally stopped or, if not, were restricted to the official statement, which rarely identified the guilty party,[51] usually the Germans. There had been thirty-two attacks on Irish ships from February 1940 to November 1941 when the *Glencullen* and the *Glencree* were attacked in the Irish Sea for the second time.[52] Following these attacks Aiken initiated a new departure in censorship policy by instructing his censors to allow stories about such incidents; his intention was to let the Germans know that the Irish people were now being made aware that the Germans were bombing Irish ships and that 'they don't like it'.[53] Irish government protests to the Germans, when their culpability was established, were met with the reply that no responsibility could be accepted as the ships had been in a German blockade zone through which the Irish had been offered free passage but on terms which were rejected.[54]

While a German victory was still a possibility Dublin protests against attacks on Irish ships and territory continued to be couched in respectful tones.[55] When German bombs fell on neutral Ireland in 1940 the Department of External Affairs gave an undertaking to the German minister that the Censorship would play down the fatal consequences.[56] Great care was taken to restrict reports to the facts of the case, usually contained in a government statement. When Campile creamery in Co. Wexford was bombed in August 1940, resulting in the death of three people, the news was not released for four hours, by which time it had already been broadcast on American radio. The news was held up in order that the identity of the plane could be verified, but even then the Irish papers were prohibited from revealing this information. When the *Enniscorthy Echo* identified the bombers as German, all issues carrying the statement were seized by the Gardaí on the direction of the Censorship.[57] Following a subsequent announcement on German radio that the German government had accepted responsibility, the Censorship informed the press that it could publish the statement as having come from German radio but to make clear that it was not issued by the Irish government.[58] Following the Sandycove bombing in December 1940 reference to the identity of the bombers was again disallowed as was speculation as to their intended target – the mailboat, Dún Laoghaire pier, etc.[59] When more German bombs fell on Dublin, and on Carlow and Kildare, in January 1941, implications that they were dropped intentionally were stopped as was 'matter calculated to incense public feeling' like the bishop of Killaloe's reference to 'these accursed bombers'. The *Kilkenny People* was directed to submit in full before publication after it published an editorial on the issue.[60]

Publicity about the motley crew which the Germans landed in Ireland for espionage purposes was also kept to a minimum.[61] In July 1940, for example, nothing beyond the announcement of the sentencing of two Germans and an Indian who had been arrested in Cork was permitted to be published. A number of stories on the affair by a Cork journalist were stopped and he was detained by the Gardaí for some days.[62] A ridiculous situation arose in 1942 following the escape from custody of German spy Gunther Schütz, alias Hans Marschner. No mention of the escape was allowed in the press for four days, after which the Department of Justice plastered the country with posters bearing his photograph and offering a reward for help leading to his recapture. Marschner remained at large for two months;

as was pointed out in the Dáil, had a photograph and description been published in the press immediately after his escape he could have been recaptured far sooner.[63]

Two Irishmen were parachuted by the Germans into Co. Clare in December 1943 for espionage purposes and were captured within hours of landing. News of this episode was kept out of the press, but it was mentioned in the so-called American Note which was presented to de Valera by David Gray, the American minister in March 1944. The note demanded the expulsion of the Axis representatives in Ireland on the basis that they posed a security threat in the run-up to the D-Day landings. Gray's intention was to get de Valera 'on the record', so as to discredit him in America and make it difficult for him to use Irish-American opinion to influence postwar policy on the partition issue. While this strategy may have succeeded in the long term, the Taoiseach turned the situation to his own immediate advantage by magnifying the threat involved and treating it as an ultimatum. Following the announcement of the note on the BBC on 10 March, there was an influx of foreign correspondents into the country. The Censorship was used to control the story from the Irish point of view and to fit in with de Valera's clever handling of the affair which was done, as one writer has put it, 'with the world's media in one hand and the ballot box in the other'.[64] Although some correspondents evaded censorship by transmitting dispatches from Belfast, most submitted their copy and did not quarrel with the censors' decisions. The basic facts of the American request were allowed along with de Valera's reply; speculation and most ancillary matter was stopped.[65] While Gray succeeded in getting de Valera bad press in the US, as was his intention,[66] Ireland and the world were to be left in no doubt about de Valera's statesmanship and bravery in standing up to the threat.

'By and large we operate this censorship', Aiken told the Seanad, '. . . to keep the temperature down internally and to prevent it from rising between ourselves and other countries.'[67] With regard to the war, this meant excluding anything which could possibly be construed as giving offence to either set of belligerents or encouragement to domestic partisans. As well as attempting to preclude divisiveness in relation to the war, the Censorship sought to exclude anything else which could have a similar effect. So, articles which might 'revive, at the present time, the animosities and bitterness of the Civil War would be disastrous to public morale and national security' and were stopped,[68] while a controversy on the subject of the Black and Tans 'may split the unity of our people' and had to be prevented.[69] Any matter which would have had the opposite and desired effect, such as praise for neutrality or criticism of partition and the Northern state, was positively encouraged. In September 1940, for example, the press censors were instructed to allow 'non-violent' criticism of the British and Northern Ireland governments, including that related to partition, the imprisonment without trial of 'anti-partitionists', advocacy of the peaceful establishment of a thirty-two county republic or the cessation of contact with the Commonwealth.[70]

In a memorandum circulated within government in January 1940 entitled 'Neutrality, Censorship and Democracy'[71] (see Appendix 1) Aiken presented the case for the legitimacy of and necessity for censorship as it was operated. He argued that, as the government was constitutionally precluded from declaring war, 'it is clearly to be inferred that it must not provoke war, and that it must use its executive authority to prevent any section of its citizens provoking war'. He went on to define propaganda as 'one of the most important weapons of war' and its expression in a neutral country, whether originating there or not, as a violation of impartiality and, effectively, an act of war. He believed that all expressions of sympathy for or antipathy against the belligerents had to be suppressed as had all discussion and debate on their respective merits, defects, morality, immorality, etc. He argued that if competition was allowed to develop between both sides, it would end up in a civil war on the issue of which side the state should declare war against.

If neutrality was essentially an expression of independence, it was, by extension, primarily an expression of independence from Britain. Since coming to power, Fianna Fáil had set about removing the symbols of British rule in Ireland, such as the oath of allegiance and the office of the governor-general. It now took the opportunity, in the name of neutrality, to wage war on the symbolic remnants of the old order, and the Anglo-Irish were to suffer at the hands of the censorship not only for their belligerence but for their Britishness.

The government's attempts through censorship to, as Smyllie put it, 'steer an even course between the Scylla of the old "Ascendency" . . . and the Charybdis of the IRA'[72] is exemplified in an episode from the summer of 1940. The *Irish Times* (which was inveterately pro-British and suffered proportionately) submitted a photograph taken at a Local Security Force (LSF) recruitment rally at College Green, Dublin. The British coat of arms from the old parliament building which featured in the photograph was scraped out by the Censorship because, claimed Aiken, the *Irish Times* had included it deliberately to 'attribute a certain complexion to the LSF'.[73] The authorities were particularly sensitive at this time as Republicans were arguing that the recruitment was to aid the British war effort and were referring to the Irish defence forces as 'John Bull's Other Army'; pro-British elements were entertaining hopes along the same lines and the *Daily Mail* correspondent's description of the meeting featured in the photograph as reminiscent of the great recruiting meetings of 1914 was not unusual. Analogies with recruitment for the British army in the First World War were particularly unwelcome and the Censorship saw it as its responsibility 'to see that nothing appeared that would give support to this view'.[74] (An amusing addendum to this episode concerns a stopped report on a debate on the liberty of the press held by a student debating society. The Rev. Savell Hicks, who presided over the debate, related the story of the deletion of the coat of arms and told how an *Irish Times* official had suggested to the censor that, in the interests of fairness, he should also cut out the figure in the photograph giving the Nazi salute. 'Who on earth is that?' asked the censor. 'Grattan', came the reply – a reference to a statue of Henry Grattan with an upraised arm.[75])

There were many organisations in Ireland whose activities, and, indeed, very existence, the government regarded as objectionable and over which the censorship cloak was pulled. These included the Irish Ex-Servicemen's and Voluntary Services Association, the Royal Naval Old Comrades Association, the Royal Artillery Association and, most prominently, the British Legion, which organised the annual Remembrance Day ceremonies. From 1941 onwards all references to the present war were deleted from Remembrance Day advertisements and notices, which could only be carried on the day immediately preceding the ceremonies, while all details were removed from accounts of the ceremonies carried in the following days papers. The approach taken is well illustrated in the treatment given to this report submitted by the *Irish Times* on 11 November 1942. The already self-censored report, as submitted, read: 'As memorial services were being held all over Éire hundreds of ex-servicemen gathered once again at the Irish National War Memorial at Islandsbridge, Dublin, to take part in the twenty-fourth Remembrance Day ceremony'. Following censorship it appeared as: 'A memorial service was held at the National War Memorial at Islandsbridge, Dublin'. Publicity was also denied to the poppy appeal, while the ban on references to the present war extended to posters and leaflets.[76]

Prohibited reports on the activities of other Anglophile associations usually related to functions, often addressed by the UK representative or his wife, at which the king was toasted or the contribution of Irish people to the war effort praised. (Before presenting his credentials to the president in 1939, Maffey had been told, 'Don't mention the war!'; his diplomatic silence on this subject, however, was not maintained subsequently!) There was also a prohibition on appeals for such as the Earl Haig British Legion Appeal, the Soldiers', Sailors' and Airmen's Families Association, the British PoW Books and Games Fund and the Spitfire Fund. In July 1941, there was a close-down on the publicity for the V (for victory) campaign which was seen as giving 'endless opportunities to certain of our citizens to show what good Britishers they are . . .'.[77] Coyne was less happy about the suppression of publicity for the less directly belligerent activities of pro-British elements, and he wrote to Aiken in March 1942 pointing out the disadvantages of this policy; the Censorship, according to Coyne, was getting a 'roasting' in the British and American press because of it, while there was little compensating benefit besides the feeling of 'putting these people in their place'.[78]

When the *Irish Times* submitted an appeal on behalf of the Royal National Lifeboat Institution – the same advertisement as was being run in the British press – the Censorship asked the paper to persuade the institution to submit something of more appeal to the Irish public, commenting that there were still English people who did not realise that 'our' did not denote English and Irish and that it 'makes any Irishman see green, white and orange . . . there is nothing our national susceptibilities can stand less than the assumption that Irishmen are a sort of provincial Englishman – West British, in fact'.[79] (The Censorship had moved quickly in the early days of the Emergency to prevent the *Irish Times* from using terms such as 'The Army', and 'our' when referring to things British.) This desire to protect 'national susceptibilities' and avoid disturbance led the Censorship, at one point, to demand the removal of a tiny Union Jack flag from an advertisement for a Raleigh bicycle catalogue, as the appearance of this microscopic emblem 'might cause resentment in some quarters'.[80]

As the war progressed Aiken warmed to the task of 'putting these people in their place' and began to change the names which they chose to apply to their places. The process began with the defensible prohibition on reference to the 'British Isles' and 'Southern Ireland', but proceeded to an insistence that the old name of Kingstown not be used in church notices for Kingstown Presbyterian Church in Dún Laoghaire and onwards to the ludicrous order to the *Irish Times* to refer to Kells, the name by which the town was known to its inhabitants, and everybody else, as Ceannanus Mór (see also pp. 166).

While what may be called the British in Ireland posed one threat to the official picture of impartiality, another was presented by the Irish in Britain and, even more so, by those serving in the British forces. From the outset of the war Irish people in their thousands crossed the border or the Irish Sea to join up, and in even greater numbers to work in war industries or as domestics. No foreign enlistment act was passed in Ireland, as it was in other neutrals, making it an offence to join the fighting services of a belligerent,[81] while the British Ministry of Labour's *National Clearing House Gazette* was displayed at employment exchanges throughout Ireland by order of the government.[82] As Salmon points out, 'Although a distinction may be drawn between state and citizens, the degree of complicity of the Irish state in this material assistance cannot be ignored'.[83] The only restriction placed on those who joined the British forces was that when they returned home on leave they had to wear civilian clothes. An arrangement was worked out with the British whereby dumps of civilian clothes were provided at Holyhead port for the returning soldiers.[84] The censorship was used likewise to disguise and 'dress down' the reality of *de facto* Irish partiality and involvement in the war.

The ban on references to Irish people in the British forces was so sweeping that it even included people from belligerent Northern Ireland.[85] In general, reference was prohibited in social columns, social announcements (births, marriages, etc.) and, most frequently, in death notices and obituaries (see pp. 163-5). Aiken explained to the Dáil that 'We have . . . to prevent some people not interested in men who die making use of obituary notices to forward propaganda . . .'.[86] Even references as minor as the letters SCF (Senior Chaplain to the Forces) in the death notice of the son of an *Irish Times* staff member who had died of a heart attack in London were removed.[87] This policy caused much resentment, particularly among the bereaved, and Smyllie, the editor of the *Irish Times*, accused the Censorship of acting with 'ghoulish malignancy'.[88] Coyne admitted to him that he was personally 'lukewarm' about this aspect of policy.[89] In response to repeated complaints that it was being 'unduly rigid and indeed ridiculous' in its treatment of announcements and photographs relating to members of the British forces, the Censorship responded by claiming that

> if matter of this kind was not strictly controlled there is a danger amounting to a moral certainty that some of our papers would be plastered day in day out with pictures and announcements about the British forces. This would have two results: it might mislead opinion abroad about the real position and feeling of this country and it would certainly provoke a counter blast at home which, in addition to making it difficult to maintain both the reality and appearance of neutrality, would be likely to give rise to internal disorder.[90]

Reference to the Irish connections of senior British army figures like Montgomery and Alexander was forbidden, while attempts to play up the Irishness of figures like Brendan Bracken, British Minister for Information who hailed from Tipperary ('Brackenalia') were stopped.[91] The playwright Denis Johnson was another who 'fell from neutral grace', by becoming a BBC war correspondent. Occasional articles by him, such as 'An Irishman Sees Desert Battle' for the *Sunday Independent*, were stopped, as was all mention of him, including in the social and personal columns when he was home in Dublin on leave.[92] Stress upon the Irishness of a handful of individuals on the other side was equally unwelcome. Most prominent in this regard was William Joyce – 'Lord Haw Haw' – the Nazi radio propagandist whose catch-phrase, 'Germany calling', was one of the most distinctive sounds on the wartime airwaves in Britain and Ireland.

With the onset of the 'blitz' – the Luftwaffe's bombing of British cities – Irish papers began to submit stories about the experiences of Irish citizens, working and living in Britain, in the raids. There was a close-down on all such stories on the basis, Connolly informed the *Irish Independent*, that

> it is not considered desirable nor in the interests of our neutrality to lay emphasis on any Irish connection with the war. The grouping of isolated incidents in which Irish people are involved is liable to give a wrong impression of the extent to which Irish people are involved.[93]

Irish people were involved, however, and continued to cross the Irish Sea in search of employment. In late 1941, against the background of a debate within government about the merits of allowing the exodus of workers to continue unhindered,[94] the Department of Industry and Commerce contacted the Censorship asking that every step be taken to stop advertisements going to outside newspapers offering Irish workers for employment and to ensure that no advertisements appeared in Irish papers offering employment outside the country. Coyne informed the press censors that he did not believe it was the government's intention to prevent people seeking employment outside the state, but merely, so far as the Censorship was concerned, to secure that our papers shall not be filled with advertisements inviting people to go to England. A year later a new employment order forbade any advertisements for over two employees and where the place of employment was not specified. It also prohibited employment agencies from placing newspaper advertisements offering Irish labour for work outside the state.[95]

The ban on appeals, referred to earlier, was not limited to those with a British flavour. In fact the issue was first raised in the early days of the war when an advertisement was submitted to the Censorship consisting of an appeal for Polish war victims, organised by the Polish Relief Fund in London. It was decided that it was 'undesirable to allow such appeals by private enterprise, in a sporadic way and in accordance with the partisan feelings and sympathies of individuals and groups'.[96] Subsequently, appeals for funds or collections for the relief of distress abroad or other humanitarian or charitable causes, except for those organised by the Irish Red Cross and authorised by the government, were banned.[97] Among the victims of this policy was an *Irish Times* story about the students of St Columba's College raising a cow on the college farm with the intention of sending it and its calves to postwar Poland to help build up its livestock resources.[98]

Other advertisements also fell foul of the censors, particularly the 'war advertisements' ('Blitz that cough with Cheks', 'Yeast-Vite: helping us to win the war', etc.) which became very prevalent in this period. These usually featured soldiers, sailors, pilots or war workers and associated a wide range of products with their activities; this had the object of linking a product with the campaign for victory, keeping up morale at home and persuading people abroad that Britain was winning the war.[99] In August 1943 the censor stopped an advertisement for Longines Watches – 'The Watch that fought in two wars' – featuring an illustration from the First World War. When the advertising company appealed the decision they were informed that the fact that it referred to another war was irrelevant as all advertisements with 'war appeal' were prohibited. In a reply which Coyne had prepared but decided was 'a bit too slick' to send, he wrote that, 'In our opinion war appeal is contra-indicated in this country at this time . . . War appeal is war appeal and like sex appeal and snob appeal it has nothing to do with a particular time or place, or person or event but with universal and innate

Blitz that Cough *with* **CHEKS**

4¹½d. per ounce, loose, from all chemists.

An example of one of the many 'unneutral' war-related advertisements which were banned during the Emergency.

instincts'. Aiken, in a rare flash of humour, suggested that they should be told that 'advertisers should appeal on grounds not contrary to the idea that the highest romance and the greatest test of men and materials is to be found in the arts and practices of neutrality!'[100]

Even advertisements in leaflet form were not immune. In June 1942 Coyne directed the seizure by the Gardaí of a leaflet advertising the 'Agrippa' incendiary bomb lifter, which featured the phrases 'Don't let Hitler's bombs scare you' and 'Hitler's messages of hate'.[101] In May 1941 a painting contractor in Dublin was prevented from advertising his business with a cartoon showing Hitler as a house painter being told '. . . about time you got back to your own job'. A direction was issued for the seizure of the leaflet and the Gardaí were told to inform the guilty party that 'he can't do that here'.[102]

In 1944 Blarney Tweeds, Hosiery and Knitting Wools ran a series of advertisements featuring cities of the world. In March the featured city was Cologne and the text contained the passage: 'And now that war has come to Cologne the machines of destruction devised by man have laid in ruins 85% of the beautiful old city. Such is the price of this thing called "war".' The advertisement was stopped because, according to Aiken, the belligerents were 'Sensitive to any stress being put upon the loss involved to civilisation and culture, as is done in this advertisement . . . [it] would undoubtedly have been held to be propaganda composed

An advertising leaflet which was seized by the Gardaí in May 1941 on the instructions of the censor. Objection was taken to the depiction of Hitler as a house-painter being told to get 'back to your own job'.

in Ireland against one set of belligerents'.[103]

In June 1940, when the country was gripped by the real fear of invasion following the fall of France to the Germans, Coyne wrote to Aiken in relation to an editorial which had appeared in the anti-British *Leader*. 'In times so dangerous as the present', he wrote,

> we cannot afford the luxury of academic discussions in the press as to whether we would benefit or lose as a result of a British or German victory . . . the freedom of the press must go by the board and . . . only one voice should be heard in respect of matters affecting our external and internal security, namely, the voice of the Government, until the present threat to our very existence has passed.[104]

The real threat did pass, but the policy of heavily censoring editorial comment and opinion on the war and foreign affairs generally continued until the very end of the Emergency. Once the immediate danger of the summer of 1940 had passed, Coyne began to have misgivings about the extent to which the Censorship was interfering with 'the free expression of opinion' with regard to foreign affairs. He still believed that the press should be prevented from blatantly taking sides and stating that a victory for either side was desirable in the interests of Ireland, but was in favour of allowing the papers to 'interpret and comment on events in a way favourable to their own point of view . . . [and] to emphasise that what is happening or may happen in the world about us is a matter of concern to the people of this country'. Just as news of a striking military victory for either side was allowed, Coyne believed that editorial comment on any such victory or opinion as to its military or political consequences should, equally, be permitted. 'I would, in short, give a full field and no favour to all our papers to write about foreign politics and international affairs provided they keep us out of it.'[105]

Unfortunately for the press the then assistant controller's proposals were shot down immediately by his superior, Connolly, who believed that Ireland could not be 'kept out of it' if free comment was allowed as it was bound 'to cause trouble' between the Irish government and one or other of the belligerents. He believed that the line should be 'to take no chances' and was unperturbed by the diminution in press freedom which this entailed. 'The preservation of neutrality', he told Aiken, 'and the determination to give no possible excuse for complaints by either of the belligerents far outweigh any temporary intellectual starvation that newspaper readers may suffer.'[106] Aiken supported this view and comment in the Irish press continued to be severely curtailed until the lifting of the censorship.

Writing shortly after, Coyne accepted that 'there is only one patriotic role for the press of this country, the role of reserve absolute and complete where foreign affairs are concerned'. He reiterated the principle that no excuse must be given for an attack, while adding that 'to seek to play the partisan in the present conflict is to endanger Irish interests and it is precisely to stop any "furore scribendi" in this direction that the censorship exists. Fortunately, the number of irresponsible journalists are few but where they are found they must be treated as mad dogs.'[107]

In April 1941 the *Irish Times* published, without submission, a leader on the defence of Athens in which it criticised the British for having been 'caught napping'. This and other criticisms of the British were cabled to America as illustrative of the view of the pro-British *Irish Times*, with the implication that the general Irish attitude was 'even worse'. Coyne wrote a reprimanding letter to Smyllie telling him that Ireland was not free to comment on 'tragic events from the touchline . . . the worse British fortunes fare in this war, the more we in the Censorship feel they are entitled to the charity of our silence'. He was equally concerned, he wrote, that the ebb and flow of the war should not be used as 'a peg on which to hang unfriendly comment about Germany'.[108] Four months later the Censorship deleted from another *Times* editorial the comment that Japan was possibly bluffing with its threat to sink American ships carrying arms to Vladivostok. 'Evidently', wrote the assistant editor, 'we are in danger of invasion by Japan.' In response Coyne wrote that 'the war is indivisible . . . the Battle of Britain is being fought at the moment by the Russians at Velikiye and elsewhere. So far as we can contrive, it is going to stay there. We are not going to have the newspapers transferring the fight to our doorstep.'[109] The danger, Aiken explained in the Seanad, was that if editors 'get an inch, they will take an ell, and we decided we would not give an inch'.[110]

With regard to actual 'war news' the Censorship set out to achieve as balanced and objective a picture as possible together with the exclusion of all blatant propaganda and propagandist terminology. Countries, their governments, leaders, armed forces, etc. were to be given their official titles and were not to be referred to by 'derogatory or propagandist names popularised by the States or organisations opposed to them',[111] or by any other title. Thus, for example, the words 'Nazi' and 'Fascist' were prohibited as were 'Hitlerism', 'Reds' and 'Bolsheviks'. Hitler was always Herr Hitler, Mussolini, Signor Mussolini and Goebbels, Dr Goebbels. In 1942 expressions like 'Fighting French' and 'France Combatante' began to be used to describe the de Gaullist forces; these were deleted and replaced with the latter phrase. In June 1943 the press censors were instructed to allow reference to the Girand–de Gaulle administration only as the Girand–de Gaulle Committee, the French North African Committee or the Committee, and not as the French Government or the National Committee for Liberation.[112] This policy with regard to names and titles was applied with zeal by the censors and was brought to some ridiculous lengths. In September 1944, for example, the *Irish Times* submitted a photograph of the pope with the caption, 'Pope Pius XII'; the censor altered this to 'The Pope' in line, according to Coyne, with policy not to allow foreign agencies to put words in the mouths of Irish editors. A stunned *Irish Times* enquired reasonably why it was more neutral to use 'The Pope' than 'Pope Pius XII'. In a reply (not issued) the assistant controller, Purcell, wrote that there was only one pope and asked the *Irish Times* to imagine the walls of Portadown bearing the slogan 'To Hell with Pope Pius XII' or the Orangemen's historic war cry being altered to read 'No Pope Pius XII. No Surrender'![113]

Balance and objectivity were sought by paring war reports as much as possible down to official statements and communiqués issued by or on behalf of both sets of belligerents. Papers were required to publish the source of their stories prominently, and to print statements by heads or ministers of states 'textually in whole or in part without commentary or gloss of any kind'[114] (these were generally exempt from censorship except where they contained abuse or charges of inhuman conduct). While not seeking a mathematical split of allotted space, the Censorship wanted both sides to receive 'a fair share of the news and a fair show in its presentation and . . . no matter how the war is going at any particular time, all the prominent displays, i.e. the big headlines, the heavy type, etc. should not be reserved for one side alone'.[115] The Censorship argued that the requisite degree of objectivity was not difficult to achieve. Both sides regularly published official communiqués, leaders made regular public statements and, given the sheer scale of the war zone, 'something newsworthy is regularly taking place on both sides, neither of which has any monopoly of skill or courage whether it be in attack or defence'.[116]

The single biggest obstacle to the achievement of 'newspaper neutrality' in Ireland was the fact that the Irish press was dependent for its war news on Allied sources. There was no Irish news agency and no Irish paper could afford a foreign correspondent. Thus, international news came entirely from the news agencies, principally British (predominantly Reuters and the Press Association) and occasionally American (Associated Press and United Press). Radio Éireann and the BBC, the other principal news sources, also depended on these agencies. This news was controlled and censored at source and was naturally slanted in favour of the Allies[117] – 'coloured subjectively through the selection and the method of presentation'.[118] The British censorship and news control system ensured that official propaganda was disseminated under the guise of objective news.[119] The propagandist function of the agencies was clearly illustrated in relation to Ireland by their habit of delivering items marked 'For Publication in Ireland Only'. These mostly fed into British propaganda efforts to heighten anti-Axis feeling in Ireland by reference to Nazi ill-treatment of the Catholic Church ('Brutal treatment of Priests in Germany', etc.).[120] The temptation was ever-present for Irish papers, for reasons of bias or convenience, to use the headings, introductions and captions provided by the agencies, thus reproducing the news with the slant provided. Also, of course, news not favourable to the Allies was often not supplied at all. (German news agency reports were supplied to the press via the German legation.)

The Irish Censorship was severely handicapped in its efforts to control newspaper coverage of the war by the fact that it did not receive any of these news services itself and so had nothing to work on until the papers submitted their material or such of it as they wanted to publish. Ideally the Censorship would have wanted all war news channelled through it, as it was through its British counterpart, before being distributed to the press. However, for logistical and/or political reasons the agencies would not have agreed to this. Another alternative would have been for the Censorship to have subscribed to the agencies itself. The cost involved was probably the main reason why this was not done, besides which it was possible that they would have refused to supply their services to a censorship such as the Irish one. As it was, the Censorship had to deal with the situation as it existed and was unhappy about having to allow the papers receive 'what was in effect, an undiluted stream of foreign propaganda'.[121]

From October 1940 the papers had to submit everything they proposed to publish related directly or indirectly to the war and it will be instructive to look at how the Censorship dealt with war news about various aspects and from various theatres of the conflict.

Information about air raids was carefully controlled by the belligerents, for security reasons and for propaganda purposes. Reports were used strategically by both sides, with a balance being struck between playing up the severity of a raid – where anger needed to be generated at home and sympathy abroad – and playing it down – to discourage the enemy and create confidence and calm at home.[122] The Irish Censorship attempted to pare down air raid stories to the bare 'facts' and where possible to just allow official communiqués from both sides. It was policy to stop reports on the destruction of church property and hospitals and of casualties to nuns, priests, doctors, nurses, women and children. 'Matter of this kind', Coyne informed the editor of the *Irish Independent*, 'can hardly fail to be propagandist in fact if not in intention'.[123]

Stories from bombed cities were stopped, including many from Irish people who had experienced the effects of the raids on British cities; the Irish press was allowed an initial 'run' on the refugees and evacuees who began arriving in Ireland from Britain, but the stories were stopped from October, 1940 except for 'special cases', while photographs were restricted to those featuring Red Cross helpers assisting refugees.[124] While denying publicity to reports which fed the legend of the 'blitz spirit', etc. the Censorship also kept out reports which cast a light on the cruel reality behind the propaganda facade; for example, reports from Coventry which accurately portrayed the panic which followed the bombing, with thousands fleeing, refusing to work and the army reading the Riot Act and seeking to impose martial law. Following a protest from the *Sunday Independent* about the stopping of a report from a Swiss paper about the effects of air raids on Hamburg, Coyne accused the editor of suggesting that

> Irish people are so deficient in imagination that unless the 't's are crossed and the 'i's dotted they may fail to realise the havoc wrought in a built up area by the dropping of several hundred tons of high explosives and remain in ignorance of the natural and probable reactions of the population of a heavily bombed city whether it be England or Germany.[125]

A heading such as 'German Arms City Bombed' was altered to read 'German City Bombed' (a reference to Frankfurt, February 1944). Coyne correctly pointed out that this was a typical example of the attempt by both sides to convince the public that only military targets were being bombed and that news agencies used such terms when describing enemy cities but not their own.[126] While British claims that they were bombing only military targets were treated sceptically the overall Allied slant was successfully put across; the actual situation, reported by German and European neutral writers, whereby a 'Bombing war against civilians'[127] was being waged, was not reflected in the Irish press.

While the Censorship's approach in this difficult propaganda war zone was often reasonable and its actions justifiable, the propensity to be farcical remained ever-present. For example, in a review of the war submitted by the *Sunday Independent* in March 1943, Aiken changed the term 'Battle of Britain' to 'the air battle over Southern England and the Channel in 1940';[128] a report in the *Standard* in October 1944 on the shortage of houses in England and Scotland had the words 'due to the bombing' deleted;[129] a photograph submitted by the *Sunday Independent* carried the caption, 'Malta Subjected to Grim Ordeal – A view from the air above Malta. In the distance a cloud of smoke from bomb burst can be seen'. The Censorship passed the photograph subject to the caption being altered to 'Malta Subjected to Bombs – A view from the air over Malta'! An earlier photograph from the battle of Malta had its caption, 'Sheltered from bombs', altered by Aiken to read 'Maltese Shelters'.[130]

When Belfast was subjected to bombs from the air for the first time in April 1941 the Irish papers were permitted to carry only the official statement; an account of 'events' following the second raid was allowed, but all the 'harrowing details' were deleted. In the aftermath of the devastating raids of the following month, de Valera authorised the allowing of reference to the aid given to civilians by fire brigades from the South, so long as no stress was laid on the part they played.[131]

While Northern Ireland was always a complicating factor for the Censorship, another was provided, because of Ireland's 'special relationship' with Rome and the Vatican, by the entry of Italy into the war in June 1940; the Press Censorship report for that month records the determination of the Censorship to 'maintain its neutral course'.[132] Much propaganda against

Italy was stopped subsequently, including many news agency 'war specials' which were, according to the Censorship, 'calculated to bring contempt' on the Italian forces and leaders.[133] The largest volume of matter up to that date was submitted in July 1943, coinciding with the beginning of the Allied invasion of Italy, the 'resignation' of Mussolini and the first attack on Rome.[134] The *Glasgow Herald* reported that 'The blue pencils of Dublin Castle were worn to stumps when the Italian surrender was announced. After the first official announcements and communiqués the censor "killed" almost everything that could be called interesting.'[135] Most interesting to Irish people was the continuing threat to 'Rome of the Popes' and the destruction of church property as the Allies advanced, but most reports on these issues were stopped. The destruction of the Monte Cassino Abbey, the parent house of the Benedictine Order and 'one of the most pictures-que monuments of Christian culture',[136] was what Coyne described as 'exactly the sort of incident that lends itself most readily to propaganda in the pathological state of society which exists in time of war'. Once the ab-bey came within the zone of military operations a propaganda battle was undertaken with regard to the actions and intentions of the other side. The Censorship closed down completely on the preliminary propaganda, but, because of the importance of the abbey to the Christian world, allowed news of its destruction. This news, however, was released only after it had been confirmed by both sides, and the Censorship let it be known that each side was blaming the other; only two statements – one by Roosevelt claiming that the abbey was being used by the Germans for military purposes, and a German statement saying that it was not – were allowed, and all subse-quent controversy on the matter was prohibited.[137]

After the Battle of Britain (or, in Aiken's terms, 'the air battle over Southern England and the Channel in 1940') Churchill and his chief of im-perial general staff made the strategic decision to commit a substantial part of the British army to North Africa as, for British imperialists, the loss of Egypt and Middle Eastern oil would have meant 'as much as losing the British homeland'.[138] For Hitler, the campaign in North Africa was 'never more than a side-show', but for Churchill and the British media it became 'the greatest theatre of war',[139] and the disproportionate amount of attention which it received from the British was reflected in the material submitted by the Irish papers. Thus, November 1942 saw the Censorship receive its largest amount of submissions up to that date, coinciding with the landings in North Africa and the fighting in the Western Desert.[140] The war here was reported in very romantic terms; it was 'the last gentleman's campaign', the German commander Erwin Rommel became the 'Desert Fox' and was saluted by Churchill as a 'great general'. In this romantic picture, where the Germans were brave and the Italians chivalrous, the missing fac-tor was provided by the arrival of hero-figure General Bernard Montgomery. 'Monty' had a keen sense of personal publicity; he managed, as Phillip

Knightley put it, to get 'a good press while appearing to hate it' and perfected the art of 'backing into the limelight'.[141] Stress on his Irish connections was prohibited by the Censorship; in August 1944, for example, when Montgomery became a field-marshal, the *Sunday Graphic*'s Dublin correspondent was prohibited from sending out an article entitled 'Ireland is proud of Monty'.[142] All eulogies of Rommel were stopped, as were reports which lay stress on his strategic prowess.[143] Overall, while the Censorship largely succeeded in making coverage of this theatre of the war more objective, it was helpless to affect the disproportionate attention that it was afforded and the importance laid on it, which were a result of the Irish press reflecting British priorities.

While the 'side-show' in North Africa received extensive coverage, the decisive battlefront of the war – the eastern front – remained the most poorly reported part of the whole conflict. This was partly because this aspect of the war did not involve the British and Americans directly and partly due to the secrecy of the Soviet authorities and their suspicion of western war correspondents. The reader in the west received mainly a rehash of Soviet official communiqués, which contained only what the Soviet leaders felt it expedient to reveal.[144] Material from the Soviet news agency was regarded by the Irish Censorship as 'doubtful', was treated with suspicion and was regularly stopped on the basis of its source.[145] War reports from the Soviet Union were often written by well-known literary figures such as Ilya Ehrenburg, Vassily Grossman and Konstantin Siminov.[146] The latter was among the small number of Russian and German reporters at Stalingrad during the siege and battle (there were none from any other country). In October 1942 the *Sunday Independent* submitted for censorship one of Siminov's descriptive reports, 'The Human Picture of Stalingrad'. Aiken was consulted and he made extensive cuts and deletions. Firstly, he changed the title to 'A Russian Picture of Stalingrad'; he deleted the final two paragraphs dealing with the suffering and courage of Stalingrad's citizens; 'women and children' became 'non-combatants', and the wrecked 'German bombers' which piled up on the streets became, for the Irish reader, unidentified 'planes'.[147]

Stalingrad's citizens were not alone in having their suffering kept from the pages of Ireland's newspapers for fear of eliciting unneutral sympathy. Reports of persecution and cruelty from across German-occupied Europe provided much work for the Censorship from the first stories of Gestapo executions of 'mental defectives' and mass executions of Polish Jews which were stopped in early 1941, onwards.[148] By the autumn of that year there were daily reports of German atrocities, perpetrated across the continent, and virtually all were stopped by the Censorship. (See 'Atrocity Stories' below, pp. 123-9) Reports of unrest, agitation and resistance in German-occupied countries began to pour in from early 1943 and many reports of underground and partisan activity in France, Yugoslavia, Czechoslovakia and Belgium were prohibited.[149] In January 1944 Aiken told his staff that too much coverage of the fighting in Yugoslavia was being allowed and he wanted these reports cut or stopped;[150] there followed a major clampdown on coverage of Tito's forces, and of partisan activity generally, especially on comments which drew parallels with the Irish guerrilla war against the British in the recent past.[151]

Following the entry into the war of the United States in December 1941, de Valera declared that 'The policy of the State remains unchanged. We can only be a friendly neutral'.[152] Coyne informed the press censors that they must be 'slow to prohibit the publication of news and views favourable to the United States' except where the impression could be given that Irish sympathy with the US was tending towards participation in the war.[153] When American troops arrived in Northern Ireland in January 1942, de Valera issued a statement, which was broadcast on radio and carried in the press, in which he declared that 'no matter what troops occupy the Six Counties the Irish people's claim for the unity of the whole of the national territory . . . will remain unabated'.[154] Elaborate publicity surrounded the arrival of the new 'occupying troops' and large numbers of Irish, British, American, Canadian and Australian media people awaited them. The Irish papers intended to give this story the prominence it deserved, using their own and agency reports. However, the Censorship restricted reports to the official announcement of their arrival,[155] and all subsequent publicity about the presence and activities of American troops in the North (as well as in the South, when they came down on leave) was kept to a minimum.[156] (Comments by Cormac Breathnach, a Fianna Fáil TD, that this US recognition of partition was a 'sinister' development were not allowed to be published in Ireland but were permitted to be transmitted to New York.[157]) In most cases reports which revealed the presence of American troops were stopped but where they were passed, the word 'American' was deleted. From October 1942 both 'British' and 'American' were deleted and replaced by 'of the occupying forces', preceded by the military rank and no name.[158]

Northern Ireland was the base for many of the American troops involved in the D-Day landings of June 1944, and 'the great flare of propaganda' which accompanied this event led to the censorship of much material from both Allied and German sources. Amongst the matter stopped was Eisenhower's broadcast to the French people and de Gaulle's call to France, as well as many reports from war correspondents who accompanied the invasion force.[159] On 11 June 1944 the press censors were instructed to stop all hostile references to the Allies and those favourable to the Germans, accompanied by a note from Coyne that the *Standard* 'will seemingly stop at nothing to create trouble for Ireland with the United Nations'.[160] A month later the censors were told of Aiken's unhappiness with the fact that much was being published from British sources but very little from the Germans. He instructed that, where possible, announcements from Goebbels indicating 'what the German people are thinking' (!) should be given publicity where they were not doctored and to allow such material from German sources as had 'news value'.[161] Much news, comment and speculation arising from the 'quickening' of the war in France – the whereabouts of Pétain, attempts on de Gaulle's life, Eisenhower's triumphant procession through Paris, 'Nazi outlook gloomy', etc. – was not allowed.[162]

Meanwhile, within Ireland, fuel supplies and transport services were gradually improving, but only official government announcements were allowed in relation to these topics; in relation to the restoration of road signs and place-names across the country, no conclusion was permitted to be drawn except that this was purely for the convenience of tourists and travellers. Speculation on the course of the war, reports of peace feelers or diplomatic moves, discussion of postwar planning, etc. had always been severely restricted and now that the war was nearing its end, Irish newspapers continued to be restrained in all these areas. Only official details of German defeats and surrenders were allowed, and although the imminence of German defeat was clear from the war news that was permitted, speculation and comment upon it and its possible aftermath were still banned.[163]

The German surrender was announced on 7 May 1945 and the following day Churchill announced the official end of hostilities in Europe. The Irish authorities, however, remained stubbornly impartial in public to the bitter end, as evidenced by de Valera's sympathy call on the German minister following the death of Hitler, reports of which were restricted to the official statement on the fact that the visit had taken place. The Censorship's final work, in its last three days, was to stop much material on Irish reaction to the end of the war in Europe. Among the reports stopped were those which laid stress on the burning of a tricolour by students of Trinity College and associated street disturbances, a retaliatory burning of a Union Jack in Cork, and the flying of a Swastika flag over the dome at University College Galway.[164] However, the Cenorship did pass an announcement for the *Independent* which was published on 7 May announcing a mass in Dublin 'for the repose of the soul of Signor Mussolini', organised by Italian fascists resident in Dublin. This provoked a protest from the Italian chargé d'affaires, who noted that while this item was passed, an Italian government communiqué regarding atrocities in Northern Italy was stopped 'on the ground of a careful practice of neutrality'.[165] Censorship policy and practice with regard to atrocity stories is the topic to which we next turn our attention.

ATROCITY STORIES

> *'The publication of atrocity stories, whether true or false, can do this country no good and may do it much harm.'*[166]   T.J. Coyne

Atrocity stories had been a prominent feature of Allied propaganda in the First World War. Between 1914 and 1918 newspapers carried horror stories about bloodthirsty 'Huns' mutilating nurses, nuns and babies, using bodies to make soap, and the like. These reports were subsequently shown to have been false and this had a disastrous effect on the credibility of reports of actual atrocities, particularly those of the Nazi death camps, during the latter part of the Second World War. In Ireland, the Censorship's policy of treating all such reports, from both sides, with equal and heavy scepticism and the continuing insistence in many circles on viewing all atrocities through the lens of the British record in Ireland widened the credibility gap. A further pertinent factor in Ireland was the need to sustain the desired sense of moral superiority which had become a corollary of its neutrality and the linked refusal to see any moral difference between the belligerents.

'While none are more easily shocked at human suffering as the Irish', wrote an Irish journalist in a dispatch heavily influenced by the Censorship, to the UPA news agency in April 1945, 'they do not want to have their own experiences recalled and are determined to adhere to their policy of no publication of details of horror stories until the end of hostilities.'[167] Atrocity stories would have given rise to 'sharp controversy'[168] and, according to the editor of the *Irish Press*, had 'no other value than to inflame passions'.[169] While the business of 'atrocity mongering' was notoriously corrupt, the levels of systematic slaughter revealed in the closing stages of the war in Europe made the Censorship policy of unbending impartiality difficult to justify, except within the narrow confines of the system's own internal logic.

In October 1942 Aiken and Coyne noted that 'It looks as if we're going to have a spate of atrocity stories' and issued detailed instructions to the press censors on how to deal with atrocity material submitted by the Irish press. They were told that details of specific atrocities were not to be allowed in most cases and that only general allegations contained in official statements or communiqués would be considered for publication.[170]

Atrocity stories began to arrive on the wires and into the Censorship in large numbers from early 1943. The majority of these reports concerned Nazi outrages in Eastern Europe (e.g. 'Nazis Gas 360 Polish Prisoners', PA, 5 March 1943; 'Germans Massacre 241 Children', Soviet news agency, 21 March 1943).[171] This continued to be the case but, ironically, it was an atrocity story from a German source which provided the Censorship with one of its largest single workloads in this area. In April 1943 the Germans found mass graves containing the bodies of an estimated 12,000 Polish officers in Katyn forest near the Soviet city of Smolensk. They had evidently been murdered by the Soviets, and the Germans, recognising its propaganda value, immediately announced their discovery to the world. All details were prohibited from publication in Ireland; the most that was allowed was reference to a German broadcast which alleged the discovery of the bodies of Polish officers alleged to have been murdered. Suppressed items included an announcement of a requiem mass being offered for the dead soldiers.[172]

In an interview in 1979 Aiken cited the Katyn atrocity in an implicit retrospective justification for his wartime policy. 'What was going on in the camps was pretty well known to us early on', stated the former minister, 'But the Russians were as bad – you only have to look at what happened in Katyn forest. There are photographs to prove that.'[173] Aiken did indeed know what was happening in the camps, and outside, as details passed through his organisation in increasing volume but were kept from the pages of the Irish press. Censorship policy remained rigid as the numbers of reported dead rose from hundreds to thousands to millions. Even official communiqués and statements from the likes of Roosevelt and Eden were shorn of all relevant detail and left as general condemnations of unspecified brutalities. Buchenwald, Belsen, Lublin, Dachau, Auschwitz-Birkenau – none could be allowed 'disturb the equanimity'[174] of the neutral Irish mind.

Atrocity stories did not, of course, emanate only from Europe. The war in the Pacific generated a whole spate of such stories. The conflict there differed from the war in Europe in the strength of its racial overtones and because of its impact on a large number of non-combatant Irish nationals, in the form of the many Catholic missionaries active in the area.

Most of the atrocity stories from this theatre of war which were stopped for the Irish papers were, again, in the main from Allied sources and thus focused on Japanese atrocities. Many of these are now well known: the Bataan death march, the Burma railway, overcrowding and starvation in PoW camps, beheadings, rapes and mass executions. All of these atrocities did occur and were the result of a number of factors: the absence of any Japanese organisation of PoWs, the code of behaviour relating to prisoners which saw them as 'provocative symbols of a detested past', and, primarily, the Japanese imperialist–racist philosophy which defined Westerners as inferior to the 'sons of Heaven' and Allied soldiers as less than human. Allied propaganda likewise dehumanised the enemy and encouraged Allied troops and the public to think of the Japanese as 'apes in uniform'. US Admiral Halsey declared at this time that 'We are drowning and burning the bestial apes all over the Pacific, and it is just as much pleasure to burn them as to drown them.' The US army and navy publicly displayed another of his sayings: 'Kill Japs, kill Japs, kill more Japs'.[175] Such attitudes and incitement inevitably led to the perpetration of atrocities, by both sides. As well as individual acts of barbarity by American and Australian soldiers, including cannibalism, we can mention well-documented acts of policy by the Americans such as the sinking of all Japanese ships on sight, including hospital and passenger ships, and the indiscriminate fire-raid bombings of Japanese cities which caused more casualties than the atomic bomb at Hiroshima. These raids left a quarter of a million dead and eight million homeless; one raid alone killed 140,000 and left one million homeless. (The Bomber Command's systematic area bombing attacks on the German civilian population, culminating in the horror of Dresden, were similarly atrocious in conception and execution.) Neither side reported its own atrocities but emphasised those perpetrated by the enemy. Here, as Phillip Knightley points out, the Allies had an advantage as they were able to use the brutal treatment of Allied PoWs to stimulate hatred of the Japanese. Japan could not retaliate as its government had told the people that no Japanese soldier was ever taken prisoner; all had died fighting.[176]

The Irish Censorship faced a formidable opponent of its own in the shape of General MacArthur's highly-skilled public relations/propaganda/censorship machine, which controlled and coloured the predominant image of the war that reached the West. While the Censorship did not interfere with the *Letter from America* propaganda bulletin which carried American reports in full, it encountered problems in 1945 as the Americans, through minister David Gray, attempted (unsuccessfully) to force atrocity stories, conveniently dealing with the deaths of Irish missionaries, through the censorship barriers and into the mainstream press. However, the fact that the victims were Irish, and religious Irish at that, did not in any way interfere with the strict application of policy towards atrocity stories.

In February and March 1945, the Censorship suppressed a story submitted by the *Cork Examiner* and the *Free Press, Wexford* dealing with the slaughter by the Japanese of over sixty people, including students, refugees, priests and brothers (a number of whom were Irish) in the De la Salle College in Manila. The stopped *Examiner* story related the experiences of Rev. Francis Cosgrove, one of the eight survivors, who had lived hidden beneath an altar for a week living on the water from flower vases and Holy Communion wafers.[177] In March 1945, an *Irish Press* story was treated thus (words deleted by the censor in italics):

> Priests and Nuns at Mandalay *Rescued* – Priests, nuns and orphan children housed in a leper colony in Mandalay were safely evacuated after *Japanese* shellfire had killed one priest and injured four others . . . They had been congregated in Mandalay *by order of the Japanese*.[178]

On 30 March 1945 the treatment of a report on the killing of four Irish priests in Manila provoked a strong protest from Gray and created some controversy about Irish policy towards atrocity stories. The priests, from the Maynooth Mission to China, had, according to a US Office of War Information (OWI) inspired report, been put inside a house and deliberately burnt to death by the Japanese. The report in the Irish papers merely announced the deaths 'during recent fighting in Manila'.[179] Gray wrote to the *Irish Press* and *Irish Independent*, quoting the OWI telegram giving details of the atrocity. This section was deleted, by the censors for the

Independent (which then refused to print the letter) and on his own initiative by William Sweetman, the editor of the *Press*; 'We merely omitted a part', he told the American minister, 'which I would consider it contrary to journalistic ethics to have published . . . You may have noticed that it is not our practice to publish news correspondents' stories against any of the belligerents. The trouble is that they are usually entirely undependable, have no other value than to inflame passions and are quite impossible for us to verify.'[180] Lee comments that 'such editorial scepticism was admirable in principle. In practice, it required by this stage a heroic determination to avert one's gaze from reality to imply that all atrocity stories were equally undependable.'[181] This, nevertheless, remained *Irish Press*, and Irish Censorship, policy until the end of the Emergency.

The censorship of the Manila story and Gray's letter provoked an amount of publicity. Associated Press carried the story of the double censorship on their wires and both the *New York Times* and the *New York Herald Tribune* gave prominence to it. The *Tribune* also ran an editorial under the heading: 'Surpassingly Neutral Éire'. It began:

> One might have thought that Éire had demonstrated her neutrality beyond shadow of doubt in the five and a half years during which the life and death of nations was being decided just beyond her chaste doorstep. Her neutrality about spies and war criminals should have prepared us for anything. Nevertheless her present neutrality about Nazi atrocities strikes Americans as plain daft.

It went on to mention the Manila story and refers to the nervousness of the Argentine government because it had

> persistently backed the wrong horse and has been neutral rather like Éire on the wrong side. Could it be that the unwillingness of the Irish powers that be to permit the Irish people to know what goes on in the world stems from a similar reluctance to be proved wrong. How else is one to explain the otherwise inexplicable Éireann [sic] Censorship of April, 1945?[182]

De Valera's expression of condolences to Hempel on the death of Hitler a couple of weeks later served to reinforce such misinterpretations, wilful or not, of the unwavering correctitude of (the outer manifestations of) Irish neutrality.

Following the lifting of censorship a number of Irish papers carried the previously forbidden details of Japanese atrocities, particularly the De La Salle College massacre and the burning of the priests.[183] The *Manchester Guardian* and the *Daily Mail* also carried the latter story, along with an account of its treatment by the censors,[184] while Longford County Council belatedly passed a resolution condemning the actions of the Japanese.[185] Gray's letter, in its original form, was printed in the *Irish*

Independent on 14 May 1945 and on the following day Setsuya Beppu, the Japanese consul-general in Ireland, wrote to that paper describing Gray's account as one-sided and calling on the Irish people to reserve judgement until the matter had been 'fully investigated by the Japanese authorities'. The war in the Pacific was, of course, continuing and in a memorandum sent to London on 21 May, Maffey, the UK representative, expressed the fear that de Valera might try to win favour with the American people by declaring war on Japan over the killing of the missionaries. The British representative noted that the headline 'De Valera Breaks with Japan' would read well in the United States.[186] The suggestion was ludicrous and de Valera had long since demonstrated his unwillingness to (publicly and officially, at any rate) jump on the Allied bandwagon.

In a dispatch to the UPA news agency in April 1945 (subsequently heavily altered by the Censorship) its Irish correspondent Charlie McDonnell wrote that 'The reaction in Éire to the wireless broadcast of scenes at Buchenwald internment camp is one of incredulity . . . the people here find it difficult to believe that atrocities such as those alleged in radio broadcasts could possibly have happened'.[187] The Irish were not alone in this reaction. People everywhere who had not directly experienced the Nazis found it hard to comprehend the scale of the horror and the fact that it was the result of a deliberate and systematic policy. There was widespread disbelief in Britain and America at the reports from the first camps to be liberated (by the Red Army); eyewitness reports and photographs were dismissed as Russian propaganda.[188]

In Ireland, the villain of the piece was always more likely to be British. Correspondence in Irish newspapers in the weeks following the lifting of the censorship gives a flavour of the disbelief felt about the pictures and reports of Nazi atrocities. Some correspondents articulated the common view that such reports were the inventions of British propagandists. Such attitudes were not (in most cases) the product of pro-Nazi sympathy, but of the narrow mind-set which clung to the myth that British inequity and Irish suffering were somehow unique. The Censorship contributed to, and also, in its policies, partly reflected this view. A Dublin doctor assured Brian Inglis of the *Irish Times* that all the evidence, descriptions and pictures from Belsen could be accounted for by a typhoid epidemic. A writer to a Kilkenny paper dismissed the same pictures as 'all propaganda'. Another wrote 'Why drag up all these unpleasant things, it's so bad for the children, life is sad enough without this beastliness.' Some months later the first prize at a local fancy-dress ball went to 'The Beast of Belsen'.[189] An anonymous letter-writer to the *Irish Times* stated that '. . . the average Dubliner would not be persuaded even though all the ghosts of Hitler's victims were to rise from the dead; he would only pour himself another drink muttering "British Propaganda".'[190] Many Irish people did avert their gaze, for many different reasons, but so too, in the preceding years, did many across wartime Europe who were far closer to the reality, with far more serious consequences.

The censors claimed that the Irish people had been kept 'fully inform-ed' of atrocities by means of belligerent broadcasts, the English press and the *Letter from America*.[191] These media, however, reached a limited au-dience, preached largely to the converted and carried the stamp of 'propa-ganda'. For the majority such stories would have lacked credibility until carried in the neutral press or on neutral radio. The Censorship ensured that this did not happen in the dubious belief that ignorance was the best policy when it came to maintaining a neutral world-view, if such a thing can be said to exist.

BOOKS, PAMPHLETS AND BOOK REVIEWS

It was not until July 1940 that the authorities took some measure of legal control over the sale of printed matter other than newspapers and periodicals. Power to control the printing and publishing of such matter was not taken until February 1942. The reasons for these self-imposed limitations were twofold. In the first place, there was a reluctance to 'alarm or antagonise either the Dáil or the public' by taking excessive powers. Secondly, the Press Censorship branch was far too small to deal with the volume of censorable material with which it would have been confronted.[192] When the first powers in this regard were taken, the effort was made to secure the desired aim, i.e. to prohibit the open sale and prominent display of books of an openly propagandist nature, by indirect methods. Thus, the Emergency Powers (No. 36) Order 1940 did not grant the power to *ban* specific publica-tions, but only to seize any publication in certain circumstances. A *modus operandi* was developed whereby booksellers could be persuaded to withdraw objectionable publications under threat of having their premises invaded by the Gardaí,[193] while the Censorship achieved its aim without incurring 'the publicity or odium' associated with the publishing of a formal ban. The power to ban *per se* was not taken because of the danger that a series of bans could have been construed as anti-German or, more likely, given the nature of most of the objectionable material, anti-British. There was the further perceived danger that if the power to ban existed, publications which were not banned could be presumed to have the implicit approval of the authorities.[194]

Relations with the booksellers were maintained through the offices of the Associated Booksellers of Great Britain and Ireland (Irish Branch), and particularly its honorary secretary, R.B. Eason. 'We are not banning propa-ganda absolutely', Coyne explained to them, '. . . we merely want you not to flaunt it.'[195] Booksellers 'voluntarily' withdrew titles such as *Inside Italy; Lies as Allies: How Hitler Makes War*, and *The Persecution of the Catholic Church in the Third Reich*. Many propagandist titles continued to be sold and displayed, however, and by late 1941 the Censorship felt that a more definite 'gentleman's agreement' needed to be made with the booksellers. A meeting to this end was held in November 1941 between representatives of the Associated Booksellers and the Censorship. It was agreed that in return for the latter refraining from carrying out a 'propaganda purge' of bookshops with the aid of the Gardaí and establishing a thorough customs check for propaganda, the booksellers would: not stock grosser forms of propaganda, especially atrocity stories and books which contained 'vulgar abuse' like *The Beast of Berlin, Under the Heel of the Gestapo* and *Men Crucified*; not stock 'official propaganda' such as that produced by the British Ministry of Information; not display openly propagandist books which by jacket or title proclaimed themselves to be anti-German, anti-British, etc. They could continue to stock such books (for example, the Oxford and the MacMillan war pamphlets series) and display the less offensive titles, but not those of the *Nazi and Nazarene* variety. No objection was taken to the display of 'important and serious' books such as *Berlin Diary* or to books dealing with the war, the RAF, the Battle of Britain, etc., provided the display of such was reasonable and 'not excessive'.[196]

It was also agreed that booksellers could be asked, through Eason, to refuse to stock or to withdraw any specific publication if expressly requested to do so by the controller of censorship. It was further agreed that booksellers could import and supply any publication whatsoever provided that it was specifically ordered for a particular customer. The Censorship nobly expressed its desire not to prevent the 'bona fide student or reader' from having access to propaganda.[197]

Among the books withdrawn on request were McGlennan's *Record Song Book* and *Victory Song Book, The Victory Chorus Book for Canteen Concerts* (these books contained typical British war songs like 'Forty Million Churchills') and a children's *Aeroplane Drawing Book*, which paid tribute to 'HM forces' and featured 'enemy' (German) aeroplanes.[198] A small number of seizures were directed by the Censorship also, for example *Comrade Genia* by Genia Demianova which was seized from bookshops in September 1942.[199] In general, however, the 'gentleman's agreement' with the booksellers, backed up by intervention from Customs and Excise and the Postal Censorship, succeeded in minimising the open sale and exhibition of crass propaganda in book form and kept it, somewhat appropriately in the context of Irish neutrality, under the counter.

Until February 1942 no legal power existed to control the printing or publishing in Ireland of objectionable material in book, pamphlet or leaflet form. Most printers, however, were in the habit of submitting doubtful matter to the Censorship to ensure against possible subsequent seizure. (The powers of the Postal Censorship provided an additional source of 'indirect' control.) In July 1941 proofs of a pamphlet containing an anti-neutrality speech by James Dillon, a Fine Gael TD and the most prominent opponent of the government's policy, were submitted to the censor by the printers. The proposed publication of this pamphlet highlighted for the authorities the 'somewhat anomalous as well as embarrassing' situation whereby the power existed to seize objectionable documents after publication, but not to prevent their being printed, even when the Censorship had advance knowledge of them.[200] Given that Dillon's speech had been passed without alteration by the censor for the Irish and external press it was decided not to attempt to interfere with the pamphlet. (A seizure or attempted seizure could have led to a court challenge, on the basis that the speech had already been allowed full publicity.) The episode provoked a discussion in government, however, regarding the extension of the powers of the Censorship to deal with books and pamphlets as effectively as it could then deal with newspapers and periodicals. A new order to deal with the censorship of printed matter of all kinds was drawn up in August 1941, but was not made.[201] The powers contained therein were subsequently incorporated into the Emergency Powers (No. 151) Order 1942.[202]

The powers of censorship were now extended to printed matter of all kinds, including books, pamphlets, leaflets and casual publications. Printers and publishers could be prohibited from printing any specified matter or classes of matter and could be required to submit matters for censorship before printing or publication. The power to direct the seizure of documents was preserved and extended to objectionable items which were not documents. The power to direct a seizure (contained in Article 4) was, however, restricted by Article 5 which stated that if a printer or publisher had submitted a document and received permission to print, the Censorship could not subsequently have it seized.[203]

Printers were still not obliged to submit anything for censorship unless they received a specific direction to submit a particular publication. Thus, the number of pamphlets, etc. received by the Censorship remained small. In December 1942 they stopped the publication of the programme of the Pan Celtic Union and a replica submitted by Clann na Saoirse (Racial Resurgence Party) in February 1943. A pamphlet entitled *Let Irishmen Defend Ireland*, produced by the Ulster Union Club and arguing for a thirty-two county defence arrangement was stopped for publication in March 1943. Coyne believed that its publication might do 'some good' in the six counties and Britain, but not in the South.[204] Such instances were exceptional and the vast majority of publications (other than newspapers and periodicals) which circulated in Ireland were printed without any reference to the Emergency Censorship.[205] A number of books did fall foul of the Censorship, however; three cases, in particular, deserve attention, having been the subject of questions and debate in the Houses of the Oireachtas.

In January 1943 Coyne issued a direction for the seizure of *Genuine Irish Old Moore's Almanac, 1943* (a separate publication to the Irish edition of *Foulsham's Old Moore*, printed and published in England), on the basis of objectionable matter contained in the monthly predictions. Having been seized, the page end predictions were crudely chopped off and the books were returned in this mutilated form.[206] The proofs of the 1944 edition were submitted in October 1943 and were passed for publication subject to the deletion of all references to the war.[207] When the 1945 proofs were submitted Coyne's attitude had softened considerably, presumably in response to the unfavourable parliamentary and external press publicity which the censorship of the 1943 edition had provoked. 'I don't think we are called upon to take this publication too seriously', he wrote to Aiken, 'or to interfere too drastically with the portentous nonsense of the prophecies which have always been regarded as part of the fun and games.'[208] Aiken, however, was determined and insisted on drastic deletions and alterations to the prophecies, commenting 'I think I have improved them'. The names of all countries were deleted and alternatives were suggested for some. Once America, for instance, had become 'the West' or 'the occident', Japan 'the East' or 'the Orient', and France 'a European country', the predictions no longer presented a threat to neutrality and the *Almanac* was passed for publication.[209]

The *Wolfe Tone Annual* was published every year since 1932 by the veteran Republican Brian O'Higgins, who had been a Sinn Féin member of the First Dáil. Its purpose, according to O'Higgins, was to perpetuate 'the Separatist Idea and the vindication of all who have sacrificed themselves for the full independence and Gaelicisation of Ireland'.[210] The 1944 edition was devoted to 'a brief, clear history of Irish Nationality'[211] and was a nationalist polemic typical of its kind. When the proofs were submitted to the censor in October 1943 Knightly was inclined to pass it for publication. Coyne and Aiken felt differently, however, and the *Annual* in its entirety was stopped. If it was, wrote Coyne, 'merely a bona fide or mala fide history it would probably do no harm as nobody reads history anyway but it is, in fact and purpose, a political pamphlet and intended and likely to have a subversive effect. This, I feel, is our real justification for preventing its publication at the present time.'[212] O'Higgins laid the responsibility for the suppression fully on the minister and believed that it was 'in retaliation for my past offences as a political opponent' of Aiken's.[213] When the matter was raised in the Dáil by James Larkin Jnr, Aiken made a number of charges in the course of his reply. He attacked O'Higgins 'as a futile old man'[214] and accused Larkin (who had been deputed by Labour Party leader, William Norton to deal with the issue) of seeking, in association with O'Higgins, to round up the remnants of a very dangerous movement throughout the country with the object of overthrowing democracy and the state.[215] Aiken's association of these two exponents of widely differing political philosophies under the banner of a common conspiracy revealed the crudity of his attitude to political opposition. The conservative nationalist and socialist internationalist were united under the common name of traitor.

Traitors of a more traditionally Irish kind were identified in the debate provoked by the treatment of *The House of Gregory*. This book, by former Royal Irish Constabulary county inspector Vere Gregory, was 'an account of the Gregory family in Ireland, interspersed with the writer's own reminiscences and comments on current affairs'.[216] The publishers, Browne and Nolan, sent galley proofs of the book to the Censorship in June 1943, as a 'precaution'.[217] Coyne's own opinion was that it was 'too unimportant' to bother with and he doubted whether it was worth 'using the Censorship to improve the book'.[218] However, having consulted 'those who are wiser than myself',[219] i.e. Aiken, a number of alterations and deletions were deemed necessary. These were duly made and *The House of Gregory*, now exempt from possible seizure (under Article 5 of the Emergency Powers (No. 151) Order 1942) was published on 20 October 1943. The Censorship then initiated a close-down on all publicity for the book. Reviews were stopped for the daily press as were mentions in the new books lists. A notice in the December issue of *The Bell*, which announced that '*The House of Gregory* comes from Browne and Nolan Ltd at 15/–' was prohibited, as was a similar notice in the publisher's catalogue.[220] The explanation for this extraordinary close-down, as given to the editor of the *Irish Independent*, was that reviews of the book 'would inevitably lead to controversy harmful of national security. No useful purpose could be served at the moment by stirring up bitter memories of the Black and Tan atrocities.' The angry editor, Frank Geary, noted that on a former occasion a ruling was made which forbade references to the civil war. Now that the Black and Tan period was a forbidden subject also, he asked at what period were newspapers to stop making references to events in Irish history: 'May we safely refer to the Land League, the Fenian period or the Insurrection of 1798, without imperilling our neutrality in 1943 or 1944?'[221]

A report on the developing controversy was carried in the *Belfast Telegraph* on 17 January 1944 and Sir John Keane tabled a motion on the matter in the Seanad, notice of which was forbidden publication in the press. The Seanad debate took place on 29 January 1944. Keane and his seconder, Donal O'Sullivan, set out to make the treatment of *The House of Gregory* a *cause célèbre*, with Keane grandiloquently comparing the figure of Vere Gregory with that of Captain Dreyfuss and John Brown.[222] The debate was prolonged and bitter. The critics focused on the inconsistency of allowing publication of the book and then denying it publicity. They questioned how the reviews represented a threat to national security and referred to other books which had also touched on the Black and Tan period – such as *Orange Terror, The Irish Citizen Army* and *The Life of Cathal Brugha* – but had not received similar treatment. The implication was that these books were written from a political perspective shared by the Fianna Fáil government and that this explained the discrepancy.

Aiken admitted that the steps taken had been 'undesirable'[223] but he stood by his actions. His defence, based on Coyne's advice, was that the book was originally passed on the assumption that it was intended for private circulation among the author's family and friends. Once it was published, however, and the reviews began to arrive into the Censorship, the minister realised the potential for 'bitter controversy', particularly on the issue of the Black and Tans and the Croke Park killings. He pointed also to the difference in potential for controversy between a fifteen shilling book and a daily newspaper – a controversy which could 'split the unity of our people'.[224] When the debate resumed on 24 February, it became very bitter. The plaster was torn off old wounds as Fianna Fáil senators raked up the past misdeeds of Albion in Ireland and current British policies in the North. The supporters of the motion were dismissed as 'birds of passage' who were 'only legally Irishmen'. They were motivated, according to their opponents, not by liberal principles but by the desire to bring Ireland into the war and, more mundanely, by the wish to promote sales of the book in question. Senator Colgan (Fianna Fáil) summed up the mood in his claim that the motion's supporters were aggrieved only because 'it is one of the natives who happens to be the Censor'. The old arguments were peppered with often vicious personal abuse, leading Keane to conclude that if the Seanad in any way reflected public opinion, then Aiken may have been justified in his actions. He declared himself satisfied, however, that 'the country' had more sense than many of the senators and that none of the book reviews would have been 'a fraction as provocative' as some of the contributions to the debate.[225]

Censorship policy in relation to book reviews in general was outlined in a letter to the editor of the *Sunday Independent* in November 1942. According to the letter, the Censorship sought to prevent the publication of reviews in cases where: the review itself contained matter the publication of which would be likely to cause offence to any of the belligerents; the book reviewed contained such matter although the review itself was unobjectionable; the review or the book were in their general tendency propagandist or likely to compromise neutrality, or publicised the exploits of Irish people serving in the war.[226] The prohibition on unobjectionable reviews of objectionable books was based on the belief that if people could be kept in ignorance about the existence of such books, then there would not be a demand for them which could upset the arrangement maintained with the booksellers.[227] While the 'international' dimension was put forth as the basis for censorship of book reviews, the treatment of *The House of Gregory* demonstrated that this was not the sole criterion; the censorship of a review of Daniel Binchy's *Church and State in Fascist Italy* was another case in point.

The *Irish Independent* submitted a review of Binchy's book in November 1941. Objection was taken to a number of passages. References to the fascist system which were 'unwelcome to the Italian government and people' were deleted, as were references to the League of Nations' sanctions against Italy, which could have had 'an unfortunate effect' on the relations between Ireland and Italy. The review had stated that 'Professor Binchy is never at pains to conceal his rooted dislike for the Fascist system. Occasionally indeed he travels rather far afield in search of a weapon or two with which to lambaste it.' The 'minor deletions and alterations' made by the Censorship produced the following: 'Professor Binchy is never at pains to conceal his rooted dislikes. Occasionally indeed one feels he travels rather far afield in search of a weapon.' The other deletions related to internal politics. In response to Binchy's claim that de Valera 'stood four-square for parliamentary democracy and popular government', the reviewer pointed out that de Valera had fought a civil war against popular government. He went on to defend the Blueshirts against Binchy's implication that they were fascist, declaring that they stood for freedom of speech against 'people who were favoured by the Government even in their blackguardly attempts upon public meetings'. The Censorship declared it 'contrary to the public interest' to allow a fresh controversy to break out in the press regarding either the civil war or the Blueshirts 'at a time when the unity of our people was more than ever called for'.[228] The *Independent* refused to publish the mutilated review and the issue was raised by Patrick McGilligan (Fine Gael) in the Dáil in February 1942. Given the nature of the deletions which had been made, his claims of party political censorship carried some weight.

While the Censorship occasionally stepped upon the civil war fault line in Irish politics (see Parliamentary Politics, Chapter 6, pp. 258-74), its treatment of book reviews in most cases was based on the desire to minimise publicity for publications which were sympathetic to one side or the other in the war. The vast majority of such books which were reviewed were published in Britain and America and were naturally pro-Allied/anti-Axis in slant. The chief culprit in the publication of pro-Allied reviews was the *Irish Times*. It published, without permission, a series of objectionable reviews, including reviews of books which had been withdrawn from sale in Ireland, like *The Persecution of the Catholic Church in the Third Reich*, which provoked a complaint from Hempel and a number of warnings from the Censorship. The *Irish Times* editor Bertie Smyllie was determined to ignore the Censorship's directions, however, and continued to refuse to submit the 'Books of the Week' Saturday feature for censorship. After he published a review of *By Order of the Gestapo* by Peter Walker on 18 October 1941, Coyne and Aiken agreed that there was no alternative but to require the *Irish Times* to submit its books page in full.[229]

In January 1943 a short review of *Worrals of the WAAF* was submitted by the *Irish Times*, and suppressed by the Censorship. Smyllie took the opportunity to set a trap for the censors. He rewrote the review, giving the women names such as Gretchen, Eva and Lilli and re-titled the book *Lotte of the Luftwaffe*. The review was submitted a fortnight later and was passed for publication. Smyllie was 'jubilant', claiming that the episode proved the anti-British bias of the Censorship.[230] Tony Gray, then editor of the books page, believes that 'all it proved was that at this particular stage of the war the Irish government ministers were far more afraid of the Germans than they were of the British'.[231] The probable truth is less dramatic. The bogus review had been included in a batch of innocuous proofs and was more than likely passed inadvertently by an overworked censor. Indeed, the fact that the *Irish Times* had attributed the publication of the 'book' to a London firm meant that the review should have been stopped on the basis of the probability that a British publication dealing with an enemy organisation would have been British rather than German propaganda. Such fine details mattered not a whit to Smyllie, however, who derived much mileage from the success of his 'experiment'. Coyne, not suprisingly, was not amused and warned Smyllie that he was considering ordering the *Irish Times* to submit page proofs and possibly the entire issue in completed form.[232] (Had this been enforced it would have amounted to suppression.) Between January 1943 and January 1945, 111 book reviews submitted by all publications were stopped by the censors or passed subject to deletions, which in most cases were of such a nature as to make the review virtually meaningless.[233]

MISCELLANEOUS ITEMS

The presence of British chain stores like Woolworths in Ireland and the less than sensitive approach of British distributors to the niceties of Irish neutrality inevitably led to some difficulties with items other than newspapers and books.

In October 1939 the display of large posters advertising 'We'll Hang out our Washing on the Siegfried Line' and 'Adolf' (illustrated with a British Tommy 'severely castigating a certain Head of State') in the record department of Woolworths in Dublin was the subject of a letter to the Censorship from the Department of External Affairs.[234] Aiken suggested that a Garda be sent to the store to suggest a less conspicuous exhibition, but the Department of Justice disagreed. Duff (Justice) pointed to the legal greyness in this area and suggested that the display was not illegal unless it was likely to lead to a breach of the peace, which was unlikely in this case. He suggested that legislation was needed to deal with such matters but warned of the danger of appearing absurd.[235]

A draft order was prepared in February 1940 (proposed as Emergency Powers (No. 22) Order 1940) which extended the powers of the Censorship to deal with effigies, gramophone records and so on. The order was not made and the proposed powers to deal with effigies, etc. were rejected as 'unnecessary and a trifle ridiculous'.[236] The danger of appearing absurd did not, however, deter the Censorship from acting against a number of items. In November 1940, for example, Woolworths were forced to withdraw a game called 'Plonk'. The object of the game, as described in a letter from External Affairs, was to get a dart into the mouth of 'a Head of State with which we are in friendly relations' (probably Hitler). The game was deemed to be a document within the meaning of the definition in the Emergency Powers (No. 36) Order 1940 and thus liable to seizure.[237]

The power to seize remained limited to documents throughout 1941, but the situation was beginning to force the authorities towards a reappraisal. Propaganda materials of various kinds began to flood into the country from Britain. Shops displayed them prominently, provoking 'repeated complaints'.[238] The items to which objection was taken included various emblems, effigies of Hitler and, most prominently, material associated with the so-called V (for victory) campaign.[239] V badges became extremely popular and fashionable in late 1941 and early 1942, provoking the Anti-British Propaganda Committee to distribute thousands of leaflets in Dublin warning young Irish people against wearing 'the sign of their only enemy'.[240] The government also was provoked into action and in February the Emergency Powers (No. 151) Order 1942 extended the power of seizure to articles which were not documents, 'the sale and distribution of which would be likely to lead to a breach of the peace or to cause offence to the peoples of friendly foreign nations'.[241] This power was occasionally utilised, for example in October 1942 when Coyne ordered the seizure of four jigsaw puzzles in the 'Epics of War' series.[242] In general, however, it was used, as in the case of books, as a threat to ensure compliance. In December 1943, for instance, a shop in Grafton Street, Dublin withdrew from sale a cheap board and dice game, 'Target for Tonight' (based on the banned film of the same name), which featured an air raid on an 'enemy city' – Berlin. The president of the Drapers' Chamber of Trade was asked to see that his members agree collectively not to stock this or similar items if they wished to avoid police raids in the pre-Christmas rush.[243] Individual Gardaí, with eyes and ears peeled for signs of unneutrality, occasionally took the initiative themselves. In November 1942 a Garda in Mitchelstown reported on the playing of a record at a funfair. It was to the tune of 'Run, Rabbit, Run' but with 'Adolf' substituted for 'Rabbit' and other uncomplimentary references to this friendly head of state. When the Garda attempted to seize the offending article its owner smashed it to pieces. No prosecution was made but it was decided that if the record was found to be on general sale its importation should be prohibited.[244]

CENSORSHIP, PROPAGANDA AND THE REPRESENTATIVES OF FOREIGN GOVERNMENTS IN IRELAND

The propaganda role of the foreign representatives in Dublin was performed in two principal, interlinked ways: firstly, by attempting to ensure the most favourable coverage in Irish newspapers for their sides' version of events; and, secondly, by disseminating propaganda bulletins directed at the press, politicians and the public. Given the heavy reliance of Irish newspapers on Allied news sources, the general pro-Allied slant of the Irish press (particularly as the war progressed), and the open availability of English newspapers in Ireland, it is not surprising that most of the protests and complaints about news treatment and presentation emanated from the Axis representatives.

The German minister Eduard Hempel's earliest complaints concerned 'the indecency of some of the anti-German propaganda appearing in British papers allowed to circulate in Ireland', specifically illustrated papers which specialised in unsubtle propaganda such as *News Review* and *Illustrated War News*. Joseph Walshe, secretary of the Department of External Affairs, agreed with him that the Irish authorities 'should make some effort to keep out what may be described as bestial propaganda'.[245] Eason, the leading wholesaler, was asked to contact such papers and warn them of the danger of prohibition unless the crass propaganda was toned down.[246] Despite the limitations placed on more openly offensive material, Axis representatives continued to have cause for complaint about the contents of English papers generally. The attitude of the Censorship was that these papers were inevitably going to be anti-Axis and that such a situation would have to be tolerated so long as they, by and large, remained within the 'bounds of decency'. It was felt that dwindling circulation would lessen the problem and that articles 'tucked away' in the middle of papers with small circulations and little influence in Ireland (like the *Sunday Chronicle* and *Reynolds News*, sources of complaint by Hempel) were 'not likely to do much harm'.[247]

The Axis representatives largely understood and accepted the situation with regard to English newspapers and their protests were, more often than not, merely perfunctory. The news policy and content of Irish newspapers, and particularly the *Irish Press*, was of far more concern to them and this issue provided the subject of most of their representations.

It was the pro-Allied bias of the war news policy of all the Irish dailies which was the primary focus of protest. This bias was revealed in a number of ways, as was repeatedly pointed out by Hempel and the Italian minister, Vincenzo Berardis. The main problem was the reliance upon Allied news sources. British news agency headlines were often used and reports were framed in such a way as to present the Allied version as fact. Reports from Axis sources were often ignored, given little prominence or printed in the form supplied by the British agencies. Thus, the Axis version of events would appear almost as an addendum to a report and invariably in the form of a 'claim'. This slant was reinforced by various techniques such as the choice of letter types, the omission or addition of quotation marks, the use of bold type and boxes, etc. The almost exclusive use of photographs from Allied sources was another case in point.

From the outbreak of war in Greece, Berardis began 'assailing' the

Department of External Affairs (DEA) about the news presentation of the Italian military campaigns, with particular emphasis on the *Irish Press*.[248] His complaints focused on the reliance on British and Greek communiqués to the exclusion of Italian material; headlines; and posters which were 'unfavourable to Italy'.[249] Frederick Boland, the assistant secretary, was dismissive of the Italian minister, suggesting to him 'that what he was really complaining about was the fact that the news of Italian defeats was printed at all!' He regarded Berardis's illustrations of bias as indicating no more than that the newspapers printed Press Association reports as they received them; yet he indicated to the Censorship that the DEA would be just as glad if the Censorship took some action 'from the point of view of avoiding friction and keeping our Italian friend in an amenable frame of mind'.[250]

Both the Italians and the Germans persistently singled out the *Irish Press* for special attention. This was not because the *Press* was more pro-Allied or anti-Axis than any other daily paper but because, in the words of an *aide-mémoire* from the German legation, it was 'looked upon as the organ of the Government Party' and should therefore have been 'pledged to particular care'.[251] By thus ascribing to it quasi-official status the Axis representatives proceeded to place upon it the demands of strict impartiality. The German legation prepared detailed reports in which the *Irish Press* war coverage was analysed and its propagandist slant identified.[252] (Hempel believed that a pro-British subeditor, whom he identified to the DEA, may have been responsible for some of the problems.) He regarded the *Irish Independent* as the most objective of the dailies, although expressed amazement, following the entry of the Soviet Union into the war, at the way in which even 'strongly Catholic papers' like the *Independent* took 'the side of Russia against Germany' by following the British propaganda line in the tone and structure of their coverage of the conflict.[253] Hempel's efforts at content analysis made some impression on Aiken who, in October 1943, noted that the German minister's complaints about Irish newspapers were 'not altogether without substance' and proposed to speak to the chief press censor and the editor of the *Irish Press* about them.[254] Boland, however, was as unmoved by Hempel's complaints as he was by those of Berardis. He saw in the pages of the *Irish Press* little more than the results of 'a kind of carelessness and negligence – the automatic publication of everything which comes to the newspaper from British News Agencies to which it subscribes without any effort to avoid giving that impression of pro-British prejudice which the exercise of a little editorial care and ingenuity could easily prevent'.[255] He acknowledged the possibility of 'a trace of definite anti-German bias' but was satisfied that editorial sloppiness was the principal factor.[256]

The situation did not improve from the point of view of the German legation as the war progressed. Hempel complained in March 1944 about the use in recent reports in Irish papers of the term 'Germany and Austria' as if the latter were a separate state. He condemned this as 'the terminology of United Nations propaganda' and stated that references to air raids on 'Austria' carried obvious political implications which were wounding to German sentiment.[257] In August 1944 the German minister was again concentrating his attention on the *Irish Press* specifically, commenting that it had become 'much less neutral since things began to go so much against Germany'. Among the cuttings sent to the DEA by way of illustration, with comments by the press attaché, Carl Peterson, was a map of Germany with its pre-1938 borders. Boland admitted that this was 'slightly premature' but hinted to Hempel that the censorship was bound to be relaxed gradually as the war approached its end and 'the time was rapidly coming when we couldn't accept any official responsibility for what was published, or not published, in our newspapers'.[258] Walshe agreed, satisfied that they need not take 'any notice' of the Germans; 'The *Irish Press*' he wrote, 'is following national feeling in not showing small countries like Austria as included in Germany'. (Walshe noted further that Peterson's comments appeared 'decidedly Prussian'.[259]) These responses reflected a general change in attitude towards the German representative and his staff from within the department. In 1940-1, when German victory was still a possibility (and one which apparently did not overperturb the secretary) Walshe and Boland had been gratuitously eager to please Hempel, making every effort, the latter noted, to forestall 'any unfavourable German attitude to Irish neutrality'. By 1944, however, with German defeat a formality, the pair had become 'brusque and rude', 'unhelpful and evasive' in their dealings with the German minister.[260]

Coyne felt that, in general, Hempel's dissatisfaction with the presentation of war news in Irish papers was 'perfectly understandable'. He pointed out, however, that the prevailing situation was unavoidable in the absence of power, on the part of the Censorship, to control the presentation of news: 'We, in the Censorship, feel that we are doing our stuff if we can succeed in preventing our papers from being positively anti-Axis, but this is very nearly all we can hope to achieve . . . We can't make them pro-German or even stop them being pro-United Nations.' He was keen to make the point, however, that the situation would have been even 'worse', from the point of view of the Axis representatives, but for the intervention of the Censorship.[261]

In November 1942 the Japanese consulate complained to the DEA about the ignorance of and lack of sympathy for Japan and things Japanese which they identified in the Irish press.[262] As the war in the Pacific area progressed, the Japanese inevitably came second best in the pages of Irish papers in the face of General MacArthur's huge propaganda machine; yet they were aided by the strict refusal on the part of the Censorship to allow the publication of the details of atrocity stories, many of which were coming from this particular theatre of war in the last months of the Emergency.

In March 1945, as was seen earlier, Irish newspapers carried a report of the deaths of four Irish missionary priests 'during recent fighting in Manila'. The report, having been doctored by the Irish Censorship, thus gave the impression that the deaths could equally have resulted from Japanese or American action or indifference to the safety of non-combatants. David Gray, the American minister, took exception to this implication and wrote to the *Irish Independent* and *Irish Press*; his letter quoted from an Office of War Information telegram from Manila, which detailed the deliberate burning to death of priests by the Japanese. The details were deleted by the censor, leaving just the bald statement that 'the telegram quoted by Mr Gray places sole responsibility for the death on the Japanese forces'. The *Irish Press* published the letter in this form, but the *Independent* refused, having not received Gray's permission to do so (in line with standard journalistic practice). The American press gave extensive coverage to the episode; the *New York Herald Tribune*, for example, ran the story with the heading: 'Éire Censors Distort News of Priests' Deaths – Americans remain suspect in Japanese murders: Envoy's Protest Garbled'.[263]

Gray believed that Aiken was pro-fascist and found it particularly objectionable that censorship policy effectively placed the Americans on the same moral plane as the Nazis and the Japanese. Following the publication in September 1942, of a speech by Cardinal MacRory in which he denounced both Britain and the US for occupying the six counties, Gray sent a letter of protest to de Valera. In reference to the censorship of a pastoral by another bishop which was critical of the Nazis, he complained that the actions of the censor 'in observing one policy toward the publication of sentiments inimical to the Axis powers and another toward the publication of sentiments inimical to the United States, is scarcely observing the benevolent neutrality which Your Excellency proclaimed upon our entry into the war'. Gray was of the opinion that the censorship worked on 'the principle that anything in the remotest way likely to hurt the tenderest susceptibilities of the Axis Ministers in Dublin must be peremptorily banned'[264] and that the 'nucleus of anti-American and anti-British influence in Éire is the censorship group, controlled by Frank Aiken'. John Maffey, the UK representative, did not concur and considered that, on balance, the effect of the censorship was to the benefit of the British. 'Anti-British feeling', he wrote in December 1941, 'was the dynamic of Irish opinion, always there though often latent. Propaganda produces counter-propaganda and the mind of the younger generation, brought up in an age and atmosphere of bitter hostility to England, would respond more rapidly to propaganda directed against us'.[265]

The dissemination of Axis propaganda in Ireland was achieved principally through the publication and distribution of bulletins or news-sheets to the press, politicians and the public. The German legation produced the *Weekly Review of the German News Agency* while the Italians published *Radio Stefani – News from Italy* (*Stefani* was the Fascist news service), also known as *Radio News from Italy* and *Italian News Review*. These publications were tolerated by the authorities so long as they remained within the same 'bounds of decency' defined for the British press.

The German bulletin was put together by Carl Peterson, press attaché at the legation. It had a reputed circulation of about 3,000 and was posted from towns all over the country to people on a mailing list who were expected to pass the material on to neutral friends and use it for 'word-of-mouth' propaganda.[266] Among those on the mailing list of the legation were government ministers, TDs and senators (a list having been supplied to the legation by the pro-German Fianna Fáil TD Dan Breen),[267] army officers, civil servants, Axis or Axis-friendly diplomatic representatives, priests, schoolteachers and creamery managers.[268] An American intelligence report asserted that apart from 'a small group of fanatically anti-British individuals' the effect of printed Axis propaganda was 'practically nil'.[269] The German bulletin had for a time been 'rather objectionable about certain personages' in Britain and the US, but this feature had disappeared following representations made to Hempel by the DEA.[270] Peterson forwarded copies of the bulletin to the Censorship; he had originally asked for it to be censored so that he could then forward it to the papers, stamped by the censor. The Censorship refused and told him to forward the messages to the press and the papers could then submit them in the usual way.[271]

In March 1941 *Radio Stefani* was being sent out 'almost daily'[272] (circulation was about 300[273]) and was becoming objectionable enough for Walshe to summon Berardis, the Italian minister, to his office. He complained to him about two recent issues, one featuring an attack on Jews and another on 'Anglo-American plutocracy'. Walshe told him that such matter constituted interference with Ireland's friendly relations with Britain and the US and was also an insult to the intelligence of the Irish people; 'It was only fit for natives and aborigines', wrote Walshe.[274]

Berardis ignored the requests made to him to tone down the propaganda (the issue of 21 April, for example, referred to Jews as 'these rodents') and in May 1941 Walshe accused him of 'violating the censorship regulations and seriously endangering the neutrality of this country . . . I have now to ask you either to refrain from publishing propaganda bulletins altogether or to submit every issue to the press Censorship before distribution'.[275] On the same day he sent a message to the Irish minister in Rome telling him to contact the Italian foreign office and inform them that while no objection was taken to 'cultural propaganda' or objective news items, Berardis was engaging in violent attacks on the US president, the American people and Jews; he was thus, according to Walshe, violating all the rules of hospitality and neutrality and endangering Irish–Italian friendship.[276] The Italians were asked to instruct Berardis to cease his activities. The foreign office, acknowledging that a minister's first duty was to be 'persona grata with the Government to which he is accredited', duly sent the requisite instruction.[277] Copies of the restrained bulletin were now sent to the Censorship (after publication) so that its excesses could be monitored. *Radio Stefani* ceased publication a year later and was replaced by a six-weekly bulletin on 'cultural matters'.[278]

Despite the 'restraint' which now characterised the Axis bulletins, the British and American representatives visited Walshe in March 1942 to seek the suppression of the German publication. In the course of the discussion Maffey suggested the possibility of withholding newsprint supplies to Ireland if the German bulletin continued to appear. He complained about the size of the bulletins and suggested that to allow them to continue in circulation seemed to go against the principle laid down by de Valera that Ireland would not be allowed to be made a base for any kind of activity against Britain. Walshe responded by showing them bulletins from legations and consulates on the Allied side and pointed particularly to the Belgian bulletin (*Bulletin de Nouvelles*) as being 'incomparably more propagandist and violent than the Axis productions'. He further pointed out that 'our people would consider it strange from the point of view of our neutrality if we suppress the relatively insignificant German propaganda and continue to allow the vast stream of British propaganda to pour into the country'.[279]

Despite his angry rejection of Maffey's and Gray's suggestions, Walshe met separately with Hempel and Berardis the following day. He spoke to them about the paper shortage and asked them to reduce their bulletins as much as possible and to at least use both sides of the paper. He went into detail with Hempel about certain items which had appeared in recent bulletins and advised him strongly against 'writing up the German Youth Movement which was suspect in this country for religious reasons about which I had frequently spoken to him'. Both agreed to shorten their bulletins and to use both sides of the paper.[280]

The Italians occasionally directed radio propaganda to Ireland, focusing on the Catholic connections of the two countries and anti-Catholic discrimination in the North. The latter was a common theme of German transmissions to Ireland throughout the war; others included the evil of partition, British historical crimes against Ireland, warnings about communism, admiration for Gaelic culture (the Germans also broadcast in the Irish language), and encouragement for Irish neutrality.[281] Lord Haw Haw's jibes against the British found an appreciative audience in the early years of the war; German broadcasts in general were listened to more in this period because the Germans were in the ascendant and their reports on the progress of the war were more likely to be truthful, while their promises about abolishing partition seemed like good news to a nationalist audience. As the war turned against Germany, and following the entry of the US, Irish listeners became far less receptive to German broadcasts, and listened more out of curiosity to learn how the once boastful Haw Haw, for example, would explain away the latest Nazi setback.[282] When the Irish writer Francis

Stuart, who broadcast to Ireland from Germany throughout the war, returned to Dublin he discovered that the details of his 'talks' were almost unknown; 'I hardly met anyone who heard me', he said later. 'I don't think anyone really listened.'[283] As the war progressed, the majority of Irish people relied on the 'neutral' news supplied by Radio Éireann, supplemented by the BBC (which also relayed American broadcasts), 'a reflection of the natural desire to get the latest from the horse's mouth, especially from the winning horse's mouth'.[284]

At the meeting between Walshe and the British and American representatives in March 1942, Gray had asked if the DEA would object to the American legation producing a bulletin of its own. Walshe replied that he would be delighted and interested to see one.[285] In the following month Gray wrote to Roosevelt outlining a contingency plan which he had been hatching in the event that Washington decided to seize Irish bases. He suggested that as any invading forces would not have much time to conduct propaganda, some preparations should be made as soon as possible. 'If we get a big propaganda shop going here' he told the president, 'it might very likely prepare things.' In a letter to the director of the OSS (the forerunner of the CIA), William Donovan, some weeks later, Gray explained that there was little chance of propagating the American viewpoint through ordinary Irish channels because Aiken would 'make any propaganda job here a difficult one as he is about as friendly as a disappointed rattlesnake'.[286]

Gray's idea was accepted in Washington and the *American Newsletter* was first published in June 1942,[287] before being replaced on 30 October 1942 by the more extensive *Letter from America*. Each week thereafter Dan Terrell, a press attaché at the legation (formerly a distinguished film and drama critic for the *Washington Herald*) who was attached to the Office of War Information, edited and organised the distribution of the newsletter to people on a mailing list, which grew from 18,000 names at first to about 30,000 by the time the last issue was published in April 1945.[288] Terrell, in a letter to the US, wrote that 'Neutrality is pretty hard to bear, of course, but I do have the pleasure of editing the only paper in Éire which can run cartoons poking fun at Hitler's whisker, Hermann's belly and Tojo's ambitions'![289]

The Americans, of course, never invaded so the newsletter never fulfilled its original 'sinister purpose'.[290] Instead, it set out to, in Gray's words, 'tell the Irish people what their Censorship did not want them to know'.[291] This included articles on Nazi and Japanese tyranny and atrocities; pro-war speeches from prominent Irish-Americans, including members of the Catholic hierarchy and accounts of the heroism of Irish people and Irish-Americans serving with the Allied forces.[292] An Irish journalist, in a censored dispatch to a London press agency in November 1942, described *Letter from America* as 'very popular and effective, and the *Irish Times* front-paged a "lift" from its very first number'. An OSS agent reported in

Letter FROM AMERICA

Vol. II.   No. 48.   September 22, 1944.

CRIMES OF LUBLIN CONDEMNED

9 Congressmen Voice Protest

Nine United States Congressmen have demanded the punishment of those war criminals responsible for the Lublin massacres—by now, except in countries where news censorship exists, common knowledge, and the object of worldwide condemnation and horror.

The Congressmen, all of Polish extraction, are Dingell, Wasielewski, Sadowski, Okonski, Monkiewicz, Lesinski, Mruk, Gordon and Gorski. Their message to Poland follows :

" A few days ago Americans for the first time visited one of the extermination centers which the Nazis built in your country. They were experienced journalists representing the most reliable newspapers in the United States. They examined the human *abattoir* in Lublin. Reports of what they saw have been published by the American press, as well as in London, and by the now liberated French press.

" Our whole nation is horrified by the unparalleled loathsomeness of the crimes which the Nazis perpetrated in that camp. We Congressmen of Polish ancestry are going to demand that the United States Government immediately make investigation of the Lublin camp and all other extermination centers that Hitler and his followers, carrying out the grim prophesies in Hitler's book, *Mein Kampf*, built in Poland. We are going to demand that no stone be left unturned in the Allied effort to obtain the name of every participant in those hideous crimes, that every one of them be tracked down no matter where they may seek a hiding place, and that they be brought to justice and made to pay with their lives for inhuman acts committed on your soil."

As more and more stories of unimaginable degradation and cruelty on the part of the Nazis come out of Poland, there has arrived in the United States a letter addressed to the President of Poland. It was smuggled out from a Warsaw prison cell and was written by a woman detained in the notorious Birkenau concentration camp. Her number was 793,350. Her letter said :

" Hunger and disease, torture and suffering, have been responsible for the death of thousands. But there are things even worse than this— the dehumanization of all.

(*Continued on page* 2.)

New York Bishop Calls for Justice

Bishop William T. Manning, Protestant Episcopal Bishop of New York City, denounced the perpetrators of the crimes of Lublin in these words :

" American public opinion flamed with a new determination as the latest, the most horrifying, the most incontrovertible story of Nazi outrage—*The Story of Lublin*—was told. The sober words of war correspondents, confirmed by a thousand grisly details, shattered the first impulse to disbelieve. Convinced beyond all doubt, outraged America called for iron justice for the perpetrators of the monstrous crime.

" The names of the guilty are noted. Punishment will be meted out.

" Hitler's goal is to involve the entire German nation so completely in his crimes that they must share the destruction that inevitably awaits him and his partners.

" The German people alone can save themselves from such a fate. They must decide to repudiate the insane leadership that has brought them to the present abyss of degradation. By unconditional surrender the German people can and must win their way back to spiritual health which will mean membership in the human family for themselves and generations to come."

A *Washington Post* editorial wrote :

" Horror stories are multiplying with great rapidity as the Allied armies close in on Germany from the west, south and east. Almost every area that is liberated has its own catalogue of atrocities.

From Lublin, Poland, come now well authenticated reports of the systematic mass murders for which the Germans' camp at nearby Maidanek has become infamous the world over, now that the camp is free of the enemy. Reporters visiting it find evidence of slaughter on a scale that leaves them baffled.

Germans are asked to shed their last drop of blood to save the bestial perpetrators of these crimes against humanity from the retribution that awaits them. Germans who have not shared the Nazi bloodlust must see that the war is being prolonged in a frantic effort to save the guilty from just punishment. There can be no other point in continued German resistance. The

(*Continued on page* 2.)

Carreau Has List Of French Victims

Ralph Parker, well-known New York press correspondent, reported recently that a list of 171 Frenchmen, murdered in Lublin's death factory by the Nazis, had been handed over to Roger Carreau, representative of the French Committee of National Liberation in Moscow. Parker said :

" The list, copied from the register of executions which is now in the hands of a mixed Polish-Soviet Commission of Inquiry, only represents a fraction of the French murdered at Lublin.

" It is an extract from a single document recording the names, identification numbers, and the date of death of 600 persons disposed of in one of the many slaughter houses at Lublin during the period of February through April, 1944.

" Paul Masure, who is twenty-sixth on the list, was put to death on February 14, 1944, in the Lublin death camp. His prison identification number is 5,335. Jacques Patis was killed ten days before. His identification number is 5,396. René Buissou was put to death fifteen days later. Identification number, 11,778. Paul Viviet was asphyxiated on April Fifth, identification number 5,175.

" The list could be continued for 150 names The Germans keep lists of people they murder, with the greatest accuracy."

Ed. Wilcox, *Warweek* correspondent, wrote this comment :

" During World War I several stories were widely circulated, informing the world of the bestiality of the German army. One was of Belgian babies with hands cut off by brutal German soldiers. The story was a fake.

" The Nazis in World War II require no fancy press agent's job to shock the world. Their entire effort ' to divide and conquer ' is based on a theory of ruthless extermination of ' inferior races ' which includes the rest of the world.

" The Goebbels radio in Berlin was quick to acknowledge the mass murder of the town of Oradour-sur-Glane, in France, which the Bishop of Limoges denounced. But the Nazis expressed regret that they had ' made a mistake ' and chosen the wrong village. They had intended to ravage Oradour-sur-Vayres, some 15 miles away.

(*Continued on page* 2.)

Thousands of pairs of children's, women's and men's shoes were found in the Lublin murder camp after capture of the city. The shoes were removed from victims for shipment to Germany.

This is one of many cremation ovens at Lublin, Poland, in which the Germans burned bodies of thousands upon thousands of men, women and children from all parts of Europe.

The front page of the US propaganda bulletin *Letter from America,* 22 September 1944, featuring accounts and pictures from the Lublin concentration camp. The bulletin's objective, according to the US minister David Gray, was to 'tell the Irish people what their Censorship did not want them to know'.

the same month that the bulletin was 'splendid and I hear praise of it from many quarters'. He warned, however, that the focus of its propaganda should be 'Nazism and its attack on religion . . . but lay off the Italians, or the effect of News from America [sic] may be greatly lessened by the instinctive subconscious grimace which anti-Italian comment looks from every Irish Catholic mind'.[293] The bulletin was four, occasionally six pages long and sometimes featured a glossy, colour supplement on topics such as women's contribution to the war effort. (The legation also distributed an occasional bulletin called *Medical News from the USA*, which featured articles with titles such as 'Massive-Dose Arsenotheraphy of Early Syphilis'!) The last issue of *Letter From America* on 20 April 1945 carried photographs and reports of plans for a German invasion of Ireland which were discovered by Allied troops in Brussels.[294]

The Censorship received complaints from individuals who had received the bulletin in the post; one objected to the fact that 'citizens of a neutral country should be the subject of such propagandist communications', while another protested against the American legation being permitted to open 'an Office of War Information of the USA in a neutral country'.[295] Despite such representations, the authorities made no attempt to interfere with the dissemination of the newsletter.

The propaganda activities of the various legations and consulates were, however, constantly monitored. In February 1941 copies of the Belgian fortnightly *Bulletin de Nouvelles* and the weekly *Nouvelles de France* were sent to the Censorship by the post office. The French bulletin was regarded as unobjectionable but the Belgian publication was objected to on the basis of its 'recruitment efforts for the Belgian forces abroad'; it was arranged that future copies be sent to the Censorship by the post office for examination.[296] The extensive surveillance carried out by G2 (Military Intelligence) on the activities of the German legation included the monitoring of its propaganda activities, and the DEA was kept informed of the details of its production and distribution.[297] In January 1942 Dan Bryan of G2 informed Walshe of the posting in Dublin of 4,000 copies of Hitler's speech of 11 December 1941 declaring war on the US (accompanied by copies of a speech given by Von Ribbentrop).[298] On 13 December the German legation had complained that Hitler's speech, with one exception, 'was reproduced in the Irish papers in a completely mutilated and insufficient form' and was hardly mentioned in the *Irish Press* despite the fact that Peterson, the press attaché, had made the complete official text available to them. A comparatively unimportant speech (according to the legation) by Churchill on the same day was reproduced in relative detail.[299]

Among the other bulletins sent out by diplomatic representatives in Dublin were the monthly *Swedish News*, made up of items from the Swedish International Press Bureau,[300] and a fortnightly *Press Circular* issued by the office of the Canadian high commissioner. From mid-October 1942 the Chilean consulate sent a weekly bulletin issued by the embassy in London to the DEA, while a Czech propaganda bulletin, issued periodically, was allowed so long as 'discretion' was used in its circulation.[301]

Five hundred copies of the British propagandist bulletin *King-Hall Letter* were sent directly to subscribers, as were a small number of *Foreign Affairs*, the journal published by the Imperial Policy Group.[302] However, the British did not have to rely on such methods for getting their message across. The propaganda work of the British representatives in Ireland was made considerably easier by the open sale and wide availability of English newspapers, the reception of the BBC and the reliance of Irish papers on British news sources. 'It was an article of faith to most British propagandists', according to Robert Cole, 'that straight news was the essential foundation upon which all other propaganda was built';[303] news, according to the British Minister of Information in 1940, John Reith, was 'the shocktroops of propaganda'.[304] The putting over of British propaganda themes in neutral countries was principally the task of the press attachés 'who were responsible for making use of the various available channels' and advised the Ministry of Information 'concerning the apparent effect on public opinion of their dissemination work and of political and military developments'.[305]

The press attaché at the office of the UK representative in Dublin from January 1941 until August 1943 was John Betjeman, who was later to become the British poet laureate. He developed a keen interest in Gaelic poetry and exchanged letters on this and other subjects of mutual interest with Coyne, with whom he established a friendly relationship. He began to sign himself 'Seán Ó Betjeman, attasé na press' (!) and used Gaelic script and Irish language phrases such as 'A Chara' and 'Is mise, le meas' in his letters.[306] 'By this time next year', he concluded a letter to Coyne in September 1942, 'my letters will be wholly in Irish if I am alive.'[307]

Betjeman supplied the Irish press with Ministry of Information propaganda circulars, including extracts from Radio Vatican broadcasts, items from the press in Sweden and other neutrals, and, in general, material which suited British propaganda purposes in Ireland.[308] One of his chief duties in this regard was to persuade the Irish that the German 'new order' was anti-Christian. He believed that *Picture Post* and the *Universe* (Catholic) newspapers were his best methods of persuasion and asked London to persuade the editor of the *Universe* to publish straightforward illustrated articles on the persecution of Polish Catholics by the Nazis. He also made 'great friends' with Peter O'Curry, editor of the influential Catholic *Standard*, and set out to persuade him of Nazi anti-Christianity and to steer him away from the anti-British slant taken in his paper.[309]

Visiting lecturers were 'always considered to be an important propaganda channel';[310] the most useful medium for the British in this regard in Ireland was the Irish Institute of International Affairs. While its lectures and meetings were not given wide coverage in the press, the propagandist intention was to appeal to the 'influential few' who would attend. Among those who lectured to meetings of the institute were Count Jan Balinski of the Polish government in exile[311] and Professor Henry Steele Commager, an American historian who lectured in Cambridge during the war; the latter took the opportunity of his visit to Dublin to write a long indictment of Irish neutrality for the *New York Times* magazine.[312] G2 monitored the activities of the institute; one report noted that 'while Neutrality is paid lip service as being Government policy, the bulk of the audience at these meetings were pro-British in sentiment'. While its meetings were regarded as generally 'harmless and open' concern was expressed at the extent to which visiting lecturers carried away with them the views of pro-Allied stalwarts of the institute such as senators Donal O'Sullivan and Frank MacDermot as representing educated Irish opinion, including the belief that censorship stifled the public expression of pro-Allied feeling.[313] By 1943 the government's tolerance of the institute's activities began to diminish. Balinski, who had visited Ireland and lectured on two previous occasions, had intended to come for a third time in January 1943. However, when the Polish embassy in London applied for a visa on his behalf they were informed by the Irish high commissioner's office that permission would not be granted. In May 1943 Monsignor Kuchar, a representative of the Royal Yugoslav government, was similarly dissuaded,[314] and on 15 June, three days before Senór de Madariaga was due to lecture, External Affairs informed the institute that: 'There are difficulties about bringing foreigners into this country for the purpose of giving lectures, and it would perhaps be better to consult the Department before issuing invitations in future'.[315] The failure to follow this procedure was used to justify the controversial banning of a lecture to the institute by Dr Jan Masaryk, deputy prime minister and foreign minister of the Czech government in exile, in October 1944.

As Masaryk was already in the country and had shared a platform with de Valera at a meeting of the Trinity College Historical Society a few days previously,[316] the case inevitably generated controversy. In his reply to charges made by Patrick McGilligan in the Dáil, de Valera made clear that the target of the government's action was the institute and not Masaryk. He took the opportunity to declare it 'a focus of propaganda devoted entirely to furthering and encouraging a particular point of view in relation to the present war'.[317] He further accused the institute of creating 'a succession of difficulties and embarrassment, positively harmful to our relations with other Governments and to the impression of this country which we would wish them to have'. As an example he cited a meeting held arising out of the Masaryk ban to which the diplomatic corps were invited, only to find themselves 'attending an organised protest against the action of the Government', thus bringing the latter into disrepute and creating embarrassment for it in its external relations.[318] The Censorship played its part in the episode by suppressing all press notices announcing the voidance of the meeting. The *Irish Times* was stopped on three successive days from draw-ing attention to 'l'affaire Masaryk',[319] while interviews with him in the *Independent* and the *Standard* were prohibited;[320] a *Bell* editorial on the affair was also stopped.[321]

British influence in Ireland extended far beyond the press, of course, and 'the totality of the relationship' (to borrow a phrase from more recent history) between the countries was exploited to the full by the British. In July 1941, for example, a letter was intercepted *en route* to the Gaiety Theatre from England regarding the sending over of Sybil Thorndike and Lewis Casson to perform in a number of plays (*Macbeth, Medea, King John*) 'for good-will propaganda purposes'.[322] The visit had been suggested by the British Council, the British cultural propaganda organisation, whose task was 'to rally allies, neutrals and other friends by explaining British life and thought'.[323] Socially as well as culturally the British scored. Maffey maintain-ed constant contact with sympathetic prominent figures like *Irish Times* editor Bertie Smyllie and Fine Gael TD James Dillon, while all the Allied represen-tatives were 'generally fêted in Dublin'. The Axis representatives, in contrast, were ostracised in the social circles in which such people usually moved; they were generally only entertained at official functions.[324] One such occasion in March 1944 was the cause of some controversy involving the Censorship.

The Irish Red Cross had circularised the various missions about a *céilidh* which it was holding in Dublin on St Patrick's Day. There was no response from the American legation, but the German and Japanese representatives purchased tickets and attended the function. Amidst the American press hysteria surrounding the American Note episode, Gray told an Associated Press correspondent, Robert Green ('off the record', according to the minister) that the government had 'deliberately slighted' the US government by not inviting an American representative to a function at which the German minister and the Japanese consul were both guests. The Red Cross rejected the allegation as did the American legation. An unpublished portion of Green's report had described de Valera's furious reaction when he received the note from Gray, a description which could only have come from the latter. The *Irish Press* ran an editorial entitled 'Denial Needed' which stated that either Green had falsified the report or Gray was guilty of undiplomatic behaviour. T.F. O'Higgins of Fine Gael attacked the government in the Dáil for having used the *Press* to give 'offence to the Minister of a friendly country in our capital and provocation to a friendly country', and the Censorship for having passed the editorial. Aiken claimed that the editorial was not stopped because it was considered that the only person to whom it could have given offence was the reporter. The Associated Press revealed that the American minister had been the source, but the latter, having denied it, refused to comment further; he was happy, he revealed to Roosevelt, that the episode gave the opposition an opportunity to attack de Valera 'for af-fronting the representative of a friendly power'.[325]

NOTES AND REFERENCES

1   NA, D/J, Press Censorship Monthly Reports, September 1939.
2   MA, OCC 7/20, Censorship to all government departments, 14 September 1939 and replies from each department.
3   NA, D/J, Directions to the Press; NA, D/T, S 11586A, Directions to the Press, 16 Septembr 1939.
4   NA, D/J, 'Press Conferences, 1939': reports on the meeting of 19 September 1939.
5   NA, D/T, S 11306, Connolly to de Valera, 19 September 1939.
6   NA, D/J, 'Press Conferences, 1939'.
7   NA, D/FA (Sec.) A 8, 'Memo on Dublin News Routine and Sources', United Press to C.T. Hallinan, 14 February 1941.
8   Eunan O'Halpin, 'Aspects of Intelligence', *The Irish Sword*, Vol. XIX, Nos. 75 and 76, 1993–4, p. 59.
9   NA, D/T, S 11445/8, Coyne memo on censorship, September 1945.
10 NA, D/J, No. 3, *Irish Times*, Connolly to Aiken, 19 September 1940.
11 NA, D/J, R 62, 'Correspondence with Army H.Q.', Knightly to McCall, 4 June 1942.
12 MA, OCC 2/86, 'Military Liaison Officer', Coyne to McCall, June 1943.
13 NA, D/T, S 9559A, Knightly to Connolly, 20 November 1939; Connolly to Aiken, 20 November 1939; Gallagher to Aiken, 30 November 1939; MA, OCC 2/38, Coyne to Knightly, 23 November 1939; Connolly to Knightly, 30 November 1939.
14 MA, OCC 2/64, 'News Items Broadcast by Radio Éireann', correspondence and memoranda, 1940–43; NA, D/J, Press Censorship Reviews: 'Work of the Censorship'.
15 Douglas Gageby, 'The Media, 1945–70' in J.J. Lee (ed.), *Ireland, 1945–70* (Dublin, 1979), pp. 124–5; Maurice Gorham, *Forty Years of Irish Broadcasting* (Dublin, 1967), pp. 130–3.
16 Fintan O'Toole, 'Our second World War finally comes to an end', *Irish Times*, 10 February 1995.
17 *Dublin Opinion*, July 1940, p. 539.
18 Maurice Gorham, *Broadcasting*, pp. 130–3; NA, D/J, Press Censorship Monthly Reports, October 1942
19 MA, OCC 2/102, Coyne to Boland, 7 August 1942.
20 R.M. Smyllie, 'Unneutral Neutral Éire', *Foreign Affairs*, Vol. 24, No. 2, January 1946, p. 324.
21 J.J. Lee, *Ireland 1912–1985: Politics and Society* (Cambridge, 1989) p. 244.
22 NA, D/J, Press Censorship Reviews: 'Work of the Censorship'.
23 Gorham, *Broadcasting*, p. 130.
24 Gageby, 'Media', p. 125.
25 *Irish Times*, 21 May 1945.
26 Discussion with John de Courcy-Ireland, August 1995.
27 NA, D/J, Press Censorship Reviews: 'Work of the Censorship'.
28 *Dáil Debates*, Vol. 77, cols. 316–17, 27 September 1939.
29 NA, D/J, No. 5A, *Cork Examiner*, proof deletion, 26 January 1945; NA, D/J, 'Instructions to Press Censors', 1 February 1945. The British censorship imposed the same restrictions on press reports of the weather. By the summer of 1940, with the Germans occupying the French coast, there seemed little purpose in continuing to ban reports of conditions in the Straits of Dover and an exception was made for this area up to and including the foreshore. This resulted in inordinate press interest in weather conditions there, particularly when there was exceptional weather in another part of the country. One London court report quoted a judge as announcing: 'It's very cold in the Straits of Dover this morning. The court is adjourned.' (George P. Thompson, *Blue Pencil Admiral: The Inside Story of the Press Censorship* (London, 1947), p. 48.)

30 Tim Pat Coogan, *De Valera: Long Fellow, Long Shadow* (London, 1993), p. 749.
31 Lee, *Ireland*, p. 244.
32 NA, D/FA (Sec.) A 11, John Betjeman to the DEA and OCC, August 1941, Walshe to Connolly, 7 May 1941.
33 MA, OCC 2/102, Coyne to Boland, 7 August 1942.
34 NA, D/J, Press Censorship Monthly Reports, June 1944.
35 John P. Duggan, *Neutral Ireland and the Third Reich* (Dublin, 1989), p. 156.
36 T. Ryle Dwyer, *Strained Relations: Ireland at Peace and the USA at War, 1941–45* (Dublin, 1988), pp. 87–8.
37 NA, D/FA (Sec.) A 26, memo, 30 January 1942, Walshe minutes, 10 May 1943.
38 Dwyer, *Strained Relations*, pp. 87–8.
39 NA, D/J, 'Directions to the Press', 'Instructions to Press Censors', and general files.
40 Lee, *Ireland*, p. 243.
41 Dermot Keogh and Aengus Nolan, 'Anglo-Irish Diplomatic Relations and World War II', *The Irish Sword*, Vol. XIX, Nos. 75 and 76, p. 119, quoting Dominions Secretary, Lord Cranborne.
42 Joseph T. Carroll, *Ireland in the War Years, 1939–1945* (Newton Abbot, 1975), p. 92.
43 NA, D/J, Press Censorship Reviews: *Irish Independent*.
44 NA, D/J, 'Instructions to Press Censors', 31 March 1942.
45 NA, D/J, Press Censorship Reviews: 'Work of the Censorship'.
46 MA, OCC 7/58, 'Notes for the Minister', 1942.
47 MA, OCC 2/57, 'Control of advertisements offering rationed commodities for sale'.
48 NA, D/J, Press Censorship Reviews: 'Work of the Censorship'.
49 NA, D/J, 'Instructions to Press Censors', October–November 1941.
50 Carroll, *War Years*, p. 92.
51 NA, D/J, Unnumbered, 'Attacks on Ships, etc.' and 'Instructions to Press Censors'.
52 Frank Forde, *The Long Watch: The History of the Irish Mercantile Marine in World War Two* (Dublin, 1981), pp. 141–2.
53 NA, D/J, Instructions to Press Censors, 10 November 1941.
54 Carroll, *War Years*, p. 91.
55 Lee, *Ireland*, p. 253.
56 ibid.
57 MA, OCC 2/37, 'Seizure of the *Enniscorthy Echo*, 21 September 1940'.
58 NA, D/J, 'Instructions to Press Censors', 3 October 1940.
59 ibid., 20 December 1940.
60 ibid., 4 January 1941; Press Censorship Monthly Reports, January 1941.
61 For details of German espionage in Ireland see Enno Stephan, *Spies in Ireland* (London, 1965); Carolle J. Carter, *The Shamrock and the Swastika: German Espionage in Ireland in World War Two* (California, 1977) and Duggan, *Neutral Ireland*.
62 NA D/J, Press Censorship Monthly Reports, July 1940.
63 *Dáil Debates*, Vol. 86, cols. 36–8 (24 March 1942) and cols. 2286–8 (2 July 1942).
64 Coogan, *De Valera*, p. 603.
65 NA, D/J, R 26, 'Censorship of Press Matter Relating to the American Note'; Monthly Reports and 'Instructions to Press Censors', February–April 1944.
66 See Dwyer, *Strained Relations*, pp. 118–45.
67 *Seanad Debates*, Vol. 24, cols. 2614–5, 4 December 1940.
68 *Dáil Debates*, Vol. 85, col. 1745, 4 February 1942.
69 *Seanad Debates*, Vol. 28, col. 759, 27 January 1942.
70 NA, D/J, 'Instructions to Press Censors', 14 September 1940.
71 NA, D/T, S 11586, 'Neutrality, Censorship and Democracy', 23 January 1940.
72 Smyllie, 'Unneutral Neutral Éire', p. 322.
73 *Seanad Debates*, Vol. 24, col. 2609, 4 December 1940.
74 NA, D/J, Press Censorship Reviews: *Irish Times*.

75 NA, D/J, R 14, 'Irish Church Dignitaries'.
76 MA, OCC 2/73, 'Armistice Day ('Poppy Day')'. There was also a ban on the carrying of unfurled banners with Union emblems, the wearing of uniforms and the display of all distinctive emblems except the poppy.
77 *Irish Times,* 3 July 1962; MA, OCC 7/47, Aiken direction, 29 September 1941; NA, D/J, 'Instructions to Press Censors', 24 July 1941, Direction to the Press, 26 July 1941.
78 NA, D/J, 'Instructions to Press Censors', Coyne to Aiken, 3 March 1942.
79 NA, D/J, No. 3, *Irish Times*, Censorship to *Irish Times*, 4 February 1940. Aiken wanted the name of the organisation changed, arguing that it was either 'royal' or 'national', but could not be both (Dermot Keogh, *Twentieth-Century Ireland: Nation and State* (Dublin, 1994), p. 126).
80 NA, D/J, No. 4, *Evening Mail*, Coyne to Connolly, 10 April 1940.
81 Smyllie, 'Unneutral Neutral Éire, p. 320.
82 T. Ryle Dwyer, *Irish Neutrality and the USA, 1939-1947* (Dublin, 1977), p. 19.
83 Trevor Salmon, *Unneutral Ireland: An Ambivalent and Unique Security Policy* (Oxford, 1989), p. 130.
84 Robert Fisk, *In Time of War: Ireland, Ulster and the Price of Neutrality, 1939-45* (London, 1985), pp. 112-13.
85 As with other subjects covered by the censorship, it is possible to find references to people from the North who fought in the war in the papers of the time. This is due to either oversight or possibly leniency on the part of censors, or non-submission on the part of the newspaper.
86 *Dáil Debates*, Vol. 96, col. 2380.
87 NA, D/J, No. 3, *Irish Times*, Smyllie to de Valera, 23 November 1943.
88 ibid., Smyllie to Coyne, November 1942.
89 ibid., Coyne to Smyllie, 23 November 1943.
90 NA, D/T, S 12381, OCC 'Note for the Minister' on censorship debate, March 1941.
91 NA, D/J, Press Censorship Monthly Reports, August 1941.
92 NA, D/J, Press Censorship Reviews: *Sunday Independent; Irish Times*, 26 May 1945.
93 NA, D/J, ibid., *Irish Independent*, Connolly to Geary, 24 December 1940.
94 Lee, *Ireland*, pp. 226-30.
95 MA, OCC 2/126, Ferguson to Censorship, 7 October 1941, Coyne to press censors, 7 October 1941, and EP (No. 24) O 1942.
96 MA, OCC 7/58, 'Notes for the Minister', 1942.
97 NA, D/J, No. 20, *Torch*, Coyne to DEA, 22 May 1943.
98 NA, D/FA 214/55, stopped for *Irish Times*, 2 December 1943.
99 NA, D/T, S 12381, OCC 'Note for the Minister' on censorship debate, March 1941.
100 NA, D/J, No. 199, Coyne, 23 August 1943; Aiken, August 1943.
101 MA, OCC 5/31, Coyne direction, 23 June 1942.
102 MA, OCC 2/56, May 1941.
103 MA, OCC 2/153, Aiken to Childers, 21 March 1944.
104 NA, D/J, No. 30, *Leader*, Coyne to Aiken, 26 May 1940.
105 NA, D/J, No. 3, *Irish Times*, Coyne to Aiken, 13 September 1940.
106 ibid., Connolly to Aiken, 18 September 1940.
107 MA, OCC 2/44, Coyne to Aiken, 3 December 1940.
108 NA, D/J, No. 3, *Irish Times*, Coyne to Smyllie, 25 April 1941.
109 ibid., Newman to Coyne, 28 August 1941, and Coyne to Newman, 29 August 1941.
110 *Seanad Debates*, Vol. 25, col. 363, 29 January 1941.
111 NA, D/J, No. 3, *Irish Times*, Aiken ruling, December 1939.
112 NA, D/J, 'Instructions to Press Censors', 15 July 1942 and 4 June 1943.
113 NA, D/J, No. 3, *Irish Times*, correspondence, September 1944.
114 NA, D/J, No. 5A, *Cork Examiner*, Coyne to *Examiner*, 6 February 1942.

115 NA, D/J, Press Censorship Reviews: *Irish Independent*, Coyne to Geary, 5 August 1943.
116 ibid.
117 Nicholas Pronay, 'The News Media at War', in Nicholas Pronay and D.W. Spring (eds.), *Propaganda, Politics and Film, 1918–45* (London, 1982), pp. 176–8.
118 Michael Balfour, *Propaganda in War 1939–1945: Organisations, Policies and Publics in Britain and Germany* (London, 1979), p. 431 quoting Goebbels on the *Times* (London).
119 Philip M. Taylor, 'Censorship in Britain in the Second World War: An Overview', in A.C. Duke and C.A. Tamse (eds.), *Too Mighty to be Free: Censorship and the Press in Britain and the Netherlands* (Zutphen, 1987), p. 174.
120 NA, D/J, Unnumbered, 'Matter stopped – "For Ireland Only"'.
121 NA, D/T, S 11445/8, Coyne memo on censorship, September 1945.
122 Balfour, *Propaganda in War*, p. 201.
123 NA, D/J, No. 2, *Irish Independent*, Coyne to Geary, 16 October 1943.
124 NA, D/J, Press Censorship Monthly Reports, October 1940.
125 NA, D/J, Press Censorship Reviews: *Sunday Independent*, Coyne to Legge, August 1943.
126 NA, D/J, No. 2, *Irish Independent*, Coyne to Geary, 17 February 1944.
127 NA, D/J, Press Censorship Monthly Reports, general and July 1944.
128 NA, D/J, R25, *Sunday Independent*, stopped and deleted proofs, 16 March 1943.
129 NA, D/J, R24, *Standard*, stopped and deleted proofs, 24 October 1944.
130 NA, D/J, R25, *Sunday Independent*, stopped and deleted proofs, 8 August 1942.
131 NA, D/J, Press Censorship Monthly Reports and 'Instructions to Press Censors', April–May 1941.
132 NA, D/J, Press Censorship Monthly Reports, June 1940.
133 ibid., December 1940.
134 ibid., July 1943.
135 MA, OCC 7/3, *Glasgow Herald*, 7 January 1944, 'Éire's Rigid Wartime Censorship'.
136 Phillip Knightley, *The First Casualty: The War Correspondent as Hero, Propagandist, and Myth Maker from Crimea to Vietnam* (London, 1975), p. 321.
137 NA, D/J, Press Censorship Reviews: *Irish Independent*, Coyne to Geary, 21 February 1944.
138 Knightley, *First Casualty*, p. 304.
139 ibid.
140 NA, D/J, Press Censorship Monthly Reports, November 1942.
141 Knightley, *First Casualty*, pp. 304–8.
142 NA, D/J, Press Censorship Monthly Reports, August 1944.
143 NA, D/J, Press Censorship Reviews: *Sunday Independent*; R 25, *Sunday Independent*, stopped and deleted proofs.
144 Knightley, *First Casualty*, pp. 244 and 245.
145 NA, D/J, No. 5A, *Cork Examiner*, Censorship to Manager, 5 November 1943, and R 61, 'Matter Submitted to the Minister'.
146 Knightley, *First Casualty*, p. 246.
147 NA, D/J, R 25, *Sunday Independent*, stopped and deleted proofs, 2 October 1942.
148 NA, D/J, Press Censorship Monthly Reports, February 1941.
149 ibid., general.
150 NA, D/J, 'Instructions to Press Censors', 5 January 1944.
151 NA, D/J, Press Censorship Monthly Reports, general.
152 Maurice Moynihan (ed.), *Speeches and Statements by Eamon de Valera, 1917–73* (Dublin, 1980), p. 462.
153 NA, D/J, 'Instructions to Press Censors', Coyne to Press Censors, 16 December 1941.
154 Moynihan (ed.), *Speeches*, p. 405.

155   NA, D/J, Press Censorship Monthly Reports, January 1942.
156   NA, D/J, Reports, Instructions, etc.
157   NA, D/J, Press Censorship Monthly Reports, January 1942.
158   ibid., October 1942.
159   ibid., June 1944.
160   NA, D/J, 'Instructions to Press Censors', 11 June 1944. The United Nations were the Allies.
161   ibid., 14 July 1944.
162   NA, D/J, Press Censorship Monthly Reports, July 1944.
163   NA, D/J, 'Instructions to Press Censors', 12 July 1944, 14 July 1944 and 4 August 1944.
164   NA, D/J, Reports, Instructions, R series (stopped and deleted proofs).
165   NA, D/FA (Sec.) A 63, 'Italian Legation and Colony', Baron Confalonieri to Walshe, 11 May 1945.
166   NA, D/J, Press Censorship Monthly Reports, May 1945.
167   MA, OCC 2/150, McDonnell to UPA, April 1945.
168   NLI, Frank Gallagher Papers, MS 18,334, Sweetman to Gray, 24 April 1945.
169   *Irish Press*, 1 April 1943, from Lee, *Ireland*, p. 266. Lee points out that this was the self-same *Irish Press* whose reluctance to 'inflame passions' was such that in April 1943 it had revealed that 'there is no kind of oppression visited on any minority in Europe which the Six County nationalists have not also endured'.
170   MA, OCC 2/42, Coyne to Chief Press Censor and staff, 20 October 1942.
171   NA, D/J, R 30 'Atrocities'.
172   NA, D/J, R 31 'Katyn Massacre, 1943'.
173   Fisk, *In Time of War*, interview with Aiken, 12 April 1979, p. 419.
174   NA, D/J, R 30 'Atrocities'; quote from Lee, *Ireland*, p. 266, referring to the concealment on the part of the Censorship of the secret co-operation with Britain.
175   Knightley, *First Casualty*, pp. 293-4.
176   ibid.
177   MA, OCC 2/150, *Cork Examiner*, 28 February 1945 and *Free Press, Wexford*, 6 March 1945 ('Stopped').
178   MA, OCC 2/150, 'Irish missionaries in the Far East'; *Irish Press*, 18 March 1945.
179   MA, OCC 2/150, ibid.
180   NLI, Frank Gallagher Papers, MS 18,334, Sweetman to Gray, 24 April 1945.
181   Lee, *Ireland*, p. 266.
182   MA, OCC 2/150, contained in telegram from Washington Legation, 26 April 1945.
183   MA, OCC 2/150, e.g. *Westmeath Examiner*, 19 May 1945: 'Irish Priests Were Burnt Alive By Japanese'; *Donegal Vindicator*, 19 May 1945: 'Seventy Two Religious Slaughtered By Japanese – Irish Priests Murdered'.
184   MA, OCC 2/150, *Manchester Guardian*, 21 May 1945; *Daily Mail*, 15 May 1945.
185   MA, OCC 2/150, *Manchester Guardian*, 21 May 1945: 'Priests Burned By Japanese – Éire Condemnation'.
186   Dwyer, *Strained Relations*, p. 167.
187   MA, OCC 2/150, McDonnell to UPA, 26 April 1945 ('Stopped').
188   Jon Bridgman, *The End of the Holocaust: The Liberation of the Camps* (London, 1990), pp. 17–20 and p. 30.
189   Brian Inglis, West Briton (London, 1962), p. 66; Hubert Butler, letter to the *Irish Times*, 14 December 1978.
190   Anonymous letter, *Irish Times*, 16 May 1945.
191   MA, OCC 2/150, McDonnell to UPA, April 1945 (Censor's additions).
192   MA, OCC 2/66, Coyne to de Valera, 30 July 1941.
193   MA, OCC 2/55, 'Requests to Booksellers to refrain from exhibiting or to withdraw from sale copies of particular publications'.
194   MA, OCC 2/66, Coyne to de Valera, 30 July 1941.

195 MA, OCC 2/55, Coyne to Eason, 13 May 1941.
196 ibid., minutes of meeting with Booksellers, November 1941.
197 ibid.
198 MA, OCC 5/37, 'Action taken under Article 4 of EP (No. 151) O 1942', July 1942 and December 1943; NA, D/J, No. 197, 'Miscellaneous Correspondence', July and October 1942.
199 MA, OCC 5/41, Coyne direction, 3 September 1942.
200 MA, OCC 2/66, Coyne to Attorney General, 26 August 1941.
201 ibid., correspondence and memos.
202 MA, OCC 5/27, Coyne to Brady, 31 October 1941.
203 Emergency Powers (No. 151) Order 1942 (Government Publications, Stationery Office, 1942).
204 MA, OCC 2/129, 'Political Pamphlets', March 1943.
205 MA, OCC 2/143, Coyne to Aiken, 18 January 1944.
206 MA, OCC 2/120, 'Seizure of document entitled *Genuine Irish Old Moore's Almanac, 1943*'; *Dáil Debates*, Vol. 89, col. 362, 3 February 1943.
207 NA, D/J, No. 176, *Old Moore's Almanac.*
208 MA, OCC 2/120, Coyne to Aiken, 20 September 1944.
209 ibid., censorship of proofs of 1945 edition, Aiken note accompanying same.
210 *Wolfe Tone Annual*, Supplement to reprinted 1944 edition (1945).
211 ibid.
212 NA, D/J, No. 21, '*Saoirse Éireann – Wolfe Tone Weekly* and *Wolfe Tone Annual,*' Coyne to Aiken, 1 December 1943.
213 *Wolfe Tone Annual*, Supplement to reprinted 1944 edition (1945).
214 *Dáil Debates*, Vol. 91, col. 2071, 11 November 1943.
215 ibid.
216 *Seanad Debates*, Vol. 28, col. 729, 27 January 1944.
217 MA, OCC 2/143, Browne and Nolan Ltd to Censorship, 18 June 1943.
218 ibid., Coyne to Aiken, 18 January 1944.
219 ibid., Coyne to Browne and Nolan Ltd, 29 June 1943.
220 *Seanad Debates*, Vol. 28, cols. 723–39, 27 January 1944.
221 MA, OCC 2/143, Purcell to Geary, 17 November 1943; Geary to Censorship, 18 November 1943.
222 *Seanad Debates*, Vol. 28, col. 711, 27 January 1944.
223 ibid., col. 762.
224 ibid., cols. 758–9.
225 ibid., Vol. 28, cols. 851–935, 24 February 1944.
226 NA, D/J, Press Censorship Reviews: *Sunday Independent.*
227 MA, OCC 2/58, 'Reviews of books of a propagandist nature'.
228 NA, D/J, Press Censorship Reviews: *Irish Independent; Dáil Debates*, Vol. 85, cols. 1982–4, 18 February 1942.
229 MA, OCC 2/58, Coyne to Aiken, 18 October 1941.
230 NA, D/J, Press Censorship Reviews: *Irish Times*; Tony Gray, *Mr Smyllie, Sir* (Dublin, 1991), p. 156.
231 Gray, *Smyllie*, p. 156.
232 NA, D/J, Press Censorship Reviews: *Irish Times.*
233 NA, D/J, R 19, 'Book Reviews (stopped and deleted proofs)'.
234 MA, OCC 7/24, DEA to Censorship, 28 October 1939.
235 ibid., Duff (Justice) to Censorship, 28 October 1939.
236 MA, OCC 5/17, Censorship memo on EP (No. 151) O 1942, January 1942.
237 MA, OCC 2/55, correspondence with the DEA, 29 August 1940 and 30 August 1940.
238 MA, OCC 5/27, Censorship memo, January 1942.
239 MA, OCC 5/17, Coyne to Attorney General's office, 9 December 1941.

240 NA, D/J, S 1/42, 'Anti-British Propaganda Committee'.
241 MA, OCC 5/27, Censorship memo, 18 February 1942.
242 MA, OCC 5/41, directions authorising seizure of certain documents, 1 October 1942.
243 MA, OCC 5/37, Coyne to President, Drapers' Chamber of Trade, 9 December 1943.
244 MA, OCC 7/24, memo, 18 November 1942.
245 MA, OCC 7/25, Walshe to Connolly, 17 Ocotober 1939.
246 MA, OCC 7/25, Connolly to Walshe, 25 Ocotober 1939.
247 MA, OCC 2/32, Coyne to Boland, November 1942.
248 MA, OCC 2/43, Boland to Coyne, 13 January 1941.
249 ibid., Berardis to the DEA, 30 December 1940.
250 ibid., Boland to Coyne, 13 January 1941.
251 NA, D/FA (Sec.) P 51, German Legation *Aide-Mémoire*, 13 December 1941.
252 NA, D/FA (Sec.) P 51, 'Report on the *Irish Press* for the month of April 1941'.
253 NA, D/FA (Sec.) P 51, memo, 12 August 1940.
254 NA, D/FA, 216/303, Aiken note following complaints from Hempel.
255 This showed how much things had changed at the *Irish Press* from its early days
     when among the directions given to subeditors by the founding editor Frank
     Gallagher were: 'Do not use agency headlines . . . ' and 'Be on your guard against
     the habits of British and foreign news agencies who look at the world mainly through
     imperialist eyes'. (NLI, Frank Gallagher Papers, MS 18361 (3), undated.)
256 NA, D/FA (Sec.) P 51, Boland to Walshe, 16 May 1941.
257 NA, D/FA 214/55, Hempel to the DEA, 25 March 1944.
258 NA, D/FA 205/84, Boland to Walshe, 14 August 1944.
259 ibid., Walshe to Boland, 16 August 1944.
260 Lee, *Ireland*, p. 253; Duggan, *Neutral Ireland*, p. 225.
261 MA, OCC 2/32, Coyne to Aiken, 2 November 1942; Coyne to Boland, 3 November
     1942.
262 NA, D/FA 205/84, complaints from foreign representatives in Ireland regarding
     misrepresentations in Irish newspapers.
263 MA, OCC 2/150, 'Irish missionaries in the Far East'.
264 F.D. Roosevelt Library, New York, David Gray Papers, 'Ireland', 'Censorship in
     Eire', undated (probably 1942).
265 Dwyer, *Strained Relations*, pp. 52–7.
266 USNA, Office of Strategic Services (OSS), Regular files, 30131, report on Axis pro-
     paganda in Ireland, November 1942.
267 NA, D/FA (Sec) A 8(1), G2 memo, 8 March 1943.
268 NA, D/FA (Sec.) P 36, Bryan to Walshe, 16 January 1942.
269 USNA, OSS (Regular) 30131, report on Axis propaganda in Ireland, November 1942.
270 NA, D/FA (Sec.) P 36, Walshe memo, 31 March 1942.
271 ibid., Coyne note, 3 April 1941.
272 ibid., Bryan note, March 1941.
273 USNA, OSS (Regular) 30131, report on Axis propaganda in Ireland, November 1942.
274 NA, D/FA (Sec.) P 36, Walshe memo, 1 April 1941.
275 ibid., Walshe to Berardis, 7 May 1941.
276 ibid., Walshe to MacWhite, 7 May 1941.
277 ibid., Rome Legation to the DEA, 12 May 1941 and 16 May 1941.
278 MA, OCC 2/118, 'Note on Bulletins', November 1942.
279 NA, D/FA (Sec.) P 36, Walshe memo, 31 March 1942.
280 ibid., Walshe memo, 1 April 1942.
281 Fisk, *In Time of War*, pp. 381–407.
282 USNA, OSS (Regular), 30131, report on Axis propaganda in Ireland, November 1942.
283 Fisk, *In Time of War*, p. 407
284 USNA, OSS (Regular), 30131, report on Axis propaganda in Ireland, November 1942.

285 NA, D/FA (Sec.) P 36, Walshe memo, 31 March 1942.
286 This is a reference to what Gray saw as Aiken's bitterness at the failure of his 1941 mission to America. The American minister believed that Aiken was now deliberately exercising a malign influence on the Irish government's attitude to the Allies out of pure spite (Dwyer, *Strained Relations*, pp. 48–49).
287 MA, OCC 2/118, 'Note on Bulletins', November 1942.
288 Copy for the bulletin came from London, by post, telegraph and in the legation pouch. In July 1943 Terrell requested the Irish authorities for permission to get his copy on a newspaper wire. His request was refused (NA, D/FA (Sec.) P 79, 'US War Information Department, Dublin: Request to use Newspaper Private Wire', July 1943).
289 Joseph Carroll, 'US–Irish Relations, 1939–45', *The Irish Sword*, Vol. XIX, Nos. 75 and 76, 1993–4, p. 103.
290 Dwyer, *Irish Neutrality*, p. 150.
291 Dwyer, *Strained Relations*, p. 57.
292 Dwyer, *Irish Neutrality*, pp. 150–51.
293 MA, G2/X/1092, '*Letter from America*', Seán Piondar to World's Press News, 20 November 1942; USNA, OSS (Regular) 30131, letter, 14 November 1942.
294 MA, G2/X/1092, '*Letter from America*'.
295 MA, OCC 2/110, '*Letter from America*, complaints from individuals'.
296 MA, OCC 3/38, '*Bulletin de Nouvelles* and *Nouvelles de France*'.
297 NA, D/FA (Sec.) P 36, G2 to the DEA, 31 October 1942.
298 NA, D/FA (Sec.) P 36, Bryan to Walshe, 16 January 1942.
299 NA, D/FA (Sec.) P 51, German Legation *Aide-Mémoire*, 13 December 1941.
300 MA, OCC 2/108, 'Swedish News'.
301 MA, OCC 2/118, 'Bulletins Circulated by Foreign Representatives in Ireland'.
302 NA, D/FA (Sec.) P 36, Coyne note on bulletins, 3 April 1941.
303 Robert Cole, 'The Other "Phoney War": British Propaganda in Neutral Europe, September–December 1939', *Journal of Contemporary History*, Vol. 22, 1987, p. 471.
304 Pronay in Pronay and Spring (eds.), *Propaganda, Politics and Film*, p. 182.
305 Cole, 'Phoney War', p. 464.
306 MA, OCC 2/107, 'Radio Vatican broadcasts, etc.'; MA, OCC 2/112, 'Ministry of Information propaganda circulars, etc.'; NA, D/FA (Sec.) A 11, John Betjeman to the DEA and OCC, August 1941.
307 MA, OCC 2/112, Betjeman to Coyne, 4 September 1942.
308 MA, OCC 2/107, 'Radio Vatican broadcasts, etc.'; MA, OCC 2/112, 'Ministry of Information propaganda circulars, etc.'
309 *Irish Times*, 28 October 1972, on the release in London of Betjeman's wartime dispatches.
310 Cole, 'Phoney War', p. 465.
311 *Dáil Debates*, Vol. 95, col. 920, 9 November 1944.
312 Carroll, *War Years*, p. 167; 'One World', *The Bell*, Vol. 7, No. 4, January 1944, p. 281.
313 NA, D/FA (Sec.) A 8, G2 report on the Institute of International Affairs, 18 February 1942.
314 *Dáil Debates*, Vol. 95, col. 921, 9 November 1944.
315 ibid., col. 922.
316 Andrée Sheehy-Skeffington, *Skeff: The Life of Owen Sheehy-Skeffington, 1909-1971* (Dublin, 1991), p. 122.
317 *Dáil Debates*, Vol. 95, cols. 926–34, 9 November 1944.
318 ibid., col. 917.
319 NA, D/J, No. 3, *Irish Times*.
320 NA, D/J, R 24, *Standard*, 7 November 1944, and *Independent*, 1 November 1944.
321 NA, D/J, R 52, *The Bell*, 14 December 1944.

322   NA, D/FA (Sec.) A 9(1), July 1941.
323   D.W. Elwood, 'Showing the World what it Owed to Britain: Foreign Policy and Cultural Propaganda, 1935–45', in Pronay and Spring (eds.), *Propaganda, Politics and Film*, p. 60.
324   Smyllie, 'Unneutral Neutral Éire', p. 325. John Ryan remembers that there were in Dublin 'aggressive little ladies of the Anglo-Irish persuasion who were doing their bit for the Allied war effort by letting out the air in the tyres of the Japanese Ambassador's car'. (John Ryan, *Remembering How We Stood: Bohemian Dublin at Mid-Century* (New York, 1975), p. 14.)
325   Dwyer, *Strained Relations*, pp. 144–5; *Irish Press*, 13 March 1944, 22 March 1944, 24 March 1944; *Dáil Debates*, Vol. 93, cols. 364–372, 23 March 1944 ; USNA, OSS (Regular), 67712, Military Attaché Report, 23 March 1944.

5.
RELATIONS WITH THE PRESS

Bertie Smyllie, editor of the *Irish Times*, argued that the main reason for the poor relations between the press and the Censorship was that 'the government simply does not trust the Press'. He described Ireland as 'probably the only democratic country in the world in which the journalist plays little or no part in politics. Here, the government has always ignored us.'[1] This lack of trust on the part of the government was certainly shared by the senior officers of the Censorship. Michael Knightly, chief press censor, believed that if the press was given the type of freedom which it sought, it 'might lead to national ruin in time of emergency'.[2] Coyne told Smyllie of the 'impossibility of getting anything like the truth from the capitalist press which flourishes and can only exist by peddling the views of its proprietors however vicious and anti-social these may be'.[3] He told the chief press censor, himself a former journalist, that he had 'the lowest opinion of newspapermen . . . not as individuals but as members of a profession whose professional interests are, in my opinion, all too frequently at variance with the interests of the public'.[4]

The mutual suspicion and distrust which prevailed between the Censorship and the press hindered the smooth operation of the censorship. G2 plans for wartime censorship in 1925 had noted that a primary requirement was an 'intelligent seeking after the co-operation of newspaper proprietors and editors in time of peace and war'.[5] This was not done, and Coyne was persuaded by his wartime experience that it was a mistake. He believed that most of the practical difficulties encountered in relations with the press arose from 'editorial or proprietorial *amour propre*' and would be likely to disappear if the press were 'taken into the conspiracy'; this could be done, as it was successfully in Britain, by establishing an advisory or consultative committee of newspaper people with whom the government could discuss its censorship plans and policies, thus cultivating the goodwill and co-operation of the press.[6]

As well as being excluded from 'the conspiracy', the press in Ireland endured many difficulties during the Emergency. The general economic downturn had a negative impact on sales and advertising revenue; the shortage of newsprint reduced the size of all newspapers to an average of four pages; the disruption of transport interfered with circulation, while the Press Censorship took a say in everything from headline size to the contents of small 'ads'. A number of papers ceased publication for the duration, but the Censorship was still faced with a list of approximately 200 Irish publications with which it had to deal. The poor state of relations between these publications and the Censorship is well illustrated by the latter's file containing expressions of appreciation which it received on the termination of censorship; it contains a letter from the *Leader* and from the *Garda Review* and a record of three telephone calls received from the *Irish People*, Hugh Smith of the *Belfast Telegraph*, and the chief subeditor of the *Evening Herald*.[7]

This chapter deals with the Censorship's relations with the various publications and its treatment of them. It also describes how the Censorship dealt with the 'external' newspapers, mostly English, which continued to circulate in the state and with the correspondents for the external press who 'exported' news from neutral Ireland.

THE NATIONAL NEWSPAPERS

The Irish Times

There would have been general surprise had the relationship between the *Irish Times* and the Censorship not been a stormy and difficult one. This was the paper which, before British withdrawal, had been (according to its editor) 'the organ of the British Government' in Ireland. Its policy was still to advocate 'the maintenance of a strong Commonwealth connection' and to stress the value of the Anglo-Irish contribution within the country.[8] It made no secret from the outset of its support for the British/Allied war effort, while at the same time acknowledging that de Valera's policy of neutrality was the sensible course to follow. Its larger-than-life, 'Hemingwayesque'[9] editor R.M. (Bertie) Smyllie had a long record of opposition to censorship in all its forms. (In Berlin during the German revolution of 1918, Smyllie, posing as an English journalist, secured an interview with Scheidemann, the president of the new German Republic, five months before any British journalist was permitted to enter the country. The scoop was lost, however, when Smyllie refused to allow his piece to be censored by the Germans.) While he reluctantly accepted the need for a wartime censorship for security reasons and to guard against breaches of neutrality, he believed, as previously noted, that it should not be done by civil servants but by the newspapers, conducting a voluntary censorship among themselves.[10] The

R.M. (Bertie) Smyllie, the legendary editor of the *Irish Times,* and the press censors' most troublesome customer.

strict demands of impartiality which the Censorship placed on the press were an unbearable burden for the *Irish Times*; the absurd lengths to which these demands were often taken, as well as the inevitable culture clash, made life even more difficult for the paper. It suffered more than any other at the hands of a system which it described on its first day 'Out of the Shadows' as a censorship 'as Draconian and irrational as anything that ever was devised in the fertile brain of the late Josef Goebbels'.[11]

In the first four months of the Emergency the *Irish Times* received several reprimands and warnings. It consistently annoyed the Censorship by carrying articles attacking Germany, failing to use the prefix 'British' when referring to 'The Army', 'The Navy', etc., and printing articles and letters suggesting that Irish neutrality was transitory.[12] When, at the end of December 1939, the paper failed to submit its report on the IRA's raid on the Irish army's Magazine Fort in the Phoenix Park, in defiance of a specific direction to do so, and carried details not contained in the official government statement, Knightly, the chief press censor, believed that the occasion 'should be availed of to make them realise that they cannot ignore the censorship with impunity'.[13] Connolly and Coyne saw the advantages of prosecuting the paper on a 'home issue' but believed them to be outweighed by the prolonging of publicity for the raid, and thus of the government's embarrassment, which a prosecution would entail.[14] When the *Irish Times* published a speech by Senator Frank MacDermot on 13 January 1940, in which he attacked the Nazis and suggested putting the ports at the disposal of the French and British, the Censorship immediately issued it with an order to submit each issue in full before publication. Following the refusal of Smyllie's request to have a press censor installed in the paper's office, the editor appealed directly to de Valera. He outlined the costs which daily sub-mission would place on the *Irish Times*, including later circulation than its competitors because of delays in publication. He also pointed out that his paper was in direct competition ('from the political point of view') with the *Daily Mail* and the *Daily Express*, both of which published 'blatant pro-paganda', and he reiterated the point made a number of times to Connolly, that it was 'not fair to muzzle the *Irish Times* when they are allowed to circulate without let or hindrance'.[15] Smyllie met with de Valera and Aiken and then with Connolly and Knightly; he promised to co-operate with the Censorship in future and the order was revoked on 1 February 1940.

Part of the agreement which led to the revocation was that Smyllie would submit his editorials. In July 1940 he complained about the persistent mutila-tion of his leaders, and referred to a recent incident when 'some bright boy cut out the following sentence: "The witches' cauldron is beginning to bub-ble with a vengeance".' He declared himself at his wits' end.[16] Coyne was uncomfortable about the mutilation of editorial comment in the *Irish Times*, and generally. He wrote to Aiken in September 1940 stating his view that

> we should give a great deal of latitude for the expression of editorial comments in the principal daily papers . . . In the case of a paper like the *Irish Times*, which is known to be pro-British in its outlook on world affairs and which is invariably referred to in the foreign press as the anglophile *Irish Times*, I feel that anything they write on foreign politics is discounted by this fact and that they can safely be given liberty to write freely on world events, including the war, even in a sense favourable to the British point of view provided they say nothing which could or might involve this country in any international dispute.[17]

Connolly, however, was unmoved. He pointed out that while the 'peculiar position' of the *Irish Times* was well known in Ireland and Britain, this was not necessarily the case in Germany, which, in any case, could claim ig-norance of the fact if it needed a reason or excuse for interfering with Irish neutrality. He informed Aiken that the *Irish Times* was the only Irish newspaper which the British were allowing to go through neutral countries to Germany and that this was reason enough to be extremely careful about what that paper was allowed to publish.[18]

Connolly's views on the situation in general held sway, but one of Coyne's specific proposals – that a senior member of staff take up duty to deal with leaders and editorial comment – was adopted. Knightly took up permanent night duty in January 1941 principally to deal with *Irish Times* leaders (which, alone among the dailies, dealt almost exclusively with international affairs), at the same time as the paper ceased to submit them. A series of objectionable leaders were published in the following months, climaxing in a 'most objectionable' article on 24 August 1941 on the British–Soviet invasion of Iran. (The Censorship considered that the comment in the article to the effect that the British and Soviets could not have behaved otherwise could have been construed into an invitation to the British to behave likewise in relation to Ireland.)[19] Aiken instructed that the *Irish Times* be ordered to submit all leading articles and editorial matter for censorship in future, and told Coyne to be as 'sticky' as possible with the paper.[20] Alec Newman, acting editor, wrote to Coyne decrying the fact that 'All this pathetic and humiliating business has started again . . . I wish to God that I was unmarried and then I could go to England and dig drains like so many thousands of others. It would be a damn sight more honourable than trying to be a journalist under this contemptible system.' Coyne, no friend of journalism, replied that he 'might do worse than switch over to drain digging: it is not the only unsavoury occupation'.[21]

In the meantime, the *Irish Times* had been allowed to continue its pre-war 'Roll of Honour' in respect of those who had died in the 1914–18 war, but was prohibited from establishing a new roll for those who fell in the latest war. Instead, the Department of External Affairs had agreed on a formula with Smyllie ('a bad one', according to Coyne) whereby the paper ran a list of those 'Killed on active service with his Britannic Majesty's Forces'. In August 1941 Aiken decided that 'the time has come to stop all this business'. Coyne wondered whether it was worth requiring the paper to list such deaths along with the ordinary death notices, as in the *Irish Independent*, as he anticipated a 'row' over the matter with the Censorship being accused of being 'petty, or even vindictive'. Knightly was also unsure; he thought that it would perhaps be better to 'let sleeping dogs lie', while recognising the use of the roll by families 'to show their sympathies in the present conflict'. Coyne suggested to Aiken that the 1914–18 roll be left and that the notices of those killed in the present war be put in the ordinary 'In Memoriam' section. Aiken was not interested; he instructed that the 'Roll of Honour' heading be prohibited, including for the First World War period, as well as the 'Killed on active service with his Britannic Majesty's Forces', and all similar headings and segregation of such announcements. All future notices were to be inserted in the ordinary 'In Memoriam' list, in alphabetical order.[22]

The rank, regiment and fact that the person had been killed on active service were still allowed, so long as the deceased had an English address. If an Irish address was given all references to the British forces were deleted. People began to evade this restriction by entering two notices: one containing rank, regiment, etc. accompanied by an English address (possibly false), closely followed by another with the Irish address and minus the military details. This 'ruse' led to a change in policy in May 1943 so that all references to rank, regiment, unit or theatre of war were deleted from death notices, obituaries, engagement, marriage and birth announcements, etc. This was irrespective of the nationality of the deceased or their normal place of residence. (Expressions like 'missing, presumed killed' continued to be allowed, however.) Exceptions to the above rules were made when the subject was a well-known Irish national whose rank dated from before the current war or when the news was of general interest; in February 1944, for example, Aiken authorised the publication of an obituary notice in the *Irish Times* for the son of Dr Gregg, the Church of Ireland primate, who had been killed in the war.[23]

By late 1942 Smyllie was adopting a generally 'defiant attitude' towards the Censorship, and Coyne met with him in an attempt to bring him into line; 'I don't want to break with him altogether', he told Knightly. 'It has always been our strength that Smyllie and Geary [the *Irish Independent* editor, Frank Geary] cannot stand each other and I don't want to force them into an unholy alliance if I can possibly avoid it.' Smyllie, however, remained 'as truculent as ever' and on 21–22 December he published three reports without submission: a statement by Hubert Morrison, British Home Secretary; a report on speech day at Portora Royal School; and a panelled announcement of the king's Christmas Day broadcast. When questioned by the Censorship Smyllie replied that he saw no reason for their submission; because of the 'unsatisfactory nature' of the reply the paper was ordered, on Aiken's instructions, on 29 December 1942, to submit each issue in full for censorship before publication. The order stayed in force until the cessation of censorship.[24]

From the outset of the Emergency, Smyllie enjoyed tricking, testing and trapping the Censorship. In a famous 'Irishman's Diary' of February 1941, the editor (using the pen name 'Nichevo') wrote the following paragraph under the heading 'Nippon Go Brath':

> In his broadcast on Sunday night, Mr Winston Churchill, the British Prime Minister (NB Britain is an island to the east of Éire) mentioned by name nine military and naval commanders who had gained fame recently in North Africa and the Mediterranean. I append the names of the gallant nine:

General Wavell	English
General Mackie	Australian
General Wilson	Japanese (North Island)
General O'Connor	Japanese
General O'Moore Creagh	Japanese
General Dill	Japanese (North Island)
General Brooke	Japanese (North Island)
Admiral Cunningham	Japanese
Admiral Sommerville	Japanese

> As the venerable member of the Samurai, San Tiok Eli [Seán T. O'Kel-
> ly, Minister for Finance] might or might not have put it: 'Quae regio
> in terra non plena laboris?'[25]

Smyllie was reprimanded for not submitting this piece and warned about
this and similar offences. He pleaded guilty and asked to throw himself 'at
your mercy as well as your sense of humour. It was not a *very* serious offence, and you will admit that it gave a few people a much needed laugh
in these gloomy times.'[26]

The editor was to get his biggest laugh at the expense of the Censorship
in December of the same year with his famous 'boating accident' story. This
concerned the fate of former *Irish Times* staff member Johnny Robinson,
who had joined the Royal Navy and went down with the *Prince of Wales*.
A cable had arrived announcing his safety and the paper carried a
photograph of Robinson accompanied by the following announcement:

> The many friends of Mr John A. Robinson, who was involved in a re-
> cent boating accident will be pleased to hear that he is alive and well
> . . . He is a particularly good swimmer and it is possible that he owes
> his life to this accomplishment.[27]

Smyllie was warned the next day that if he tried such a 'trick' again the
Irish Times would be ordered to submit in full.[28] (As we have seen, this
fate later befell it.) However, the damage had already been done as far
as the Censorship was concerned and the story spread far and wide. In
a letter to Smyllie, two months later, Coyne wrote that

> Your jeu d'esprit about 'The Boating Accident' to the *Prince of Wales*
> in which your pal Robinson was involved is still going round the world
> to the tune of a hymn of hate against this country and is doing us
> a hell of a lot of harm. Hardly a day passes without a variation of
> the theme being obtruded on my notice from some obscure corner of
> the globe.

He asked Smyllie to 'use discretion in future' and to 'temper your high
spirits with a modicum of meditation on the natural and possible consequences of a jape of this kind'. He admitted that the linen got dirty from
time to time, but asked Smyllie to 'keep the washing at home' and to keep
his problems with the Censorship 'in the family'.[29]

The *Irish Times* regarded the ban on references to Irish people involved
in the war as 'unjust, if not *ultra vires*' and continued, in Smyllie's words,
'to resort to subterfuge to get around it'.[30] His favourite ploy was to use
'lead poisoning' when referring to bullet or shrapnel wounds.[31] In
December 1943 the paper named one of the Irish men who had been
parachuted into Co. Clare by the Germans for espionage purposes; it
reported that he was in Ennis county hospital recovering from back in-
juries 'received in a fall'. The paper was threatened with prosecution for
publishing that report.[32]

A recurring difficulty faced by the paper throughout the period was that posed by the use of place-names. While all papers had from the outset been prohibited from using terms like 'Southern Ireland' and 'British Isles', the policy took a new turn in 1942. In May of that year Aiken instructed that Maryborough, Queen's Co. be altered to Portlaoighise, Co. Laoighise, and Christchurch, Kingstown (in a funeral announcement) be altered to Christchurch, Dún Laoghaire, in an *Irish Times* proof. Knightly informed the paper that 'insistence on repudiating the legal names was subversive'.[33] In June 1944 'Nichevo', in an 'Irishman's Diary', referred to a poker game in his home town of Kells; 'I suppose', he continued, 'in deference to the Minister for the Co-ordination of Defensive Measures, I ought to say this correspondent hails from Ceannanus Mór; but I just can't'. On Aiken's direction this comment was deleted and Kells was replaced with Ceannanus Mór in the first instance. Although Coyne was unhappy about this aspect of censorship, he explained to Smyllie that it was policy to prevent the publication of place-names 'aggressively imposed and disloyally maintained in the interests of compulsory English and in the process of a campaign to deny the right of the Irish people to rule themselves in their own way'.[34] In September 1944 Aiken instructed that the *Irish Times* be told that if it continued to submit proofs with 'British Isles' and 'Kingstown', a direction to submit final page proofs would be issued to it.[35] Smyllie was refused written directions on place-names, and threatened to invoke 'outside assistance' and to take High Court action on the issue. He was convinced that the Censorship was abusing its powers in this matter, and Coyne was in agreement with him. Following more trouble about 'Maryborough' and 'Queen's Co.' in December 1944 the controller expressed his unhappiness to Aiken, pointing out that there was no statutory authority for most place names and that they were determined in most cases by custom and usage.[36] Aiken was unrepentant and told Coyne that if usage by the inhabitants was a legal basis, then the Censorship was quite right to prevent the *Irish Times* from 'foisting unwanted names' on the people.[37] The trouble with the place-names continued, but in January 1945 the *Irish Times* 'had a score' when it pointed out that the *Iris Oifigiúil* (an official government publication) had used the name 'Royal Marine Hotel, Kingstown'. The Censorship duly informed the news editor that he could publish what appeared in the *Iris Oifigiúil*.[38]

The behaviour of the Censorship with regard to place-names provoked Smyllie into some of his most vitriolic attacks against the organisation. He saw the Kells incident as a clear illustration that policy towards the *Irish Times* was 'dictated entirely by the bile secretions of an individual [Knightly] whose mind is obsessed by a pathologically malignant Anglophobia'. He referred to the chief press censor's 'frenetic diatribes' on the telephone, including an attempt by Knightly to hold Smyllie personally responsible for the alleged forging of the Casement diaries! Following the stopping of the Kingstown funeral announcement, he referred to 'delving into graves for purely politico-Gaelic purposes' and wrote to Coyne that 'if we are to have a political censorship acting under the aegis of the Gaelic League, let us be clear on the point at any rate'.[39]

Following deletions to a leading article in July 1942 Smyllie wrote to Coyne and referred to the occasion when he met Arthur Griffith after the ratification of the Treaty. Griffith had told him that

> 'the next step must be the elimination of the Yahoo'. . . if he had been alive today and could have seen the deletions that were made in our leading article this morning, he would have realised that it is not the elimination, but the enthronement of the Yahoo that has been achieved.[40]

He reserved particular scorn for the Press Censorship staff whom he described variously as 'troglodytic myrmidons', 'moronic clodhoppers', 'ignorant bosthoons', and 'poor cawbogues' whose blue pencils were their 'only claim to literacy'.[41] Smyllie regarded Connolly, like Knightly, as 'a bitter Anglophobe'[42] and found Aiken ('your ministerial stooge'[43]) 'unintelligently impossible';[44] the minister, he believed, 'smelt treason and conspiracy against the State behind every sentence' printed in the *Irish Times*.[45] (Aiken told Robert Fisk many years later he 'had a lot of fun with Smyllie. When he was censored, he would always write a letter about it. So I would sentence him to one or two pages of Coyne. We used hop off each other.'[46]) De Valera, in contrast to Aiken, he found 'more than anxious to be fair'[47] and Smyllie doubted that the Taoiseach 'ever realised the extent to which its [the Censorship's] powers were abused'.[48] Coyne he held in high esteem and repeatedly appealed to him 'to quit this filthy job with which you have been saddled'[49] and to 'go back to an honest job'.[50] He pointed out to him at one stage that while the Censorship was acting in a petty fashion, 'grand men are getting killed for something in which they and I . . . and for that matter yourself . . . believe with a passion'.[51] Smyllie knew that Coyne was uncomfortable about a number of aspects of the Censorship policy which he was forced to implement and defend. He admitted to Smyllie that he disliked interfering with obituary notices, but consoled himself with his belief that the *Irish Times* exploited the living and the dead for the gratification of its 'West British readers'.[52] Coyne constantly refuted Smyllie's accusations of anti-Britishness against the Censorship; he told the editor on one occasion that censorship policy was nothing more or less than 'pro-Irish'. 'Must you always forget', he asked him, 'that you have a country of your own?'[53]

In the last days of the censorship Smyllie celebrated VE Day (8 May 1945) with a little victory of his own. The seven pictures of Allied leaders which he submitted in proof were passed as unobjectionable and appeared at random in the country edition. However, for the city edition Smyllie personally remade the front page so that the photographs of King George,

The front page of the *Irish Times* (city edition) on VE Day, 8 May 1945. The photographs of Allied leaders, which had been passed for publication by the censor, were arranged into a giant V (for victory) by Smyllie in a final gesture of defiance.

Eisenhower, Field-Marshal Alexander, Stalin, Montgomery, Churchill and Roosevelt formed an enormous V which spanned the whole page under the neutral heading, 'Peace To-Day in Europe'.[54]

The Irish Press

The *Irish Press*, founded in 1931 by de Valera, was the Fianna Fáil newspaper. Given its close links with the government the relationship between this paper and the Censorship was bound to be a delicate and unusual one. The general expectation among opposition newspapers and politicians that 'Pravda' (as it was once described by James Dillon) would receive preferential treatment ensured, in turn, that this would not happen. The Germans also made it clear that as the *Irish Press* was 'looked upon as the organ of the Government party' it was expected to be 'pledged to particular care',[55] as was the Censorship in its treatment of it. The editor, William Sweetman, came to believe that such expectations led the Censorship to discriminate against his paper in an attempt to prove its impartiality. The situation was further complicated by the fact that the chief press censor, Michael Knightly, had, for a number of years, worked as a journalist on the *Irish Independent*, the only mass circulation daily which out-sold the *Irish Press*.

Relations between the Censorship and the *Irish Press* were 'unpleasant' in the early days of the Emergency. This was chiefly because of Sweetman's persistent allegations that Knightly was showing favouritism towards the *Irish Independent*. Knightly resented the accusation that he was 'activated by any motive other than the discharge of my duty to the Government'; he asked Coyne to bring the matter to the attention of Aiken and through him, to the management of the *Irish Press*.[56] There was a subsequent reduction in the accusations against Knightly personally but Sweetman continued to complain about anomalies which arose in the treatment of both papers.

The main reason for the occurrence of such anomalies was the fact that the *Irish Independent* submitted little matter, particularly in the early years, and largely carried out its own censorship. Sweetman, however, began to believe that his paper was being used as a sacrificial lamb by the Censorship as part of its strategy in dealing with its more troublesome competitors, the *Irish Independent* and the *Irish Times*. Following the censorship of an *Irish Press* report on the Moscow Declaration in November 1943, the editor accused the Censorship of killing the report because the story, as submitted by the *Irish Times*, was objectionable. 'It was killed because the Press Censorship is afraid of the *Irish Times*', he wrote. 'It was killed so that the Press Censorship, if questioned by the *Irish Times*, could answer: "but see what we have done to the *Irish Press*" . . . Our reputation as a newspaper has on several occasions been injured for no better reason than that a censor was afraid of hurting the susceptibilities of another paper.'[57] Coyne dismissed the charge as 'offensive nonsense'.[58]

The use of Allied news agency reports and the tight rein maintained by the Censorship resulted in an overall tone in the *Press* which upset some of its more virulently anti-British readers. In a letter to the editor, stopped by the censor in June 1942, Dan Breen, the Fianna Fáil TD, war of independence and civil war veteran, and prominent pro-Nazi, attacked the paper: 'Your paper today', he wrote,

> is more British than the British . . . You are guilty of crimes that would make Irishmen who gave their all for a free Ireland hang their heads in shame . . . Your paper of today is the rag of the forties that the *Daily Mail* was in the last war. You out-do the British in their lies and are at times more red than Stalin. May God save Ireland from the trash you print. May God save the people and guide them away from the rotten pro-British element that your paper panders to.[59]

Dan Bryan of G2 believed that Henning Thomsen, a Nazi who was Hempel's second-in-command at the German legation, was 'the inspiration of Breen's effusion'.[60] Although M.J. McManus, the paper's literary editor, was a close friend of John Betjeman, the press attaché at the office of the UK representative, and Hempel believed that a pro-British subeditor was giving the paper's war coverage a pro-Allied slant, a number of the paper's journalists had pro-Axis sympathies and were watched closely by G2.[61]

Although the *Irish Press* was never subjected to an order to submit in full, its publication, without submission, of a photograph of Dr Goerdeler, who was involved in the plot to assassinate Hitler, led to an order on 12 August 1944 to submit all photographs and pictorial matter for censorship (it was revoked on 17 October 1944).[62] Sweetman wrote directly to Aiken to complain about the direction and the treatment of the paper in general: 'You can imagine what capital Mr Dillon would have made of them in the Dáil had the Censor behaved in a similar manner towards the *Irish Independent* or *Irish Times* . . . It seems clear that in taking care to be right with the other newspapers the Censor is careless as to the injury he may cause the *Irish Press*.'[63] Sweetman's persecution complex was not eased when on 14 January 1945 the paper was directed to submit its 'Film Notes' (following an unauthorised reference to ENSA, the organisation which provided entertainment for British and American troops in the North), which it did until the cessation of censorship.[64]

The editor's personal relationship with the censors never improved. In October 1944 Coyne enquired of Aiken whether Sweetman was a Quaker! 'At any rate', wrote the controller, 'he does not appear to believe in making the truth any more palatable by any of the customary, if insincere, expressions of formal politeness.'[65] This was in contrast to the editorial staff of the *Irish Times* who, despite being 'off-side' politically, prompted Coyne to write 'Toujours la politesse' beside their New Year greetings to the Censorship for 1944.[66]

In spite of the poor personal relations between the editor and the censors and the former's belief that his paper had suffered reverse discrimination, the *Irish Press* moved immediately, on the cessation of censorship, to perform its party political function. While the first post-censorship leaders in the *Irish Independent* and *Irish Times* on Saturday, 12 May 1945 condemned the operation of the censorship, the *Irish Press* toed the party line. Its editorial praised the success of the censorship in 'opposing efforts to create a partisan spirit at home' and declared that it 'fully justified itself, no matter what minor errors or irritations we may have had to complain about'. The leader writer went on to pay tribute to the organisation's 'good sense', 'honesty' and 'impartiality', before concluding that:

> It was not a case of suppressing the truth: in fact, probably ninety per cent of the 'news' which came under the ban of the censor was false. In a time of war the news agencies of the belligerent countries are not so much concerned with the truth or falsehood of the reports they send out as with making propaganda for their own side.[67]

The editorial fails to mention, of course, that the 'Truth in the News' itself was among the chief offenders in carrying, unedited, such reports.

The Irish Independent

The *Irish Independent* was the largest-selling Irish paper (circulation, 1942: 140,000; *Irish Press*: 108,000) and the one most closely associated with the principal opposition party, Fine Gael. While the other dailies submitted a considerable amount of matter the *Irish Independent* largely did its own censorship, particularly of agency messages carrying war news. It 'did it reasonably well', according to the Censorship, but this situation inevitably led to a stream of complaints about unequal treatment. The paper was frequently reminded to submit doubtful matter but it refused to change its policy.[68]

The first serious trouble arose in August 1940, when the paper carried a detailed report of the bombing of the SS *Kerry Head* by the Germans off the Cork coast, prior to the official release of the story. Immediately before this incident the paper had published a photograph of an Irishman in the uniform of the Grenadier Guards; because of the frequency of such occurrences a direction to submit in full before publication was issued to the *Irish Independent* on 6 August 1940. A long exchange of letters ensued, during which Knightly admitted that the paper was 'generally doing the censorship quite well – quite possibly better than we would do it'; furthermore, as *Irish Independent* editor Frank Geary pointed out, the latest direction to the press covered most matters arising out of the war so that a considerable amount would be submitted in any case. On Knightly's recommendation Aiken revoked the order to submit in full on 30 August 1940.[69] There followed a series of what Coyne described as 'offensive and ill-mannered letters' to the Censorship which he believed were intended to provoke replies in such terms as to provide the *Irish Independent* with sources of complaint to Fine Gael members of the Defence Conference.[70] Material was certainly forwarded to James Dillon and other opposition deputies and senators who raised them in parliament. Relations with the paper improved, according to the Censorship, only after the chief subeditor, Hector Legge, was promoted to the editorship of the *Sunday Independent* in August 1940.[71]

Following constant complaints from the *Irish Press* and *Irish Independent* about matter stopped for one being allowed for the other, a policy of advising all papers when an item submitted by one paper was censored was adopted. This, however, did not eliminate anomalies, particularly in relation to first editions.

In December 1940 an *Irish Independent* series by their 'Special Correspondent' in London was stopped because it dealt with the experiences of Irish citizens during the air raids there.[72] Another of the paper's features which fell foul of the censors was its articles by military correspondents. The Censorship sought to prevent the inadvertent supply of material to propagandists arising out of the correspondents' analyses and forecasts. In the latter case the fear was that they 'might just happen to be right and the premature disclosure by accident of the plans of military operations in the press of this country would . . . be extremely awkward and might have serious consequences'.[73] German radio quoted from *Irish Independent* military articles on a number of occasions; on 23 January 1944, for example, it quoted the correspondent as saying that by means of excellent staff work the Germans had so far smashed any Soviet prospects of achieving victory. Among the military articles stopped for the paper was a piece on the disastrous Dieppe raid in which the correspondent presented it as an attempted invasion; such a contention fitted in perfectly with the German view of the incident.[74]

In July 1943 the Censorship raised the hackles of the editor by ordering the reduction in size, from five columns to four, of a banner heading relating to the fighting in Sicily. Geary challenged the censor's right to act in this way and pointed out that the *Irish Independent* had always made its style of captions a particular feature of its journalism. He accused the Censorship of an unwarranted interference with its tradition in this area. The Censorship, of course, was not on strong grounds here as its legal powers were restricted to news content and not presentation. Aiken, however, had always felt that such a lack of legal power should not deter the Censorship from imposing its preferred presentation by the indirect method of refusing to pass matter which a paper proposed to present in 'objectionable' form. Although this was the first occasion on which headline size had been at issue, Oscar Traynor (the Minister for Defence, acting in Aiken's absence) supported the action of the censors.[75]

Geary's temper was not improved in the next weeks following a series

of petty acts of censorship, including the deletion of references to bad
weather in an August bank holiday write-up, but the passing of references
to good weather. Geary vented his anger in a reply to a long letter from
Coyne which had addressed his various complaints:

> Stripped of all the lectures, the sneers, the alleged jokes, the gratuitous
> advice and the offensive suggestions, [your letter] just means that what
> you say must always be right; that what you like, we must like; that
> what you dislike, we must dislike; that all regard for the interest and
> safety of this country is entirely vested in you, and you only, and that
> regulations or no regulations what you think must be the Law. That
> is our Censorship.[76]

On 20 January 1941 a leading article, 'Our Charges Against the Censorship', written in the week before a debate on the subject in the Seanad,
was stopped. The article charged that the Censorship was biased against
the *Irish Independent* and that it exceeded its powers by issuing orders which
it had no authority to issue (in relation to 'requests' regarding captions
and the display of news).[77] In the course of that debate, Frank MacDermot read out extracts from the stopped editorial. Aiken, in reply, raised
the old chestnut of the *Irish Independent*'s call for the execution of James
Connolly following the 1916 Easter rising: 'If the Senator had been here
at a certain stage in Irish history, he would remember another leading article which the Irish people would have been glad to see stopped in 1916'.
Aiken denied Senator Hayes's charge that he was 'punishing the *Independent* in 1941 for something which was written in 1916'.[78] In his notes for
the minister before this debate Knightly had written that, 'As long as
Irishmen live two newspaper articles will live in their memories, one the
notorious article in the *London Times* gloating over the disappearance of
the Celt from Ireland and the other the article of the *Independent* calling
for the blood of the 1916 leaders.'[79]

On 26 January 1941 another leader, headed 'A Minister on Censorship',
was stopped. This related to observations made by Seán Lemass, Minister
for Supplies, at an Institute of Journalists' dinner to the effect that while
a wartime censorship was necessary, 'a free Press and a good Press was
essential to the conduct of democracy'. Knightly informed the editor that
the article was stopped 'because it has been decided not to allow newspapers
to criticise the Censorship either directly or by implication' and to forestall
a 'hostile newspaper campaign' which could undermine the authority of
the Censorship.[80] It is not clear whether Lemass intended his comments
to be an implied criticism of the Censorship or not, but the *Irish Independent* certainly intended to present them in this way. On 10 December of
the same year cuts were made to a leader which could, according to Coyne,
have had 'the effect of preventing farmers from growing the wheat that
the nation requires'; he informed Geary that 'it is up to editors who want

to see the nation strengthened to encourage farmers to grow as much wheat as possible'.[81] From February 1942 the *Irish Independent* adopted a policy of going to press without a leading article in cases where the Censorship had interfered in some way with it. Following deletions or stoppages it carried no leading article on 21 February and 10 November 1942, on 14 February and 16 July 1944 and on 14 February 1945.[82]

This last omission followed the deletion of comments 'calculated to cause offence to the US and Great Britain as well as to Russia' in an editorial on the Crimea Conference headed 'New Partition of Poland'. Coyne wrote to Geary telling him that 'much mischief' could be created by the *Irish Independent* giving the impression that the Censorship had stopped a leader on the Crimea Conference. He asked for an assurance that there would be no repeat.[83] Geary replied that a newspaper could not be held responsible for impressions made on the minds of unnamed persons or the rumours and wrong conclusions affecting the Censorship.[84] Fortunately for the paper the course of action discussed by Coyne and Aiken, in the event of an assurance not being forthcoming (court action based on a contravention of the prohibition on revealing the actions of the Censorship), was not pursued.[85]

On Saturday, 12 May 1945 the *Irish Independent* availed of its new freedom to condemn the Censorship for its incompetence and partiality. The editorial claimed that the Censorship had been frequently inspired 'not by national but by party political motives' and implied, as an extension of this, discrimination against the *Irish Independent*, the paper most closely associated with the Fine Gael party. 'We gladly bid good-bye to the Censorship', the leader concluded, 'not only because its departure marks the restoration of the freedom of the Press – a fundamental right and need of a democratic community – but also because of the disappearance of powers which were unreasonably and unfairly exercised.'[86]

The Sunday Independent

As the only Irish Sunday newspaper the *Sunday Independent* was in direct competition with the English Sundays which were sold openly in Ireland but were not subject to Irish censorship; this resulted, the paper complained, in unfair competition. Further cause for regular complaint arose when stories broke at the weekend and the authorities decided to delay publication 'in the public interest' or until the Government Information Bureau issued a statement on a particular matter. 'If we think it right to stop a story on Saturday night', Knightly told the editor, 'and release it on Sunday we have no alternative but to do so even if the result is to deprive the *Sunday Independent* of a story.'[87]

Despite these problems arising from the *Sunday Independent*'s unique position, relations between the paper and the Censorship were initially most friendly. This relationship began to sour, however, on the accession of Hector

Legge to the editorship in August 1940. The new editor demanded extended hours for the censors on duty on Saturday night, he published censorable matter without submission and his general attitude, according to the Censorship, was 'hostile'. He gave curt replies to the censors' complaints about his behaviour and continued to ignore directions and requests. Legge's attitude as summed up by Coyne was that it was 'a case of his judgement against ours and he preferred his own judgement'.[88]

Despite repeated warnings, the *Sunday Independent* continued to publish censorable matter without submission and in June 1943 Knightly warned Legge that if he persisted an order to submit in full before publication would be served on his paper.[89] The editor, in reply, claimed that he did not 'seek to publish anything that would not be passed by the Censor'. He continued to prefer his own judgement and to question that of the Censorship, accusing it a couple of months later of being 'very squeamish about "hurting the feelings" of the people of certain countries' (i.e. Axis states). 'Does it ever think', Legge asked Coyne, 'that it hurts the intelligence of its own people?'[90]

In October 1943 Coyne wrote to Legge stating that 'Soviet Russia – who would believe it – is all the rage today and I notice that the *Sunday Independent* is in the fashion'. He was referring to an article published on 10 October entitled 'Dubliners are Acquiring a Knowledge of Russian'. 'Maybe there is not much to which the Censorship can take exception in the article', admitted Coyne, '. . . but I think it is as well to tell you that we expect you to submit this sort of thing for censorship beforehand in future and that you will find us wholly unsympathetic to the idea of a "build-up" for a particular belligerent no matter what form it may take.'[91]

One of the final clashes with the *Sunday Independent* occurred in March 1945 when the censor deleted portions of a speech by Basil Brooke, the Northern Ireland premier. Legge wrote that though 'the authorities here may disagree with what Sir Basil Brooke says, censorship of his speeches raises the big question of freedom of speech and freedom of the Press'. Coyne replied that it was the existence of a Censorship which raised the 'big question' and not this specific act and indeed settled it 'so long as the Censorship continues to exist for, as everyone knows, the two things are wholly incompatible'.[92]

The Cork Examiner

The *Cork Examiner* was the only Irish daily newspaper published outside Dublin and thus bore a 'heavy burden' in relation to the censorship. It had to submit doubtful matter by telephone at night and was often discriminated against because of delays in informing it about stopped matter arising from proofs submitted by the Dublin papers. There were also problems when, for example, a report was held over pending an official government statement and the *Cork Examiner* was not informed of the lifting of a prohibition on a story until it was too late. The paper found such delays 'most annoying', but the Censorship was satisfied that these were 'difficulties inseparable from Press Censorship'.[93]

The *Cork Examiner* had its own private wire from London and matter received on it occasionally caused 'embarrassment' for the Censorship. In September 1940, for example, its 'London Letter' referred to 'invasion rumours' and stated that a vast armada was destined for an attack on the British and Irish shores. This, according to Coyne, was 'Churchill's thesis but not ours' and he requested the paper to impose 'a self-denying ordinance' in respect of matter of this kind received on its private wire which it did not intend to submit before publication.[94]

Headings were a constant source of trouble and a number of readers complained to the Censorship about them. In April 1941 an anonymous reader forwarded examples like 'Cobh a Dead Town', 'Poor's Plight' and 'A Desperate State of Affairs', with the comment: 'Can anything be done to stop this kind of defeatism? Half an ounce of tea a week is bad enough without having this for breakfast'!![95] It was difficult for the Censorship to deal with headings over the telephone. This also applied to reports of broadcasts where the British and American agencies introduced sections with prefatory comments. The Dublin papers' submissions often did not carry these comments and the reported broadcasts were passed for the *Cork Examiner* without knowledge of the 'objectionable interpolations'. In January 1942, for example, it featured a broadcast by Hitler in the form supplied by the Associated Press, which had a sort of running commentary, prefacing quotes from Hitler with comments like, 'In a sneer at democracy . . . '. Aiken told Coyne to 'Tell off and warn the *Cork Examiner*' and in a letter it was reminded that in reporting pronouncements by heads of state, newspapers were required to 'print the pronouncement textually in whole or in part without comment or gloss of any kind'.[96]

In November 1943 the Censorship sent the manager of Cork Examiner Publications a letter listing twenty-five instances from January 1942 (the Hitler broadcast) to October 1943 ('a sneer at the Italians') in which the *Cork Examiner* and its sister paper, the *Evening Echo*, had contravened the printed directions and *ad hoc* directions given to members of staff, and had published items which were 'intrinsically objectionable having regard to the purpose for which the Censorship has been established'. All the examples listed related to war/international news and all were deemed objectionable on the basis of their pro-Allied, anti-Axis bias. 'The fact that foreign-controlled international news agencies are the source of much of the news which is carried by the press', wrote the censor, 'makes it very necessary to take particular care that the papers of this country are not used as sounding boards for the propaganda machines of the various belligerents.'[97]

In spite of the various problems and difficulties which were encountered, relations between the Cork and Dublin staffs of the *Cork Examiner* and the censors remained, according to the latter, 'cordial throughout the Censorship'.[98]

The Evening Herald

The *Evening Herald*, which was the third of Independent Newspapers' titles, was, according to the Censorship, 'the most satisfactory of the daily newspapers with which we had to deal. Except in one instance, a ready willingness to co-operate was shown and relations with the staff throughout the Censorship were quite friendly.'[99]

The 'one instance' referred to occurred in September 1942 when the paper submitted its report of the shooting by the IRA of the well-known Special Branch detective Denis O'Brien in Ballyboden with the heading 'Rathfarnham Shooting – Detective Killed'. The censor refused to pass the report unless it described 'the crime by its proper name', i.e. 'murder'. The paper refused to use this word and went to press without any report of the assassination.[100] As an Independent Newspapers' title, the *Herald* was certainly not sympathetic to the IRA's cause. The apparent reason for the editor's action was that the press had previously been stopped from describing the killing of an RUC man in the North as murder, and wished to be (awkwardly) consistent. The editor lodged a protest, stating: 'The Censor may delete but so far as I am aware, he has no authority to insert words of his own choice in substitution for words to which he objects.'[101] The Censorship sent a simple acknowledgement to the editor, but the controller took the opportunity to clarify for the press censors policy with regard to such matters. He reminded them that the Censorship powers were purely negative and that they had no right to insist on their own choice of words. The suggestion of alternative words was, according to Coyne, a convenient *modus operandi* to save time and effort for both the censors and the newspaper staff. The paper could accept the censors' words, submit an alternative unobjectionable formula of its own, or, as in the case above, refuse to run the report except in its original form.[102]

The Evening Mail

The (Dublin) *Evening Mail* had a stormy relationship with the Censorship in the first years of the Emergency and was subjected to repeated warnings and a threat to compel it to submit in full before publication. The principal source of trouble was the paper's repeated publication of items containing a pro-British bias.

On the outbreak of war it published an article which stated that 'Germany is at war with the British Empire of which we are a part, and we are just as liable to an air raid as England, France or Poland.' On 18 September 1939 the *Mail* published a letter from the Earl Haig's British

Legion Appeal and on 20 November it carried a letter advertising that the British War Office was seeking recruits for the Irish Guards. This led to a warning that further contraventions of the directions would lead to an order to submit in full before publication. A further warning was issued in February 1940 following the publication of a report on Nazi atrocities perpetrated against the Catholic Church in Poland. After the publication of an advertisement for a Cumann na mBan mass offering for the IRA hunger strikers in Mountjoy Jail (stopped for the *Evening Herald*) and a war-related advertisement for Milk of Magnesia (stopped for the *Irish Times*) a direction to submit in full was drafted, but was not issued following an apology from the editor.[103] Connolly continued to believe that there would be 'no peace' until the *Evening Mail* was forced to submit[104] but, following a meeting between Knightly and the chief subeditor in March 1941, 'better co-operation' ensued and, although minor contraventions continued, 'no serious cause for complaint arose'.[105]

Following the lifting of censorship Aiken invited the editors of the major newspapers to a 'celebratory dinner' which all of them, except one, attended. Smyllie, remembers C.S. Andrews, 'was the *clou* of the party. All the schemes devised to defeat the censorship were revealed and all the counter ploys recounted. Smyllie was hilarious and the evening was hilarious too. Frank smiled benignly on the proceedings.'[106]

THE PROVINCIAL PRESS

The small Press Censorship staff was primarily occupied with the work of censoring the daily newspapers. It thus relied heavily on the willingness of the weekly, provincial press to effectively censor itself along the lines of the Censorship directions. This arrangement suited the local papers as, given the logistics of their production, large scale submissions of doubtful matter to the Censorship in Dublin would have made regular weekly publication extremely difficult, if not impossible. The provincial papers on the whole behaved with 'admirable restraint',[107] according to the Censorship, thus substantially easing its workload. When these papers published censorable matter they were given reminders, admonishments and warnings, and were required, in return, to provide explanations, apologies and assurances that they would not re-offend. When 'serious' contraventions of the directions occurred, orders to submit all matter for censorship before publication were issued. Six such orders were issued to provincial papers in 1940–1; a number were also directed to submit all editorial matter at various stages. In January 1942 a direction was sent to all the provincial papers compelling them to submit before publication all matter connected with foreign affairs; this direction deterred many of the papers from dealing in any way with issues related to the war or international affairs.

According to Coyne there was no provincial paper 'too obscure to be quoted next day for a propagandist purpose by a hostile news agency in Oysterville, Tennessee and from China to Peru as the authentic voice of the Irish people and garbled and represented as official, if needs be, in the process'.[108] In a memo to staff in November 1941 he wrote that 'the harm that results from the indiscretions of these provincial papers is often out of all proportion to their circulation or importance'.[109] A *Skibbereen Eagle*-type intervention into international affairs (i.e. its legendary warning to the Tsar that it was 'keeping its eye' on him) was no longer to be viewed with amusement. (An American intelligence report from Ireland in 1942 claimed that the Germans had 'assiduously cultivated the Irish provincial papers and I have heard it said that they have subsidized some'. The evidence for these assertions, provided in the report, is flimsy.[110])

The direction which forbade any reference to people serving with belligerent forces (invariably British) was contravened on a regular basis ('Meathman Killed in Action in Libya',[111] 'Carrick man Prisoner in Java',[112] etc.). As well as news reports, this prohibition extended to marriage, birth, death and general social announcements. Papers were reprimanded for the publication of the most obscure and insignificant references; the *Leinster Leader*, for example, was rapped on the knuckles for publishing a comment from the mother of a juvenile defendant in a court case which revealed that the boy's father was away serving with the RAF.[113] The extent to which this rule interfered with local reporting is well illustrated in the following extract from a letter sent by the exasperated editor of the *Drogheda Independent* to the chief press censor:

> So many people in my circulation area are either dying for foreign powers or marrying other people who are preparing to die for foreign powers or are having christened the children of people who are feared to have been lost in the service of foreign powers, I have to be continually on the look-out . . .[114]

Other common contraventions in the provincial papers included the publication of references to recent weather conditions, crash landings of belligerent planes, belligerent activities in local waters, the names of Department of Supplies inspectors, and the inadvertent disclosure of the location of military camps.

The false presumption on the part of many provincial paper editors that matter which had appeared in the daily press was automatically passed for publication gave rise to repeated difficulties, as did the 'lifting' of stories from external newspapers that circulated in Ireland. Feelings of unfair competition emanating from this situation were felt even more acutely by newspapers published in the border counties, which were directly competing with Northern Irish papers that circulated in their districts.[115] The grievance felt by the editor of the *Donegal Vindicator* was centred upon the *Derry Journal*. The latter, although published in the North, circulated mainly in Donegal, carried Irish government advertisements and was known, throughout Donegal, as 'The Official Éire Government Organ in the North'; it was also styled 'The Official Fianna Fáil Organ' and 'The Derry Fianna Fáil Organ'.[116] When the *Donegal Vindicator* was threatened with seizure and an order to submit in full in October 1942, following the publication of a story relating to a US soldier which was lifted from the *Derry Journal*,[117] the editor complained that 'a paper subsidised by the Éire government may carry news to my doorstep which is banned to me'[118]. The authorities in the South did not wish to exclude six-county papers for political reasons and for fear of retaliation, and managed instead to receive 'a fair amount of voluntary co-operation' from the editor of the *Derry Journal*, including the occasional publication of separate Northern and twenty-six county editions.[119]

The issuing of a direction to submit in full each issue for censorship before publication was the most serious penalty which could be imposed on an offending newspaper. The implementation of such a direction would have been tantamount to suppression in the case of most of the provincial papers. The Censorship did not seek to put papers out of business but saw submission orders as 'the best way to give a paper a good fright'[120] and ensure future compliance.

In September 1940 the *Southern Star* was issued with an order to submit in full following its revelation of the actions of the Censorship in stopping a story about the bombing of a West Cork boat in the Irish Sea; the order was lifted after a week following an apology.[121] In the same month (on 21 September) the *Enniscorthy Echo* published, without permission, the following paragraph:

> *Germany Admits Liability for Campile Bombing* – The *Echo* learned on Thursday night that the German government has admitted liability for the bombing in Campile and other parts of South Wexford on August 26, when three girls were killed in the Campile Co-operative's premises.[122]

The issue was seized by the Gardaí on the direction of the Censorship and an order to submit in full was issued.[123] Following the receipt of a letter from the managing director in which he proffered apologies and claimed that the order was tantamount to suppression of the paper, the order was revoked on 24 September.[124] Coyne impressed upon him the necessity of complying with directions and warned that if another order were issued it would be enforced.[125] On 16 November 1940 the *Enniscorthy Echo* ran a leader headed 'Glorious Greece' which began 'You can lead the Italians to the battle, but you can't make them fight'. Another order was issued for submission in full. It was revoked after the submission of one week's issue on the basis of an assurance from the paper that all editorial matter would be submitted in future.[126]

On 14 October 1940 the *Donegal Democrat* was issued with a submission order following its publication of a local scoop headed 'Boat attacked near Killybegs'. The order was lifted two days later following an appeal from the proprietor and a local judge who told the Censorship that the order had brought the proprietor to the verge of a nervous breakdown; following the lifting of the order the judge wrote again, thanking God for 'a Government Department endowed with real understanding and humanity'![127] The *Connaught Tribune* repeatedly published articles which contravened the regulations in the first years of the war and was warned on a number of occasions. In February 1941 the publication of a poem entitled 'Hitler' (which ended with the lines 'That stupid cry, "Heil, Hitler, Heil"') provoked a complaint from Hempel and an order to submit in full on 7 February. Following the submission of two issues and a written guarantee of future good behaviour, the order was lifted.[128]

The 12 April 1941 issue of the *Tipperary Star* carried two items which had been stopped for other papers: a report on the visit of the Australian prime minister to Dublin and a reference to the bombing of Belfast. An order to submit in full was issued on 16 April. One issue was submitted, accompanied by an assurance from the editor that he would in future submit all doubtful matter, especially that relating to foreign affairs and the war; the order was revoked on 24 April.[129] The paper's Dublin correspondent created problems again when the 'Dublin Letter' of 6 June 1941 made reference to the case of Charlie McGuinness, brought before the Military Tribunal accused of 'selling information to Germany'. The case was held *in camera* and the Dublin newspapers had been prohibited from disclosing any information about it. A direction was issued on 8 June compelling the *Tipperary Star* to submit in future the full text of its 'Dublin Letter'.[130]

E.T. Keane, editor of the *Kilkenny People* for half a century, was 'a living legend in his own lifetime' and 'arguably the outstanding provincial editor of this century'.[131] He was also 'an irreconcilable political opponent'[132] of Fianna Fáil and 'the most troublesome gentleman with whom the Censorship had to deal'.[133] He consistently ignored directions and published censorable matter but 'because of his record and age he was allowed great latitude'.[134] The patience of the Censorship ran out in January 1941 when Keane published an editorial with 'an anti-Axis bias' on the bombs dropped on Dublin, the Curragh and Borris, Co. Carlow; he also expressed doubt about whether

> the powers invested in the Heavenly Twins drest in the little brief authority of the Censorship, Mr Aiken the Defence Minister with the polysyllabic tail to his title like a forlorn comet looping the loop, and Mr Connolly, have not been exercised unfairly and in a manner not free from political partisanship.[135]

A direction to submit in full was issued to the *Kilkenny People* on 13 January 1941; it was revoked two days later on the strength of assurances of future good behaviour from Keane.[136] He continued to offend, however, and was frequently reprimanded and warned. On 28 March 1942 Keane, in the course of a leading article, referred to the action of the Censorship in stopping one of his items. He was directed, on 31 March, to submit in future all leading articles and editorial comment before publication. The next issue carried no leader but the following week he submitted an editorial entitled 'The Liberty of the Press', based on debates in the British houses of parliament concerning the freedom of the press. The censor, on the instruction of Aiken, suggested a number of alterations and additions, including the changing of the title to 'The Liberty and Licence of the Press' and the addition of the following:

> Another curious phenomenon which has been observed recently is that certain Editors understand liberty to mean no more than licence to hurl abuse at the Government and representatives elected by their own people which they would not have dared to hurl at a foreign tyranny when robbing and dragooning the country.[137]

An outraged Keane refused to adopt the 'suggestions' and the article was stopped in its entirety. He wrote to Knightly condemning this 'audacious attempt to make me the medium of attacking other newspapers and making charges against them which I know to be false' while 'you, the real author of it, skulk in the background'.[138] In place of the leader Keane published, under the heading 'The Voice of the People', a verse of Yeats's ('Was it for this the Wild Geese spread/The grey wing on every tide . . . Romantic Ireland's dead and gone/It's with O'Leary in the grave'), and an extract from Swift's 'Fourth Drapier's Letters', which ended: 'although a man upon the rack was never known to be refused the liberty of roaring as loud as he thought fit'.[139]

Keane continued to ignore the direction regarding leaders, submitting them only sporadically and for certain periods stopping publishing editorials at all. On 16 December 1944 he published a leading article under the title 'Partition', in which he wrote of the debt owed to Northern Ireland by the British and Americans. It was quoted with approval in the *Belfast Telegraph* and the *Londonderry Sentinel*.[140] Knightly wrote to Keane on 16 January 1945 threatening him with prosecution for prejudicing the interests of the state by 'justifying the occupation of the six north-eastern counties on the grounds of the strategic convenience of that territory to the belligerents'.[141] Keane's wife died the following week and no further action was taken.[142]

At the war's end Coyne pointed to the history of the Censorship's relations with Keane and the *Kilkenny People* as an illustration of the problems which arise when the authorities lack the power to enforce directions that are given. Keane ignored the Censorship directions despite the threat of prosecution 'in the evident hope', wrote Coyne,

> that the prosecution would never be brought or would fail or else would turn out to be a pyrrhic victory because of public sympathy with the editor . . . Here was a man on the brink of the grave (he has since died), his fortune and fame established, with almost nothing to lose and a lifetime of controversy behind him. What was there to fear? Jail was almost out of the question. The mere institution of proceedings would, indeed, be represented as a political persecution. And if he had to suspend publication for a time and get rid of his staff what of it? Perhaps he could get the staff back on better terms later on . . .

(The latter was reputed to have happened when the paper was suppressed by the British censor in 1920.) Short of taking the power to suppress the paper and seize its printing presses, the threat of which would probably have proved sufficient, Coyne believed that the only way Keane could have been 'brought to heel' was by empowering the Censorship to enter the paper's premises and see that its directions were being carried out by supervising production. Fortunately for Keane, no such power was available.[143]

In a letter to Knightly in December 1941 Keane had written that if he 'had the protection that Minister Aiken gave the *Dundalk Examiner . . .* I would not be subject to these annoyances'.[144] Aiken was a director of the *Dundalk Examiner* which on 1 November 1941 ran, according to the Censorship, 'an extremely mischievous leading article' under the heading 'Roosevelt's Cock and Bull Story'. The writer took issue with the American president's 'ludicrous' claim that the Nazis had plans for the partition of South America and the destruction of all religion. Having declared the impossibility of destroying religion and identifying the Soviet Union as the greatest threat to it, the article went on to give a qualified defence of the Nazi record with regard to the Catholic Church. The editor was strongly remonstrated with for having published this article without submission and was directed to submit all leading articles and editorial matter for censorship in future (the editor having apologised and explained that the article had been written and published in his absence).[145] The matter was raised in the Dáil by Patrick McGilligan in November 1941 and again at adjournment in February 1942. Like Keane, he compared its treatment with that of the *Kilkenny People* and implied that the Dundalk paper had received preferential treatment because of its links with Aiken. The Censorship was in fact careful not to appear to give preferential treatment to Fianna Fáil-linked papers like the *Dundalk Examiner* and the *Irish Press*. The direction to submit editorial matter issued to the *Dundalk Examiner* was revoked in January 1944, following an appeal by the editor and on the understanding that it was still necessary to submit matter relating to international affairs or any subjects specified in the directions.[146]

The censorship regulations were lifted on 11 May 1945; on the following day the *Nationalist* (Clonmel) published an editorial entitled 'We Heave a Sigh', which gives a flavour of how the censorship affected and frustrated the work of the provincial press for over five years, with its 'most rigid and frenzy-making' regulations. The editor celebrated that they were now free from

> the haunting fear that in our previous issue we may have committed 'A MAJOR CRIME' – we might even have gone so far from the 'straight and narrow' as to blazon forth that the weather, apart from a few showers, was summer-like or that the week's fine spell should do great things for the crops!!

He acknowledged the necessity of a censorship in time of war, 'but when that censorship was so bound up with characteristically stuffy, nonsensical, idiotic and what-have-you red-tape regulations which fairly reeked of the professional civil servant as to make an Editor's everyday life a kind of prolonged mental torture', he asked readers to appreciate how it felt 'at this moment of release from bondage'.[147]

OTHER IRISH PUBLICATIONS*

The *Leader*, D.P. Moran's famous Irish–Ireland paper, was ordered to submit in full before publication on 26 June 1940 following its publication without submission of an editorial which suggested the advantages to Ireland of a German victory.[148] A publication called *News and Views* was likewise directed in July 1943; this paper consisted of a collection of news cuttings, compiled by journalist Sidney Czira, and included matter which had been stopped for the Irish papers.[149] *The Progressive Printer and Newspaper Publisher*, a trade paper with private circulation, was the only publication of its type to be ordered to submit in full; this occurred in February 1941, following its publication of a feature on the 'Spitfire Fund', sponsored by the *Belfast Telegraph*;[150] *The Bakery Trades Journal* was the only trade union paper to meet a similar fate (see Chapter 6 p. 255). Few publications, however, managed to escape the attention of the censors.

The *Irish Tobacco Trade Journal* was warned on a number of occasions for publishing censorable matter without submission; in October 1944, for example, an explanation was sought for its publication of a reference to non-smoker Montgomery making a gift of one million cigarettes to the troops in Normandy.[151] The *Licensed Vintner and Grocer* was warned about referring to the export of beer,[152] while the *Screen* was instructed to stay off the subject of the war record of stars like Jimmy Stewart, Henry Fonda, Clarke

---

* Religious, Republican and left-wing publications are treated in chapter 6 pp. 220-57.

Gable and Tyrone Power.[153] In November 1944 the *Irish Agricultural and Creamery Review* was warned following its publication of an article entitled 'Taking the Mystery out of Bacteriology'; the author, an American professor, had written that 'Bacteria are the Hitlers and Hirohitos of the organic world', and that 'milk is a virtual "Poland" for these microscopic "Hitlerites"'.[154] The professor of bacteriology at Trinity College, Dublin was employed by the British forces in the fight against the 'Hitlerites' of the non-microscopic variety, a fact which the *Journal of the Free State Medical Union* was prohibited from publishing.[155] The *Irish Farmer's Gazette* apologised for referring to the effect of the German invasion on Danish dairy farming,[156] while the *Garda Review* was prohibited from publishing extracts from the *German Police Gazette*; following publication of objectionable matter in its 'International Comment' the *Review* was instructed to submit all matter related to international affairs to the Censorship before publication.[157]

The *Bell*, edited by Seán O'Faoláin, is famous for having championed the struggle against literary censorship in Ireland; its main difficulties with the emergency political censorship arose from the contents of O'Faoláin's 'One World' editorials. Following the mutilation of his editorial on the Masaryk affair, and in defence of the Irish Institute of International Affairs (see Chapter 4, pp. 147-9), O'Faoláin declared that he would move to Belfast to publish if he was going to be silenced in the South; Coyne commented that he refrained from saying that he wished he would.[158] Another editorial in the same month, December 1944, was likewise heavily censored. Its criticisms were directed at de Valera and his Department of External Affairs; in one of the deleted portions O'Faoláin had written:

> Mr de Valera's peasant love for secrecy and hugger-mugger, combined with his natural turn for benevolent despotism, has turned our Ministry of External Affairs into a machine for that peculiarly tiresome and dangerous type of secret diplomacy which is being dispatched in Europe at the very time that we are apparently bringing it to a fine art.[159]

An article from the previous edition, 'What it means to be a Jew', by A.J. Leventhal was so heavily censored that it was not worth publishing. The article dealt with anti-Semitism, past and present, in Ireland and abroad. While some of the deletions are explicable by reference to censorship policy (e.g. references to the Nazis) the deletion of other sections, like those dealing with aspects of Jewish culture,[160] are less easily understood or explained.

One of the two most organised groups of anti-Semites in Ireland at this time – the other being Ailtirí na hAiséirighe – was the organisation styling itself the People's National Party. This Irish Nazi group, led by George Griffin, was secretly preparing for the arrival of a German invasion force, and included among its number Eoin O'Duffy, founder of the Blueshirts and first leader of Fine Gael; Alex McCabe, a former Cumann na

The front page of the January 1941 edition of *Penapa,* the paper of the Irish fascist People's National Party, featuring a typically crude anti-Semitic caricature. All copies of the paper were seized by the Gardaí as the cover and much of the content had not been submitted to the censor before publication. Blatant anti-Semitic material was banned because it was regarded as prejudicial to the maintenance of public order.

nGaedheal TD; a number of Fianna Fáil party workers and several police officers.[161] It launched the first issue of its paper, *Penapa*, in December 1940. Proofs were submitted to the Censorship and a number of anti-Semitic references and articles were deleted, in pursuance of censorship policy which regarded the promotion of anti-Semitism as prejudicial to the maintenance of public order. The paper went ahead and published a good deal of poisonous anti-Semitic matter which had not been submitted, including the cover which featured 'The Uncrowned King', a crude caricature of a rich Jew sitting on bags of money over the Irish economy. When this came to the notice of the Censorship, *Penapa* was ordered to submit all matter in full before publication. Certain items were submitted, but when the January issue came out it featured the same cover as the previous issue and a series of anti-Semitic articles which the censor had not seen. These included court reports on moneylending cases involving Jews, articles on 'The Jewish Nation and Freemasonry', an anti-Semitic apostolic letter of Pope Gregory XIII from 1581 and a poem entitled 'The Hibernicised Jews'. A direction for the seizure of this issue was made by Coyne and over 8,000 copies were seized from the printers in Drogheda and the party's offices in Dublin; Griffin and other members of the executive were questioned by the Gardaí regarding the contravention of the December order to submit in full. The Censorship was flooded with more of the same type of matter for the next issue, but the Gardaí in Drogheda had received an assurance from the printers that they would not print any more issues until they were satisfied that the contents had been passed for publication. Most of the submitted items were stopped and Griffin obviously saw little point in continuing to attempt to publish *Penapa*; no further issues appeared.[162]

Griffin and company did not disappear, however, and in June 1942 they resurfaced as the Irish Christian Rights Protection Association. The *Irish Times* reported on a leaflet they were circulating that attacked the 'pernicious evils' of moneylending and hire-purchase, which were in the control of 'aliens'. Coyne signed an order for the seizure of the leaflet on 29 June 1942, on the basis that it contained matter 'likely to lead to a breach of the peace', and 320 copies were seized.[163]

Anti-Semitism continued to be an ugly, though censored, presence in Ireland. In January 1944, for example, the Censorship deleted remarks made by a number of delegates at the Fine Gael árd fheis; one had stated that it seemed impossible to get a Jew convicted in the Special Criminal Court and that aliens fleeing 'justice' in Central Europe were setting themselves up as successful businessmen in Ireland and employing slave labour. In the following month reports were prohibited of a number of anti-Semitic actions in Dublin; 'Jews' had been painted in two-foot letters across a number of Jewish-owned premises on Grafton Street and labels with the words 'Perish Judah' were stuck on the windows.[164]

EXTERNAL NEWSPAPERS

Arthur Griffith once said that the British had built a paper wall around Ireland; on the inside they painted what they wanted the Irish to know about the rest of the world, on the outside what they wanted the rest of the world to know about Ireland.[165] The news agencies which supplied international news to the Irish press, and news of Ireland to the world, provided one part of this double-sided mural; the other part was provided by the British press. After independence English daily and Sunday newspapers and the various periodicals continued to have a high circulation in the new state. The war was to have a serious impact on circulation figures for a number of reasons, the press censorship being only a minor factor. In fact there was a pre-war background of falling circulation of English newspapers, beginning in 1929. This was the year that the Censorship of Publications Act became law and it led to the banning of two Sunday newspapers, the *Sunday Pictorial* and *Thompson's Weekly News*. (Objection to the contents of English Sunday newspapers had been the main driving force of the campaign which resulted in the Act.) Other pre-war factors included the Betting Act of 1931, the imposition of a newspaper import tax in 1933 (and its increase in the following year) and the increase in the price of newspapers in May 1934.[166]

With the onset of war in 1939 circulation figures began to drop dramatically so that by September 1941 the total circulation of English dailies and Sundays in Ireland had fallen by about 60 per cent.[167] The principal operative causes of this decline were the disruption of transport and the scarcity of newsprint.

By the outset of 1940 the mailboat delivering the English dailies no longer arrived on time to connect with the early morning trains which distributed the Dublin dailies countrywide. By July 1940 the cross-channel newspapers were being delivered on the afternoon trains and by September, as the mailboat arrived later and more irregularly, many of the English newspapers were held over for distribution with the Dublin dailies on the following morning. This led directly to a 15–20 per cent drop in circulation. Efforts to counteract the problems caused by the mailboat by importing newspapers through Belfast were hampered by the deterioration in the train service between Belfast and Dublin. As coal shortages began to bite, this service was severely reduced as were train services within the state, with the result that newspapers increasingly were delivered by lorry and bus.[168] Petrol shortages soon affected these services and transport difficulties so disrupted deliveries to rural areas that circulation was practically killed there.[169]

Newsprint shortages were severe and heavy restrictions were imposed in Britain on the use of paper.[170] The supply of newspapers in Britain thus fell far short of demand; given this fact, and the deterioration in the advertising position, it is remarkable that so many English publications continued to circulate in Ireland. The principal reason for their doing so was, presumably, to maintain their share of the market with a view to the postwar period. For example, the *Daily Mail*, which continued to circulate in Ireland throughout the war, increased its share of the Irish market during the Emergency. After the war it outsold the *Daily Express*, which had ceased Irish circulation in 1941, while in England the *Express* had established a far greater circulation than the *Mail*.[171] The political objective of presenting the 'British perspective', news being seen as 'the shocktroops of propaganda', was also a factor.

By late 1940 newspapers were made non-returnable. A system of forced orders was introduced, special deliveries were cut out altogether and the casual purchase of cross-channel newspapers became virtually non-existent. Supplies from the publishers were constantly cut back in the light of all these difficulties and the cost of distribution in Ireland was becoming considerable relative to the revenue from sales.[172] In March 1941 both the *News of the World* and the *Daily Express* discontinued supplies to the twenty- six counties and other newspapers, temporarily or permanently, discontinued Irish parcels. Neither the *Daily Mirror* nor *Cavalcade* resumed supplies after bans on them were lifted in September–October 1941, while in May 1941 *Picture Post*, unable to meet demand in England, held back supplies to Ireland. This was a severe blow to its Irish distributors as the *Post* had the largest circulation at that time of any illustrated general-interest weekly. It had already encountered difficulties with Irish censorship on 'moral grounds' and John Eason, managing director of Eason and Son, the leading Irish newspaper wholesalers, concluded that 'the publisher was not willing to take the risk of his paper being stopped on either of the two grounds of censorship with which he had experienced difficulty'.[173] (The issue of 27 July 1940 had been seized under emergency powers.)

The onset of war had led to a huge upsurge in the popularity of illustrated papers, which became, in the main, 'virulent propaganda' organs. The problem for Ireland was that it, unlike other neutrals, possessed virtually no indigenous 'picture-press' and was totally dependent for such material on the British. In the first months of the war the free circulation of these papers created some difficulties for the Censorship. Following complaints from Hempel, in October 1939, Joseph Walshe of External Affairs contacted Connolly suggesting that 'we should make some effort to keep out what might be described as bestial propaganda'. The power existed under the Emergency Powers (No. 5) Order 1939 to prohibit the importation of named external newspapers and to seize any copies already in the country.[174] The Censorship, however, decided at first to take an informal approach and asked Eason to contact the chief offenders. Eason had earlier in the month written to Odhams, publishers of *News Review*, explaining his 'apprehension' about its 'vigorous' propaganda.[175] He now wrote to the circulation manager of *Illustrated War Weekly* pointing out that there was a danger of the paper being banned in Ireland on the basis of its propagandist content.[176] As we shall see, however, no official action was taken against any English publication until March 1940.

In the meantime, newspaper posters became the main source of difficulty in relation to crass propaganda. The Press Censorship was becoming 'somewhat embarrassed', according to Knightly, by anti-German posters which, he believed, could not 'with propriety be allowed to be displayed on the public streets of a neutral state'. As well as slogans such as 'Huns Must Hang', objection was taken to phrases like 'How Hitler Hopes to Wipe Us Out' which took for granted that Ireland was a belligerent at war with Germany.[177] As early as 15 September 1939 the local *Daily Express* correspondent had been warned that posters such as 'Hitler Bombs Children' could lead to a prohibition of the newspaper.[178] Such posters, however, continued to be displayed and were the subject of a complaint by Senator Margaret Pearse on 23 November 1939; she was assured by the minister that action was being taken on the issue.[179]

The Gardaí seized the *Cavalcade* poster 'These Huns Must Hang' at the request of the Censorship and on 1 December 1939 Knightly wrote to the principal importers of English newspapers to enlist their help in dealing with 'the poster nuisance'. They were asked to communicate to the publishers that the Irish authorities wished them to drop posters altogether in relation to Irish sales, or to at least restrict them to the title of the paper and inoffensive matter. Meanwhile the importers/distributors were asked to refrain from distributing objectionable posters.[180] A circular was sent to the English publishers calling attention to the matter and this, allied to a paper-saving wartime reduction in poster production,[181] put an end to the 'poster nuisance'.

Problems remained, however, with the content of cross-channel newspapers themselves. On 5 January 1940 the *Daily Mirror* ran an item on a 'Mystery Ship Hunt in Éire', regarding a search by the army and Gardaí for a ship crewed by IRA members who were planning to use it to dump arms and ammunition. The story was regarded as dangerous, if true, and mischievous, if false. It led to a complaint to the British authorities by the Irish high commissioner in London and the 'good offices' of the importers and distributors were again enlisted on the strength of their success on the posters issue. They were asked to convey to English newspaper publishers that if any newspaper in the future published any matter which was considered detrimental to the security and interests of Ireland steps would be taken to seize issues or ban importation of the newspaper altogether. All of the English newspapers were notified of the position through the various newspaper associations and the Irish distributors were told that there should be no further cause for complaint.[182] In fact the 'causes for complaint' increased and from March 1940 to June 1944 there were fifteen bannings and five seizures of cross-channel newspapers under the emergency powers orders.

While Hempel had been promised that if English newspapers became 'too offensively' anti-German they would be stopped, all the bans and seizures were related to articles which dealt with Ireland. Most occurred between April and September 1940 when the British press campaign against Irish neutrality was at its height. Problems arose again in 1944, around the period of the American Note affair.

The first action taken against a non-Irish publication was on 7 March 1940 when copies of the British weekly news magazine *News Review* were seized by the Gardaí after distribution.[183] The cause of the seizure was an article carried in the 7 March edition headed 'Éire's German Agents', which outlined 'the remarkable activities of Hitler's two chief envoys in Éire', Hempel and Henning Thomsen. The article described how Hempel curried favour with de Valera and the Irish and how both men held strategic positions of prime importance to the German intelligence service.[184]

On 9 April 1940 an order was issued which prohibited the importation of the weekly *Reynolds News*, because of an article on the IRA hunger strike in its English and Irish editions, published in contravention of the directions to the press. The article was written by the papers Irish correspondent, who was a subeditor in the *Irish Press*, Brian O'Neill. He appealed the decision on the grounds that he was ignorant of the particular direction which required prior submission to the censor of all matter relating to the hunger strike. He was told that the ban would be revoked for the next issue provided *Reynolds News* gave an undertaking to comply with the directions in future.

The ban was lifted, but in the following week's issue *Reynolds News* claimed the right to publish any item on the basis of its veracity, irrespective of whether its publication was expressly forbidden by the Irish Censorship. The latter pointed out that truth or falsehood were not the only factors that had to be considered in the enforcement of censorship; they explained that external newspapers could not circulate in Ireland in competition with Irish newspapers and contain matter on Irish affairs which those newspapers could not carry. Thus, another prohibition order on *Reynolds News* was issued on 23 April 1940 and it remained in force until 20 May when the publishers declared themselves 'aware' of the restrictions and their intention to abide by them.[185] (*Reynolds News* provided cause for complaint again in the issue of 24 August 1941, but on this occasion the authorities took no further action. The objectionable article related to the bombs which fell on Dublin on 31 May 1941. It stated that the Irish government had claimed £400,000 compensation from the Germans and had received only £23,000. 'The balance', wrote the author, 'apparently represents the price of Irish neutrality.'[186])

On 17 April 1940 two orders were made prohibiting the importation of the *Sunday Times* and the *Daily Mirror*.[187] The *Mirror* on that day carried a cartoon showing a Nazi figure lying across a map of Ireland, hand to ear towards Britain. The caption read: 'The Enemy Within – Spies in Éire are having a free hand to send Britain's war secrets to Germany via the Dublin Legation'. As copies of this issue had already arrived in the country arrangements were made for these to be seized. In response the editor of the *Mirror* wrote that there was never any intention to reflect on 'the good faith of the neutrality of the State of Éire – indeed nothing was further from our thoughts'! He apologised and pointed out that in the same issue they had deleted reference to the hunger striker Tony D'Arcy's death due to a communication from the Censorship and that this had required a special change of the page and other emergency action.[188] He gave an assurance that nothing would appear in the *Mirror* in future which would cast doubt on Éire's neutrality or provoke internal disorder.[189] The prohibition order was revoked on 19 April.[190]

The ban on the *Sunday Times* was lifted on 18 April, but on that day the *News Review* was in trouble again. The Gardaí were directed by Coyne to seize all copies of the issue from the distributors and to destroy them. The magazine had carried an item, 'Nazis in Éire', which had appeared in *The People* on the previous Sunday, suggesting again that Ireland was being used as a centre for German espionage activities (both papers were published by Odhams, Ltd). An order prohibiting the importation of *The People* was made on 19 April 1940. This ban was regarded as an 'absolute disaster' by Harry Hughes, *The People*'s main distributor, as this popular Sunday newspaper had a circulation of up to 60,000 in the twenty-six counties at this time. It was taken so seriously by the publishers that they sought a meeting with the Censorship and Aiken. Two representatives travelled to Ireland and met with Connolly and Coyne on Saturday, 20 April. It was pointed out to them that the article was highly offensive and mischievous, particularly in the light of the efforts being made through the postal, telegraph and press censorship to prevent espionage activities. They were told of the suspicion on the part of the Censorship that this article was 'part of a campaign to spread the idea that Éire was being made the centre for information being made available to the Germans' and that such a campaign had the effect of creating 'bad blood' between the governments and peoples of both countries.[191]

The Odhams representatives were profuse in their apologies and were prepared to give any guarantees sought by the Censorship. The guarantees required were: nothing would appear in future which cast doubt on the genuineness of Irish neutrality or the state's capacity to maintain it; there would be no further suggestions of the government permitting espionage activity; and nothing dealing with internal disturbances or problems would be published unless passed by the Irish censor. The representatives agreed to give these guarantees, and on the understanding that they would send written conformation of this undertaking on return to England, the ban on *The People* was raised.

At the meeting an informal discussion then took place about the British press attitude to Irish affairs. It was pointed out by Connolly and Coyne

Extract from Daily Mirror
of 17ᵗʰ April, 1940

THE DAILY MIRROR — 17.4.40   Page 9

The Enemy Within!

Spies in Eire are having a free hand to send Britain's war secrets to Germany via the Dublin Legation.

A cartoon in the *Daily Mirror* of 17 April 1940, presenting neutral Ireland as a base for Nazis spying on Britain, a common theme in the British press during the war. All copies of the paper were seized in Ireland and its importation was banned because of the cartoon.

that the press had 'considerable power for good and evil in the present difficult time', and on their return to Fleet Street the representatives might do something to remove 'the absurd rumours and mischievous publicity' which were current there. They gave an undertaking to do their utmost to dispel any wrong impressions that existed in English press circles, which, given that Odhams controlled a large number of newspapers and weekly journals, was regarded by Connolly as a valuable promise.[192]

A review of the work of the Censorship, prepared at the end of the war, suggested that 'the most important work done by the Censorship was in calming a British Press infuriated by lying stories' about Ireland. This was achieved through personal contact, as in the above case, and by making influential newspapers like the *Times, Sunday Dispatch, Daily Mail, Daily Express* and *Manchester Guardian* 'see the error of their ways' and having 'friendly' articles published in them.[193]

Although Coyne had suggested to Aiken that the exclusion of offending newspapers would not be 'an effective remedy' in countering the British press campaign, such actions continued to be taken, despite fears expressed by the distributor Tivy that, given the newsprint shortage, there was a danger of losing supplies of British newspapers altogether.[194]

On 2 May 1940 a prohibition was placed on the importation of *News Review*. This ban increased Tivy's fears, as the publishers had informed him personally that they would stop sending the magazine to Ireland if it was again seized (it having already been seized twice, as we have seen). Solicitors acting for the publishers (Odhams) in Dublin, however, informed the Censorship that *News Review* was now in possession of the official requirements and would conform in the future. Aiken felt that the ban should be lifted; Coyne wrote that 'at the back of his [Aiken's] mind . . . is the idea that if we can secure a friendly press, or even a neutral press, on the other side without abating any of our sovereign rights, it is worthwhile doing so'. The prohibition order on *News Review* was duly revoked on 3 June 1940 and the Government Information Bureau was requested to 'secure such publicity as possible' for the revocation. The *News Review* offended again in May 1944 and on the eighteenth of that month was the last newspaper to be seized during the Emergency (having also been the first).[195]

The *Daily Mirror* fell foul of the Censorship again on 11 May 1940. Its English edition of that day carried an article entitled 'Britain Buys Bases in Éire'. It claimed that Britain had paid the Irish government fifty million pounds for the right to take over camps, fortresses and air and sea bases formerly held by the British. The deal, claimed the article, would strike a blow at the activities of German nationals living under the cloak of the German legation and mentioned, in conclusion, that Britain had large concentrations of troops in Northern Ireland 'ready to move in any direction from which danger threatens'. Although the article was not carried in the Irish edition, its appearance in the English edition at this particularly sensitive time was considered serious enough to justify a punitive ban on the paper in Ireland.[196] This time there were no apologies and assurances, as the difficulties with the Censorship, allied to newsprint shortage, transport difficulties and dropping circulation led the *Mirror* to cease sales in Ireland until after the war.[197] (The ban was, however, lifted in September 1941 – in interesting circumstances, as shall be seen.)

On 22 July 1940 importation of the periodical *Cavalcade* was prohibited by order. In the issue of 20 July it had carried 'an inaccurate and mischievous' article under the caption 'Ireland's Peril' in its 'World Behind the Headlines' series. It dealt with advanced German plans for an invasion of Ireland with the co-operation of Seán Russell and other IRA men in Germany, as well as fifth columnists within Ireland.[198] The order was revoked in October 1941 and Easons communicated with the publishers, Argus, with a view to resuming supplies to Ireland; the latter, however, did not see fit to take any action and *Cavalcade* remained unavailable to Irish readers.[199]

The issue of 27 July of another illustrated periodical, *Picture Post*, carried an article by Tania Long, London correspondent of the *New York Herald Tribune*. The objectionable subject was again the threat of German invasion and the activities of fifth columnists. An order for seizure of the issue was made and the Gardaí seized over 4,500 copies from around the country. Aggrieved retailers seeking compensation arising out of losses from the seizure were told to apply to the publishers through the wholesale suppliers.[200]

The last publication to be banned in 1940 was *News Chronicle*, for an article headed 'Dublin Lights Point the Way' in the issue of 24 October. The article referred to the absence of a blackout in Dublin, which made it a signpost for night bombers on raids over Liverpool and other northwestern English towns. The prohibition order was made on 29 October and revoked on 13 November after an apology was given by *News Chronicle*.[201] Coyne, in recommending the revocation to Aiken, wrote that given the small circulation of the *Chronicle* (approximately 700), it was more in the interests of the Irish authorities than of the newspaper that the publishers' goodwill be retained, 'or, at any rate, their neutrality in respect of their English circulation'. In September 1941 *News Chronicle* submitted a proof for censorship of an article for its Irish edition entitled 'Éire Wants British Guns'. It was the first time that an article had been submitted by an external newspaper, and in reply the Censorship pointed out that, while it was not the practice to censor external newspapers, action would be taken if there was an attempt to circulate the matter in Ireland.[202]

Hempel, meanwhile, continued to complain about the anti-German propaganda contained in British publications. Following one complaint in April 1941 (in relation to 'Hitler's Childhood Exposed' in *Reynolds News* and 'Hitler's Most Brutal General' in the *Sunday Chronicle*) Coyne wrote to Boland at the Department of External Affairs. He explained that they expected English newspapers to be anti-German 'and if they become too offensively so we may be forced to stop them altogether. We want to avoid this if possible as such an action would be bound to be misinterpreted by our enemies both in England and America.' He expressed the hope that the newsprint shortage might solve the problem for them and pointed out that 'an article tucked away in the middle of a paper which has little or no circulation and no influence here is not likely to do much harm'.[203] In November 1941 Coyne wrote that he did not expect an English paper not to be offensive to the Axis; 'what we do require is that, in their Irish editions, at any rate, they shall not outstep the bounds of decency'. These bounds began to be outstepped as atrocity stories started to appear with increasing frequency in the English press. On 9 November 1941 the *Sunday Chronicle* carried an article by Beverley Nichols entitled 'They [the 'Huns'] Crucified a Priest'. Coyne contacted Doran O'Reilly, the *Chronicle*'s local correspondent, and explained that this article had 'crossed the line'. As a result of representations from the Censorship in relation to atrocity stories the *Chronicle* arranged for a new 'Irish page', in Irish editions, to take the place of the atrocity material – an action which obviously pleased the Irish authorities.[204]

In the autumn of 1941 Senator Frank MacDermot, an outspoken critic of Irish neutrality and censorship, was on one of his many wartime visits to the United States. In speeches, broadcasts, articles and interviews MacDermot aired his forthright views on the situation in Ireland, with particular reference to neutrality, attitudes to the war and the activities of the Censorship. His activities were kept under close scrutiny by the Irish authorities and in August 1941 a cablegram from the Washington legation gave details of an interview with the senator which was published in the *New York Post* on 29 August. During the course of the interview MacDermot claimed that the popular support for neutrality was due in great measure to the Censorship; 'Arguments against neutrality and news that would create anti-Nazi sentiment simply are not printed.' In order to counter this claim the Washington legation sought details of the circulation of English newspapers in Ireland and on 16 September Walshe asked Coyne for the names of the papers and their circulation figures so that the legation could publicise them and say that all English newspapers were allowed to circulate freely in Ireland.[205]

Coyne sent on to Walshe the approximate circulation figures, but pointed out that the *Daily Mirror* had been banned since May 1940. 'The existence of this single exception', wrote Coyne, 'seems to me to spoil what would otherwise be a perfect case', and he suggested, subject to Aiken's presumed approval, that the order prohibiting the importation of the *Mirror* be revoked, backdated to 15 September 1941, the day Coyne had become controller, 'as a sort of amnesty gesture'. The Department of External Affairs could then inform Washington that not a single English newspaper was excluded by the Censorship. Walshe thought that Coyne's suggestion was 'an excellent one', anticipated Aiken's approval, and informed Washington that all English daily and Sunday newspapers were allowed to circulate freely in Ireland.[206]

The revocation of the *Daily Mirror* ban was in fact backdated to 13 September, the day of Connolly's retirement, thus making it appear as 'a last executive act of grace on Connolly's part' rather than a first act of generosity on the part of the new controller. In October, Coyne realised that one other blot on the perfect picture in fact remained – the ban on *Cavalcade* was still in place. He contacted Knightly to sign the revocation order on 24 October and asked him to backdate this also to 13 September.[207]

In November 1942 issues of *Irish Freedom* were seized by customs and detained by the postal censor on Coyne's orders. This was the paper of the Connolly Association, an Irish republican communist group in Britain, which during the war sought to organise Irish immigrant workers. Among its most well-known members was the labour historian and political activist, C. Desmond Greaves.[208] Coyne had a particular dislike for this organ and believed that its 'particular brand of Irish Republican Communism was entirely bogus'. He told Aiken in December 1942 that he thought it was subsidised by the Soviet Union and by Scotland Yard 'which finds it convenient to have politically-minded left-wing Irishmen grouped together in a single organisation whose activities can easily be supervised by the police'. *Irish Freedom* was banned in the North and Coyne very much wanted it banned in the South also, 'and nothing I suspect, would be more unwelcome to the British government as it would expose a very obvious manoeuvre'. Following the entry into the war of the Soviet Union the paper increased its arguments in favour of a maximum British war effort, though continued to defend Ireland's right to remain neutral. However, Coyne maintained his personal campaign against the paper and found small references which were critical of neutrality to bolster his case for its banning. Although supplies to Ireland had ceased at the beginning of 1943, a prohibition order was placed on *Irish Freedom* on 29 March 1943. The paper was renamed the *Irish Democrat (incorporating Irish Freedom)* and was banned under that name on 1 February 1945. The ban remained in place until the lifting of censorship in May 1945.[209]

In the issue of the *Sunday Dispatch* for 5 September 1943 there was an article by Dorothy Crisp entitled 'I See the Tragedy of Ireland'. In it she challenged Ireland's right to be neutral, to refuse the ports to the Royal Navy and to harbour the 'King's enemies' in the shape of the German and Italian legations. Crisp claimed that the economic situation was hopeless and that 'informed people everywhere wanted only one thing – the British to come back and impose one government on the whole country'. She also reported the words of a Dublin journalist who said that Ireland was 'under an iron dictatorship and a censorship that could teach Goebbels all the tricks'. A further article was announced for the following week in which Crisp would 'prove' the unconstitutionality of the presence of the legations in a part of the British empire and show that 'there is a very simple way out'.[210] The local distributor of the *Dispatch*, Kirwan, protested to the paper and advised suspension of supplies to Ireland until this series had finished. On Kirwan's instigation the Manchester editor contacted Coyne and gave an assurance that there would be no more of these articles in either the Irish or English editions. His decision, however, was overruled by the editor-in-chief in London who was determined, as a matter of principle, to run the second article. Aiken duly authorised the order prohibiting importation of the *Sunday Dispatch* on 11 September 1943. The next issue, on the following day, carried a front page 'Statement by the Editor' under the bold heading 'BANNED!' The editor, Charles Eade, accused the Irish government of blackmail and stated that 'British newspapers have played a worthy part in the war against the dictatorship of Hitler and Mussolini. They are not willing to bow to the dictatorship of Mr de Valera.'[211]

When the Manchester editor flew to Dublin to see Coyne with a view to the removal of the ban, the controller suggested that he should obtain an article from 'some competent Irish journalist' setting out the 'Irish point of view' in answer to Dorothy Crisp's articles. John T. Grealish of the *Irish Press* was suggested and the editor duly obtained an article from him and returned with it to Coyne. Grealish had written a spirited defence of Irish neutrality entitled 'Ireland Has Taken Her Decision' and, after some minor alterations by the censor, it was brought back to England. The article appeared in the *Sunday Dispatch* on 1 October 1943 and the prohibition order was revoked on the following day.[212]

In 1944, during the period of the American Note controversy and following the Allied D-Day landings, a number of British journals again took up the habit of running articles attacking Ireland's neutrality and were duly punished. On 2 March 1944 *Everybody's Weekly* (which had a high circulation of approximately 12,000) was banned because of a number of attacks on Irish policy in recent issues. In a letter to the publishers the Dublin Wholesale Agency, in words supplied by the censor, wrote that the articles represented 'an unwarranted attack upon neutrality and the rights of Irish people and [were] bitterly resented as a caddish and lying account'. In April 1945 Eason wrote to Coyne pointing out that *Everybody's Weekly* had been out of circulation for over twelve months, that recent issues had contained no anti-Irish propaganda and he suggested that the ban could be lifted. Coyne and Aiken agreed and the order was revoked on 6 April 1945.[213]

The June 1944 issue of *Strand Magazine* featured an article by A. Beverley Baxter MP with the heading 'Back from Éire, I Ask: Will England Forgive?' and a drawing showing the Dublin skyline with a Swastika flag flying from the rooftop of the German legation. A prohibition order was made on 3 June. In a letter to the publishers on 14 June Eason justified the actions of the Censorship and accused the magazine of indulging in 'political propaganda against this country'. 'Good for you, Jack Eason', commented Coyne,[214] but the circulation manager of the publishers took a different

view, retorting that 'I did not ask for your political opinion. As our principal wholesale agents in Éire I sought your advice as a businessman.' Eason
replied that 'I can find no business solution to a political difficulty'.[215] He
sent the circulation manager some material on the Irish point of view on
neutrality and in February 1945 sent Coyne the previous three issues of *Strand*
suggesting that in the absence of any more 'anti-Irish propaganda' the ban
could be lifted. This was duly done on 12 February 1945.[216]

Interestingly, Eason performed a similar role during the civil war, explaining and justifying the Provisional Government's censorship to an unco-
operative English press,[217] at a time when that government was at war with
the Republican forces led by, among others, Frank Aiken. Eason was again
involved in the lead-up to the prohibition of the *World Digest*, the last English
publication to be banned under the emergency powers. On 19 June 1944
he sent to the Censorship a copy of the *Digest* pointing out that it contained an article critical of Irish neutrality. The *Digest* was banned that very
day and the order was not revoked until April 1945.[218] In common with a
number of other prohibited publications, copies of this were seized by
Customs *en route* to individuals.[219] Prohibited publications could only be
imported under licence, and these licences were granted on only three occasions: to an advertising agency for one copy a week of *Reynolds News*; to
the Trinity College library for copies of *News Review* for its files, on provision that they would not be made available to readers and to Easons to
import one copy of *News Chronicle* for a doctor living in Ireland who acted
as its medical correspondent.[220]

Technically, of course, papers published in the North were also external
publications, although the authorities did not like to admit it. Fortunately
for them, the only Northern papers which had any significant circulation
in the South were nationalist publications like the *Derry Journal*, which,
not surprisingly for a paper dubbed the 'Derry Fianna Fáil Organ',
voluntarily co-operated with the Southern Irish censorship.[221] The *Ulster
Protestant*, which carried articles on the 'Éirish-Germanic Menace' and co-
operation between the 'Celtic Romanists and Jesuit-controlled Germany'
would have been less inclined to co-operate; the 'uncivilised Éirish' authorities
considered the question of banning its importation but decided they would
only degrade themselves by taking 'any notice of it whatsoever'. It sold only nineteen copies a month in the South and its only other market outside
the North was in Orange areas of Canada. A ban by 'Papist Éireland' would
have delighted the publishers, boosted its circulation and could, the
authorities feared, have misled opinion in the US and Canada. Interestingly, David Gray, the American minister and implacable critic of the Irish
Censorship, complained vigorously to the British on a number of occasions
about the failure of their censor to stop some of this journal's more scur-
rilous sectarian outbursts.[222]

CORRESPONDENTS OF THE EXTERNAL PRESS

Coverage of Irish affairs for external newspapers was provided by a variety of correspondents. There were only three full-time staff reporters for outside publications; most of the correspondents were staff reporters on Irish newspapers, and their coverage was supplemented by material from freelance journalists and reporters, mainly British and American, who visited the country for short periods, especially when Ireland was a centre of interest. There was a large influx, for example, in the summer of 1940, as journalists came to find stories of Nazi espionage and Irish aid to the German U–boat campaign, with which to fuel the British press campaign against Irish neutrality. The activities of these correspondents, and the control of 'exported news' in general, presented a particular problem for the Irish Censorship.

As the Press Censorship began to take shape in September 1939 the correspondents had their attention drawn to the terms of the Emergency Powers (No. 5) Order 1939 and the directions to the press issued thereunder. It was made clear to them that material sent out of the country was subject to the same censorship restrictions as material intended for publication within the state; they were thus compelled to submit all such matters as came under the purview of the directions.[223] Given the wide gaps in the censorship net around the state there was ample opportunity for correspondents to evade control. The Postal Censorship was limited, there was no general telephone censorship, while correspondents could smuggle stories out on their own or another's person. Another alternative was to simply write the story after leaving the country. The principal evaders of censorship were visiting foreign journalists who in this way stole a march on their Irish competitors who acted as correspondents for external newspapers.[224]

In an effort to address the problem of censorship evasion in the export of news the government made the Emergency Powers (No. 67) Order 1941, on 29 January. Its provisions made it an offence for any person to send out of the state by post, telegraph, telephone or any other means, any press message relating to 'any event arising out of or connected with the war or internal public order . . . or relating to any actual or alleged attack on the State or to the supply of commodities in the State', without first submitting it for censorship. It did not apply to official government statements or to matter which had already been printed in Ireland. While it was uncertain whether convictions could be obtained under this order, it was made in the belief that it would deter 99 per cent of potential offenders and that things could be made 'very uncomfortable' for the other 1 per cent.[225] In the following month action was taken to implement the terms of the Emergency Powers (Restrictions on the Conveyance of Informative Articles) Order in relation to bus and rail carriage of press letters to places outside the state, i.e. Northern Ireland. Arrangements were made whereby press matter carried in this way had first to be presented to the Press Censorship for treatment.[226]

Most correspondents found that it paid to co-operate with the Censorship and not indulge in 'sharp practices'. A United Press correspondent told a colleague that he had 'lots of stuff really on thin ice approved because it was handled with restraint and in proper perspective'.[227] Others, however, persisted in transmiting 'contraband news', in breach of regulations and undertakings given to the Censorship. Coyne believed that 'by granting facilities or privileges to pressmen the authorities are in some position to control them, especially if the privileges accorded them are real and of substantial value as in this event a withdrawal or threat of withdrawal should operate as a useful deterrent'.[228]

Press cables were filed at the Post Office and were sent from there to the Press Censorship at Dublin Castle, a process which took about an hour. In the case of 'hot' stories, correspondents went directly to the censors and had their copy censored before filing it. With trustworthy correspondents the Censorship was quite informal; short items or individual details were read over the telephone and verbal approval received.[229]

The three full-time staff reporters of external newspapers – Joseph Kenny of the *Daily Express*, John Murdoch of the *Daily Mail* and Hugh Smith of the *Belfast Telegraph* – all enjoyed special, unrestricted facilities for communicating with their newspapers, on the understanding that such facilities would not be used to evade the censorship. They undertook to carry out the agreement made with the authorities in the spirit, as well as the letter, by refusing to give news over the telephone by way of replies to questions from the other end. While the undertaking was 'carried out scrupulously by the representative of the *Belfast Evening Telegraph*',[230] both Kenny of the *Express* and Murdoch of the *Mail* were less scrupulous and, in the case of the latter, paid a price.

In December 1941 Kenny telephoned two stories to the *Express* without prior submission; one concerned the attack on the S.S. *Cambria* (mailboat) and the other a flying boat disaster off the Clare coast. In a letter to Murdoch, the *Daily Mail* correspondent, about the evasions, Coyne pointed out that there was 'nothing but a sense of honour and interest stopping a particular correspondent ignoring an agreement and stealing a march on colleagues and rivals if he's prepared "to get the school a bad name"'. Coyne warned that Kenny was risking having his long-distance telephone facilities, and those of the press generally, withheld altogether; 'Perhaps it is too much to expect a newspaper man to accept a self-denying ordinance like we tried to impose as long as the physical means of communication are ready to hand.' It was 'British rather than Irish interests' that were primarily involved in these stories and Coyne guessed that Kenny assumed that, if the stories were passed by the British censor and thus appeared in the *Express*, the Irish Censorship would not object. This was not the case. The Censorship was in constant contact with the Press Association and frequently passed messages for them before allowing them to be published in Ireland so that the British censor could decide on the question where British interests were involved; but the Press Association, as a news agency, was, in Coyne's words, 'one thing and the *Daily Express* another and we have never overlooked the fact that reporting and newspaper production is a competitive business'.[231]

Coyne continued in this vein when he reprimanded Kenny personally, pointing out to him that the agreement made with the cross-channel corespondents at the time of the making of the EP (No. 67) O 1941 was primarily in their own interests, i.e. to ensure that none would 'scoop' the others. In the case of the *Cambria* and air boat stories the *Express* had scooped its rivals unfairly, and Kenny gave an undertaking not to evade the censorship in such a manner again. He pointed out, however, that when matter which was initially stopped or held over was subsequently released the Censorship invariably omitted to notify the cross-channel correspondents because they had not submitted in writing and therefore the censors had nothing before them to remind themselves. He gave the example of Dillon's anti-neutrality speech in the Dáil in July 1940. It was decided that only those correspondents who had been in contact with the Censorship and were informed that a story was stopped should be told of a subsequent release, so as not to 'hand' the story to those who had not originally worked for it.[232]

In August 1942 Kenny was in trouble again having been heard telephoning uncensored messages to his office regarding six IRA men sentenced to death in Belfast and the activities of the reprieve committee. Coyne wrote to Kenny warning him that he was considering prohibiting incoming calls to cross-channel correspondents altogether and restricting outgoing calls to the text of a pre-censored message which had been submitted to the Censorship in writing.[233] This drastic action was not taken in relation to all cross-channel correspondents but Murdoch of the *Mail* was not so fortunate.

His troubles began in June 1941 when the *Mail* carried a story about the Irish government's compensation claim in respect of the North Strand bombing. Murdoch was warned by Coyne that if he reoffended, his communications with his paper by telephone and telegraph would be cut off.[234] When in April 1942 Murdoch sent out an unauthorised story about the German spy Hans Marschner, 'on the run' in Ireland at the time, Coyne suggested to Aiken that he be prosecuted or, if not, interned. Aiken, however, restricted the penalty to the disconnection of Murdoch's telephone at his home (on 2 May), while the Post Office was told not to put through calls to the *Daily Mail* without authorisation from the Censorship.[235]

On 22 May Murdoch wrote an apology and undertook to submit all further items.[236] The order was revoked and his telephone restored the following day. According to agreed practice cross-channel correspondents telephoned in their stories and they were censored over the telephone. In August 1942 Murdoch telephoned in a particularly long piece and Coyne

requested that he submit it in writing. When Murdoch accused him of being unreasonable, the controller informed him that all his future messages
would have to be submitted in writing and in duplicate for censorship.[237]
The other cross-channel correspondents continued to be facilitated as before,
except in exceptional cases or where there was no urgency. In February 1944
the exceptional obligation of Murdoch was lifted, but he was in difficulty
again the following month.

On 12 March 1944 he telephoned a message to Coyne which related to
the possibility of economic sanctions and Irish vulnerability to them, in the
wake of the American Note. Coyne told him to omit the references to
sanctions because of the 'very difficult and delicate situation' created by
the note. Murdoch urged Coyne to consider the expediency of giving him
a certain amount of latitude so that his paper would not be tempted to send
someone down from Belfast as before. (He neglected to mention that he
had spent the previous evening with the Belfast correspondent of the *Mail*,
who had come to Dublin on just such a mission.) Coyne said that he refused
to be blackmailed. Murdoch proceeded to telephone the *Mail* and tell them
that he could not be objective and that all he was permitted to convey was
'one-sided'. He was disconnected in the middle of his call; had he not been,
according to Aiken, this latest breach, at the time of the American Note,
'might have helped bring a disaster to this country' as Murdoch was implying that there was alarm and despondency in the country and that Irish
resistance to outside pressure was likely to collapse at the first turn of the
screw. Murdoch's telephone was disconnected by ministerial order for the
second time.[238]

When telephonic communications with Britain were suspended in April
1944, in the run-up to the Normandy landings, Murdoch requested re-
connection as he could not now telephone Britain, but neither could he
use his telephone for internal communications. His repeated requests, accompanied by representations on his behalf by politicians and Irish
newspaper people, were refused until February 1945, when his telephone
facilities were restored.[239]

Correspondents in the press room of the Dáil usually co-operated with
each other in carrying out decisions of the Censorship. Occasionally they
submitted copy jointly for censorship and generally conveyed to each other
whether a story had been passed or stopped. All correspondents were treated
alike so that a story passed for one was invariably passed for all. Occasionally
the system broke down as when Murdoch telephoned a message to the *Mail*
on 4 May 1945, containing the official communiqué about de Valera's expression of condolences on the death of Hitler, with the additional fact that
the swastika flag was flying at half-mast from the German legation. He had
acted on the announcement of a colleague that it was 'OK with the Censor'.
When he discovered that it had not, in fact, been 'OK' and that only the
government statement declaring that the visit had taken place was allowed

he moved quickly to cancel the copy and apologised profusely to the Censorship.[240] Fortunately for Murdoch the censorship restrictions were lifted the following week and the burden of this particular correspondent was substantially lightened.

David Gray, in a memo on the Censorship, wrote that correspondents of American and British papers were 'all treated as potential or actual spies and saboteurs' who were constantly threatened with arrest and intimidated by visits from the police.[241] However, a number of correspondents who visited Ireland for short periods had a good relationship with the authorities, co-operated fully and wrote objective, accurate articles about the situation in the country. Others indulged in racist stereotyping and deliberate propaganda using a mixture of half-truths, fantasies and lies. Others again fell victim to a variety of practical jokes, deceptions and exaggerations at the hands of 'natives' who regarded the picture of Ireland which was presented in the foreign press far less seriously than did the authorities.

A 'blackguardly deception' was worked on a special representative of the *Daily Mail* in July 1940, when the British press campaign against Irish neutrality was at its height. The *Daily Mail* man was among the influx of journalists who poured into the country at this time. His first piece, telephoned in from Limerick to Murdoch for submission, was a 'fantastic story' about parachutists. It quoted a farmer who, when asked if he had seen any parachutists, replied 'Oh Lord, yes. One came down near the creamery last evening. At first I thought it was a bag of hay in the air.' The Censorship realised that the journalist was being 'taken for a ride' and stopped the story. He next visited Co. Kerry where more tales were served up for his benefit. On his return to London he wrote that in the remote bogs of Kerry he had heard enough stories of 'fraternisation' with U-boats to make any Briton's hair stand on end. He was shown a pub near Dingle, he wrote, where Nazi sailors had toasted the downfall of John Bull, and he recounted the tale of the U-boat commander who regularly called at one of the islands for fresh vegetables. He paid with English money and 'men who have seen his boat tell his usual hail on being pulled into the tiny fishing jetty is "Come on, Maggie, hurry up with those cabbages"'![242]

A dominant theme of many stories was the refuelling of U-boats with petrol along the west coast; these dried up once it was realised that U-boats did not use petrol! These were followed by accounts of how the lights of Irish cities guided German bombers on raids on Britain and, persistently, of the leakage of military information from the Axis legations in Dublin and the espionage activities of their staffs, whose numbers were often grossly exaggerated to maximise the impact of their supposed activities.

One correspondent, J.L. Murray of the *Daily Mirror*, refused to indulge in the 'type of "hot" news story so favoured by some of my colleagues here'. In an article on 'Axis propaganda in Éire', which was stopped in April 1942, he argued that 'every intolerant word, whether by a British newspaper or British politician, which betrays lack of sympathy or understanding of Ireland's case, is seized upon by the astute propagandists to bolster up the Axis cause'. He contended that wildly exaggerated spy stories were counter-productive and that it was only by establishing 'bonds of sympathy and understanding' that the pro-Allied feeling in Ireland could be properly harnessed; 'Meantime the best British propaganda of all in Irish eyes is military enterprise instead of strategic withdrawals, victories instead of evacuations.' Murray's frustration with the situation led him to quit his position as *Mirror* correspondent in April 1942. In his letter of resignation he defended his decision not to send 'hot' news stories:

> they are easy to do and require nothing more than a fertile imagination . . . Most British (and American) pressmen view Dublin through an upended glass in the Palace Bar . . . As a pyrotechnical display of in-tellectual dishonesty the backroom of the Palace Bar is probably unique. But a quite definite menace. It no more represents Dublin, let alone Ireland, then that fine old 'Irish ballad' – 'Did your mother come from Ireland?' [243]

In July 1943 John Betjeman, the press attaché at the office of the UK representative, submitted an article on behalf of Joan Haslip, an English journalist, which was intended for publication in the *World Review*. Purcell (assistant controller) was directed by Aiken to inform Betjeman that the article, 'De Valera's Other Island', had been stopped. Purcell went on to tell Betjeman 'that if there is much more of this sad-sympathy-with-the-mists-that-do-be-on-the-Irish-bogtrotters type of propaganda in the British press regarding Irish neutrality, it will be necessary to let the Irish people know about it and allow Irish publicists reply'.[244]

As well as controlling what was presented to the Irish people about the outside world, the Censorship sought to influence the picture of Ireland which was painted on the outward-facing side of Arthur Griffith's 'paper wall'. 'Friendly' articles by 'Irish publicists' were published, at the instiga-tion of the Censorship, in the *Daily Mail, Times, Manchester Guardian* and *Daily Express*.[245] As has been seen, an article by John T. Grealish which the *Sunday Dispatch* published in October 1943 in order to have the ban on it lifted was entitled 'Ireland Has Taken Her Decision', and contained some contributions from the Censorship. The article, which was carried in the English and Irish editions of the paper, contrasted the British attitude to other neutrals with the attitude taken to Irish neutrality:

> Sweden could let foreign troops through her territory. Britain 'under-stands'. Turkey can have an alliance with Britain and a treaty of friendship with Germany. Britain 'understands'. Spain can have a 'Blue Legion' fighting Britain's ally. Britain 'understands' . . . Switzerland

can close its frontiers to escaping British prisoners in Italy. Britain 'understands' . . . All the wrath is reserved for the Irish.[246]

In May 1943 journalist Cobbet Wilkes visited Ireland and wrote an article for the *Spectator* entitled 'Censorship in Éire'. (The article also appeared, in condensed form, in *World Digest* in September 1943.) He described how the censorship, 'much more severe than in any other neutral country', was doing 'a great deal to drive Ireland out into the Atlantic mists which will cut her off from both Europe and America'. He outlined how emergency powers were being used to 'weed out all survivals of the old order' (like coats of arms and references to the royal family), discussed the film censorship and gave examples of how the Press Censorship 'tends to favour the Axis at the expense of the Allies'. He argued that the censored press lacked a tone of authority and that the Censorship encouraged ignorance, apathy and scepticism among the population. All in all, he saw in Ireland 'a crumbling of moral values in a cloud-cuckoo land'. In response, Coyne wrote a letter to the *Spectator*, using one of his 'customary aliases', M. O'Brien. That portion of his letter which the magazine regarded as constituting a direct reply to the article was printed in the *Spectator* of 18 June. Coyne introduced himself as 'an Irishman living in Ireland and one who served with the Royal Air Force in the last war'. Having established his credentials he went on to defend the Irish against Wilkes's 'cloud-cuckoo-land' slur and predicted a major Irish contribution to the postwar world. He rejected the charge of pro-Axis bias by the Censorship and pointed out that practically all war news printed in Irish papers was supplied by British and American news agencies; British and American newspapers were imported and circulated without restriction; and British and American propaganda, like the *Letter From America*, was circulated in far greater proportion than any Axis material. He contrasted this with the situation in Switzerland. Coyne went on to defend the film censorship on the basis of 'the temperamental and emotional' nature of the Irish, and concluded by questioning the moral superiority of the Allied belligerents over the neutrals.[247]

Wilkes had the last word, in a letter to the *Spectator* on 2 July 1943. He pointed out that in Switzerland the authorities were equally strict in keeping out both Allied and Axis propaganda, but that the Swiss press was doing 'a magnificent job' in keeping the people well informed. The Swedish and Turkish press were equally courageous and outspoken, according to Wilkes, and his submission was that this was not the case in Ireland, because of the Censorship. He concluded that the pro-Axis bias was based not on malice but on the fact that the Germans were more likely to retaliate and on the tradition of hostility to British arms which survived in Ireland. Coyne sent copies of this correspondence to his colleague Philip O'Donoghue, in the Office of the Attorney General, noting that he had 'participated in this controversy – alas with no great success'.[248]

When 'unfriendly' articles bypassed the Censorship and appeared in external newspapers efforts were always made to lodge complaints, refute allegations or present the Censorship, or Irish government, case. This was frequently done through the offices of Irish representatives, usually in London and Washington. (Irish diplomatic representatives were expected to act in this regard on their own initiative also.) For example, on 15 April 1940 the *Washington Times Herald* carried an unsigned article stating that Germany was counting on the aid of a fifth column in Ireland for the purpose of launching an attack on Britain and that 'German Submarine Officers have been fêted in certain western Irish cities'. Robert Brennan, the Irish minister in Washington, telephoned the editor who promised to omit the article from later editions. Brennan then issued an official statement to all news agencies countering every point made in the article.[249] During the American Note affair, Brennan was called to the State Department to explain a Reuter report that 3,000 Japanese had landed in Ireland and were living in disguise! Brennan's reaction was to ask: 'Is there no limit to the credulity of Americans?'[250]

Most American correspondents who visited Ireland either came across from London or dropped in to Ireland on their way back from the continent. On arrival in Ireland, they were usually briefed on the situation there by the US minister, David Gray, an individual whom the Irish authorities regarded as singularly unfit for such a task. In a letter to Robert Brennan in June 1945, Joseph Walshe, secretary of the Department of External Affairs, wrote of Gray that 'he brought over to Ireland from London every few months a troop of journalists whom he conditioned on each occasion with anti-Irish venom, the consequences of which you have so often had to report'. Hugh Curran (of the *Irish Times*) in a press telegram to the *Chicago Tribune,* wrote that most American journalists accepted Gray's 'lowdown', which often took a mischievous angle and misrepresented the situation.[251]

The vast majority of visiting correspondents were British and American, but a small number of journalists from the continent of Europe did visit Ireland, while a number of Europeans resident in the country wrote, or sought to write, for external publications.

A Spanish journalist, F.F. Armesto, who came to Dublin in August 1940 and wrote articles on British and Irish affairs, was informed by the Censorship that the Irish authorities did not want foreign journalists coming to Ireland and writing about the internal affairs of any of the belligerents and he left prematurely after two weeks.[252] A Hungarian, Vera de Rudnyansky, was allowed to continue writing apolitical pieces for a Hungarian publication, provided she submitted her articles in translation before transmission.[253] Kurt Werner, a German national resident in Ireland who wished to act as foreign correspondent for certain Swiss newspapers, was not so easily accommodated. He was the subject of an order made under the Aliens Order

1939 in April 1940 by the Minister for Justice. The order prohibited him from any correspondence whatsoever with any newspaper or magazine. Coyne suggested that 'any alien who claims to have an intimate knowledge of our political, economic and social life is worth watching'.[254] One writer prudent enough not to visit Ireland was Sebastian Hoffner, a German refugee resident in England, who had published a book entitled *Offensive Against Germany* in which he urged the forcible occupation of the Irish ports by the British. In a letter to the Department of Justice in April 1941, Coyne suggested that if Hoffner did visit Ireland 'you will lose no time in locking him up so that he may revert to his legitimate obscurity from which he should never have emerged'.[255]

Carl Peterson was the press attaché at the German legation and the representative in Ireland of the German news agency. When a press telegram of his to New York in July 1941, on the subject of the Soviet entry into the war, was stopped by the Irish Censorship, Peterson was not informed. Connolly explained that the stoppage would 'no doubt' be attributed to 'others', through whose channels the telegram had to pass, and it was mainly because it was going through those channels that it was stopped; to have allowed it, according to Connolly, would have indicated 'a neglect of Irish censorship functions'.[256]

A number of freelance Irish journalists catered for what the Censorship described as 'a British market in imaginative stories served up as news'. These were the so-called 'provincial correspondents' whose messages were often drastically cut or stopped. They were not advised as to the treatment of their messages on the basis that this would be 'gratuitously handing them a weapon' with which to 'attack' the Press Censorship.[257]

A 'local correspondent with a very fertile brain' by the name of Doyle wrote a weekly article for English newspapers, including the *Sunday Graphic* and *Sunday Dispatch*, from his home town of Roscrea, Co. Tipperary. He wrote 'the most picturesque stories' about happenings, real and imagined, across the thirty-two counties. One article, describing a reception given to Daniel Giles O'Sullivan, deputy prime minister of New Zealand, was submitted the day before he arrived in Ireland. On VE Day Doyle described thousands marching through Dublin carrying the flags of many nations, while 'from the British, American, French and *Russian* embassies flags were hoisted'. (Ireland did not establish diplomatic relations with the Soviet Union for another twenty-eight years!) He constantly played up the Irish connections of international figures like Montgomery, Mrs Truman and Brendan Bracken, whose family home in Templemore, Co. Tipperary, Doyle saw fit to point out on one occasion, was only a few dozen yards from the site of a miraculous apparition which had cured 80,000 pilgrims. His final wartime story concerned the 'arrival' in Ireland of Lord Haw Haw. He stated that Joyce had been dropped from a plane into the country, and explained that he had got the story from 'a man who was waiting for a bus'.[258]

A local correspondent who was particularly disliked by the Censorship was Vivian O'Connell of Cork, described by chief telegraph censor, Cussen, as 'a very dangerous man [who] . . . specialises in vilifying this country in the low-class English press'. He was regarded as a 'sensation-monger' and his messages were dealt with severely, the Censorship causing him as much inconvenience as possible. Typical of his articles was one written for the titillation of *News of the World* readers dealing with the laxity of morals of the young people of Cork in the blackout and tales of young girls 'going down the quays'.[259]

Seán Piondar was a freelancer who wrote articles for *News Review,* the *News of the World,* the *People,* the *Daily Telegraph* and *World Press News, London.* His pieces constantly caused problems for the Censorship and many were stopped or suffered deletions. In October 1943 the Censorship stopped a Piondar article which reported on that year's All-Ireland Football Final. In it he described the rough, bad-tempered game between Cavan and Roscommmon which he claimed was damaging to the image of the GAA and of the country. Piondar protested strongly at the stopping of a sports report. In relation to the reply Aiken unsportingly instructed Knightly to 'take the gloves off – and squash 'im!' Knightly continued the sporting metaphor, asking Piondar if it was 'playing the game' to take money 'for holding your own fellow country-men up to contempt and ridicule in the columns of an English Sunday newspaper at a time when all the anti-Irish elements everywhere are actively engaged in trying to influence public opinion against this country?'[260] The stopping of this article would seem to have been yet another example of the Censorship moving the goalposts to suit its game.

Prosecution of a number of correspondents was considered at various stages, but never pursued. Among them was the 'itinerant *Daily Telegraph* correspondent', Cornelius Ryan, who reported from Dublin when at home on holiday. (He went on to cover the D-Day landings for the *Telegraph,* the subject of his famous book *The Longest Day*.) When two special articles appeared in the *Telegraph* on 11 and 14 March 1944, concerning the alleged presence of a German plane over Dalkey and the reported stopping of leave for the Irish army (in anticipation of an American invasion following the rejection of the American Note), Ryan was immediately suspected of being the conveyer of these 'contraband' items. He was interviewed by the Special Branch and the Garda involved reported his satisfaction that Ryan was not responsible for these 'alarming reports'. Nevertheless, Coyne had not 'the slightest doubt' that Ryan was the author. The stories had not been sent out by George Burrows, the *Telegraph*'s Dublin correspondent, nor by telegraph or telephone from Dublin; yet no action could be taken in the absence of legal proof, 'which Ryan takes care not to make available by carrying his stories to Belfast and transmitting them from there'.[261]

This practice, of a reporter coming into the state and literally taking a story out, was common. Robinson, the Belfast correspondent of the *Daily Mail*, regularly came south and wrote stories on his return which the Dublin-based John Murdoch would never have got past the censor.[262] A *Daily Express* feature on the Hans Marschner 'wanted' posters had been supplied by Joseph Kenny to an *Express* representative who came from Belfast or England specifically to get it.[263] In January 1942 Montague Lacey, a special reporter from the London office of the *Express*, visited Ireland for a couple of days and wrote an article dealing with arms supplies. Coyne passed the article, aware that Lacey was on his way to Belfast and would have had the whole article published anyway. If the Irish Censorship had interfered with it the feeling was that Lacey would have made it 'more sensational and less friendly'. Coyne believed that

> expediency must be the only guide in dealing with English newspaper men and that, in cases like this, we have simply to make the best bargain we can. Certainly if Murdoch submitted an article to me denouncing partition and calling for a better deal from England for this country, I would let him go very far if he wanted to include in the same article a story about the recent arrival of arms.[264]

In passing an article by the communist Seán Nolan for the *Daily Worker* (New York) in November 1944, Coyne pointed out that it drew attention to the 'evil of partition' and that in that regard, 'any publicity – even in the *Daily Worker* – may be better than none'.[265]

The majority of correspondents for external newspapers were staff reporters of Irish newspapers. They were invariably conscientious and co-operative with regard to submitting copy. This, presumably, was chiefly because they had to operate under the Censorship in their daily work as Irish press people and did not wish to antagonise the authorities. There was also an element of patriotic loyalty, often from the most unexpected quarters. In December 1941, Bertie Smyllie, *Irish Times* editor and correspondent for the *Observer* and the *Times* (London), transmitted to the latter the story of the attack on the SS *Cambria* mailboat, unaware that the story was being 'held'. When he discovered this he attempted to cancel the story, but was too late. It was subsequently released and, according to himself, only his 'guilty conscience' stopped him from having 'a crack at the Censor for giving the evening papers the scoop'. He wrote to Coyne:

> I am sorry that the story should have anticipated the fall of the official flag, but will ask you to acquit me of any desire to outwit you in the matter. I happen to be rather punctilious in regard to exported news, although I will plead guilty to a certain elasticity of conscience where my own newspaper is concerned. In fact, I regard your department as I regard the Income Tax Wallahs; but I will not do the dirty for the Sasanach.[266]

A number of Smyllie's *Irish Times* staff acted as Irish correspondents for external newspapers and agencies. George Burrows was the *Daily Telegraph* correspondent, while Alec Newman wrote for the *Havas Agency*, Berne. Hugh Curran contributed regularly to the *Chicago Tribune* and his articles often fell foul of the censor. In October 1943 he wrote an article for the *Tribune* entitled 'Irishmen's Exploits in the War', which was stopped *in toto*. It dealt with the publication of a thirty-page pamphlet giving a record of the distinctions won by Irish people in the war. In an explanatory letter Coyne wrote that he was 'not prepared to pass an article which referred directly or indirectly to the pamphlet'. He questioned Curran's implication that the thousands of Irishmen fighting in the war were volunteers, fighting 'for conscience sake'. He referred to the existence of many 'mercenaries' among the 'volunteers' and indicated that 'by introducing the question of conscience you cease to be objective and become tendentious with a cause to be advanced, a prepossession to be expressed and a moral judgement to be passed – the war ceases to be a war and becomes a crusade'.[267]

One who certainly, and openly, believed the war to be a crusade was the independent senator Frank MacDermot, a constant critic of the Censorship as both politician and Irish correspondent of the *Sunday Times*, in which position he constantly fell foul of the blue pencil. On 23 June 1940 the *Sunday Times* published an article of his entitled 'Ireland and Defence'. The article had been submitted in telegram form and heavily censored, but MacDermot had obviously taken the precaution of posting or telephoning the original version, which duly appeared in the paper. Aiken instructed that MacDermot be verbally warned that if he 'again resorts to tricks of this nature the *Sunday Times* will be banned'.[268] After one of his articles was stopped in December 1940, Connolly wrote to Aiken stating that 'the Country is getting rather tired of his efforts to carry on what is nothing more or less than fifth column activities. There are men behind bars who have not been any more dangerous to the neutrality of the State than Senator MacDermot'.[269]

Prominent Irish individuals were occasionally asked to contribute articles on Irish affairs to British newspapers. In April 1940 the *Sunday Chronicle* began a new feature entitled 'In Ireland Today', written by General Eoin O'Duffy. He could not have made a worse start, from the point of view of the Censorship, than his first article, 'When Censorship Defeats Itself'. He argued that the Censorship was self-defeating as it led people to distrust newspapers and rely on rumour, true or false, for information on such matters as the IRA hunger strikes. On Aiken's suggestion, Doran O'Reilly, the *Chronicle*'s Irish representative, was telephoned and warned that the paper might be banned if further 'offending matter of this sort' appeared.[270]

The writer Frank O'Connor was initially stopped, but subsequently allowed (after censorship of his script) to broadcast a 'talk' for the BBC from the Radio Éireann studios on St Stephen's Day 1940. A year later, however, he wrote an essay entitled 'The Future of Irish Literature' for a *Horizon* (Cyril Connolly's English literary magazine) special edition on Ireland in January 1942. That issue also featured a poem by Patrick Kavanagh called 'The Old Peasant' (which later was extended and published as *The Great Hunger*); 'that filthy poem' was identified by the authorities as the basis for the banning and seizure of the issue, on the grounds of its supposed obscenity. However, O'Connor's full-frontal attack on Irish society, politics and culture could not have pleased the authorities either, and soon after he began to experience the results of that displeasure with the initiation of a particularly nasty form of indirect censorship. (He was already a victim of the Censorship of Publications Act, was frowned upon because of his marriage to a divorcee, and was the subject of Garda surveillance for suspected espionage activity.) O'Connor had been broadcasting talks and readings regularly on Radio Éireann, a welcome source of income in difficult times for writers; suddenly, from February 1942, he was no longer allowed to broadcast for no stated reason. The unofficial ban was extended to broadcasts to the BBC from the Radio Éireann studios, while he was blocked from obtaining a permit to travel to London to broadcast.[271]

Seamus Ó Braonáin, director of broadcasting from 1941, has recorded that the war years saw a steady flow of newspaper representatives and correspondents of outside broadcasting organisations coming to report on 'this land of ours, flowing with milk and honey – not to mention the beefsteaks'. They were granted facilities for broadcasting on condition that they submitted their scripts for censorship by the director. The scripts, according to Ó Braonáin, were 'occasionally highly coloured' and it fell to him to 'get them right and suggest amendments'; he notes that the correspondents were occasionally a little 'concerned' at this curbing of their freedom, but in general the system worked smoothly and they always parted 'on the best of terms'.[272]

In general, the Censorship found the situation with regard to 'exported news' 'highly unsatisfactory' and it was felt that, in any future emergency, the controls over correspondents would have to be radically increased. Coyne suggested, as a first step, the provision of a room in a convenient centre, close to Leinster House (where parliament sat), for example, from which the correspondents could communicate with their newspapers or agencies. The room would be fitted with telephone booths connected through a central table at which censors would monitor the conversations, which would be restricted to matter contained in a script that had been submitted for censorship beforehand. He further suggested the taking of power to compel the registration of the local representatives of the foreign press as well as local freelance contributors; visiting correspondents would be required to register on arrival and undertake to comply with censorship requirements. As it would continue to be impossible to prevent a visiting journalist from writing a story after leaving the country, Coyne suggested that in such cases a correspondent be excluded from the country after he or she had once given cause for offence and that, where possible, the newspaper or agency which employed him or her be penalised in some way. Such a system, Coyne felt, would also have a deterrent effect.[273]

NOTES AND REFERENCES

1   'Meet R.M. Smyllie', *The Bell*, Vol. 3, No. 3, December 1941, pp. 183–4.
2   NA, D/J, R 25, *Sunday Independent*, Knightly to Aiken, 2 September 1943.
3   NA, D/J, 'Controller's Correspondence', Coyne to Smyllie, 30 October 1942.
4   MA, OCC 2/79, Coyne to Knightly, 13 September 1941. This low opinion was articulated in a callous manner by the controller when referring to the fact that no press people had been allowed near the scene of the Strand Street bombings for twenty-four hours after the incident; 'whoever was responsible was being unnecessarily fussy', wrote Coyne. 'I would still think this if a damaged building had collapsed on a party of pressmen. After all, news hunting is a dangerous profession and the loss of a couple of dozen pressmen need not be too deeply deplored.'
5   MA, G2/P/21560, 'Organisation – Censorship', 'Notes on the press and propaganda during war', 27 December 1925.
6   NA, D/T, S 11445/8, Coyne memo on censorship, September 1945.
7   NA, D/J, No. 200, 'Letters of appreciation on the termination of censorship'.
8   'Meet R.M. Smyllie', *The Bell*, Vol. 3, No. 3, December 1941, p. 185.
9   Horizon, Vol. V, No. 25, January 1942, p. 9.
10   *The Bell*, December 1941, pp. 184–5.
11   'Out of the Shadows' (editorial marking the cessation of censorship), *Irish Times*, 12 May 1945.
12   NA, D/J, Press Censorship Reviews: *Irish Times*; D/J, No. 3, *Irish Times*.
13   NA, D/J, No. 3, Knightly to Connolly, 30 December 1939.
14   ibid., Connolly to Aiken, 30 December 1939.
15   ibid., Smyllie to de Valera, 15 January 1940.
16   ibid., Smyllie to Censorship, 5 July 1940.
17   ibid., Coyne to Aiken, 13 September 1940.
18   ibid., Connolly to Aiken, 18 September 1940.
19   NA, D/J, Press Censorship Reviews: *Irish Times*.
20   NA, D/J, No. 3, Aiken to Coyne, 26 August 1941.
21   ibid., Newman to Coyne, Coyne to Newman, 28 August 1941.
22   MA, OCC 2/68, *Irish Times* 'Roll of Honour'.
23   MA, OCC 2/130, 'Obituary, etc. notices relating to members of belligerent forces'.
24   NA, D/J, Press Censorship Reviews: *Irish Times*; D/J, No. 3, *Irish Times*.
25   *Irish Times*, 11 February 1941.
26   NA, D/J, No. 3, Censorship to Smyllie, 11 February 1941; Smyllie to Censorship, 14 February 1941.
27   *Irish Times*, 17 December 1941.
28   NA, D/J, No. 3, Coyne meeting with Smyllie, 18 December 1941.
29   NA, D/J, 'Controller's Correspondence', Coyne to Smyllie, 16 February 1942.
30   *Irish Times*, 19 May 1945.
31   Tony Gray, *Mr Smyllie, Sir* (Dublin, 1991), p. 154.
32   NA, D/J, No. 3, *Irish Times*.
33   NA, D/J, 'Controller's Correspondence', 15 May 1942.
34   NA, D/J, Press Censorship Reviews: *Irish Times*, Coyne to Smyllie, 12 June 1944.

35 ibid., 11 September 1944.
36 NA, D/J, No. 3, Coyne to Aiken, 8 December 1944.
37 ibid., Aiken to Coyne, 12 December 1944.
38 ibid., Purcell to Brown, 27 January 1945.
39 NA, D/J, 'Controller's Correspondence', Smyllie to Coyne, 16 June 1944 and 16 May 1942.
40 ibid., 14 July 1942.
41 ibid., 27 November 1942.
42 UCD Archives, Richard Mulcahy Papers, P7/C/113, Smyllie to Mulcahy, 20 May 1941.
43 NA, D/J, Controller's Correspondence, Smyllie to Coyne, 29 January 1943.
44 UCD Archives, Richard Mulcahy Papers, P7/C/113, 20 May 1941.
45 *Irish Times*, 19 May 1945.
46 Robert Fisk, *In Time of War: Ireland, Ulster and the Price of Neutrality, 1939-45* (London, 1985), p. 168.
47 UCD Archives, Richard Mulcahy Papers, P7/C/113, 20 May 1941.
48 *Irish Times*, 12 May 1945.
49 NA, D/J, 'Controller's Correspondence', Smyllie to Coyne, 27 November 1942.
50 ibid., 30 October 1942.
51 ibid., 16 November 1943.
52 ibid., Coyne to Smyllie, 24 November 1942.
53 NA, D/J, No. 3, Coyne to Smyllie, 13 April 1944.
54 *Irish Times*, 8 May 1945; Gray, *Smyllie*, pp. 160-1.
55 NA, D/FA (Sec.) P 51, German Legation *Aide-Mémoire*, 13 December 1941.
56 NA, D/J, Press Censorship Reviews: *Irish Press*, Knightly to Coyne, 6 March 1940.
57 ibid., Sweetman to Censorship, 9 November 1943.
58 ibid., Coyne to Sweetman, 12 November 1943.
59 NA, D/J, Press Censorship Reviews: 'Work of the Censorship', Breen to editor, *Irish Press*, 8 June 1942.
60 NA, D/FA (Sec.) A 8(1), Bryan to Walshe, 1 July 1942.
61 NA, D/FA (Sec.) A 8, Archer (G2) to Walshe, 18 June 1941, memos on four *Irish Press* employees.
62 NA, D/J, Press Censorship Reviews: *Irish Press*.
63 NA, D/J, No. 1, *Irish Press*, Sweetman to Aiken, 22 September 1944.
64 NA, D/J, Press Censorship Reviews: *Irish Press*.
65 NA, D/J, No. 1, *Irish Press*, Coyne to Aiken, 19 October 1944.
66 NA, D/J, No. 3, *Irish Times*, Coyne note, 1 January 1944.
67 *Irish Press*, 12 May 1945.
68 NA, D/J, Press Censorship Reviews: *Irish Independent*.
69 ibid.; D/J, No. 2, *Irish Independent*; NA, D/T, S 12043, complaint from *Irish Independent* regarding the treatment of a report on the bombing of the SS *Kerry Head*, August 1940.
70 NA, D/J, No. 2, *Irish Independent*, Coyne, 24 December 1940.
71 NA, D/J, Press Censorship Reviews: *Irish Independent*.
72 NA, D/J, No. 2, *Irish Independent*, Connolly to Geary, 24 December 1940.
73 NA, D/J, Press Censorship Reviews: 'Work of the Censorship'.
74 ibid.
75 NA, D/J, Press Censorship Reviews: *Irish Independent*, Geary to Censorship, 26 July 1943, Coyne to Geary, 28 July 1943.
76 NA, D/J, No. 2, *Irish Independent*, Geary to Coyne, 9 August 1943.
77 ibid., 20 January 1941.
78 *Seanad Debates*, Vol. 25, cols. 216-17, 241-3, 29 January 1941.
79 MA, OCC 7/58, Knightly, January 1941.
80 NA, D/J, No. 2, *Irish Independent*, Knightly to Geary, 12 February 1941.

81 NA, D/J, Press Censorship Reviews: *Irish Independent*, Coyne to Geary, 13 December 1941.
82 NA, D/J, Press Censorship Reviews: *Irish Independent*.
83 ibid., Coyne to Geary, 14 February 1945.
84 ibid., Geary to Coyne, 15 February 1945.
85 NA, D/J, No. 2, *Irish Independent*, Coyne to Aiken, 16 February 1945.
86 *Irish Independent*, 12 May 1945.
87 NA, D/J, Press Censorship Reviews: *Sunday Independent*, Knightly to editor, 6 August 1940.
88 NA, D/J, Press Censorship Reviews: *Sunday Independent*.
89 ibid., Knightly to Legge, 7 June 1943.
90 ibid., Legge to Coyne, 11 August 1943.
91 ibid., Coyne to Legge, October 1943.
92 ibid., Coyne to Legge, 12 March 1945.
93 NA, D/J, Press Censorship Reviews: *Cork Examiner*.
94 NA, D/J, No. 5A, *Cork Examiner*, Coyne to *Cork Examiner*, 27 September 1940.
95 NA, D/J, Press Censorship Reviews: *Cork Examiner*.
96 NA, D/J, No. 5A, *Cork Examiner*.
97 ibid., Censorship to McGrath, 5 November 1943.
98 NA, D/J, Press Censorship Reviews: *Cork Examiner*.
99 NA, D/J, Press Censorship Reviews: *Evening Herald* and *Evening Mail*.
100 NA, D/J, No. 5, *Evening Herald*.
101 NA, D/J, Press Censorship Reviews: *Evening Herald* and *Evening Mail*.
102 NA, D/J, No. 5, Coyne to Press Censorship Staff, 12 September 1942.
103 NA, D/J, Press Censorship Reviews: *Evening Herald* and *Evening Mail*; D/J, No. 4, *Evening Mail*.
104 NA, D/J, No. 4, Connolly to Knightly, 7 March 1941.
105 NA, D/J, Press Censorship Reviews: *Evening Herald* and *Evening Mail*.
106 C.S. Andrews, *Man of No Property: An Autobiography (Vol. Two)* (Dublin and Cork, 1982), p. 124.
107 NA, D/J, Press Censorship Reviews: 'Provincial Papers', p. 1.
108 NA, D/T, S 11445/8, Coyne memo on censorship, September 1945.
109 NA, D/J, Press Censorship Reviews: 'Provincial Papers', p. 42.
110 USNA, OSS (Regular), File 30131, Report on Axis propaganda in Ireland, November 1942.
111 NA, D/J, No. 25, *Meath Chronicle*, 4 August 1942.
112 NA, D/J, No. 45, *Munster Express*, 27 August 1943.
113 NA, D/J, No. 63, *Leinster Leader*, 25 September 1943.
114 NA, D/J, No. 24, *Drogheda Independent*, editor to Chief Press Censor, 7 June 1943.
115 NA, D/J, Press Censorship Reviews: 'Provincial Papers', p. 35.
116 ibid.
117 NA, D/J, No. 34, *Donegal Vindicator*, Censorship to editor, 27 October 1942.
118 NA, D/J, Press Censorship Reviews: 'Provincial Papers', p. 35.
119 ibid., p. 36
120 NA, D/J, No. 44, *Westmeath Examiner*, Coyne to Traynor, 19 May 1941.
121 NA, D/J,, Press Censorship Reviews: 'Provincial Papers', pp. 6–7; D/J, No. 74, *Southern Star*.
122 NA, D/J, No. 60, *Enniscorthy Echo*, 21 September 1940.
123 NA, D/J,, Press Censorship Reviews: 'Provincial Papers', p. 7.
124 NA, D/J,, No. 60, *Enniscorthy Echo*.
125 ibid., Coyne to Managing Director, 24 September 1940.
126 NA, D/J,, Press Censorship Reviews: 'Provincial Papers', pp. 8–9; D/J, No. 60, *Enniscorthy Echo*.

127 NA, D/J,, Press Censorship Reviews: 'Provincial Papers', pp. 34–5; D/J, No. 37, *Donegal Democrat*.
128 NA, D/J, Press Censorship Reviews: 'Provincial Papers', p. 4.
129 ibid., p. 10.
130 ibid., pp. 10–11.
131 Tomás Ó Duinn, 'Irishman's Diary', *Irish Times*, 16 January 1992.
132 NA, D/T, S 11445/8, Coyne memo on censorship, September 1945.
133 NA, D/J, Press Censorship Reviews: 'Provincial Papers', p. 12.
134 ibid.
135 ibid., p. 15.
136 ibid., pp. 16–19.
137 UCD Archives, Donal O'Sullivan Papers, P20/17.
138 NA, D/J, Press Censorship Reviews: 'Provincial Papers', p. 26; UCD Archives, Donal O'Sullivan Papers, P20/18, Keane to Knightly, 21 April 1942.
139 D/J,, Press Censorship Reviews: 'Provincial Papers', p. 27.
140 ibid., p. 32.
141 ibid., pp. 32–3, Knightly to Keane, 16 January 1945.
142 ibid., p. 33.
143 NA, D/T, S 11445/8, Coyne memo on censorship, September 1945.
144 NA, D/J, Press Censorship Reviews: 'Provincial Papers', p. 21.
145 ibid., pp. 39–40.
146 ibid., p. 43.
147 NA, D/J, No. 51, *The Nationalist*, Clonmel, 12 May 1945.
148 NA, D/J, No. 30, *The Leader*.
149 NA, D/J, No. 174, *News and Views*.
150 NA, D/J, No. 127, *The Progressive Printer and Newspaper Publisher*.
151 NA, D/J, No. 186, *The Irish Tobacco Trade Journal*.
152 NA, D/J, No. 156, *The Licensed Vintner and Grocer*.
153 NA, D/J, No. 157, *The Screen*.
154 NA, D/J, No. 66, *The Irish Agricultural and Creamery Review*.
155 NA, D/J, No. 41, *The Journal of the Free State Medical Union*.
156 NA, D/J, No. 61, *The Irish Farmers' Gazette*.
157 NA, D/J, No. 39, *The Garda Review*.
158 NA, D/J, R 52, *The Bell*.
159 NA, D/FA(Sec.) A 9(2), deletions from *The Bell*, 13 December 1944.
160 NA, D/J, R 52, *The Bell*, censored proof, 8 November 1944.
161 Fisk, *In Time of War*, pp. 432–6.
162 MA, OCC 2/47, '*Penapa*', Coyne to Inspector Reynolds, 16 January 1941 and other correspondence, memos and reports, December 1940 to June 1941; copy of *Penapa*, January 1941.
163 MA, OCC 5/32, 'Seizure of leaflet issued by the Irish Christian Rights Protection Association', June 1942.
164 NA, D/J, Press Censorship Monthly Reports, January–February 1944.
165 R.M. Smyllie, 'Unneutral Neutral Éire', *Foreign Affairs*, Vol. 24, No. 2, January 1946, p. 317.
166 NA, D/FA (Sec.) P 6, Coyne to Walshe, 19 September 1941.
167 ibid., 18 September 1941.
168 L.M. Cullen, *Eason and Son: A History* (Dublin, 1989), pp. 360 and 362.
169 NA, D/FA(Sec.) P 6, Coyne to Walshe, 19 September 1941.
170 Cullen, *Eason*, p. 359.
171 ibid., p. 361.
172 ibid.
173 ibid., p. 369.

174   MA, OCC 7/25, Walshe to Connolly, 17 October 1939.
175   Cullen, *Eason*, p. 366.
176   MA, OCC 7/25, Connolly to Walshe, 25 October 1939.
177   MA, OCC 2/8, Knightly to newspaper wholesalers, 1 December 1939.
178   NA, D/J, No. 7, *Daily Express*.
179   MA, OCC 2/8, Pearse to Aiken, Ennis (Aiken's secretary) to Pearse, 23 November 1939.
180   ibid. , 'External Newspapers and Posters', correspondence and memos, December 1939.
181   Cullen, *Eason*, p. 367.
182   MA, OCC 2/8, correspondence, January 1940.
183   MA, OCC 2/52, 'Seizure of extern newspapers'.
184   ibid., *News Review*, 7 March 1940, extract.
185   MA, OCC 2/70 and NA, D/J, No. 53, 'Reynolds News'.
186   ibid.
187   MA, OCC 2/8, 'External Newspapers and Posters'.
188   MA, OCC 2/52, *Daily Mirror*, 17 April 1940, extract, and editor to Censorship, 17 April 1940.
189   NA, D/FA(Sec.) A 9(1), editor to Censorship, 19 April 1941.
190   MA, OCC 2/8, 'External Newspapers and Posters'.
191   ibid. , Hughes to Censorship, 18 April 1940 and Connolly memo on 'The Banning of *The People* and the removal of same', 27 April 1940.
192   ibid., Connolly memo.
193   NA, D/J, Press Censorship Reviews: 'Work of the Censorship'.
194   MA, OCC 2/8, Coyne to Aiken, 18 April 1940 and Tivy to Coyne, 25 April 1940.
195   ibid., Tivy to Coyne, 25 April 1940, Coyne notes, 21 April 1940 and 3 June 1940, and Censorship to the Government Information Bureau, 3 January 1940.
196   MA, OCC 2/52, *Daily Mirror*, 11 May 1940.
197   Cullen, *Eason*, p. 369.
198   MA, OCC 2/8, Censorship to Argus, publishers of *Cavalcade*, 13 August 1940.
199   Cullen, *Eason*, p. 369.
200   MA, OCC 2/33, *Picture Post* seizure, 27 July 1940.
201   MA, OCC 2/8, *News Chronicle*, 29 October 1940; OCC 2/52, extract from the latter.
202   NA, D/J, No. 59, *News Chronicle*, Coyne to Aiken, 6 November 1940 and Coyne to *News Chronicle*, 25 September 1941.
203   NA, D/FA (Sec.) A 9(1), Coyne to Boland, 5 May 1941.
204   NA, D/J, No. 55, *Sunday Chronicle*, Coyne to Doran O'Reilly, 27 November 1941 and O'Reilly to Coyne, 10 December 1941.
205   NA, D/FA (Sec.) P 6, 'Senator Frank Mac Dermot-Visits to the US, 1940–42', DEA and G2 reports and correspondence with the Censorship.
206   ibid., Coyne to Walshe, 18 September 1941 and 19 September 1941, and Walshe to Coyne, 20 September 1941.
207   MA, OCC 2/8, Coyne to Knightly, 22 September 1941 and 24 October 1941, and Coyne to the Revenue Commissioners, 28 October 1941.
208   Anthony Coughlan, 'C. Desmond Greaves – Politician and Historian' in Daltún Ó Ceallaigh (ed.), *Reconsiderations of Irish History and Culture* (Dublin, 1994), pp. 157–8.
209   MA, OCC 2/127, *Irish Freedom*, Coyne to Aiken, 8 December 1942 and 26 March 1943, and Coyne to Walshe, 25 January 1943.
210   MA, OCC 2/125, *Sunday Dispatch*, 5 September 1943; Coyne memo, 14 September 1943; NA, D/J, Press Censorship Reviews: 'Extern Newspapers'.
211   ibid., correspondence, memos and extracts.
212   ibid.; NA, D/J, Press Censorship Reviews: 'Extern Newspapers'.

213 MA, OCC 2/135, *Everybody's Weekly*, Dublin Wholesale Agency to publishers, 3 March 1944, Eason to Coyne, 3 April 1945 and Coyne to Aiken, 5 April 1945.

214 MA, OCC 2/138, *Strand Magazine*, Eason to publishers, 14 June 1944 and Coyne note on same.

215 Cullen, *Eason*, p. 370.

216 MA, OCC 2/138, Eason to Coyne, February 1945.

217 Cullen, *Eason*, pp. 212–16.

218 MA, OCC 2/140, *World Digest*, correspondence and memos, June 1940 to April 1945.

219 ibid.

220 MA, OCC 2/24, 'Licences for the importation of prohibited newspapers'.

221 NA, D/J, Press Censorship Reviews: 'Provincial Papers'.

222 MA, OCC 2/48, *The Ulster Protestant*, November 1941 and Coyne to Roche (Justice), 21 January 1941; T. Ryle Dwyer, *Strained Relations: Ireland at Peace and the USA at War, 1941–45* (Dublin, 1988), p. 55.

223 NA, D/T, S 11586A, memo on the sending abroad of uncensored press messages, 25 January 1941.

224 MA, OCC 2/13, Censorship to the representatives of the external press in Ireland, 22 September 1939.

225 NA, D/T, S 11586, memo, 25 January 1941.

226 MA, OCC 2/54, 'Conveyance of press letters by rail and omnibus to and from places outside the State'.

227 NA, D/FA (Sec.) A 8, United Press to C.T. Hallinan, 'Memo on Dublin News Routine and Sources', 14 February 1941.

228 MA, OCC 2/79, Coyne to Knightly, September 1941.

229 NA, D/FA (Sec.) A 8, United Press to C.T. Hallinan, etc., 14 February 1941.

230 NA, D/J, Press Censorship Reviews: 'Extern Newspapers'.

231 MA, OCC 2/13, Coyne to Murdoch, 8 December 1941.

232 ibid., Coyne to Knightly and press censorship staff, 8 December 1941. The three full-time staff reporters (Kenny, Murdoch and Smith) suffered discrimination in another way also, as highlighted in February 1944 when the *Daily Telegraph* carried a front-page account of the Dáil discussion about the Irishmen from the Channel Islands who were parachuted into Clare by the Germans. This was an example of a story which was prohibited for export but released, partly, for publication in the home papers. The Irish dailies went across the border and over to Britain on the day of publication, where any paper or correspondent could then use fully the matter which the staff reporters in Dublin had been prohibited from sending (Kenny, Smith and Murdoch to Censorship, February 1944).

233 MA, OCC 2/109, Coyne to Kenny, 8 September 1942.

234 MA, OCC 2/94, Coyne to Knightly, 21 June 1941.

235 ibid., Coyne to Aiken, 2 May 1942.

236 ibid., Murdoch to Censorship, 22 May 1942.

237 ibid., Coyne to Knightly and press censorship staff, 18 August 1942.

238 ibid., Coyne memo, 12 March 1944.

239 ibid., Aiken to William Davin, 8 May 1944, and various correspondence and memos, April 1944 to February 1945.

240 ibid., Murdoch to Purcell, 4 May 1945.

241 F.D. Roosevelt Library, New York, David Gray Papers, 'Ireland': 'Censorship in Eire', undated (probably 1942).

242 NA, D/J, Press Censorship Reviews: 'Extern Newspapers'.

243 MA, OCC 2/104, 'Axis Propaganda in Eire' by J.L. Murray, April 1942, and Murray to the *Mirror*, 10 April 1942.

244 MA, OCC 2/139, Purcell to Betjeman, 17 July 1943.

245 NA, D/J, Press Censorship Reviews: 'Extern Newspapers'.

246 ibid.; MA, OCC 2/125, 'Banning of the *Sunday Dispatch*, September 1943'.

247 MA, OCC 2/132, '*The Spectator* and Censorship in Eire': Cobbet Wilkes, 'Censorship in Eire', *The Spectator*, 4 June 1943, reply from Coyne, 9 June 1943, reply as published in *The Spectator*, 18 June 1943.

248 ibid., Wilkes letter to the editor, *The Spectator*, 2 July 1943, and Coyne to O'Donoghue, 4 August 1943.

249 MA, OCC 2/13, Brennan to the DEA, 15 April 1940.

250 *Irish Press*, 21 March 1944.

251 NA, D/FA (Sec.) P 48 A, 'David Gray, US Minister – 1940–47': Walshe to Brennan, 11 June 1945; D/FA (Sec.) A 9(2), Curran to *Chicago Tribune*, 25 March 1944.

252 MA, OCC 2/13, Coyne to Knightly, 31 August 1940.

253 MA, OCC 2/13, correspondence regarding Vera de Rudnyansky, April 1940.

254 MA, OCC 7/31, Coyne to Duff (Justice), April 1940.

255 ibid., Coyne to Duff, 29 April 1941.

256 NA, D/FA (Sec.) A 9(1), Connolly, 18 July 1941.

257 NA, D/J, No. 197, 'Miscellaneous Correspondence', McAteer (Press Censorship) to Coyne, 9 March 1945.

258 NA, D/J, Press Censorship Reviews: 'Extern Newspapers'.

259 MA, OCC 4/17, O'Connell press messages, and Cussen to Coyne, September 1939. A file on O'Connell in the Military Archives remains closed to researchers.

260 NA, D/J, R 37, 'Sean Piondar', Piondar to *The Fortnightly*, May 1941, Piondar to the *People*, 12 October 1943, Knightly to Piondar, 18 October 1942 and Aiken note on same.

261 MA, OCC 2/136, 'Cornelius Ryan, *Daily Telegraph*', Garda report, 6 April 1944, and Coyne to Aiken, 14 April 1944.

262 MA, OCC 2/94, 'Mr J.H. Murdoch, *Daily Mail*'.

263 MA, OCC 2/109, Coyne to Aiken, 13 April 1942.

264 ibid., Coyne to Knightly, 7 January 1942

265 NA, D/J, R 61, 'Matter submitted to the Minister', Coyne to Aiken, 8 November 1944.

266 MA, OCC 2/13, Coyne to Smyllie, 8 December 1941 and Smyllie to Coyne, 9 December 1941.

267 ibid., Coyne to Curran, 8 October 1943.

268 NA, D/J, No. 16, *Sunday Times*.

269 MA, OCC 2/13, Censorship to MacDermot, 10 April 1941.

270 NA, D/J, No. 55, *Sunday Chronicle*.

271 James Matthews, *Voices: A Life of Frank O'Connor* (Dublin, 1983), pp. 173–5 and 185–191.

272 Maurice Gorham, *Forty Years of Irish Broadcasting* (Dublin, 1967), pp. 131–2.

273 NA, D/T, S 11445/8, Coyne memo on censorship, September 1945.

6.

'KEEPING THE TEMPERATURE DOWN'
PRESS CENSORSHIP, POLITICS AND SOCIETY

THE CATHOLIC CHURCH

The devil will not be allowed quote scripture in Ireland for the duration of the war.[1]

T.J. Coyne

Sir John Maffey described Ireland as a society where the visit of a cardinal or the death of a leading churchman took precedence over all contemporary history in the world.[2] Given the dominance of the Catholic ethos in the political culture and the social power wielded by that church it is not surprising that the censorship of ecclesiastical pronouncements, Vatican statements, influential Catholic publications, and so on, should have been one of the more controversial aspects of the work of the wartime censors. It should be noted, however, that the question of church–state conflict did not arise in this regard and that the actions of the Censorship did not represent a challenge to church power. Rather, they were carried out within a context of reverence and were informed by, among other things, an expressed 'duty' to the 'Holy Father'. Nevertheless, some Catholic feathers were ruffled and the episode is of further interest for the spotlight thrown on a number of pertinent issues; for example: the occasional difficulties raised by the fact that Ireland was politically partitioned but subject to the one hierarchy; the strength of Catholic-inspired anti-communism; the anti-Semitic thread in the Christian tradition; the issue of morality in the war; and the use made of the various churches and religious concepts in the propaganda of the belligerents.

The Irish Catholic hierarchy – in contrast to its English counterpart, for example – did not speak out as a body on what was happening in Europe and tended in general to concentrate on local pastoral concerns.[3] With regard to the war, the Irish hierarchy supported the neutral position adopted by the Vatican and the Irish government. In June 1940, when Irish neutrality

220

seemed in greatest danger following the collapse of France, the Irish bishops issued a statement in response to a request by the government. It endorsed neutrality, rejoiced in the unity of purpose among the political parties, and enjoined upon Irish Catholics to give full obedience to the state and to co-operate in whatever measures were proscribed 'for the common safety'.[4] Among those measures was a censorship so strict that when some of the bishops did occasionally speak out on aspects of the war, they were treated 'with no more ceremony than any other citizen'.[5]

In his first monthly report on the operation of the press censorship, the chief press censor wrote that in dealing with the East European war situation the Censorship 'has had regard for the natural sympathies of our people with Poland' and avoided excising matter which might ordinarily be seen as contravening the directions in the belief that it was the better of two evils.[6] In the following month the dangers inherent in allowing the press to carry statements by Irish bishops on the issue was highlighted. Bishop Fogarty of Killaloe, in the course of a sermon in Ennis cathedral, made reference to the destruction of Poland. The sermon was reported in the British press the following day under such headings as 'Hitler's Greatest Crime – By a Bishop', 'Enemies of God' and 'Bishop Brands Hitler a Murderer'.[7] The Censorship realised that Ireland's 'natural sympathies', as expressed by some of its bishops, were potential weapons in the propaganda war and closed down on publicity for such statements. The only episcopal pronouncements on the war which were subsequently allowed publicity were those made in what has been called 'the periphrastic manner' of the Vatican.[8] Specific belligerents could not be identified and the statements had to be vague and general, such as condemnations of 'the law of the Sword' and the lack of Christian principles on the part of 'the great nations'.[9] In January 1941 Bishop Fogarty was censored again when, following the death of three people in Borris, Co. Carlow as a result of German bombs, he wrote an open letter to the parish priest of the area asking 'What do these accursed bombers mean by bombing our poor country? It is, I fear, the inception of bigger and more ruthless assaults'.[10]

Problems were also created by the broadcast of religious services on Radio Éireann. Following the transmission of an unneutral sermon which featured an attack on Hitler early in the war, the director of broadcasting tried to get advance scripts of sermons on the grounds of ensuring that they ran on time. The ecclesiastical authorities refused but they promised that ser-mons would keep strictly to the alloted time; the next sermon which was carried on the station overran its time by some forty minutes![11]

In 1940 the reporting of the bishops' Lenten pastorals was subjected to censorship for the first time in the history of the state. In that year the bishop of Killaloe's pastoral letter referred to universal ill-feeling towards 'the two powers which had savagely assaulted the life of two helpless nations – Poland and Finland'. The bishop of Cloyne alluded to the 'victim of aggression by two countries whose governments were pagan in outlook and spirit', while the bishop of Elphin mentioned the 'powerful aggressor states' who had violently conquered their small neighbour and violently prevented its inhabitants from practising their religion. Reports of these comments did not appear in Irish newspapers.[12]

In his 1941 Lenten pastoral (on the theme of Christian marriage) Bishop Morrisroe of Achonry made reference to Germany's 'godless plans' and to the persecution of the church in Poland and Germany. He asked whether Catholics could 'view with easy minds the possibility of a victory which would give brute force the power to control Europe and decide the fate of small nations'.[13] This portion of the pastoral was submitted for censorship by the *Irish Independent* and permission to publish was refused. This provoked a storm in the Houses of the Oireachtas, with questions being put down, Dillon reading the offending section into the Dáil record and Senator MacDermot tabling a motion which deplored 'the partiality shown by the Censorship in its treatment of the Bishops' Lenten pastoral letters'.[14] (The motion was ruled out on a technicality.) The Censorship was in no doubt that the censored portion was partisan, 'and so partisan as to afford every justification for offence being taken by one of the belligerents'. It pointed to the fact that the portions selected for publication by the *Independent* were those only which gave offence to Germany. If the pastorals were printed in their entirety the Censorship suggested that it might pause before interfering; but so long as newspapers were selective the authorities were determined that 'if any censorship is going to be done it should . . . be done by the State'.[15]

The state did continue to censor the pastorals and other pronouncements of the Catholic bishops, as well as those emanating from the Church of Ireland, for the remainder of the war. Bishop Coholan of Cork was censored in January 1942 when he wrote for the *Sunday Independent* that the evil done by the 'Totalitarian leaders' was inconsiderable when compared with 'the evil caused and transmitted by two other leaders, Martin Luther and John Calvin'.[16] (It was, of course, the reference to 'Totalitarian leaders' and not the sectarian attack contained in this comment which led to its censorship.) The bishop of Galway transgressed by referring to the recruitment of Irishmen for the British army. A report on the passing of a resolution expressing sympathy with the Norwegian bishops by the Church of Ireland synod was censored, as was a reference to Catholic girls marrying American soldiers in the North by the bishop of Down and Connor.[17] Other deletions from pastorals in the following years included references to neutrality, the emergency services, the price paid to farmers for wheat, starvation and oppression in Europe, the persecution of Jews, the position of the Vatican, the course of the war and the prospects for peace. In February 1945, in the final months of the censorship, the bishop of Elphin's call for prayers for the millions of Catholics living under the despotic rule of those who 'hate and despise Christianity' and the bishop of Ferns' criticism of the Soviet Union and the partition of Poland[18] were the final pastorals to fall foul of the blue pencil.

Deletions from press reports of episcopal pronouncements, though relatively frequent, were only made after prior consultation with Aiken and 'for the gravest reasons'. In reply to criticisms the censors were keen to stress that, in any case, newspapers were not the medium by which pastoral letters were conveyed to the bishops' flocks.[19] The point was made that the Censorship had never interfered with pastorals *per se*, but that the Northern Ireland authorities had done so when they held up a letter in the course of its transmission through the post – a fact which evoked a protest from Cardinal MacRory.[20]

Partition and the treatment of the Catholic minority in the North were issues which complicated the strict application of censorship in relation to the church. MacDermot's charge of 'partiality' on the part of the Censorship in relation to bishops' pastorals, quoted earlier, is explained in an article he wrote for the *Sunday Times* in December 1940 (which was stopped by the censor). In it he wrote that the

> great prestige of Catholic bishops in this country does not always save them from the attention of the Censor. Our newspapers, however, have been allowed to feature a tirade delivered last Sunday by the bishop of Down and Connor in which he attacked the government of Northern Ireland (and by inference the British government whose tools they are supposed to be) for interning suspects without trial and for 'violating the sanctity of Catholic homes' by police raids during the hours of night. The extremely bitter tone of the speech was little in keeping with the desire to keep the political temperature from rising which was expressed a few days earlier by our minister in charge of Censorship. Similar criticisms of our own government in connection with our own internments and police raids or of the German government in connection with their proceedings in countries under German occupation would stand no chance of being permitted to appear . . .[21]

Similar statements in connection with the treatment of Northern Catholics were contained in published pastorals by Cardinal MacRory and the bishop of Derry.[22]

In the eyes of the Censorship the answer to MacDermot's charges was 'relatively simple'. All three of the Northern bishops had been referring to 'the internal position within their own dioceses, the intolerable position of their Catholic people within their own "flocks"'. There was no parallel, in the censor's opinion, between the passing of such matter and the deletion of passages such as those in the 1941 pastoral of Bishop Morrisroe. The former contained 'irrefutable statements' while the latter represented 'a gratuitous attack based on war propaganda on one of the belligerents'.[23] The genuine plight of Polish Catholics was invalidated in the eyes of the

Censorship, and many Irish people, by the exploitation of their suffering by British propaganda. In a draft letter to the American Catholic weekly, *Commonweal*, Coyne warned American readers against believing that the British had become eleventh-hour champions of the Catholic faith. By way of illustration, and in order that the plight of Polish Catholics be seen in 'proper perspective', he quoted from the aforementioned pastoral by the bishop of Down and Connor on 'the plight of Catholics, not in the Pripet marshes, but in Belfast'.[24] John Betjeman, press attaché at the office of the UK representative, reported that 'even among the most sincere Catholics' there was 'a refusal to believe in stories of German persecution'.[25] When Count Jan Balinski visited Ireland in January 1941 for the Polish Research Centre (a branch of the exiled Polish government in London) he was angered by the Irish insistence on viewing all persecution via the lens of British repression in Ireland. 'Sometimes when I spoke of the persecution of the Poles', he wrote, 'I was told by Irishmen that they know by experience what persecution meant. I reacted with some heat to such assertions'.[26]

The assertion that Britain's war defended Christian civilisation against the anti-God Nazis formed one of the broad themes of British propaganda. The line was that while Catholics, Protestants and Orthodox might differ doctrinally they were as one as Christians under threat from the common neo-pagan foe. The Ministry of Information (MOI) boasted a religions division, and bishops and priests were asked to write 'uplifting materials for dissemination'.[27] The MOI compiled extracts from Vatican Radio broadcasts and Catholic publications world-wide and supplied them to Irish newspapers, with particular emphasis on the Catholic press, via the office of the UK representative.[28] Both sides claimed to have moral right on their side and utilised every pertinent utterance from all religions for use in the propaganda war. The pronouncements of church dignitaries from every country – belligerent, occupied and neutral – which referred to the war were ruthlessly censored in Ireland, from the Bavarian catholic bishops to the archbishop of Canterbury and the patriarch of the Russian Orthodox Church.[29]

One of the most prolific of the clerical propagandists was the Catholic archbishop of Westminster, Cardinal Hinsley. His treatment at the hands of the Irish Censorship gave rise to an amount of comment in the Dáil and Seanad as well as in the British and American press. The attitude of the Censorship towards the cardinal was clear-cut. He was, in Coyne's words, 'a highly patriotic Englishman in addition to being a prince of the Church. In the latter capacity he is, no doubt, a high spiritual authority; in the former he is a pure jingo.' Coyne went on to describe him as 'the most tactless member of the Sacred College' who was 'constantly identifying Catholic interests throughout the world with the success of the British cause – this despite the fact that there are a majority of Catholics and an overwhelming preponderance of cardinals on the other side who almost certainly do not share his views'.[30] Typical of Hinsley's numerous pronouncements that were censored was a report of a broadcast to America in which he declared that 'neutrality of the heart' was impossible in 'this great struggle' between light and darkness, and a report of a broadcast he made to the British forces in August 1940 in which he declared them to be 'on the side of the Angels against the pride of rebellious Lucifer'. The reply to the latter from a German radio station (reports of which were also stopped) stated that it was strange that the three million Catholics in England were on the side of the angels while the forty million Catholics in Germany and Italy were on the side of Lucifer. 'In the present circumstances', wrote Michael Knightly, the chief press censor, 'we think that our newspapers should ignore these controversies.'[31]

Some of Hinsley's statements arrived on the wire marked 'For Publication in Ireland Only'. When Aiken pointed this out in the Seanad following complaints about censorship of the archbishop, a statement was issued on Hinsley's behalf denying that this was so. A report of the denial was stopped for the *Irish Times*.[32] (Marking certain press messages in this way was a habit of British news agencies and had nothing to do with Hinsley himself.)

In 1944 Hinsley's successor as archbishop of Westminster, Dr Bernard Griffin, drew the ire of the Belfast government (and, possibly, wry smiles from the Irish censors) when he drew parallels between Nazi persecution of Catholics in Germany and Poland and the persecution of Catholics in Northern Ireland.[33]

When Hinsley died in March 1943 D'Arcy Osborne, the British representative in the Vatican, wrote that he had done much to counteract the unfavourable effects abroad of the Vatican's hypersensitive neutrality.[34] In Ireland great store was set by what the Vatican thought and did in the field of diplomacy and it was no accident that its wartime neutrality so closely resembled the model adopted by the papal state.[35] Under the Lateran Treaty the pope had undertaken to 'remain outside temporal conflicts unless the parties concerned appeal in unison for the pacifying mission of the Holy See'.[36] As Pope Pius XII was treaty-bound not to publicly criticise Mussolini he adopted the same position with regard to all other heads of state. He followed the path of caution and compromise, refusing to name any of the belligerents in his pronouncements and would only 'enunciate general principles which implied condemnation rather than utter condemnations of particular acts'.[37] Yet, no matter how vague and general such pronouncements were, belligerent propagandists, particularly the British, always found useful material in them.

The Irish authorities were aware that 'both parties in the present conflict are anxious to harness the Vatican and Catholic opinion to their chariots'[38] and the Censorship was as anxious to protect the image of Vatican neutrality as it was to protect the Irish version. 'There is no more Catholic country in the world than Ireland', wrote Coyne, 'and nowhere is there greater devotion to the Vatican and to the person of the Holy Father.'[39] The Censorship perceived it as its 'duty', not merely to Ireland 'but also to the

Holy Father to do what we can to prevent his position and attitude from being misrepresented to the Irish people'.[40] This approach was misinterpreted (perhaps deliberately, on occasion) and the Censorship was heavily criticised whenever it appeared that the Vatican or the pope had been censored. James Dillon, for example, accused it of losing 'all sense of proportion' by censoring the Vatican in a 99 per cent Catholic country,[41] while the American Catholic weekly *Commonweal* charged that 'the Irish Censorship has indeed shown a strange discrimination against the Vatican'.[42]

The basis for such claims lay primarily in the treatment given to items which originally emanated from Vatican Radio and the Vatican newspaper *Osservatore Romano*. Both were generally viewed as being official mouthpieces of the pope, thus censorship of them was seen as censorship of the pontiff himself. In fact, neither was authorised to speak for the pope and matter lifted from both was treated on merit. In February 1941, for example, the Censorship stopped the publication in the *Irish Press* and the *Irish Times* of a Vatican statement which had been issued through the *Osservatore Romano*. The statement was a denial of rumours (which had originated from a statement by the Protestant bishop of Chelmsford and had been developed by the Germans) regarding papal support for the Axis powers. The Censorship had stopped publication of the original rumours and thus felt totally justified in stopping the Vatican statement in order to prevent giving the rumours fresh currency.[43]

Osservatore Romano had been the only Italian newspaper to carry reports from Allied sources and attitudes to Germany which were not found in the rest of the Italian press (which was subject to Fascist censorship). It was thus highly valued by the British as a drag on Mussolini's entry into the war. Once Italy became a belligerent (and even shortly before) Fascist pressure ensured that it carried only official military communiqués and no comment,[44] thus making its coverage of international affairs closely resemble that of the Irish press. Vatican Radio, however, continued to be very useful to the British. 'The Vatican wireless', wrote A.W.G. Randall, who was in charge of Vatican affairs at the British Foreign Office, 'has been of the greatest service to our propaganda and we have exploited it to the full.'[45] While it was not overtly pro-Allied and attempted to sound neutral and impartial, its transmissions on the persecution of the church in Poland were especially useful to the British in 'the struggle to influence European and American opinion and in raising scruples about the Nazis in the propaganda war'.[46] The BBC quoted extensively from Vatican Radio; it 'touched up' stories, made others more pointed and invented more.[47] As mentioned earlier, the MOI compiled extracts from these broadcasts which were supplied to the Irish press. From September 1942 the Censorship arranged to be supplied directly with these compilations so that a check could be kept on the amount of British-supplied material which was being used, particularly by the *Standard*. Each item, origin notwithstanding, continued to be treated on its merits.[48]

Translations of Vatican Radio broadcasts on the persecution of the church in Poland, together with reports from Swedish travellers which had been presented to the pope in 1940, formed the basis of the book *The Persecution of the Catholic Church in German-Occupied Poland* (1941). It was distributed by the MOI and featured a fiery anti-Nazi preface by Cardinal Hinsley.[49] The book's effective banning in Ireland provoked much criticism in the Dáil and in the Catholic press abroad. In a letter issued through the Government Information Bureau and published in the *Commonweal* and the *Tablet*, Coyne described the illustrations in the book as 'examples of Continental blasphemy' and stated that it would not be allowed into Ireland 'in peace or war'.[50] Two papal encyclicals of the seventeenth and eighteenth centuries were stopped in late 1940. They had been submitted by the short-lived Irish Nazi paper *Penapa* and highlighted the anti-Semitism present in the Christian/Catholic tradition[51] – an updated version of which could be found in the pages of the *Standard*. The Censorship later forbade the publication of all reports concerning the Vatican following the occupation of Rome by the Germans. This ban was extended to include all reports of the damage done to church buildings and shrines throughout Italy during the Allied advance, as a propaganda war raged about which side was most destructive of church property.[52] At this time, incidentally, the Vatican was concentrating its efforts on saving Rome from the ravages of war and found the Irish government 'of special help' in its attempts to influence the British and Americans to this end.[53] De Valera appealed to the Allies to refrain from bombing Rome, and both he and the Catholic Church expressed far more concern about the threat to the architecture of that city than about the holocaust, the details of which were well known to them by this time although they were kept from the Irish public.

It was primarily the pope's association with moral right which made him so attractive to both sides in the war. All belligerents want their cause to be seen as moral; belief in a righteous fight or just cause served as a morale booster on the battle front and the home front, while the sympathy of the neutrals was more likely to be with the belligerent with right on its side.[54] The Irish government, however, refused to accept that morality motivated either side. Aiken suggested in the Dáil that if moral issues were at stake then it was the duty of the heads of state involved, who were not censored, to present their case. He implied that their failure to do so proved his case and justified the censorship of all others who attempted to fit the conflict into a moral framework.[55] Irish policy, in any event, was driven by the notion, as articulated by Joseph Walshe, secretary of the Department of External Affairs, that 'small nations like Ireland do not and cannot assume the role of defenders of just causes except their own'.[56]

Although Ireland's 'just cause' was self-preservation, a morally superior, self-righteous attitude permeated much official and popular thinking. In November 1940 Elizabeth Bowen sensed a certain Catholic self satisfaction about neutrality which stressed the 'spirituality' of Ireland's attitude to world affairs.[57] She identified 'smugness' as the most disagreeable aspect of this 'official "spirituality"'. Once the Soviet Union entered the war and Britain allied with it, this was proof positive for many in Ireland that the war, after all, was not being fought on behalf of democracy, not to mention Christianity. With the Nazis on one side and the communists on the other the war became even more of an 'ungodly struggle' and Irish neutrality became even more puritanical.[58] The Axis propagandists attempted to present the attack on the Soviet Union as a crusade against communism[59] and German propaganda broadcasts fed into Ireland's well-known Catholic hostility to the godless creed, inviting it to join in 'the fight against Bolshevism'. The call fell on deaf ears, although former Blueshirt leader General Eoin O'Duffy, true to form, did plan to raise a Green Division to go and fight on the eastern front.[60]

The anti-communist crusade was, however, waged on the home front, particularly in the pages of the *Standard*. This Catholic paper had been allowed 'fairly wide scope'[61] in this area until the entry of the Soviet Union into the war, after which its belligerent status entitled it to the same 'protection' by the Censorship as all the other belligerents. (It was policy to restrict criticism of belligerent countries, their governments and systems of government.) The *Standard* and the *Irish Catholic* were allowed an anti-Soviet 'bite' in June–July 1941 (balanced by a pro-Soviet 'bite' from the Communist Party's *Irish Workers' Weekly*) after which pro- and anti-Soviet items were to be stopped. However, the Censorship regarded the *Standard* as 'a recognised organ of Catholic opinion' which deserved to be treated liberally 'in the matter of theological and ethical questions'.[62] Thus, taking account of the Irish people's 'natural . . . antipathy towards Communism',[63] 'authoritative criticism' of it as a philosophy was allowed. Many articles that were passed under this umbrella were in direct contravention of the Censorship rules which forbade criticism of the systems of government of other states. There was permitted, for example, a lengthy tirade by the papal nuncio to Chile in which he stated that 'as a system and as a politico-social organisation, Communism is the most impious aberration and most brutal tyranny that the world has ever seen. As defined by the Pope it is intrinsically evil.' He went on to refer to religious persecution in the Soviet Union and signed off on the optimistic note that 'Russia will be converted'. (While the latter statement was allowed, a direct 'quotation' from the message of 'Our Lady of Fatima' in an advertisement for the book of the same name, which read: 'if the people attend to my petition Russia will be converted and there will be peace . . .' was deleted.)[64] The occasional permitted publication of references to religious persecution in the Soviet Union stood in stark contrast to the zealous suppression of all such references in relation to the Nazis. Besides the 'natural' antipathy of the Irish people towards communism, the actual distance of the Soviet Union from Ireland (which minimised any

" Standard "

22 May 1944

CHURCH IS VICTIM OF WAR

In Cervaro, Italy, two American infantrymen observe artillery in the Cassino region, before the ruins of a demolished church. The altar of the church, under timbers to the left of the square steeple, was unharmed by the shelling and bombardment of the town. Army Signal Corps photo. (N.C.W.C.)

A photograph submitted by the *Standard* in May 1944. The censor refused to pass it for publication because such imagery, linking the Catholic Church to the war, was regarded as propagandist and objectionable.

possible physical threat) and the absence of a Soviet diplomatic representative were probably influential factors in this regard.

The *Standard* was probably Ireland's most influential Catholic paper. It had a high circulation of up to 50,000 copies per week and its declared aim was the creation of 'a united public opinion in the cause of Catholic reconstruction'.[65] It propagated the monetary theories of its chief contributor, Alfred O'Rahilly and, under the influence of the Catholic social teaching of *Quadragesimo Anno*, displayed 'a distinct tendency towards corporatism'.[66] The *Standard* had the distinction of being the first newspaper to be directed to submit in full before publication, on 23 September 1939; it complied immediately and the order was revoked leaving it to submit only 'doubtful matter'; because it featured 'highly controversial political articles' large submissions were necessary each week.[67]

Most controversial in the first years of the war were its articles on the state's financial and economic policy. The Department of Finance was a particular target, and in a letter to Coyne in March 1942 its secretary, James McElligott, complained that the *Standard* had been 'conducting a violent campaign' against his department. He took particular exception to items about the control exerted by the senior civil servants at Finance which implied that the department was 'seeking to perpetuate the spirit of Dublin Castle and looks down upon the mere native Irish'.[68] McElligott and the other senior officials were worried at the effect O'Rahilly's public and provocative attacks on fiscal policy were having on the public in general and the Fianna Fáil party in particular.[69] Unfortunately for them Frank Aiken was among those influenced by O'Rahilly's ideas on monetary reform,[70] a fact which must have influenced his belief that the expression of criticism of financial policy was a lesser evil than its suppression.[71] He thus allowed articles which could easily have been construed as being calculated to undermine public confidence in the national currency and financial institutions, as suggested by McElligott.[72] Given this situation, the Censorship was unable to act on McElligott's request to stop such articles and Coyne suggested that he get his minister to raise the matter at cabinet level.[73]

Other matters 'stopped' for the *Standard* included a wide range of predictable issues: the persecution of Catholics in Europe, war damage to missions in the Far East, damage to church property in Italy, Irish chaplains in the British forces, criticisms of 'American lifestyles', anti-Semitic references, US soldiers in the North, speculations on 'the peace', etc.[74] Letters and articles which argued for a policy of anti-Semitism in Ireland were prohibited. Most anti-Semitic items, however, particularly in the *Standard*, were thinly disguised as criticisms of the evils of moneylending, the abuses of hire-purchase trading, and so on. As long as such articles and letters did not attack these activities as specifically Jewish they were allowed to appear.[75] Among the anti-Semitic articles stopped for the *Standard* was a piece entitled 'Another Conquest of Ireland', in which it was suggested that farms across Ireland were being bought up for Jewish clients.[76]

At the war's end the Censorship acknowledged the 'loyal co-operation' of the *Standard* with it throughout the period.[77] This co-operation was both official and unofficial. In February 1943 Professor Joad, the British author of the charter for rationalists, visited Dublin and was interviewed by the *Standard*. Joad's charter, among other things, argued for the legalisation of abortion, increased access to contraception and divorce, the abolition of censorship and the repeal of anti-homosexual legislation. Coyne believed that Joad's arguments for the latter in his interview should be deleted but realised that such censorship was outside the scope of his authority. He therefore chose to do the next best thing and approached the editor, Peter O'Curry, in a 'personal way', and asked him to omit the references, which he duly did. The *Standard*, of course, wished to present Joad as a representative of British degeneracy. It described him as a British propagandist, which provoked a complaint from John Betjeman, press attaché at the office of the UK representative. He pointed out that Joad was not representative of British opinion and asked that no further publicity be given to him. The Censorship thus instituted a close-down on Joad, on the basis of preserving 'good relations' with Britain.[78] (Interestingly, a G2 memo in the following month noted that Joad had come to Ireland with the approval of the British Ministry of Information and that this fact added significance to the favourable remarks about Irish neutrality and de Valera which he had subsequently made, i.e. that they indicated a more favourable British attitude towards neutrality.[79])

The *Standard*'s antipathy to most things British, American and Soviet, its corporatist tendencies and its anti-Semitism led observers, not unreasonably, to regard it as a pro-Axis paper; it won a libel action against the *Daily Mail* for making this allegation.[80]

Ireland's second biggest selling Catholic newspaper was the *Irish Catholic* (with a circulation of approximately 30,000 per week).[81] It was a more general, 'straight' paper than the *Standard* and less an advocate of a particular point of view. Although less 'controversial' the *Irish Catholic* encountered censorship difficulties similar to those of the *Standard*. Articles on the Soviet Union frequently overstepped the acceptable boundaries as did many on the effects of the war on the Vatican and the church in Italy.

In July 1943 the *Irish Catholic* reported that the Virgin Mary had appeared again to one of the 'shepherd children of Fatima' and revealed that the war was nearing its end; the Censorship stopped the story.[82] The journal dedicated to Mary, *Maria Legionis* (quarterly organ of the Legion of Mary) broke the rules on a number of occasions, but in March 1944 Knightly wrote to Jack Purcell (acting controller of censorship) to say that the question of taking action was a difficult one and that he was inclined to accord the journal 'generous treatment'. He believed that a direction to submit in full would appear drastic and feared that the Censorship would be 'charged with hindering a very laudable religious movement'. Purcell was inclined to agree but in consulting Aiken warned of the dangers of being accused of favouritism. The editor was León Ó Broin, a principal officer at the Department of Finance, and Aiken was sure that 'a friendly chat' with him should suffice. Purcell explained the position to Ó Broin, but the fears he expressed to Aiken were realised in May when the *Missionary Annals* magazine was stopped from publishing a photograph of a priest in a British army chaplain's uniform. The editor pointed out that such pictures regularly appeared in *Maria Legionis* and Purcell immediately arranged for the legion journal to submit all such matter before publication.[83] In January 1945 Ó Broin submitted three photographs along with the page proofs. Two of the pictures were mutilated by Aiken 'in order to indicate the manner in which they could be passed for publication'. (He ripped out figures in military uniform from the photographs which showed the apostolic delegate inspecting a legion stall.) The photographs, it then transpired, were not the property of the legion and had been given to them on loan; an embarrassed Censorship apologised and attempted to repair them as well as possible! Most of the deletions from the *Maria Legionis* proofs related to the British forces and the war, including the serialised story of Stalag 383, 'the PoW camp which introduced the Legion to Germany', which had previously been allowed.[84]

The presence of large numbers of Irish Catholic missionaries in the Pacific area began to create difficulties for the Censorship as the conflict spread and Irish missionary magazines increasingly infringed upon the regulations. The editor of *Ricci Mission News* was informed, following upon an article he had published in April 1945, that 'the Censorship does not allow hospitals, still less children's hospitals to be shelled or bombed in our press by either side whatever the facts may be'.[85] In June 1943 *Island Missions*, the organ of the Marist Missions in the South Seas, featured an article on 'The Solomons Massacre' which provoked a complaint from the Japanese consul. The magazine was asked to submit such matters in future.[86] The Censorship was aware of the dangers posed to Irish nationals in this theatre of war and wrote in November 1943 to Irish Jesuit Publications asking them to submit matter that they proposed to publish which touched upon events such as the occupation of Hong Kong by the Japanese. The censor expressed his desire to prevent 'the publication of matter which might make it more difficult to secure favourable or even fair treatment of our nationals in the various countries and territories which have been occupied by one or other of the belligerents'.[87]

The principal non-Catholic religious publication of the period was the *Church of Ireland Gazette*, which showed, according to the Censorship, 'a markedly anti-German bias'. The editor was called in and remonstrated with in September 1940 following the publication of a series of articles which were 'offensive to Germany'. He gave a 'promise of amendment' and, enjoying the greater latitude afforded to such organs as his own and the *Standard*, avoided the ire of the Censorship until May 1941 when he published 'a most outrageous letter'. The offending writer suggested that a choice would have to be made between loyalty to Éire and loyalty to the British crown and indicated that the latter was the appropriate choice for members of the Church of Ireland. The letter was regarded by Coyne as 'seditious libel and subversive in its general tenor'; its publication led to an order to submit in full before publication being issued to the *Gazette*. The order was revoked on 19 June 1941 after the editor had expressed his regret and gave an assurance that he would not reoffend. The paper encountered no further difficulties with the Censorship for the remainder of the Emergency.[88]

In the treatment of church-related matters the Censorship, for the most part, adhered stubbornly to its strict policies. The most pertinent in this area was the absolute refusal to allow moral motives to be ascribed to the policies or actions of any of the belligerent states. The propagandists were handicapped in their efforts to win Catholic opinion in Ireland – as Coyne put it, the 'devil' was forbidden to 'quote scripture'. In relation to the Vatican, the Censorship acted upon its perceived duty to the pontiff and was constantly vigilant of propagandist attempts to exploit the ambiguity of papal pronouncements. Ireland's apparently innate anti-communism and the seemingly unique perniciousness of the treatment meted out to Northern Catholics provided the basis for most of the anomalies which arose. The significance or effect of the censorship of episcopal pronouncements should not be overestimated. The number of pastorals and other statements of the bishops which were censored was small relative to their overall output, and they continued to pontificate unhindered on most issues. It is worth repeating the point that the pastorals and statements themselves were not interfered with, only reports of and quotes from them in the press. The fact that the latter was not the medium through which the hierarchy communicated its messages to its flocks was referred to by officials and doubtless served to salve the consciences of those civil servants and politicians accused of the cardinal sin of interfering with the work of the Catholic church or infringing on the 'freedom of religion', as independent TD Patrick Cogan once suggested in the Dáil.[89] Such charges were groundless; there was no challenge to church power nor even an infringement upon it. It was the press and the propagandists who lost out, though it was unusual to see the Catholic Church, for once, at the receiving end of censorship in Ireland.

THE IRA

The publication of anything which could give anyone an excuse for sup-
porting the so-called IRA of today can only do harm at the present
time . . .[90]

T.J Coyne

While many of the factors influencing the maintenance of Irish neutrality
lay outside Irish control, one area in which the state could take effective
measures to protect itself was in dealing with its main internal enemy, the
IRA. The principal threat which they posed in the early years of the war
arose from the German view of them as their 'natural ally' and the possibility
that this could lead the British to make a pre-emptive strike or, perhaps,
use the excuse of the IRA to occupy Irish bases. The IRA had 'declared
war' on Britain in January 1939 and had been engaged in a bombing campaign there which continued until shortly after the war had begun. This
posed a direct threat to de Valera's pledge that Ireland would not be used
as a base for attacks on Britain.

They also posed a serious threat to the 'unity of the people' in the state
and to the much sought-after position of 'national leadership' which de Valera
was to achieve through popular and cross-party support for his wartime
policy of neutrality; he was determined to avoid the fate of John Redmond,
the Home Rule leader, who had been driven from the political stage by de
Valera's own generation of rebels.[91] The full force of the newly legitimised
state was brought to bear on militant Republicans as de Valera set about
implementing the 'rule of order' with a new ruthless authoritarianism;[92]
the Emergency provided the impetus and the opportunity to eliminate the
IRA from Irish politics. G2's brief was extended to deal with this internal
security threat, particularly its links with Germany, and both it and the Garda
Special Branch were given additional powers and resources. De Valera appointed the tough, uncompromising Gerald Boland as Minister for Justice
and among the general repressive measures adopted by the state were internment without trial, military courts, the death penalty and censorship.

The Offences Against the State Act (OASA), made in June 1939, already
provided censorship powers with regard to 'incriminating', 'treasonable' and
'seditious' documents and the publication of matter by or on behalf of 'an
unlawful organisation'. The emergency censorship, however, was utilised in
a far more general fashion to minimise the impact of actions taken by the
IRA and its supporters; to 'keep the temperature down' and deny them and
their views the life-blood of publicity and any suggestion of legitimacy. 'There
is a public interest to be preserved', Coyne told the editor of the *Standard*

which requires that nothing should be published at the present time
which would encourage the idea that the so-called IRA of today is in
apostolic succession to the pre-truce or even the pre-1931 body . . . The

publication of anything which could give anyone an excuse for supporting the so-called IRA of today can only do harm at the present time . . .[93]

Among the matters 'which could give anyone an excuse' and were suppressed were reports which implied that IRA gunmen were anything other than murderers; coverage of Easter rising commemorations; reports on hunger strikes and 'blanket' protests; and much more. In conjunction with repression Fianna Fáil countered the threat from its Republican opponents by taking every opportunity to play the 'green card', and the Censorship played its part in this process also. Thus, while matter relating to the internment and imprisonment of Republicans in the North was published, similar material relating to the same issues in the South was suppressed; while campaigns for the reprieve of IRA men facing death sentences in Britain and the North received full publicity, there was no coverage allowed for similar campaigns for those facing an identical fate in the southern state. Meanwhile, Fianna Fáil played politics with the partition issue, the education system continued to glorify the physical force tradition in Irish nationalism, and press publicity about the oppression of Northern nationalists and the 'evil of partition' was positively encouraged.

In the first weeks of the Emergency the Censorship contacted the various government departments seeking particulars of any matters 'which it is desirable to prohibit from the point of view of the welfare and protection of the State'. The Department of Justice replied on the same day (14 September 1939) with two specific requests.[94] It wanted the submission of all news items with reference to the arrest, detention, trial and treatment of persons dealt with under the OASA or the Emergency Powers Act (EPA) 'in order to prevent these matters being dealt with in such a way as to impede the administration of justice or create unnecessary alarm'. A direction to this effect was issued to the press on 19 September 1939. The second request was that no future issue of the *Wolfe Tone Weekly*, the Republican paper of the time, should be published without prior submission. A direction to submit was issued to the paper on 19 September. However, the proprietor, prominent and life-long Republican Joseph Clarke, was in Arbour Hill prison and the paper ceased publication following the issue of 30 September 1939.[95] The *Weekly* had been founded in 1937 by Clarke and Brian O'Higgins (who continued to publish the *Wolfe Tone Annual*; see p. 132); following its demise in 1939 Republicans were without their own paper until the launch of the *United Irishman* in 1948.[96] (The IRA's clandestine *War News* began in 1939 but ceased publication the following year.[97])

Clarke had been imprisoned in August and was among a total of some 1,100 people who were interned or imprisoned between 1939 and 1945.[98] Given that such a high proportion of Republicans were behind bars, the struggle was inevitably carried into the prisons. Those held in Arbour Hill and Mountjoy jails and at the Curragh internment camp were allowed wear their own clothes, but the top IRA prisoners held in Portlaoise were expected to wear convict uniforms. The 'blanket' protest which they staged as a result was allowed no publicity throughout the war years. Prisoners in Mountjoy and Arbour Hill began the first in a series of wartime hunger strikes in October 1939 and the government, discomforted by the ghosts of Thomas Ashe and Terence MacSwiney, closed down on all publicity for these protests also. This mainly took the form of coverage of the support campaign spearheaded by Cumann na mBan and reports on the medical condition of the strikers. Exceptions were made when 'the circumstances favoured publicity'; for example, a report on attempts by protesters to disrupt a St Vincent de Paul meeting at the Mansion House, Dublin addressed by de Valera was allowed because it was believed that this action was 'generally resented'.[99] Despite public pronouncements to the contrary, de Valera was still tending towards leniency at this early stage and six hunger strikers were released between October and December 1939, most notably 1916 veteran Patrick McGrath – a decision de Valera would come to regret. The desire to suppress reported links between the IRA and Germany was farcically illustrated in November by the Censorship's treatment of an *Irish Press* report on the case of Seán Dunne, charged at Bray with possession of a German Mauser pistol; the word 'German' was deleted.[100] Later on, more serious evidence of these links was suppressed with the close-down on publicity about the various agents from the Reich who arrived in the country seeking contact with their 'natural ally'.

On Christmas Eve, 1939 the IRA severely embarrassed the government by stealing a large proportion of the Irish army's ammunition stores in an audacious raid on the Magazine Fort in the Phoenix Park. This incident, described by Dan Bryan of G2 as 'our Pearl Harbour',[101] allied to the seizure of an IRA pirate radio station in Dublin and the fatal shooting of a Garda in Cork, tipped the balance away from leniency and led the government to amend the Emergency Powers Act to allow the internment of Irish citizens on 5 January 1940.[102] Meanwhile, the press had been instructed not to publicise the Magazine Fort raid and to restrict coverage to the bare official announcement. The *Irish Times*, however, published a report which contained details not in the official statement; this transgression, allied to another two weeks later, led to the paper being directed to submit in full before publication.[103]

The next event of major significance occurred in England, with the hanging of Peter Barnes and Frank Richards (whose real name was James McCormick) on 7 February 1940 for their part in causing an explosion in Coventry in August 1939. (They had not been involved in the actual bombing.) Their sentencing had aroused a wave of bitterness in Ireland, and public bodies across the country appealed for clemency. De Valera made representations on the men's behalf to Maffey, Eden and Chamberlain, Fianna Fáil TDs appeared on protest platforms and the *Irish Press* gave 'massive coverage' to the protest campaign.[104] The Censorship allowed all matter likely to influence a favourable decision and stopped anything 'likely to militate against a reprieve'. Following their execution Ireland went into national mourning; flags were flown at half-mast, theatres and cinemas were closed, sports events were cancelled.[105] Some publicity was allowed for protests but a check was put on utterances 'likely to aggravate the situation'. Deletions were made to such statements from several Fianna Fáil TDs; Councillor Corry's comments that he hoped Hitler would blow the British to hell were stopped as were those of Richard Corish, the Labour TD, who described the men as patriots. Calls for the recall of the Irish high commissioner in London and the expulsion of John Maffey, the UK representative, from Ireland were also prohibited.[106]

Meanwhile, the struggle of IRA prisoners for political status was continuing in Ireland's prisons and on 25 February 1940 a new hunger strike was launched. Two of the original eight protesters abandoned their fast on 5 March but the other six held out. The strike provided the Censorship with the bulk of its work during March as most matter relating to it, barring official statements, was stopped. Cumann na mBan was again to the fore in the support campaign and speeches and statements of prominent nationalist women like Maud Gonne, Mary MacSwiney and Anne Ceannt all fell foul of the censorship.[107] Despite intense 'behind the scenes' pressure, de Valera did not relent this time; Tony D'Arcy died on 16 April 1940 followed by Jack McNeela three days later. The strike was abandoned after the other four received word (which turned out to be false) that their demands had been granted. On the day before the ending of the strike Coyne had passed an *Irish Times* editorial on the protest, as he wanted to allow editorial comment which urged the abandonment of the strike while suppressing anything that might encourage them to persist.[108] On the day of D'Arcy's death a direction was issued to the newspapers instructing them to submit all matter 'in any way relating to the death and burial of any person who has died while in lawful custody'.[109] Severe censorship was used to 'kill public interest' in the deaths, leading to strong protests. Letters, resolutions and reports of demonstrations were stopped, including a report from a protest in Dublin at which Peadar O'Donnell called on the Dublin Trades Council to organise a mass demonstration 'to burst the Censorship'. Coverage of the hunger strikes in the *Irish Workers' Weekly* and the *Torch* led to them being directed to submit in full before publication, while the importation of *Reynolds News* was prohibited for the same reason. The hunger strikers' deaths were marked only by half-column death notices, with no prominence or pictures. All other matter, including resolutions of sympathy, was stopped.[110]

The suppression of news on the hunger strikes led the IRA to issue threatening letters to the management and staff of all the Dublin dailies on 6 April. The letter to staff warned that the IRA would ensure that 'if newspapers are to appear at all, they will be representative of all shades of thought . . . When newspapers deliberately accept a censorship that is calculated to mislead the public and impair the right of all the people to live in freedom, we have no alternative but to intervene'. The IRA, the letter went on, was 'very loath indeed to take any action that would deprive fellow workers of the opportunity to earn a living in Dublin. But if the cause of the suppression is the censorship, organised labour through its Union and its Parliamentary group has the remedy in its own hands'. The Garda commissioner considered that it was incumbent upon the Gardaí to provide protection at the newspaper printing works and in connection with deliveries, and all Gardaí were directed to be 'on the alert' to prevent interference with circulation.[111]

One of those who had abandoned the hunger strike was Thomas Mac-Curtain, son of the former lord mayor of Cork who had been killed by the British in 1920. On 13 June 1940 he was sentenced to death for the killing of a Garda in Cork. Coverage of his sentence in the press was restricted to one-third of a column with no prominence. A reprieve campaign developed and was denied all publicity,[112] yet de Valera gave in eventually (apparently, following a decisive intervention on MacCurtain's behalf by Cardinal MacRory) and on 19 July 1940 a government statement announced that the sentence had been commuted to penal servitude for life.[113]

Following the fall of France and the onset of the Battle of Britain the German threat to Ireland never appeared more real and the government was determined that the IRA would not add to the danger. That summer of 1940 saw the failure of two German attempted link-ups with the IRA – the Goertz and Russell–Ryan missions[114] – the seizure of arms dumps, the internment and arrest of hundreds more IRA men and the formation of the Local Security Force, signalling the arrival of a new type of patriotism, which had an effect on IRA recruitment. G2 and the Garda Special Branch were given additional resources; the latter adopted a 'shoot first, ask questions later' approach and what amounted to street warfare developed between them and the IRA. A pattern of 'provocation, retaliation and vengeance' was established[115] and between May and August there were twenty-six incidents involving IRA men and the police, with people dying on both sides.[116]

The Censorship heavily censored all references to the shooting dead by the Special Branch of an unarmed IRA man, John Kavanagh, while engaged in digging a tunnel in the direction of Cork jail on 3 August.[117] On 16 August three Gardaí were shot, two fatally, in a shoot-out during a raid in Rathgar in Dublin. The press was prohibited from implying that the Gardaí had died in a 'fair fight', and only the bare minimum coverage was allowed for the case of the two men charged with the killings[118] – Thomas Harte and the man who de Valera had released the previous December, Patrick McGrath. The government responded to the shootings by giving the military tribunal the right to pass sentence of death without appeal and the Censorship moved to close down on all discussion in the press on the issue of capital punishment. McGrath and Harte were executed in Mountjoy jail on 6 September 1940. The official announcement of the executions was the only coverage permitted, and it was not allowed any prominence. The lord mayor of Dublin, Kathleen Clarke, flew the city flag at half-mast on the day of the executions, a fact which Senator Frank MacDermot believed should have been made known to the voters of Dublin.[119]

The next death occurred in December 1940 following an outbreak of rioting in the Curragh; an IRA internee, Bernard (Barney) Casey, was shot in the back by military police. Coverage of his funeral was restricted to giving the names of the priest and chief mourners; all other names were cut, as were references to the IRA, the tricolour on his coffin and all other details.[120] The following July Richard Goss was arrested for shooting at and wounding a soldier during a bank raid in Co. Longford and was sentenced to death. The Censorship permitted just the bare announcement of his sentence and closed down on coverage of the campaign for his reprieve.[121] He was executed on 9 August 1941.

The IRA's fortunes declined even further in the aftermath of the 'Hayes Confession' débâcle in the summer of 1941. At the end of June leading members of the organisation had kidnapped and court martialled chief of staff, Stephen Hayes. He was sentenced to death for treachery and betraying the IRA to the southern Gardaí. He escaped his captors before they could shoot him and turned himself in to the Gardaí. The IRA subsequently published the lengthy 'confession' he had been forced to write, creating further confusion and demoralisation in the organisation.[122] No coverage of the affair was allowed in the press.[123] Arising out of details contained in the 'confession' George Plant was sentenced to death for the killing of an IRA man in Waterford. The usual restrictions were placed on coverage of the case[124] and Plant was put to death in Portlaoise prison on 5 March 1942. Supporters, intent on circumventing the censorship, produced a leaflet setting out the facts of the case from their point of view; they scattered 5,000 copies down over Dublin from the top of Nelson's Pillar while de Valera was attending St Patrick's Day mass in the nearby pro-cathedral.[125]

By the autumn of 1941 the IRA, 'gutted by arrest and splintered by the Hayes affair', no longer presented a threat to neutrality or even to civil order.[126] Although at a very low ebb its actions, and particularly the reaction to them from the British, could still arouse strong feelings; by now it was not the IRA itself that de Valera feared, but 'its power to mobilize Republican support in time of crisis'.[127] In August 1942, a group of six IRA men, all aged under nineteen, were sentenced to death for the killing of an RUC man in Belfast.[128] 'If any action could revive the IRA', Longford and O'Neill wrote in their official biography of de Valera, 'a mass execution on that scale would be sure to do so.'[129] De Valera did all in his power to stop the executions and managed to persuade the American government to take up the case. Practically full publicity was allowed for the strong reprieve campaign which developed in the South. However, 'unhelpful matter' which exposed the hypocrisy of the Irish government's position was stopped, like the comments of a speaker at a Labour meeting in Clones who pointed out that the government's arguments to the British were lessened in force because the British could point to the same actions by them.[130] Five of the six were reprieved, but Thomas (Tommy) McWilliams was hanged on 2 September, despite a last-minute personal appeal to Churchill by de Valera.[131] The reprieve of the other five had 'stabilised public opinion', yet Dublin experienced demonstrations and unrest, including Garda baton charges, following the execution. The Censorship closed down on reports of these events, and those relating to shooting incidents in Belfast and near the border were confined to the RUC statements.[132]

Although the IRA threat on both sides of the border had been largely neutralised, both states continued to keep up the pressure with the object of eliminating them entirely as an organised force. By this stage also many policemen had developed a personal interest in wiping them out.[133] One of the most notorious and effective of the IRA's Special Branch foes was Detective Sergeant Denis (Dinny) O'Brien. On 9 September 1942 he was shot dead as he left his home in Rathfarnham, Co. Dublin. The press censors were instructed to stop the word 'gunmen' being used in reports and to replace it with 'murderers'. The *Irish Independent* omitted passages of its report where this change had been made, while the *Evening Herald* went to press with no report rather than obey the Censorship and describe the killing as murder.[134] This was because the press was discouraged from describing the incident for which McWilliams was hanged the previous week as murder. 'Apparently', wrote David Gray, the American minister, '. . . murder by the IRA is murder only in Eire and not when committed north of the border.'[135]

In the following November Maurice O'Neill was sentenced to death by the military tribunal for shooting dead a detective at Donnycarney in Dublin. (There was no evidence that he had fired the shot.[136]) The campaign for clemency, centred on his native south Kerry, was denied all publicity. Following his execution in Mountjoy the heading 'Death Sentence Carried Out' was altered to read 'Donnycarney Shooting Case: Sentence Carried Out'; the fact that Kerry County Council adjourned its quarterly meeting as a mark of respect was suppressed, and the words 'who was shot at Mountjoy' were deleted from a mass notice for the dead man.[137]

A number of IRA men were charged at various times in connection with the killing of Dinny O'Brien, but only one, a 26-year-old Kerryman called Charles Kerins, was sentenced to death for his part in it, in November 1944. At the time of the shooting Kerins was deputy chief of staff and head of what was left of the IRA in Dublin. The authorities were sure that he had given the order to kill O'Brien even if he had not fired the shot. By the time of his arrest in June 1944 he had become chief of staff, but was virtually a lone operator – 'Chief of Staff of a one-man army'. Units across the country had disintegrated and the long-lived IRA infrastructure was broken, disillusionment, disorganisation and state repression having taken their toll.[138]

In the meantime, the Censorship had been busy ensuring that nothing was published which cast doubt on the 'fact' that the Republican tradition was vested in the one, true church of Fianna Fáil, in 'apostolic succession' from the 'old' IRA, and not in that organisation which had 'usurped' the title. The clearest illustration of this policy was the stopping of advertisements, notices and reports in connection with all Easter rising commemorations, except for the official one.[139] References to the IRA were deleted in all circumstances, from ministerial speeches to the interjections of hecklers and even a court report which mentioned that a drunken Jack Doyle, the famous boxer, had shouted, 'Have you heard of the IRA?', during an encounter with a bus conductor![140] On 21 November 1942, after the *Irish Press* had been allowed to use the heading 'Three Kerrymen Convicted', Coyne told the press censors that 'the use of headings which appeal to local patriotism in connection with law-breakers and misdemeanants is something which is repugnant to man and most hateful to God and the Minister says he will chop the head off the next member of staff to pass a heading of this kind'.[141] The *Irish Times* heading to its report on the trial of Kerins, 'Kerryman Charged with Murder', was deleted in October 1944 for being 'tendentious and mischievous . . . What, I wonder', Coyne asked Smyllie, 'would you think of the caption, "Freemason charged with abortion"?'[142] When IRA man Seán McCool, who was chief of staff before his arrest, contested the 1943 general election in Donegal, only his name and candidature were allowed to be published; no mention could be given to the fact that he was an internee and hunger striker.[143] Reports of Jim Larkin Jnr's maiden speech in the Dáil, during which he called for the release of the hunger strikers in the Curragh, were suppressed.[144] The fact that Seán O'Tuama was an internee at the time of his election as president of the Gaelic League in October 1941 most certainly did not fit the official picture, and although his name and election were publicised, his current place of residence was not.[145] Publicity for appeals by the National Aid Society, which provided relief for the dependants of political prisoners, was also denied.[146]

Following the sentencing to death of Charles Kerins, 'The Boy from Tralee', a reprieve campaign was established under the auspices of Kerry County Council. A public meeting in support of a reprieve was held in the Mansion House on 27 November 1944 and was attended by 'several thousand people'; it was chaired by the lord mayor of Dublin, Martin O'Sullivan of Labour, and the platform included the lord mayor of Cork and a number of TDs, including Fred Crowley, Pat Finucane (Independent), Dan Spring (National Labour) and both Jim Larkins, senior and junior (Labour). The authorities clamped down heavily on the reprieve campaign, viewing it as a front which the IRA was using in order to reorganise itself and garner support. All matter relating to the campaign was kept out of the press, including advertisements for that public meeting in the Mansion House and the petition campaign organised by Kerry County Council; notices about a series of masses being said for Kerins; and an advertisement from the Kerryman's Association announcing simply that 'A meeting of all Kerrymen and women resident in Dublin will be held in Clery's, O'Connell Street on tomorrow, Thursday at 7.30 p.m.'[147]

Having been denied press publicity the campaign undertook to publicise its activities with posters and leaflets. In response, the authorities brought the censorship onto the streets; posters and leaflets were seized by the Gardaí and twenty-one people were arrested. Petitioners were also arrested and the campaign was prevented from using a loud-hailer mounted on a cab; the police even went so far as to baton charge a rosary meeting for Kerins outside the GPO on the night before his execution.[148] When Jim Larkin Jnr attempted to raise these issues in the Dáil on 30 November he was suspended for refusing to accept that the issue was not urgent![149] While Kerins was being hanged in Mountjoy the next day, Labour Party leader William Norton raised the issue of censorship on adjournment and a lengthy debate ensued.

The approach taken by the government speakers – Gerald Boland, the Minister for Justice, Aiken and de Valera – was to verbally criminalise the reprieve campaign. (Ironically, the leading member of the reprieve committee was the businessman Denis Guiney, a strong financial supporter of Fianna Fáil and a personal friend of Boland.) They persistently strayed from the issue at hand to speak about the IRA (though the term was never used) and the threat which they posed to democracy and the state. 'The advertisements were stopped', according to de Valera, 'by virtue of our right to maintain order and preserve the State, to prevent organisations getting ahead and using this as a cloak for reorganisation.'[150] The individuals and groups who supported reprieve, but were obviously not IRA supporters, were, according to the ministers, being duped. Boland accused Norton and others in the Labour Party of being 'tools' of the IRA.[151]

The death of Kerins broke the line of IRA continuity; there was no longer a chief of staff, a GHQ, an army council or even an IRA.[152] The organisation had been temporarily crushed and the Censorship had played its part.

In the course of the Kerins debate, de Valera had returned to the old theme of young people being 'misled' and not 'understanding' the changed position. 'We were willing to do everything we could to make allowance for them and to try to wean them off; but they have resisted every effort of ours to induce them to obey the law and to accept the constitutional position of the Irish people.'[153] The main culprits, according to this approach, were older Republicans who led the young astray. Stephen Roche, secretary of the Department of Justice, wrote in 1938 that the main object of the special powers legislation which was then in preparation (and became the Offences Against the State Act) was 'to prevent a small group of older people, who make a hobby of violent political agitation from leading the younger generation into folly and crime in order to gratify their own vanity and drive for leadership'.[154] A prime example of those he had in mind was Brian O'Higgins, the life-long Republican who published the *Wolfe Tone Annual*. That publication was banned, according to Aiken, because O'Higgins was 'inciting the young men of this country or leading them to believe they have a right to overthrow the constitution . . .'[155] Such comments arose from the same paternalistic attitude which de Valera adopted towards the IRA on his accession to power. 'He spoke of them', according to Fanning, 'much as a benevolent schoolmaster might speak of a spirited but naughty schoolboy', and sought to lead them 'on the right path'.[156] The benevolence turned to malevolence, however, when they continued to refuse his lead, would not accept the legitimacy of his state and put it under threat at its moment of greatest danger.

As Lee points out, so many young people could not have been so 'misled' were they not already predisposed in that direction.[157] While de Valera had mastered the political 'art of the possible' and successfully bridged the gap between *de facto* position and *de jure* claim,[158] the official political culture, and especially the education system, continued to trade in nationalist mythology and glorification of the tradition of violence.[159] While the Censorship suppressed the position which refused to accept the preservation of a twenty-six county state as the primary national goal, the 'fairy tale text books' of Irish history[160] continued, in their approach, to justify that refusal.

THE LEFT AND THE WORKING CLASS

> . . . *the greatest menace to us, the fifth columnist aiding our capitalist foe, is the authority that would gag us.*
>
> John Swift (editor),
> *Bakery Trades Journal*,
> March 1941

The war impacted heavily on the Irish economy and, as always in times of economic difficulty, it was the poorer sections of the community which bore the brunt. Employment fell heavily, prices rose sharply while wages and social welfare payments were pinned down. Basic working-class foodstuffs were strictly rationed and profiteering and black marketeering became rife. The lack of adequate housing was accompanied by overcrowding, insanitary conditions and rack-renting. Many working-class people suffered acute poverty, with disturbing levels of malnutrition, tuberculosis and infant mortality occurring in city slums. T.J. Coyne, in a letter of July 1941, described poverty and hunger as 'fairly widespread';[161] such a description would never have been allowed publication.

The reality of social hardship in wartime Ireland has traditionally been hidden behind tales of the legendary 'glimmerman' (an inspector who monitored the unauthorised use of gas) and good-humoured ditties of the 'Bless de Valera and Seán MacEntee, for giving us brown bread and a half ounce of tea' variety.[162] The quaint picture of Irish society united in its hour of peril, good-humouredly shouldering an equally shared burden is a false one which still persists. Its origins lie partially in the contribution of the Censorship to the maintenance of the 'united front' image. The publication of matter which highlighted the social inequality of the Emergency regime was considered undesirable because of its 'demoralising' effect on 'the public'. Actions taken by sections of the working class in defence of their interests were treated in the context of the threat which such actions posed to public order, essential supplies and services, and so on. The efforts of the left to force class issues on to the national agenda were counteracted by the Censorship in the interests of political consensus and ostensible unity.

The wartime censorship, however, was but the most obvious impediment to the left in the communication of its messages. The fervent, Catholic church-inspired anti-communism of the time ensured that socialism was effecively a taboo concept within Irish political culture, its doctrines alien, sinful and suspect. The left, therefore, suffered an implicit, prior censorship which marginalised and invalidated its arguments. This 'structural censorship' was far more effective than any explicit prohibitions. Reinforcing it was the shared discourse of twenty-six county nationalism which developed between Fianna Fáil and important sections of the trade union movement, for whom the 'preservation of the state' became the shared primary concern. The need to defend specific working-class interests was superseded by the imperative of defending 'national interests'; defence of the state meant defence of the status quo – political, economic and social – with obvious implications for revolutionaries.

In 1940 James Larkin Snr and the left-wing Dublin Trades Council approached the government with a proposal to bring up to 2,000 British evacuee children to live with workers' families in Dublin. The scheme was rejected by the government and all publicity for it was denied.[163] Aiken stated in the Seanad that the government had been negotiating with its British counterparts about the reception of refugees and did not want 'a body like the Dublin Trades Unions Council butting in on that matter until the government here had settled the major question with the British government'.[164] Aiken was supported by the trade unionist, Senator Seán P. Campbell, who served on the Irish Trade Union Congress (ITUC) executive. Campbell spoke in favour of the censorship of 'certain bodies' which, he claimed, were out to cause 'disaffection' not only in the state but among their fellow workers. He proceeded to characterise parliamentary opponents and critics of the Censorship as a liberal coterie indulging in 'high-falutin' talk' about the freedom of the press and who represented 'choleric colonels' and not the 'ordinary' people.[165] (Following this speech the senator received a message from the editor of a Dublin newspaper accusing him of being 'very much worse than Mr Aiken himself'.[166]) This episode is illustrative of the alliance of interests between Fianna Fáil and leading trade unionists and is a good example of the 'double censorship' faced by those who challenged it. The experiences of the *Torch*, which are discussed later, provide another case in point.

As well as supporting the Censorship, the ITUC gave qualified approval to the Construction Corps forced labour scheme and collaborated in the implementation of wages controls, while the Irish Transport and General Workers' Union (ITGWU) provided the government with a substantial loan of £50,000 to help it through the Emergency.[167] In a memo to the government in January 1942 congress stated that 'in the present crisis confronting the state . . . the unions and wage earners are prepared to . . . bear their fair share of the burden imposed by the exigencies of the present emergency and . . . are willing to make all the necessary sacrifices'.[168] This view was not shared by all in the trade union movement, however, and in a circular distributed at a demonstration against the Trade Union Bill and the Wages Standstill Order in June 1941, the organising Council of Action stated that 'The Irish trade union movement will not sacrifice its independence and the rights of its members at the behest of any group, party or government, outside the working class, not even to preserve national unity, because the Irish working class is the basis of the Irish nation . . .'.[169] That demonstration was the climax of a period of working-class militancy which briefly forced class issues on to the agenda and temporarily threatened the consensus about 'national interests'.

There was a high level of strike activity in the first seven months of the Emergency, culminating in a strike by municipal workers in Dublin in March 1940 which caused major disruption to the city. The Minister for Industry and Commerce Seán MacEntee responded with proposals for draconian legislation for controlling strikes and trade unions. The cabinet rejected many of the more drastic elements of MacEntee's proposals and the legislation was eventually divided, resulting in the Trade Union Bill, the terms of which were published in April 1941, and the Wages Standstill Order (Emergency Order 83) which was introduced on 7 May 1941.[170] The Trade Union Bill aimed to 'whittle away the smaller unions and to eliminate trade union multiplicity'[171] through a system of state licensing, and was seen by many as an attack on freedom of association.[172] However, it had the covert support of William O'Brien (ITGWU), the president of the ITUC, who was suspected by his opponents in the labour movement of being 'in league with the government in an attempt to achieve the "One Big Union" by statutory means'.[173] The congress executive favoured a low-key protest and wished the

Labour Party to shoulder the burden of opposition. The official leadership was overtaken, however, by a wave of rank and file dissent which was building against the Bill and the wage freeze. This opposition soon began to centre around the Council of Action, which had been established by the Dublin Trades Council (with the support of the Dublin constituencies council of the Labour Party) and was led by the Larkins. The wave of resistance culminated in the demonstration of 22 June 1941 when an estimated 20,000 people, including members of fifty-three unions, marched in Dublin. In College Green Jim Larkin Snr struck a match on the seat of his pants and burnt a copy of the Trade Union Bill,[174] while the moderate Labour TD James Hickey reportedly called for the overthrow of capitalism.[175] This was the 'biggest demonstration of working class resolve since 1923'[176] and provoked Labour leader William Norton and his party to adopt a position of blanket opposition to the Bill as opposed to selective criticism.

The Council of Action gradually relinquished its leading position to the Labour Party administrative council and the ITUC executive. The Labour Party wanted the congress executive to make the measure unworkable by refusing to take out state licences, but they refused. In the face of the widespread and unexpected opposition to the Bill, the Minister for Industry and Commerce, Seán MacEntee, had 'explicitly and gratuitously redirected the venom of the Bill from the small unions to the amalgamateds'.[177] Legislation thus weighted in favour of larger and Irish based unions and against smaller and British based unions suited O'Brien's purposes very well. He took the position of waiting for the protest movement to taper off, which it rapidly did in the absence of any direction from its nominal leadership.[178] The more conciliatory Seán Lemass returned to Industry and Commerce in August 1941 and, following consultations with congress, removed 'some of the objectionable provisions of the Act of 1941'.[179] He introduced a new Trade Union Act in 1942 under the terms of which most unions took out licences, and by October 1942 the trade union leadership was collaborating in the implementation of both the Trade Union Act and the wages controls.[180] The eventual acceptance of the wages freeze was a matter of some relief, for, as R.F. Ferguson, secretary of Industry and Commerce admitted in private: 'We didn't think we'd get away with it.'[181]

The left failed to provide a focus for the discontent over the official leaders' handling of the struggle. The Communist Party of Ireland (CPI) in the South had become stagnant and isolated, as its policies increasingly reflected the demands of Soviet foreign policy and not the interests of the Irish working class. (The CPI, of course, believed that the latter were best served by following the former.) It dissolved in the autumn of 1941 and embarked on an entryist strategy; most of its members joined the Labour Party and increasingly adopted reformist politics in line with the Stalinist popular front strategy. Most other Irish socialists were also to be found within the Labour Party. This was particularly so in Dublin where activists like Mick Price,

Owen Sheehy-Skeffington and the Trotskyist, Paddy Trench served on the constituencies council. The ranks of the left in the party were swelled in 1941–2 with the influx of prominent socialists and communists like James Larkin Snr and Jnr, John de Courcy-Ireland and other former CPI members, and many workers politicised by the struggle against the Trade Union Bill and wages freeze.[182] There occurred 'a brief but memorable flowering' of left-wing politics in Dublin,[183] and with the Labour successes in the 1942 local elections many on the left came to believe that the party could become the vehicle for the task of social, economic and political transformation in Ireland. It was a forlorn hope, however, for this vehicle was wheel-clamped by its reactionary leadership and the domination of conservative trade unions, as well as being hampered by structural factors such as late in-dustrialisation, a small working class and the political and social dominance of the Catholic Church and the rural bourgeoisie. The conflicting forces within the 'broad church' of the Labour Party were personified by Larkin and O'Brien, whose long-running feud came to a head as Larkin's star rose briefly with that of the left within the party. O'Brien engineered a split, a purge of the left was undertaken and the folly of those socialists who had put their faith in the Labour Party was exposed.

The CPI's *Irish Workers' Weekly* and the Labour Party's *Torch* were the two main left-wing papers of the period. They fell foul of the Censorship on a regular basis and both were subjected to orders to submit in full before publication. These publications were given a little more latitude, because of their specific concerns, than what Coyne described as 'the more reputable papers';[184] nevertheless, they encountered many difficulties on the basis of their treatment of both domestic and international issues.

On 29 April 1939 the first issue of the new CPI paper, *Irish Workers' Weekly* (*IWW*) declared that 'we cannot be neutral against fascism, for peace and against war'. This remained the party's position until the Hitler–Stalin non-aggression pact ensured that, by the end of September 1939, Britain's 'just', 'democratic' and 'anti-fascist' war had become 'imperialist'. The primary duty of communists in each country was once again to struggle against their native ruling class. By October 1939 then, the CPI was calling for peace (on Hitler's terms), had readopted a militant stand on workers' economic struggles and had rediscovered its opposition to British imperialism in Ireland. Support for and co-operation with the IRA was again possible, a campaign for the withdrawal of Northern Ireland from the war was begun and Irish neutrality under Fianna Fáil was staunchly endorsed. When Hitler invaded the Soviet Union in June 1941, and the Anglo-Soviet pact for mutual aid was signed in July, Britain's imperialist war again became just and democratic. The CPI dropped its campaign for the withdrawal of Northern Ireland from the war, began opposing strikes and Irish neutrality and discovered that the IRA were, after all, 'agents of Hitler'.[185]

In April 1940 the IRA were still 'freedom fighters', and the *IWW*'s anti-British line and support for illegal strikes in wartime industries led to its banning in Northern Ireland in that month.[186] On 3 April the *IWW* was served with an order to submit in full before publication to the censorship authorities in the South because of an article published in support of the IRA hunger strikes. The next two issues were submitted and thereafter the order was ignored. On 27 April the Department of Justice took exception to another article on the hunger strikes and the Censorship began to consider the possibility of prosecuting the *IWW* for its failure to submit as ordered, with a view to making an example of it and deterring 'more reputable papers tempted to work in the same way'. A case was prepared by the chief state solicitor but in September Coyne wrote to the attorney general asking for the case to be dropped; he suggested that instead a new order be served against the paper accompanied by a written warning that failure to comply would result in criminal proceedings. 'The Minister', wrote Coyne, 'is chiefly concerned in this matter to avoid the appearance of acting oppressively or to be discriminating against what might be described as a working class paper and, of course, he is anxious to avoid, at all costs, an unfavourable or even an unsatisfactory verdict.' A new direction to the *IWW* to submit in full was issued on 11 November 1940 and remained in force until the paper ceased publication in November 1941.[187]

In March 1941 the Censorship prevented publication in the *Evening Mail* of two advertisements for CPI-organised public meetings, one of which was entitled 'Hunger in Dublin'. Two of the speakers, Jim Prendergast and Seán Nolan, editor of the *IWW*, visited Coyne to protest. The men argued, with some justification, that if the meetings were allowed by the police and no disturbance occurred, the advertisements should not have been stopped. Coyne responded by saying that the words 'Hunger in Dublin' were likely to cause 'alarm and despondency'. He then went on to make 'a couple of friends for life' by pointing out 'these were dangerous times and they were dangerous men'![188]

The CPI's temporary support for working-class struggle at home created further difficulties in the following months. CPI member Neil Goold was chief organiser of the tenants' committee of the Cabra–Kimmage–Crumlin and North Crumlin area of Dublin. His involvement in organising a campaign for rent reductions and social welfare increases led to his arrest. The CPI issued a bulletin on May Day calling for his release. Coyne described the publication of the bulletin as an attempt to evade the censorship of the *IWW* by slipping it into a 'passed' issue. On 2 May a direction was made for the seizure of the bulletin.[189]

With the invasion of the Soviet Union in the following month the position of the CPI/*IWW* was drastically altered and a whole new set of fronts were opened on which it would fall foul of the Censorship. Being now a supporter of the British war effort it no longer supported the IRA. However, the Soviet Union was now a belligerent, so pro-Soviet articles took on a new meaning, while the *IWW*'s new-found opposition to Irish neutrality was unlikely to find favour with the censors.

With the entry of the Soviet Union into the war the Censorship decided to allow 'both sides' a 'bite' at the issue before closing down on all pro- and anti-Soviet articles. Thus, the *Irish Catholic* and the *Standard* were allowed attack the 'Godless Communist' state; the *Torch* was permitted to present its 'moderate' position, while the *IWW* was given one chance to strike a blow for the Soviet war effort. Thereafter, Coyne informed the *IWW* that it 'would have to stick to generalities about the capitalist hell and Com- munist heaven, not forgetting the imperial maggots'.[190]

Its new opposition to Irish neutrality left the CPI more isolated and unpopular than ever and on 10 July 1941 its national committee recommend- ed the dissolution of the Dublin branch which effectively meant the liquida- tion of the CPI in the South. Despite some opposition the party soon dissolved,[191] but the *IWW* under Seán Nolan continued to publish. Its sup- port for the Soviet Union and the Allies, its opposition to neutrality and advocacy of Irish entry into the war resulted in heavy censorship, including the seizure of the issue of 16 August 1941.[192] In October Coyne wondered whether it was desirable that Nolan and his associates should 'remain at large'[193] and in the following month the decision was taken to cease publication of the *IWW*. Nolan et al., however, did not disappear.

Most of the members of the CPI joined the Labour Party and concen- trated on building its electoral support; they continued to meet and organise within the party, recruiting and successfully building up communist in- fluence, particularly in Dublin.[194] Labour did very well in the local government elections of 1942 and Martin O'Sullivan was elected as the first ever Labour lord mayor of Dublin. His election agent was Seán Nolan,[195] who continued to work within the Labour Party until his expul- sion in 1944. He also ran New Books, a communist bookshop which was opened in Pearse Street, Dublin in January 1942. A series of lectures and public meetings on such topics as 'Lenin – the Man and his Works', 'Trade Unions in Russia' and 'Women in the Soviet Union' were held at the shop beginning in late 1942,[196] leading Nolan and his comrades into conflict with the Censorship once again.

When a series of advertisements for these meetings was prevented from publication in the *Evening Mail* in late 1942 and early 1943, Nolan wrote to Aiken complaining that Coyne had acted on the basis of 'private pre- judice' and that the suppression of the advertisements was an abuse of the powers of censorship and an 'infringement of ordinary constitutional rights'. Coyne's position, supported by Aiken, was that these meetings were 'part of a propaganda campaign on behalf of one of the groups of belligerents' and that 'an organisation which is subservient to the policy of a foreign state can hardly be expected to be permitted publicity during the present emergency for its subversive activities'. When Nolan denied subservience to the policy of any foreign government, Coyne pointed to the US Communist Party money sent to Nolan on a monthly basis (observed in the Postal Censorship) and the fact that the speakers were all prominent in the CPI (which was still organised in the North). On that basis, Coyne argued, it was safe to conclude that, under democratic centralism and the structure of the Comintern, New Books followed the 'Moscow line'. Publicity was denied to all the New Books' meetings, while a number of pro-Soviet pamphlets addressed to the shop were held by the censor.[197]

Following the demise of the *IWW* Nolan continued to write for communist publications like the *Daily Worker* (US) and *Irish Freedom* (Britain). The importation of *Irish Freedom* into Ireland was prohibited by order in March 1943 and it was banned under its new title, *The Irish Democrat* in February 1945 (see Chapter 5, p. 197).[198] Towards the end of the war the Irish communists re-launched the *IWW* as a 'monthly *REVIEW* of current affairs'. It continued in this form for about three years under the editorship of John de Courcy-Ireland.[199]

The *Torch* was the weekly newspaper of the Dublin constituencies council (DCC) of the Labour Party. It had been launched in May 1939 and claimed to be, as well as the organ of the DCC, 'the mouthpiece of all organised workers'. While it played its part in the growth of the Labour Party in Dublin and the flourishing of socialist politics at grassroots level, it was, in the words of Andrée Sheehy-Skeffington, 'often flabby . . . too full of ideological and historical matter'. Its dullness was highlighted by the liveliness and topicality of *Workers' Action*, a supplement to the *Torch* produced by the Council of Action, which came out on six occasions between June 1941 and May Day 1942.[200] While, as we shall see, the *Torch* was badly affected by the Emergency Censorship, it is appropriate to deal briefly first with the 'prior censorship' which limited its effectiveness.

The principal problem lay in the control exercised over the paper by the large unions (particularly the ITGWU) through their financial support. At the height of the struggle against the Trade Union Bill and the wages freeze in 1941 Owen Sheehy-Skeffington was in a socialist minority of one on the three-person editorial board; the other two members were Robbins and Macken of the ITGWU. As a result many major labour issues were ignored; the activities of the Council of Action, for example, were barely covered while the *Torch* virtually ignored the controversial ITUC conference of July 1941 when the national executive was attacked and O'Brien acted like a dictator. When an attempt was made to voice criticism in an article the ITUC immediately withdrew its grant to the paper. At subsequent special meetings of the DCC held to discuss the future of the *Torch*, Owen Sheehy-Skeffington argued that 'freedom from financial subsidy was essential for freedom of expression and an independent policy'. His efforts were frustrated, however, and he resigned from the board in November 1941.[201] The *Torch* continued until April 1944; despite its limitations, it was the main left-wing publication of the period and encountered many difficulties with the official censorship.

On 10 April 1940 it was served with its first order to submit in full before publication by the Censorship because of a report on a Dublin Corporation discussion on the IRA hunger strikes.[202] Cathal O'Shannon, then editor of the *Torch*, had written in September 1939 that the censorship would have to be endured 'with good grace'.[203] Having fallen foul of it his good grace deserted him and the *Torch* challenged the right of the Censorship to prevent references to the hunger strikes. Coyne gave the official line in response, which was that the issue of the hunger strikes touched upon the questions of public safety and the maintenance of public order. References to the hunger strikes and criticisms of the Censorship were deleted from subsequent issues, and on 25 May the order to submit was revoked.[204]

In reply to complaints from the Department of Industry and Commerce in January 1941 regarding matter published in the *Torch*, Coyne explained the desire of the authorities to avoid 'a head-on collision' which would result in the suppression of a newspaper, particularly a representative paper like the *Torch*; 'A victory achieved by closing down or prosecuting such a paper would, we feel, be a Pyrrhic victory.' He went on to explain that the Censorship had always distinguished between different types of publications; 'thus, we allow more latitude on their special subject to the *Standard*, the *Church of Ireland Gazette*, the *Irish Workers' Weekly* and the *Torch* than we would allow to, say, the *Irish Times* or *Irish Independent*'.[205]

The *Torch*, however, continued to fall foul of the Censorship and in April 1941 the Labour Party requested the cessation of the 'most irritating and at times childish censorship of the contents of the *Torch*'. Deletions included: criticism of the Unemployment Relief Works Bill; an attack on the organisers of the Spitfire Fund in Dublin; a reference to Chaplin's film *The Great Dictator* (banned in Ireland); an article on 'Morals and the Class Struggle'; a reproduction from the paper of the Minneapolis Teamsters Union calling on workers to defend themselves and not the bosses and imperialism; and a piece on the 'grim realities of the Third Employment Order' which stated that 'the de Valeras and MacEntees of today are very different from what they were in 1927 or 1928'.[206]

On 26 April Michael Price, secretary of the Dublin constituencies council, wrote to the controller drawing attention to a resolution carried unanimously at the national conference of the Labour Party which demanded that the use of the Press Censorship against the 'activities of the working class in their struggle for better conditions be withdrawn, and that the Emergency Powers be not utilised against organisations working for the economic betterment of the working class'. Joseph Connolly replied that the Censorship had not been or would not in future be used to the detriment of the working class and that deletions had been limited 'to those which the neutrality and safety of the State in the present difficult times made necessary'.[207]

Among the 'activities' mentioned by Price was a rent strike among municipal housing tenants, organised by the Kimmage–Crumlin Tenants' Association. The association demanded that 'All rents . . . be reduced to pre-war level and all unemployment benefit and assistance, widows, orphans' and old age pensions, sick benefit and soldiers' marriage allowances . . . be raised by not less than 50%.'[208] The *Kimmage–Crumlin News*, a broadsheet published by the tenants' association, was directed to submit in full in March 1941,[209] all publicity was denied to the rent strike, while its chief organiser, the communist Neil Goold, was interned.

On 6 May Michael Price wrote an open letter to de Valera which he sent to the daily newspapers and the *Torch*. In it he called, on behalf of the Dublin constituencies council, for jobs and rent allowances for the unemployed. He referred to the poverty, destitution and appalling living conditions of municipal housing tenants and stated that the Kimmage–Crumlin rent strike was 'quite understandable' and likely to spread unless the government acted. The letter was stopped, after consultation with the Taoiseach, prompting Price to remind the Censorship of Connolly's assurance that its powers would not be used against the struggle of the working class for better conditions. Price was informed that his letter was believed to have advocated unlawful actions and had been stopped on that basis.[210]

The chief concern of the authorities, however, was more general. The rent strike itself was a relatively small affair, easily handled. What worried Coyne was the issue of precedent in relation to the prospect of a general strike, which was being mentioned in relation to the Trade Union Bill and which the Department of Industry and Commerce feared would render 'impossible the enforcement of the [Wages Standstill] Order'. What Coyne now sought was to establish a principle in relation to 'working class activities bordering on the criminal' and to institute guidelines 'with respect to the publication of such matter including calls to action for political purposes'. He wrote to Philip O'Donoghue, legal adviser to the attorney general, in this regard seeking an indication of where 'the line should be drawn by us in allowing the press to advocate the frustration of a particular law by holding the whole community to ransom by general strike action'.[211] O'Donoghue was in 'no doubt' that the action of the Censorship in stopping Price's letter was justified on the grounds that its publication would have been prejudicial to the maintenance of public order. He contended that actions which were a menace to the public peace on a large scale assumed a 'grave complexion' in the light of the emergency, which was the key issue rather than the intrinsic nature of the acts themselves. 'This would be my approach to the question of a general strike', he concluded.[212]

Meanwhile, the struggle against the Trade Union Bill and the wages freeze was reaching a climax with the large demonstration in Dublin on 22 June 1941. The leader of the Labour Party William Norton, as noted earlier, was impressed by the demonstration and in the Dáil on 24 June he and his fellow Labour TD Richard Corish made statements to the effect that if the Trade Union Bill became law they would advocate non-recognition and non-observance of it.[213] Oscar Traynor (acting for Aiken) and de Valera agreed that the deputies' remarks should not be published in the press and the Censorship duly informed the papers, first by telegram and then by official direction, that this was the case.[214] At the following day's sitting Norton read out the text of the telegram sent to the *Torch* and protested that the actions of the Censorship constituted 'an invasion of the rights of this House' and a wanton breach of the assurance given by the Taoiseach during the passage of the Emergency Powers Act that Dáil debates would not be subject to censorship. Norton concluded by stating that the censorship was being used as an instrument of the government party in preventing publication of criticism of the government.[215]

De Valera's assurances aside, there was in fact no law or parliamentary privilege which granted immunity from censorship to press reports of Dáil proceedings. (The published *Dáil Debates* themselves were not censored.) The deputies' remarks were regarded as censorable on the basis that they were an 'exhortation to break the law'. It was recognised that this was not strictly the case, as the law which Norton and Corish urged non-observance of had not yet been made – hence their comments referred to a hypothetical case. Nevertheless, the Censorship was adamant, stating that 'a deputy who has announced his intention of urging his followers to disregard an enactment if it is passed by parliament is being impudently cynical in deploring the Censor's lack of respect for parliament in preventing this announcement from getting publicity'.[216] The following week Norton (with William Davin) put down a motion in connection with the second stage of the Emergency Powers (Continuance) Bill 1941, which read:

> That Dáil Éireann refuses to give this Bill a second reading until such time as this House obtains from the Government adequate assurances that the powers conferred upon them by the Emergency Powers Act, 1939 will not be employed in future for the purpose of reducing real wages or of suppressing expression of opinion concerning the social and economic consequences of Government policy.

In a letter to Maurice Moynihan, secretary of the Department of the Taoiseach, in relation to this motion, Coyne expressed his concern that de Valera should understand the background, and felt certain that Norton and Davin were 'not altogether sincere in their criticism of the censorship'. He claimed that Norton was aggrieved at having been 'branded' by name in the direction to the press in relation to his 'reckless and foolish incitement to his followers' with regard to the Trade Union Bill, and that he was under pressure from 'the Irish Trotskyites' in the Dublin constituencies council whom he was too weak to resist and who had a 'special bone' to pick with the Censorship over the stopping of the Price letter. Coyne was satisfied to dismiss the motion as a product of 'personal pique on the part of Deputy Norton and irresponsible Leftism on the part of the *Torch* and its backers'.[217]

Coyne argued that 'a lot of the matter which they publish or seek to publish in the *Torch* is directed to stirring up class warfare and fomenting social unrest and disorder';[218] not suprisingly, the paper continued to encounter difficulties with the Censorship, in relation to both domestic and international items. Articles on bread and fuel shortages, unemployment, the Construction Corps, the wage freeze and the Trade Union Bill were all stopped. On the international front, most matter relating to the Soviet Union, war-related or not, was stopped subsequent to the *Torch*'s 'bite' on 1 July 1941. That article presented the *Torch*'s position, which was that the Soviet Union was a degenerated workers' state that could best be defended by fighting for the working class at home and not by joining Britain's imperialist war. Other casualties included items on famine conditions in Belgium and the Spanish civil war. In December 1943 Knightly declared that the *Torch* was 'becoming out and out Bolshie'; Aiken agreed and on 23 December made an order for it to submit all issues in full before publication.[219]

This occurred at a time of severe convulsion in the Labour Party. William O'Brien and the ITGWU, having successfully isolated and excluded the Larkins and their Workers Union of Ireland within the trade union movement, now sought to have Larkin Jnr expelled from the Labour Party, along with John de Courcy-Ireland, on a technicality concerning the way in which they had nominated Larkin Snr as an election candidate. Despite ITGWU opposition to their selection and a rigged selection conference, both Larkins had stood successfully as Labour candidates in the June 1943 general election. They were among seventeen Labour TDs elected. The expulsion motion failed and the ITGWU left the party, citing communist infiltration as the reason. Five of the union's eight Labour TDs left with them and formed the National Labour Party (NLP) in January 1944. The NLP challenged Labour to accept an investigation into communist influence in the party by 'the bishops or any impartial body'. Norton established an internal inquiry. Against a background of red scare mongering, led by the McCarthyesque exposures and inquisitions in the pages of the *Standard* (penned by Alfred O'Rahilly), a witch-hunt was undertaken to uncover those in the party who had been tainted by communism. By the time of the party's annual conference in April 1944 six leading members had been expelled (though not the Larkins) and the left had been largely silenced. A week after the expulsions the *Torch* ceased publication on the order of the administrative council and was replaced by the 'tightly controlled and conciliatory' *Irish People,* produced by the leadership.[220]

Labour faced into the June 1944 general election in total disarray and lost 70,000 votes and four seats, including Larkin Snr's; the NLP lost one of its five seats.[221] Labour's hopes of continued growth and progress had been shattered, as had the dreams of the left of building a socialist Labour Party which could bid for power. The split in the party prepared the way for the split in the trade union movement in April 1945. This was also spearheaded by the ITGWU which led other Irish based unions away from the ITUC and its 'anglified labour thinking' and into the new Congress of Irish Unions, with its 'pointedly indigenous labourism, distinguished by emphases on corporatism, nationalism, Catholicism and anti-Communism'.[222]

John Swift, who was a member of the Dublin constituencies council of the Labour Party and the Dublin Trades Council as well as serving on the editorial board of *Workers' Action*, edited his union paper, the *Bakery Trades Journal*. Given Swift's socialist politics it was inevitable that his paper would fall victim to the censors; he had been singled out by the Special Branch report on the Council of Action march as a 'dangerous agitator'.[223] Swift used the paper to criticise government policy in general and their policy towards trade unions and profiteering in flour in particular. In the issue of March 1941 he launched a fierce attack on the Censorship, provoked by the lack of publicity given to a bakers' strike in Waterford. He blamed the Censorship and stated that there was a policy of limiting references to trade disputes:

> Organised Labour, we regret to say, has defaulted in not standing up to this gagging of publicity by Fascist bureaucrats and their counterparts in the Dáil. Organised Labour ought not let the war become an alibi of inept and frightened authority . . . And the greatest menace to us, the fifth columnist aiding our capitalist foe, is the authority that would gag us.

The Censorship immediately imposed an order on the *Journal* to submit in full before publication on the basis of its 'recklessness' and the fact that no direction had been issued to the press with regard to trade disputes.[224]

While the latter was strictly true, virtually every trade dispute, strike or other action taken by workers, farmers, the unemployed or tenants' organisations could be interpreted as a threat to internal order or the maintenance of essential supplies and services. Thus, for example, reports of a strike by Dublin dockers in April 1941 in solidarity with the dismissed crew of the *Irish Elm* were stopped at the request of the Department of Supplies on the grounds that it was 'not in the public interest' to allow publicity to claims about the unseaworthiness of Irish ships.[225] Publicity was denied to calls for increased wages for turf-cutters and to a protest meeting held by workers at Castlecomer colliery regarding the threat to their livelihoods posed by a coal rationing order in 1942;[226] all references to the heavy unemployment at collieries in 1944 were censored as, according to Aiken, such reports were 'likely to cause misunderstanding concerning the position in respect of coal supplies'.[227] The campaign for increases in and the extension of the soldiers' marriage allowance (which was restricted to soldiers who were over twenty-three) was denied publicity because it was aimed at 'disrupting the country' and was a front for 'a subversive anti-recruiting campaign'.[228] In November 1939 there was a censorship close-down on publicity for the farmers' strike: an action undertaken by the Irish Farmers' Federation, in support of the Association of Milk Producers, which had the object of securing higher payments to farmers by the withholding of supplies of milk and other agricultural produce. The stoppage of the strike notice and manifesto of the Farmers' Federation was requested by the Department of Agriculture and approved of by de Valera and Aiken, with the intention of frustrating 'the danger to the community, pending the provision of essential supplies'.[229]

The case of supplies is an interesting one. At the outset of the Emergency the government promised to 'set its face against the effort of any class to obtain compensation for the rise in prices at the expense of the community'. Profiteering, however, became rife and in May 1941 Lemass revealed that since the beginning of the war his department (Supplies) had investigated 426 cases of profiteering and had found 72 companies guilty.[230] The ITUC annual report for 1942 stated that 'open profiteering and the black market in rationed and unrationed commodities had reached the dimensions of a national scandal'.[231] Fines for overcharging were so small as to present little or no deterrent, while in some cases the profiteer was officially encouraged; take, for example, the case of white flour.

Large quantities of this commodity were smuggled across the border from the outset of the Emergency with the knowledge of the Southern authorities. It was then sold openly and at 'extremely high prices'. The Department of Supplies was, according to Coyne, 'all in favour of the smuggling and urged that nothing should be done which might stop it'. That department considered it was in the national interest that the country should obtain all the supplies of white flour it could, and to have allowed the situation to be publicly criticised could have forced the Northern Irish authorities to tighten up border controls. John Swift was chief among the critics of this policy. He argued for an end to profiteering and a pooling of all supplies crossing the border which could then be disposed of equitably by the state, either separately or mixed with the existing stocks of non-white flour. Until 1941 the Censorship deferred to the views of the Department of Supplies on the issue; eventually, however, a decision was taken that suppression of criticism of 'the white flour racket' was unjustified and the policy was reversed.[232] (The publication of the term 'black bread', or the word 'black' in relation to bread, which was the commonly used term to describe the bread resulting from the use of the entire ear of wheat, was banned in January 1941.[233])

Articles which dealt with unemployment, emigration, poverty and hunger were described as 'atrocity stories and defeatism'. Coyne believed that 'picturing thousands of starving Irish workers flocking across to the bombed areas of England or to join the British forces, or maybe to throw themselves into the sea, have simply got to be stopped if public morale is not to be hopelessly compromised'.[234] Yet, the reality was not too far removed from Coyne's sarcastic exaggeration and the Irish authorities were very glad that Britain's war industries and armed forces were able to absorb Ireland's surplus labour. De Valera acknowledged, in a meeting with bankers in 1940, that the unemployed were 'a danger in our midst',[235] while McElligott, secretary of the Department of Finance, described emigration as 'a safety valve against revolution'.[236]

Publicity about an outbreak of typhus in 1942 was considered 'undesirable' by the Department of Local Government and Public Health, particularly in light of comments in the House of Commons which linked the disease to a lack of cleanliness among the emigrant Irish 'working classes'.[237] Reports of rickets and tuberculosis, malnutrition and infant mortality were equally undesirable. Highlighting the plight of the poor at a time when the 'unity of the people' was the priority was considered divisive; such reports were carried in the left press 'with the object of promoting class hatred and civil war'.[238] Attacks on the Construction Corps forced labour scheme were detrimental to the national effort. The questioning of government policy and propaganda in the face of widespread suffering encouraged 'defeatism', as when the *Torch* responded to the Department of Supplies slogan 'Fill Your Larders!' with the reasonable question: 'With What?'[239]

In his letter to Maurice Moynihan in July 1941 Coyne touched upon the central issue: 'With unemployment, poverty and hunger already fairly widespread and perhaps likely to increase it is not always easy to draw the line between what is legitimate criticism and what is defeatism and anti-social agitation.'[240] Within a year Coyne would have no problem in drawing the line. He was writing during a period of temporary crisis between Fianna Fáil and organised labour; the dangers of class conflict began to concern the authorities and the left appeared to be on the ascendant. The storm had passed by mid-1942, however, as the 'moderates' reasserted control. 'Legitimate criticism' and 'legitimate defence of working class interests' became the preserve of the conservative trade union leadership, particularly that of the largest union, the ITGWU. Working class militancy and class conflict threatened their position and 'the nation', i.e. the state, the stability of which was essential for the pursuit of 'orderly' trade unionism. 'Legitimacy' and a close relationship with Fianna Fáil was the reward for delivering 'disciplined' trade unionists and a working class 'willing to make all the necessary sacrifices'.[241]

PARLIAMENTARY POLITICS

This democracy business can be overdone too.
Democracy, overdone, can be a great menace . . .[242]

Seán McEllin (Fianna Fáil),
Seanad Éireann, 30 January 1941.

In meeting the extra parliamentary challenge presented by militant Republicans and socialists Fianna Fáil was supported by the opposition parties who shared a common interest with the government in opposing these elements. Cross-party support was also given to the policy of neutrality and the defence arrangements put in place to uphold it, including the establishment and operation of a censorship. The handful of parliamentary mavericks who opposed neutrality were also, in the main, those who were most prominent in opposing and criticising the censorship as it came to be operated. The exercise of censorship by a single-party government, above all other repressive powers put at its disposal, inevitably created problems, as the dividing line between government and state, party interests and national interests, often became blurred. Fianna Fáil rejected the idea of an emergency coalition, believing that it could provide 'whatever national government was required',[243] and the dangers, in parliamentary terms, were obvious when a political censorship was in the control of a party which often appeared to have difficulty in accepting that it did not, in fact, embody the nation in itself – a party led by a man who once famously claimed that he only had to examine his own heart when he needed to know what the Irish people wanted.

Given the government's power to legislate by decree, cross-party support for Fianna Fáil on the major issues of foreign policy, defence and security and the danger that 'opposition beyond a certain limit could always be branded as a danger to national solidarity and security', and even as treason,[244] parliamentary opposition during the war years was often little more than perfunctory. Fine Gael was caught between a rock and a hard place; its support for neutrality represented an implicit abandonment of its Commonwealth position – its 'remaining distinguishing mark';[245] yet, for it to have openly opposed neutrality would have been highly unpopular and politically futile. The only political pay-off for its support of the government was participation, along with Fianna Fáil and Labour, in the National Defence Conference – a poor substitute for genuine national government which Fianna Fáil never took seriously. It was a frustrating and dispiriting period for the main opposition party and it lost out heavily in the wartime elections, unable, as it was, to capitalise on the disillusionment with Fianna Fáil, particularly on the socio-economic front, which existed. The new farmers' party Clann na Talmhan took up the slack in rural areas while Labour looked briefly like stealing back its natural urban working-class constituency from Fianna Fáil with a strong showing in the 1943 election. However, as already noted, Labour split in 1944 against the background of a red scare campaign and, with Fine Gael in disarray, de Valera called a snap election in May 1944 and regained the majority he had lost the year before.

As revelations about and criticisms of the operations of the Censorship were strictly prohibited from the press, the Dáil and Seanad became important as the only public fora where the Censorship could be brought to task and made somewhat accountable for its actions, and where newspaper people, through friendly parliamentary representatives, could have their grievances aired. It was a common occurrence for censored copy to be read into the parliamentary record by TDs and senators. While the official reports were not subject to censorship (they could only be altered with the agreement of the Ceann Comhairle/Cathaoirleach and the TD/senator or his/her party)[246] newspaper reports of parliamentary proceedings were censored and the Censorship ensured that it was not evaded in this way. Once they transgressed the rules of the Censorship, politicians, no less than the bishops, were treated with no more ceremony than anybody else.

Aiken declared his dislike of secret sessions, stating that 'I would rather have public sessions and then cut out anything that is indiscreet'; 'Especially if you do it yourself', retorted Senator J.G. Douglas,[247] and this was an important point. The Censorship not only deleted statements which it believed presented a danger to the state and public safety, but rejected reports that it saw as unbalanced, deleted what it considered to be misrepresentations of ministerial statements, and so on. In February 1945 the entire proceedings in the Seanad in relation to a question from Sir John Keane on postal censorship were denied publicity. Aiken was charged with having unconstitutionally put the house into private session with no consultation and was condemned for having committed 'an outrage on our Parliamentary liberty'. The question had concerned the holding of two letters by the Postal Censorship; the only details which were revealed were that there was censorship of mails exchanged with England and that in this particular case it was the addresser (unnamed) who was in question. Aiken declared it a matter which affected national security and told the Seanad that he had stopped publication of reports on the issue 'among other reasons to teach him [Keane] a lesson'. Keane accused him of using his powers in the manner of Goebbels and Himmler.[248]

The minister was often accused of having dictatorial tendencies and one school of thought among critics saw the person of Aiken as the main problem with the Censorship. Having supported the granting of such extensive powers to the government, the first shock to the opposition, according to T.F. O'Higgins of Fine Gael, was the choice of Aiken as the minister with responsibility for censorship. 'It is a Department which needs tact, experience and a mentality capable of giving and taking', he declared. 'A more unsuitable selection, in my opinion, could not have been made . . .'.[249] Senator Michael Hayes regarded him as 'narrow', 'biased' and 'foolish',[250] while Professor Joseph Johnson told the Seanad that 'When a man with Cromwell's temperament, such as the Minister seems to have, is on the warpath, nothing in our Constitution or in our parliamentary institutions is safe'.[251] James Dillon was an old adversary of Aiken's, and one of his more complimentary descriptions of him was that he was 'a public menace'.[252] Senator T.C. Kingsmill-Moore, a former censor himself, declared that 'unless censorship is used with the greatest possible caution and the greatest possible discretion it becomes a monster and turns on the people responsible for it – a Frankenstein monster or, as was suggested to me, a Frank-aikenstein monster'.[253]

The arguments of the Censorship's critics were far more substantial than the simple blaming of the individual in charge; Fianna Fáil, however, refused to accept most of these arguments on their own terms, constantly accusing critics (not always without justification) of harbouring ulterior motives and working to hidden agendas. In his notes for the minister prior to a Seanad debate on the Censorship, the chief press censor, Michael Knightly was unequivocal: 'The attack on the Censorship has only one object, the destruction of our neutrality.'[254] The fact that the two most prominent critics (and domestic parliamentary political victims) of the Censorship, James Dillon in the Dáil and Frank MacDermot in the Seanad, also favoured the abandonment of neutrality, lent weight to such crude assertions. (Both MacDermot and Dillon had been leading members of the short-lived Centre Party, which was founded in 1932 and merged with Cumann na nGaedheal and the Blueshirts in 1933 to form Fine Gael. MacDermot resigned from the party in 1935 and was nominated to the Seanad as an independent senator by de Valera in 1938.) Other critics, who came from all parts of the political spectrum, were accused variously of war-mongering, propagandising for the belligerents, disloyalty, party political point-scoring and conspiring to overthrow democracy and the state.

The situation was certainly complicated by the fact that those who put forward the classical liberal arguments against censorship in the Seanad were closely associated with the era of British rule in the South and were supporters of the Commonwealth connection. They represented in parliament what the *Irish Times* represented in the press. When Aiken entered the Seanad, according to Hayes, and saw Frank MacDermot (a major in the British army in the First World War), 'he sees him in British uniform and immediately finds himself back in 1921. When he sees Senator Sir John Keane, he sees generations of landlords.'[255] Aiken described MacDermot as 'a monument to the past' who 'blew in here from some part of the world'.[256] (MacDermot was born in Dublin but was educated and lived in England until his return to Ireland in 1932, at the age of 46.) He was one of those whom Senator William Quirke denounced as 'birds of passage in this country . . . They are only legally Irishmen. They live within the walls of the British colony and can never possibly see outside it.'[257] Another senator who raised his voice was Kingsmill-Moore, who had been a press censor in Ireland during the First World War. According to Quirke (Fianna Fáil), the only reason he and the others were complaining about the Censorship was 'because it is one of the natives that happens to be the Censor'.[258] Peadar O'Lochlainn (Fianna Fáil) agreed, and wondered whether 'we should not cut short the activities of men of this character who come here and pillory the Minister'.[259] Michael Hearne (Fianna Fáil) saw their activities as 'a gross breach of the hospitality of this country on the part of people who were formerly associated with the British military machine . . . it is time that the efforts of the Quislings . . . and of the Fifth Columnists . . . to embroil us should cease'.[260]

Their minority position and liberal outlook was used as another stick with which to beat them by Fianna Fáil and its allies like the trade unionist, Senator Seán Campbell, who prided himself on representing the 'vast majority' of 'ordinary people'. 'There is a little coterie in this country', announced Campbell, 'who affect to be devotees at the shrine of liberal thought and who do not like the censorship of books, nor the divorce laws nor many other things which the people of this country favour.'[261] These were 'fine theorists' whose arguments were 'the squealing of propagandists . . . the squealing of people who know they have no right to speak for the people of this country'.[262]

Confusion and suspicion reigned when these 'wailing shoneens'[263] addressed matters outside their alleged brief, and were supported by representatives of the 'ordinary people' on the basis of principles of democracy and free speech. When Sir John Keane made reference in the Seanad to the suppression of publicity for the Kimmage–Crumlin Tenants' Association, and contrasted the suppression of information on the number of IRA internees held in the South with the fact that publicity was allowed for such information in relation to the North, Aiken replied that 'if I saw a wolf's tail sticking out through a lamb's skin, I would not be more suspicious than if I saw Sir John Keane's head sticking out from an IRA plus Communist robe'.[264] When the trade unionist Sam Kyle supported Keane in a Seanad debate on the censorship of reports on parliament, Hearne marvelled at the 'united front . . . [by] what might be described as the white hope of capitalism joined with the red star of the proletariat . . .'.[265] Following James Larkin Jnr's election to the Dáil in 1943, and his re-election in 1944, the Censorship was among the issues he raised, particularly the banning of the *Wolfe Tone Annual* and the suppression of publicity for the reprieve campaign for Charles Kerins. Because he addressed these particular issues, with the support of his party, Aiken and Justice minister Gerald Boland identified a 'new alliance' between communists and Republicans, a common conspiracy to overthrow the state, using the likes of Labour leader William Norton as 'tools'.[266]

The parliamentary Labour Party was satisfied with the operation of censorship with regard to war news and belligerent propaganda and restricted its occasional criticism to the censorship of domestic matters, particularly when it affected itself and its constituency. Fine Gael's leading critic was James Dillon who, following his resignation from the party in 1942, continued his crusade as an independent. (He rejoined the party in 1953, becoming leader in 1959.) Patrick McGilligan was another consistent critic of the censorship in general, while Paddy Belton pursued the issue of censorship in relation to the campaign with which he was involved for farmers to receive higher prices for wheat.

The critics in the Seanad, mostly independents, put forward the liberal argument that freedom of expression and freedom of the press should be interfered with no more than was absolutely necessary for the safety of the state. Some believed that the scope of the censorship needed to be delimited by the establishment of agreed principles which would govern its operation, backed up by a parliamentary committee in an advisory or consultative role. Fine Gael supported the idea of a committee and Aiken declared that he would be willing to consult such a body.[267] Fine Gael never pursued it, however, probably mindful of their frustration in the Defence Conference where they had to 'grub for information', in Richard Mulcahy's phrase, 'like hens scratching'.[268] In the Seanad Frank MacDermot proposed the creation of a list of censorable matters covering the disclosure of military secrets; treason, sedition or incitement to disobey the law; violence and intemperance of language tending to excite civil commotion or provoke external attack; and the dissemination of unfounded rumours, likely to produce disaffection or panic.[269] The Censorship rejected a specific classification like MacDermot's because it was too limited, omitting as it did reference to propaganda, matter affecting supplies and financial security, shipping, matter affecting the interests of the belligerents and, thus, indirectly, Irish interests, etc. They pointed to the vital importance of context and circumstance in dealing with news, as these gave each item 'its distinguishing colour and discriminating effect'. The danger, according to the Censorship, was that 'the devil can always quote scripture for his purpose'.[270]

Another approach of the critics was to seek to specify a number of areas which should be declared immune from censorship. First among them was criticism of government policy and administration. The government and the Censorship flatly denied that they attempted to 'hush up' mistakes by the government or incompetence on the part of the civil service. They admitted prohibiting publication of criticism of the Censorship, because such criticisms would undermine its effectiveness and thus present a danger to the state. It was also argued that the Censorship was enjoined by the constitution to interfere in cases where the 'public authority' was being undermined. (The issue of party bias in the operation of the Censorship is treated later.)

The second major freedom sought was that which allowed publicity for criticism of neutrality, and advocacy of an alternative policy, by the press, the public and, crucially, by parliamentary representatives. It was argued that it was anti-democratic to suppress such arguments, especially as arguments in favour of neutrality were not only allowed but encouraged. Another point was that neutrality and strict censorship were not necessarily in the best interests of the state and could in fact be detrimental to its safety; that the government did not have a monopoly on knowing how national interests could be best served and that in the fluid and changeable international situation, the rigid application of censorship in the protection of a particular policy was not necessarily serving the interests which it was established to protect.

The third major issue which the critics addressed was that of 'moral neutrality'.[271] It was argued that people had a right to the information which would enable them to formulate moral judgements on the war and the issues at stake, and a duty to argue for a particular policy on the basis of those judgements. They advocated this freedom firstly in terms of Ireland's obligation, as a small Christian country with little other power, to exert its moral influence. It was seen, secondly, as being a practical necessity. It was pointed out that by keeping the people in ignorance about the moral issues at stake in the war, and by preventing open discussion around them, the censorship was having a detrimental effect on morale which, in turn, 'will make our mental equipment for meeting invasion, if it does come, very bad indeed'.[272] It was pointed out that strict censorship had had such an effect on France and Holland and had led to these countries being overrun all the more easily. Dillon and MacDermot, in particular, argued that Germany was the most likely invader and public opinion needed to be educated about the 'bestial nature' of the Nazi regime and the danger it posed. They stressed the need to distinguish between the belligerents, both morally and in practical terms because Ireland's interests were so bound up with those of Britain. The much-vaunted unity of the people, a prerequisite for opposing an invasion, was essentially artificial, according to the critics, because of the censorship and the 'moral neutrality' which it created.

On the prohibition of criticisms of neutrality, the Censorship argued that its case was based 'not on logic but on expediency and has an internal as well as an external aspect'. A small and powerless country could not enjoy the benefits of neutrality and the 'luxury' of unrestricted comments on the belligerents, while a public controversy on the issue of neutrality could lead to internal disorder. Because an alternative policy had not been 'seriously put forward' in the Dáil or Seanad, publicity could not be allowed for the questioning of neutrality, 'simply because, in the present circumstances, the Government believes that this is the only policy that is compatible with the security of the State', and could not be allowed to be jeopardised by 'subterranean sabotage'.

The freedom to pass moral judgements on international affairs would, according to the government, have been 'positively dangerous'. If a certain section of the population was allowed to talk offensively about the morals of Germany, argued Aiken, then 'we can be quite sure that others would try to express in even more offensive terms their detestation of British morality. If we were a nation of Dillons words would only lead to words. But we are not'; if such freedom were given Aiken anticipated a civil war on the question of which belligerent Ireland should declare war upon.[273] On the question of 'moral neutrality' Coyne stated the position clearly: 'We do not see this war as a clear cut moral issue, but rather what the belligerents themselves admit it to be – no more than a struggle between the great powers which will be determined by the survival of the fittest.'[274]

James Dillon saw a clear moral difference between the belligerents and was the only one of a number of Fine Gael TDs who opposed neutrality to openly criticise it and advocate its abandonment. The foreign press wrongly placed great significance on his speeches against neutrality in the belief that, as deputy leader of the second largest party, he was an influential figure who represented a large body of opinion. The British, and later the Americans, courted him in the belief that he might be the instrument to bring about the desired change in Irish politics which would lead to the country entering the war. He remained an isolated figure, however, and following his resignation from Fine Gael because of his stance, became, in his own words, 'a minority of one'.[275] (Aiken, delighted with Dillon's isolation, referred to him as 'our boy who wants to be different'.[276]) Not surprisingly, Dillon was the most censored of all politicians, with heavy treatment given to his letters to the press and reports of his speeches and contributions to debates inside and outside the Dáil. While all his criticisms of the German and Soviet governments were stopped, he was allowed some laudatory references to Britain and America,[277] in line with general policy which allowed 'greater latitude to matter favourable to either belligerent or to any foreign state than to unfavourable matter'.[278]

In January 1940 Dillon submitted to the Censorship the manuscript of a speech which he proposed to publish in pamphlet form. Portions of the speech had been deleted from press reports and Dillon was informed that these portions could not be published in pamphlet form either; he was given no reason and no authority was cited, as none existed.[279] At around the same time the *Irish Times* was ordered to submit in full before publication following its publication of an anti-neutrality speech by MacDermot. In anticipation of parliamentary controversy provoked by the censorship of these prominent politicians, Aiken prepared a memorandum 'for the information of the members of the Government'. The memo, entitled 'Neutrality, Censorship and Democracy' (reproduced in full in Appendix 1), anticipated and addressed the arguments about censorship and neutrality as outlined earlier. It also argued that the survival of democracy made the actions of the Censorship both 'legitimate and necessary'. Addressing himself to the critics, Aiken wrote of 'some self-styled democrats who would hold on to the peace-time liberalistic trimmings of democracy while the fundamental basis of democracy was being swept from under their feet by the foreign and domestic enemies of their democratic State'. He noted that these 'trimmings' were wisely discarded when the government was given the right to legislate by decree, and stated that 'Whoever says he is not satisfied with such a system of democracy in "time of war" is either a very foolish democrat or an agent provocateur for those who want to overthrow democracy or to embroil us in civil or foreign war'.[280]

The only indication of unease within government about Aiken's approach and his search for further powers was a 'Memorandum regarding Censorship' from Seán MacEntee which was circularised by his Department of Industry and Commerce on 7 February 1940. It consisted of passages, without comment, from a speech delivered in the House of Lords by the Parliamentary Under-Secretary for the colonies; MacEntee had underlined the following:

> I do believe that if every time an abuse of freedom is committed, we allow that to be an opportunity for further government control, further censorship, further denial of liberty, then I do believe that you are going to erode in a very few years perhaps the whole rock of personal liberty.

The underlined passage went on to mention 'a slippery slope' and concluded that 'there is nothing more worth fighting for, whether in the field or in politics, than the personal liberty of the public, liberty of expression and freedom'.[281] (MacEntee himself was censored later in the year when his comment during a Local Security Force meeting that there was a danger that when the war was over Ireland might find herself without any friends was deleted from newspaper reports.[282])

In January 1941 Aiken, during a Dáil debate on essential supplies, stated that 'The Lord had given us resources, and we have the means at the moment, so that even if every damn ship were at the bottom of the sea, we could have twice as high a standard of living in a few years . . .'.[283] (Following this speech, one provincial newspaper dubbed him 'Admiral Aiken'.[284]) The Censorship closed down on all publicity for these comments, and MacDermot claimed that he deliberately included them in one of his articles for the *Sunday Times* in order to make Aiken censor himself.[285] A few days later the minister made a speech in Drogheda bemoaning the unemployment situation there, brought about by the lack of imported raw materials. Dublin councillor and former Cumann na nGaedheal TD and Senator Seán Milroy wrote a letter to the *Irish Independent* asking whether the Minister for the Co-ordination of Defensive Measures could co-ordinate with Frank Aiken and 'find out whether he means what he says in Dáil Éireann or what he says in Drogheda'. 'This perfectly valid piece of political jocularity' was stopped, prompting Dillon to ask 'Is it treason in this country to pull Frank Aiken's leg?'[286]

In March 1941 Aiken set off on his 'mission' to America, which involved a doomed effort to secure arms and supplies and a three-month coast-to-coast speaking tour under the auspices of Irish-American isolationist groups.[287] David Gray had informed Roosevelt that Aiken was pro-German and he looked forward to the minister being exposed to the chill winds of American opinion;[288] any chance of his being exposed to chill winds at home were denied by the Censorship. On his departure to the US Aiken gave an instruction to his censors, in his own handwriting, not to allow anything to appear in the press during his absence which might impair the success of his mission and, in particular, 'to prevent personal attacks and criticism of him during his absence'. Coyne told the Minister for Defence, Oscar Traynor, who was deputising for Aiken, that even if he had not done so,

> We would have taken appropriate steps on our own initiative to see that there was no sabotage or stabbing in the back while he was away. Mr Aiken knew that he was bound to have a hostile press in America and that he might as well not cross the Atlantic at all if the local press were to be let loose in full cry after he had gone.[289]

In his St Patrick's Day broadcast to America in 1941 de Valera made reference to Ireland being blockaded by both sides in the war (as a result of their blockades on each other). His comments were criticised by J.G. Douglas in the Seanad and in a letter to the press by T.F. O'Higgins of Fine Gael. The letter was stopped after consultation with the Taoiseach while deletions were made to reports of Douglas's criticisms in the Seanad,[290] and the heading 'Broadcast to America Criticised' was altered to read 'Reference to Broadcast to America'.[291] De Valera defended these actions by saying that his comments had been misrepresented for party political purposes and that it had been implied that he was being anti-British. 'It is not in the interests of the community', he told the Dáil, 'that the head of the Government, in circumstances like these, should be misrepresented by anybody, or that an attempt should be made to build up a case to represent him as being biased . . . it is not in the interests of the State.'[292] 'Since when', Dillon asked, 'has the safety of the State demanded that the Taoiseach should not be criticised?'[293]

When Paddy Ruttledge resigned as Minister for Local Government in August 1941 MacEntee replaced him and de Valera acceded to pressure from Seán Lemass, Minister for Supplies – who told him that he did not have enough to do! – by restoring Industry and Commerce to him;[294] he held it jointly with Supplies for the rest of the war. In a leading article in October 1941 which was submitted for censorship, the *Irish Times* had written, 'Mr Seán Lemass, Minister for Industry and Commerce, who in his spare time also is Minister for Supplies . . .'. The censor deleted the words 'in his spare time' prompting *Irish Times* editor Bertie Smyllie to enquire whether the Censorship 'prohibits even sidelong criticisms of Ministers'. He accused it of gross abuse of its powers and of attempting to stifle political criticism. Coyne drafted a reply to the effect that the jibe was capable of mischievous interpretation as Smyllie was implying that the burden of two departments was too much for Lemass. Aiken, however, was becoming sensitive to charges of misusing the Censorship to protect the government and refused to authorise the sending of Coyne's reply. Instead, Smyllie was told that the words had been deleted in error, the justice of his protest was admitted and regret was expressed.[295]

Throughout 1942, with an election only a year or so away (under the constitution, a general election would have to be held in or before June 1943), opposition deputies began to suspect that the Censorship was increasingly being operated in a party political fashion. A number of Fine Gael statements regarding bread shortages and cereal prices for farmers had been suppressed,[296] while general criticism was made of the 'distorted version' of reports on Radio Éireann and in the press of parliamentary proceedings: undue coverage was being given to ministerial statements, deputies' names were not being given in Question Time reports and the impression was being given that ministers had volunteered information which had often been given only reluctantly and after repeated questioning.[297]

The most glaring example of alleged bias ironically related to a speech which had been passed in full by the censor. This was James Dillon's famous speech at the Fine Gael árd fheis on 10 February 1942, following US entry into the war, when he declared that: 'Whatever the sacrifice, whatever America may want from us to protect her from her enemies, she will get for the asking.'[298] While the speech was allowed to be published in full, it was denied undue prominence; an introduction in one paper was deleted because of the 'bias' shown in not referring to the repudiation of Dillon's views by two delegates, while references to the speech being greeted by applause on two occasions were also deleted; much subsequent comment on the speech in the press was also stopped.[299] T.F. O'Higgins claimed that the speech was allowed because it would

> create embarrassment for the political Opposition in this House and provided it could create sufficient political embarrassment . . . then it did not matter one bit whether it jeopardised the neutrality of this country or caused offence and provocation abroad . . .'[300]

Dillon himself agreed, stating that Aiken,

> judging the Fine Gael Party by his own standards . . . thought that because I deemed it my duty to tread a different path from that of my colleagues, by giving publicity to the fact, he could wreck the Fine Gael Party . . . he naturally expected a dog-fight. That is what would happen in the Fianna Fáil Party, but in that expectation he was, of course, disappointed.[301]

Aiken, of course, denied political motivation, claiming that it was his duty to decide, after taking all the surrounding circumstances into account, whether the interests of the state were best served by permitting or suppressing the publication of particular matters. In this case, the speech was allowed because the powers were not then available to effectively stop the export of reports; it was a premeditated and deliberate statement of policy on an important occasion by the deputy leader of the second largest party; it would have been represented abroad that the Irish government was afraid to let the Irish people know the views expressed by Dillon.[302] Overall, Aiken argued that it would have done more harm than good to neutrality to have made an unsuccessful attempt to stop the publication of the speech.[303]

The government dismissed the general charges of party censorship as 'utter nonsense'.[304] It was concerned about the allegations, nevertheless, and in April 1942 Aiken made an urgent request to Coyne to prepare a collection of newspaper clippings containing criticisms of the government which he could use to defend himself against the charges.[305] The collection which was prepared contained published criticisms covering the supplies situation, black marketeering, prices, ministerial cars, 'jobs for the boys', government spending, local government, the Irish language, and so on. Aiken could then claim that only important matters affecting the interests of the state were censored and that 'ordinary day to day' criticisms of the government were allowed.[306] In a retrospective review of its work the Censorship dismissed the allegations of party censorship as 'ill founded' and trawled the files to find examples of the prohibition of matter disobliging to the opposition politicians and parties, which were stopped 'in pursuance of the policy of maintaining a united front on the main national issue – the maintenance of neutrality and internal security. If matter which might be considered anti-Government received similar treatment it was only for the same reason.'[307] Following the non-censorship of Dillon's speech Patrick McGilligan of Fine Gael condemned the 'united front' as a farce, a pretence exemplified by the Defence Conference, and stated that if this so-called unity was to be made an excuse for 'an outrageously partisan type of censorship' then it should be got rid of immediately.[308]

It was certainly the case that anything which cast doubt on Fine Gael's commitment to neutrality would be to the advantage of Fianna Fáil in what it knew would be a tough election in 1943. (De Valera's fears about the election made him postpone it until the last possible moment, contrary to his normal practice.) The social hardship of the emergency regime, the economic grievances of farmers and workers and the 'irksome intrusions of bureaucracy'[309] into people's everyday lives, all combined to threaten Fianna Fáil electorally; in such a situation the party inevitably attempted to use neutrality to its own advantage. 'The thesis was developed that only de Valera's achievements had made neutrality feasible in the first place and only his leadership would see the country safely through the war.'[310] The Fianna Fáil slogan for the 1943 election campaign was 'Don't change horses when crossing the stream', which implicitly cast doubt on Fine Gael's ability to maintain neutrality, and its commitment to doing so; another election jingle ran 'If you vote Fianna Fáil, the bombs won't fall'.[311]

On 14 November 1942 Aiken instructed his press censors to bring all matter relating to neutrality to his personal attention.[312] He was conscious of the accusations of party censorship and realised there was a danger of the Censorship being portrayed as being part of the Fianna Fáil election campaign, even if this occurred inadvertently. Thus, while neutrality certainly became an election issue, the press was prohibited from conveying this fact; claims and counterclaims about who was responsible for neutrality, who was not, who used it, and so on, were prohibited publication.

In November 1942 a Labour Party newspaper advertisement which read: 'Labour's Foreign Policy: Labour is the keystone of the national arch of Neutrality' was altered to read: 'Labour's Foreign Policy: Neutrality'.[313] Another of the party's advertisements, which read: 'Labour policy is the people's policy of strict neutrality' was stopped in its entirety.[314] Deletions were made to a report of a Clann na Talmhan meeting in Tuam in which a speaker was reported as criticising Fianna Fáil claims to be responsible for neutrality, as farmers and workers had won it by fighting the economic war and forcing Britain to hand back the ports.[315] Two days later, on 13 October 1942 Aiken sanctioned the censorship of a report of a speech by his colleague the Tánaiste and Minister for Finance, Seán T. O'Kelly, in the Seanad, during which he attributed the success of the neutrality policy to the wise and prudent statesmanship of de Valera and implied that Fine Gael had not supported the policy at the outset.[316] On 21 January 1943 Aiken instructed his censors to stop an *Irish Times* leading article that criticised a speech by de Valera in Ennis in which he implied that an effort was being made to starve Ireland into abrogation of its neutrality. Smyllie accused them of party political bias and asked whether the press could comment freely on pre-election speeches. In a reply, drafted by Aiken, Coyne rejected the 'impudent assertion' of bias and accused Smyllie of confusing 'party bias' with 'loyalty to Ireland'.[317]

The issue of censorship of pre-election speeches was raised in the Dáil by Dillon a few days later. Aiken told him that the Censorship would continue to stop matter which was prejudicial to the public safety and preservation of the state, but refused to answer directly Dillon's enquiries as to whether the issue of neutrality could be freely discussed; 'What's the use of pretending to have a free election', he asked, 'when only the Government can speak its mind?'[318] In response Aiken asked, 'Is the Deputy trying to make the case that subversive influences – the action of fifth columnists, if you like – should be allowed disrupt the State?'[319]

On the day following these exchanges the Censorship stopped an *Irish Times* editorial which effectively supported Dillon's position and stated that

'Yesterday's dialogue between Messrs Dillon and Aiken, democratic integrity versus national (or, at worst, political) expediency, displays more clearly than anything else the illogical and dangerous folly of the impending contest'. The same argument put forward by Smyllie in an article for the *Observer* was stopped the next day and a fortnight later another of his articles for the same paper, in which he wrote that it was absurd to speak of a free election when a party government was in a position to censor speeches 'and the competent Minister is the sole judge of what is or is not in the national interest', was not allowed out of the country.[320] (A cartoon appeared in that month's *Dublin Opinion* featuring a gagged election candidate at the hustings being introduced as knowing 'so much of what it is in the public interest to hear that we have had to gag him'![321]) A couple of weeks after the initial exchanges Dillon again pursued the minister on the issue, but Aiken continued to be evasive and flippantly dismissive; 'As far as I can see', he stated, 'what the Deputy wants to do is lie in a bed of roses down in Ballaghaderreen and dream he is in the snows of Russia.'[322]

On 15 February 1943 the Department of External Affairs presented a memorandum and draft statement to de Valera.[323] The memo addressed two questions: '(i) whether, election speeches advocating the abandonment of neutrality should be allowed in the Press, and (ii) whether speeches, even

"——and *our* candidate knows so much of what it is not in the public interest to hear that we have had to gag him."

Dublin Opinion, February 1943, taking a gentle swipe at the censorship of election speeches.

if professedly pro-neutral, should be censored if their publication would seem likely to weaken or compromise Ireland's position as a neutral State'.

On the first question, it was pointed out that neutrality did not have the 'sacrosanctity of a constitutional right' and that censorship of speeches advocating its abandonment could not be defended on that basis. Pro-war speeches could only become censorable, i.e. contrary to the provisions of the Emergency Powers Act 1939 (EPA), when they fell into the second category under question – speeches whose publication would seem likely to weaken or compromise Ireland's position as a neutral state. 'It is impossible to admit that speeches of this kind, even at election time, and even when they pretend to accept the neutrality policy and position, are suitable for publication.' The memo goes on to note the 'theoretical argument' against this position, which involved the contention that the EPA did not specifically provide for the maintenance of neutrality at all, but for the securing of the public safety, preservation of the state, etc. Moreover, no defined rule of international law compels a neutral state to suppress 'unneutral' comments within its jurisdiction. While these arguments were accepted as being 'plausible' by the Department of External Affairs, they were rejected as an argument against the censorship of the type of speeches in question. The author declared it 'contrary to all commonsense to suggest that, because the Emergency Powers Act 1939, does not specifically refer to "neutrality", it does not in fact relate almost entirely to the implementation of that status', and that three and a half years of day-to-day operation of the Act put it beyond doubt that this was the case. Even if this argument were not accepted, the memo suggests that the censorship of 'unneutral' speeches could be justified in another way. This involved the contention that the publication of anything which might involve Ireland in the war could be said to endanger the public safety, the preservation of the state and the maintenance of public order, and thus lead to the destruction of those objects which the EPA set out to achieve. This logic, however, demanded the prohibition of even perfectly inoffensive pro-war speeches, but the author believed that this would be going 'too far, at least in the context of a General Election'. He pointed out that the preservation of the state, as constituted in 1937, implied the existence of a sufficient measure of free speech at election time to enable candidates to rally electors in favour of any policy, including ones which were contrary to those adopted and implemented by the outgoing Dáil. The censorship of inoffensive pro-war speeches would clearly have been undemocratic and probably unconstitutional, as Article 28 provides that the assent of the Dáil must be given to a declaration of war; how could that article become effective unless people could elect deputies who they knew would declare war? Indeed press censorship could theoretically have led people to unwittingly vote for pro-war candidates.

The memorandum went on to suggest that, 'In all the difficult circumstances, the most politic course might well be to promise freedom of the press to all 100% inoffensive pro-war speeches. There will, in the nature of things, be very few such speeches, if any.' Even if a few pro-war speeches were made and publicised, the author suggested that the success of the Censorship in keeping out the bulk of belligerent propaganda made it unlikely that they would have any effect on the mass of public opinion, an opinion shared by John Maffey, the UK representative, when, in a dispatch to London on the upcoming election, he noted the difficulties involved in swinging a public opinion 'drugged by the Censorship'.[324] Finally, it was noted, in the words of the draft statement, that

> the very fact that our censorship has been strict – which I do not for a minute deny – would render its relaxation, even temporarily, all the more liable to be taken by outsiders as a definite departure from that attitude of correct restraint which the Irish people, through their elected representatives, have imposed on themselves.

On 27 May 1943 Aiken told the Seanad that it could be 'quite sure that during the election we will relax somewhat the rules that have been operated by the Censorship to date'. He was merely playing politics, however, as when he referred to allowing publicity for pro-war speeches he was alluding to 'inoffensive' ones, while he specified that 'statements bordering on the treasonable or that would have an adverse effect on our neutrality will have to be censored'.[325] It should be noted that Irish electoral politics was still very much based on direct contact with the voters and the era of election campaigns being conducted largely through the media was a long way off in the future. The rationing of newsprint had, in any event, reduced newspapers to a fraction of their normal size (on average, four pages), while the campaign was further hindered by the restrictions on transport caused by wartime shortages.[326]

The election was held on 22 June 1943 and, despite the success of neutrality, de Valera's attacks on the instability of coalitions – the only viable alternative to Fianna Fáil – and MacEntee's 'red scare' attacks on Labour, Fianna Fáil's vote dropped by 10 per cent and it lost ten seats, putting it in a minority position in the Dail.[327] The low turnout (a result of transport difficulties as well as apathy) and the absence of hundreds of thousands of emigrants, who might have voted their dissatisfaction with de Valera other than with their feet, both helped to reduce Fianna Fáil's losses.[328] As the other parties and independents were unable to coalesce, it remained in power as a minority government. Fine Gael also lost heavily and on 19 January 1944 William T. Cosgrave resigned as leader and was replaced by Richard Mulcahy, who had lost his seat in the election.

On the day before Cosgrave's resignation, Senator Donal O'Sullivan of Fine Gael, who wrote under the pen-name of 'OUTIS', submitted an article to the *Times Pictorial* (an *Irish Times* publication) on the subject of party names. On hearing of Cosgrave's resignation, he inserted additional paragraphs into his piece to mark the occasion. To a sentence which began: 'he succeeded to the leadership of the new State . . .', the Censorship wanted added: 'under the British threat of "immediate and terrible war" '. The editor refused to add these words and was duly ordered to delete the entire sentence. In the section on party names OUTIS had written: 'Fianna Fáil means Warriors of Fál, which does not suggest very much, except, perhaps, a tendency to look backward down the centuries instead of forward to the immediate future.' The Censorship instructed that the first six words be altered to 'Fianna Fáil means Warriors of Destiny',[329] and the rest of the paragraph deleted. The official who gave the instruction went on to dictate the following (which was written by Aiken) over the telephone:

> Note to 'OUTIS': Fianna Fáil means 'Soldiers of Destiny', which suggests that its members do things, do them now and do them themselves, despite the groanings of wailing shoneens whose minds keep running back to the 'Good Old Days' before Quislings were called Quislings.

The official, according to O'Sullivan, inadvertently revealed that the note had been written by Aiken; when the editor said that he would print the passage in brackets as a note from the censor to OUTIS, the horrified censor formally prohibited publication of the whole piece.[330]

Having ceased to control the west of Ireland for the first time since its foundation, due to the success of Clann na Talmhan,[331] and uncomfortable in a minority position, the Soldiers of Destiny, so-called, set out to 'do things' to rectify the situation. Labour were in disarray and Fine Gael were drifting, so de Valera, riding the success of the American Note episode and armed with the rural electrification scheme,[332] called a snap election in May 1944. The *Irish Times*, in a leader submitted for censorship, argued that the calling of the election would encourage the intensification of 'that introspective condition of mind that has become so noticeable over the last five years'. It deplored the fact that while the rest of the world was thinking about the fall of Sebastapol and the imminence of the second front, Ireland was thinking in terms of Fianna Fáil, Fine Gael and the split in Labour; 'If post-war Ireland is not prepared to think internationally, it can have no future as an independent State. This ought to be borne in mind by every citizen who has the vote.' These and many other comments were deleted,[333] while election matter going abroad was 'rendered unobjectionable from a national point of view'.[334] The election saw the lowest turnout since 1923 and although Fianna Fáil recovered less than half the votes it had lost the previous year, it managed to regain its overall majority.[335]

The fact that the government was empowered to legislate by decree, the cross-party agreement on the major issues, the sense of shared danger and general participation in the defence effort all helped to diminish the importance of party politics during the war years. The Censorship contributed to this situation by dampening political controversy in pursuit of the goal of 'keeping the temperature down'. It could be argued that it also contributed, in a broader sense, to the diminution of democracy. Government policy became synonymous with the security of the state; the authoritarian strain in Irish political culture and the majoritarian approach adopted by Fianna Fáil allowed the Censorship to smother democratic discourse and dissent in the 'national interest'. The majority had spoken and the right to challenge or question set policy was effectively removed; dissidents were expected to 'put up or shut up'. When they did speak out they were faced with what Dillon described as a 'hypocritical shell . . . the right to speak with the assurance that you will not be heard'.[336] A central point about censorship, of course, is that both the speaker and his/her intended audience are deprived.

The object of the government was to carry the state, with its democratic institutions, through the emergency intact. When it spoke of 'preserving democracy' it had in mind the structures and machinery of parliamentary democracy or 'the shell'. The democratic 'guts' – free speech and a free press, the right of the minority to challenge the majority, etc. – had the potential to burst the shell and were thus removed, as 'trimmings' swept aside, to be re-injected once the danger had passed.

The generality of the principles which governed the operation of the censorship allowed Aiken and his censors to become the sole arbiters of the 'national interest'; those who questioned their actions were thus undermining that interest and were liable to legitimate suppression. The fact that such powers were vested in a single party was inevitably problematic for the conduct of parliamentary politics. The Taoiseach and his ministers, by virtue of their offices, were representatives of the state, yet they were also party politicians implementing party policy and the use of a 'national' power for party purposes was a real danger. Was it legitimate for de Valera to claim that criticism of the Taoiseach was not in the interests of the state, and for the Censorship to prohibit it? Did Aiken genuinely believe that he was protecting national interests when he suppressed criticism of himself? The evidence suggests that the temptation to use or abuse the powers of censorship for party purposes was not always avoided – a situation which was probably not helped by the personality of the particular minister in charge.

Robert Fisk, in his history of wartime Ireland, points out that the suppression of political opinion was such that it called into question the very nature of neutrality. 'If Éire's policy of non-intervention was intended to preserve the freedom and parliamentary democracy of the twenty-six-county state', he writes, 'then how far could the Government go in restricting the democracy in order to safeguard its neutral shield?'[337] The question is valid and important. We have seen how far the government went; whether it went too far is obviously a moot point and will be further addressed in the Conclusion.

NOTES AND REFERENCES

1   MA, OCC 2/67, Coyne to Walshe on the replies to the charges made against the Censorship in the *Commonweal*, August 1941.
2   Dermot Keogh, 'Profile of Joseph Walshe, Secretary, Department of Foreign Affairs, 1922–46', *Irish Studies in International Affairs*, Vol. 3, No. 2, 1990, p. 79.
3   Dermot Keogh, *Twentieth-Century Ireland: Nation and State* (Dublin, 1994), p. 128.
4   Ronan Fanning, *Independent Ireland* (Dublin, 1983), pp. 132–3.
5   J.H. Whyte, *Church and State in Modern Ireland, 1923–1970* (Dublin, 1971), p. 375.
6   NA, D/J, Press Censorship Monthly Reports, September 1939.
7   NA, D/J, No. 58, extracts from various newspapers dealing with Fogarty's sermon, November 1939.
8   Anthony Rhodes, *The Vatican in the Age of the Dictators, 1922–45* (London, 1973), p. 237.
9   MA, OCC 7/58, extracts from published reports in 'Notes for the Minister', March 1941.
10 *Seanad Debates*, Vol. 25, col. 224, 29 January 1941.
11 Maurice Gorham, *Forty Years of Irish Broadcasting* (Dublin, 1967), p. 131.
12 MA, OCC 7/58, deletions from Bishops' Pastorals.
13 NA, D/J, Press Censorship Monthly Reports, January 1941; MA, OCC 7/58, 'Notes for the Minister'.
14 NA, D/T, S 12381, Notes for Taoiseach on MacDermot's motion, March 1941.
15 ibid.
16 NA, D/J, R 14, 'Censorship of Irish Church Dignitaries', 11 January 1942.
17 ibid., 14 June 1942.
18 NA, D/J, Press Censorship Monthly Reports, February 1945.
19 MA, OCC 7/58, Notes for Taoiseach on MacDermot's motion, March 1941.
20 MA, OCC 2/101, Coyne to Aiken, 9 May 1942.
21 NA, D/T, S 12381, Notes on MacDermot's motion, March 1941.
22 ibid.
23 ibid.
24 MA, OCC 2/67, Coyne to Walshe and Gallagher, August 1941.
25 *Irish Times*, 28 October 1972.
26 Robert Fisk, *In Time of War: Ireland, Ulster and the Price of Neutrality, 1939–45* (London, 1985), p. 439.
27 Robert Cole, 'The Other 'Phoney War': British Propaganda in Neutral Europe, September–December 1939', *Journal of Contemporary History*, Vol. 22, 1987, p. 461.
28 MA, OCC 2/112, 'Ministry of Information propaganda circulars received from the Office of the UK Representative'; MA, OCC 2/107, 'Radio Vatican – extracts prepared by the BBC Monitoring Service, supplied by the Press Attaché at the Office of the UK Representative'.
29 NA, D/J, R 5, 'Censorship of British Church Dignitaries'; NA, D/J, R 15, 'Censorship of Church Dignitaries of all Countries'; MA, OCC 7/58, Notes for the Taoiseach on MacDermot's motion, March 1941.
30 NA, D/T, S 12381, Coyne memo on the censorship debate, March 1941.
31 MA, OCC 7/58, Knightly, March 1941, 'Cardinal Hinsley'.
32 ibid.; NA, D/J, Unnumbered, 'Matter Stopped: "For Publication in Ireland Only"'.
33 Fisk, *In Time of War*, p. 459.
34 Owen Chadwick, *Britain and the Vatican during the Second World War* (Cambridge, 1986), p. 220.
35 Dermot Keogh, *Ireland and Europe, 1919–1948* (Dublin, 1988), p. 181.
36 Rhodes, *Vatican*, p. 78.

37 Chadwick, *Britain and the Vatican*, p. 199.
38 NA, D/T, S 12381, Coyne memo on the censorship debate, March 1941.
39 MA, OCC 2/67, Coyne to Walshe and Gallagher, August 1941.
40 ibid.
41 *Dáil Debates*, Vol. 82, col. 1439, 3 April 1941.
42 MA, OCC 2/67, Coyne to Walshe and Gallagher, August 1941.
43 ibid.
44 Chadwick, *Britain and the Vatican,* pp. 107, 113, 144; Rhodes, *Vatican*, p. 246.
45 Rhodes, *Vatican*, p. 246.
46 Chadwick, *Britain and the Vatican*, p. 144.
47 ibid., pp. 146-7.
48 MA, OCC 2/112, 'Ministry of Information circulars received from the Office of the UK Representative'; MA, OCC 2/107, 'Radio Vatican – extracts prepared by the BBC Monitoring Service, supplied by the Press Attaché at the Office of the UK Representative'.
49 Chadwick, *Britain and the Vatican*, p. 143.
50 MA, OCC 2/67, *The Tablet*, 1 November 1941.
51 NA, D/T, S 12381, Coyne memo on the censorship debate, March 1941.
52 NA, D/J, R 65, 'Reports regarding the position of the Vatican following the German occupation of Rome, 1943'.
53 Chadwick, *Britain and the Vatican*, p. 285.
54 ibid., p. 198.
55 *Dáil Debates*, Vol. 85, cols. 691-3, 13 January 1941.
56 Keogh, *Ireland and Europe 1919-1948*, pp. 188-9.
57 Fisk, *In Time of War*, p. 430.
58 ibid., p. 429.
59 Rhodes, *Vatican*, p. 256.
60 Fisk, *In Time of War*, p. 387; Keogh, *Ireland and Europe 1919-1948*, p. 97.
61 NA, D/J, Press Censorship Reviews: *The Standard*.
62 ibid.
63 NA, D/J, Press Censorship Monthly Reports, September 1939.
64 NA, D/J, R 24, *The Standard* (stopped and deleted proofs).
65 Whyte, *Church and State*, p. 70.
66 ibid.
67 NA, D/J, Press Censorship Reviews: *The Standard*.
68 ibid.
69 J. Anthony Gaughan, *Alfred J. O'Rahilly, Vol. 2: Public Figure* (Dublin, 1989), p. 338.
70 ibid., p. 367.
71 NA, D/J, Press Censorship Reviews: *The Standard*.
72 ibid.
73 ibid.
74 NA, D/J, R 24, *The Standard*, stopped and deleted proofs.
75 MA, OCC 2/42, 'Instructions to the Chief Press Censor', 11 October 1940.
76 NA, D/J, Press Censorship Monthly Reports, September 1941.
77 NA, D/J, Press Censorship Reviews: *The Standard*.
78 MA, OCC 2/123, 'Visit of Professor Joad, 1943', correspondence regarding.
79 NA, D/FA (Sec.) A 8(1), G2 memo, 8 March 1943.
80 Joseph T. Carroll, *Ireland in the War Years* (Newton Abbot, 1975), p. 93.
81 Whyte, *Church and State*, p. 71.
82 NA, D/J, Press Censorship Monthly Reports, July 1943.
83 NA, D/J, No. 178, *Maria Legionis*.
84 ibid.
85 NA, D/J, No. 201, *Irish Jesuit Publications*.

86   NA, D/J, No. 179, *Island Missions.*

87   NA, D/J, No. 201, *Irish Jesuit Publications.*

88   NA, D/J, Press Censorship Reviews: 'Provincial Papers', *Church of Ireland Gazette.*

89   *Dáil Debates*, Vol. 87, col. 2235, 2 July 1942.

90   NA, D/J, No. 19, *Standard*, Coyne to Curry (ed.), 19 June 1940.

91   Seán Cronin, *Washington's Irish Policy: Independence, Partition, Neutrality* (Dublin, 1987), p. 105.

92   Ronan Fanning, "The Rule of Order": Eamon de Valera and the IRA, 1923–1940', in John P. O'Carroll and John A. Murphy (eds.), *De Valera and his Times* (Cork, 1983), pp. 167–8. He was supported in this task by the bishops who issued a statement in June 1940 reminding all Catholics 'that it is a sin against the law of God to conspire against the legitimate authority of the state'. (Fanning, *Independent Ireland*, p. 133.)

93   NA, D/J, No. 19, *Standard*, Coyne to O'Curry, 19 June 1940.

94   MA, OCC 7/20, Censorship to Departments, Justice to Censorship, 14 September 1939.

95   NA, D/J, No. 21, '*The Wolfe Tone Weekly and the Wolfe Tone Annual*'.

96   J. Bowyer Bell, *The Secret Army: The IRA, 1916–1979* (Dublin, 1979), pp. 140 and 247.

97   ibid., p. 176.

98   Tim Pat Coogan, *De Valera: Long Fellow, Long Shadow* (London, 1993), p. 620.

99   NA, D/J, Press Censorship Monthly Reports, October–December 1939; MA, OCC 2/7, 'Matter Suppressed, November 1939'.

100 MA, OCC 2/7, ibid.

101 Eunan O'Halpin, 'Aspects of Intelligence', *The Irish Sword* , Vol. XIX, Nos. 75 and 76, 1993–4, p. 61.

102 A constitutional challenge to the OASA internment clause had led to the release of 53 IRA internees from Arbour Hill on 2 December 1939. The EPA, unlike the OASA, was not subject to judicial review and could not be challenged in the courts. Future internments were carried out under the amended EPA and a detention camp was established at Army HQ at the Curragh for these internees (Tim Pat Coogan *The IRA* (London, 1971), pp. 179–80.)

103 NA, D/J, Press Censorship Reviews: *Irish Times*; NA, D/J, Press Censorship Monthly Reports, December 1939.

104 Coogan, *The IRA*, p. 172, *De Valera*, p. 621; The Earl of Longford and Thomas P. O'Neill, *Eamon de Valera* (Dublin, 1970), p. 359.

105 Bell, *Secret Army*, p. 175.

106 NA, D/J, Press Censorship Monthly Reports, February 1940.

107 ibid., March 1940. As well as the usual arguments, de Valera was criticised by Josephine Mary Plunkett for allowing those men remain in Mountjoy, 'where sexual degenerates are also imprisoned'. De Valera assured Cardinal MacRory that there was no danger of 'depravity' (whatever about death) as IRA prisoners in Mountjoy were kept segregated (J.J. Lee, *Ireland 1912–1985: Politics and Society* (Cambridge, 1989), p. 222).

108 MA, OCC 2/25, Coyne to Aiken, 18 April 1940, Connolly memo, 24 April 1940.

109 NA, D/J, 'Directions to the Press', 16 April 1940.

110 NA, D/J, Press Censorship Monthly Reports, April 1940.

111 NA, D/J, S 164/40, IRA to Staffs, IRA to Managements, 6 April 1940, Commissioner's Office to the Department of Justice, 9 April 1940.

112 NA, D/J, Instructions to Press Censors, 13 June 1940; Press Censorship Monthly Reports, June 1940; 'Directions to the Press', 19 June 1940.

113 Coogan, *The IRA*, p. 190.

114   See Seán Cronin, *Frank Ryan: The Search for the Republic* (Dublin, 1980), pp. 188–91 and Fisk, *In Time of War*, pp. 339–44 and 348–61.

115   Bell, *Secret Army*, pp. 183, 187 and 191.

116   Coogan, *The IRA*, p. 193.

117   NA, D/J, 'Instructions to Press Censors', 7 August 1940; *Seanad Debates*, Vol. 25, col. 223, 29 January 1941; Bell, *Secret Army*, p. 187.

118   NA, D/J, 'Instructions to Press Censors', 22 August 1940.

119   NA, D/J, Press Censorship Monthly Reports, September 1940.

120   NA, D/J, 'Instructions to Press Censors', 17 December 1940.

121   ibid., 6 August 1941; NA, D/J, Press Censorship Monthly Reports, August 1941.

122   See Cronin, *Washington's Irish Policy*, pp. 82–9 and Coogan, *The IRA*, pp. 195–205.

123   NA, D/J, 'Instructions to Press Censors', 9 September 1941.

124   ibid., 2 March 1942.

125   Coogan, *The IRA*, p. 299.

126   Bell, *Secret Army*, p. 216.

127   Cronin, *Washington's Irish Policy*, p. 105.

128   Among them was Joe Cahill, a prominent member of the present-day Sinn Féin.

129   Longford and O'Neill, *De Valera*, p. 399.

130   NA, D/J, Press Censorship Monthly Reports, August 1942.

131   Longford and O'Neill, *De Valera*, p. 399.

132   NA, D/J, Press Censorship Monthly Reports, September 1942.

133   Bell, *Secret Army*, pp. 216–7.

134   NA, D/J, Press Censorship Monthly Reports, September 1942; 'Instructions to Press Censors', 10 September 1942 and 12 September 1942.

135   F.D. Roosevelt Library, New York, David Gray Papers, 'Ireland', 'Censorship in Eire', undated (probably 1942).

136   Cronin, *Washington's Irish Policy*, p. 103.

137   NA, D/J, R 37, 'Execution of Maurice O'Neill, 1942' (stopped and deleted proofs).

138   Bell, *Secret Army*, pp. 229–34.

139   NA, D/J, Instructions, Directions, Reports: 1940–43.

140   NA, D/J, No. 1, *Irish Press*, 11 January 1945 (the *Press* published the report without submission).

141   NA, D/J, 'Instructions to Press Censors', 21 November 1942.

142   NA, D/J, No. 3, *Irish Times*, Coyne to Smyllie, 23 October 1944. This was probably a reference to Dr Ashe, found guilty of being an accessory before the fact on a charge of procuring an abortion. The exigencies of the war period led to an increase in illegal abortions in Ireland because of the added difficulties which Irish women faced in procuring legal abortions in England.

143   NA, D/J, R 37, 'General Elections, 1943'.

144   NA, D/J, R 36, 'Deletions and Stops, Ministers, Ex-Ministers, TDs and Senators'.

145   NA, D/J, Press Censorship Monthly Reports, October 1941. The Gaelic League had been founded by Douglas Hyde in 1893. Hyde was now president of Ireland, while de Valera spent much of 1943 touring the country attending commemorations marking the fiftieth anniversary of the founding of the organisation.

146   NA, D/J, R 25, *Sunday Independent*, 21 May 1942, stopped letter.

147   *Dáil Debates*, Vol. 95, cols. 1407–71, 1 December 1944; NA, D/J, Press Censorship Monthly Reports, November–December 1944.

148   *Dáil Debates*, Vol. 95, cols. 1407–71, 1 December 1944.

149   ibid., cols. 1222–6, 30 November 1944.

150   ibid., col. 1459, 1 December 1944.

151   ibid., cols. 1424–5.

152   Bell, *Secret Army*, p. 234.

153   *Dáil Debates*, Vol. 95, col. 1462, 1 December 1944.

154 Lee, *Ireland*, p. 224.
155 *Dáil Debates*, Vol. 91, col. 2072, 11 November 1943.
156 Fanning, *Independent Ireland*, p. 164.
157 Lee, *Ireland*, p. 224.
158 Fanning, *Independent Ireland*, p. 171.
159 Lee, *Ireland*, p. 224; T.D. Williams, 'Conclusion' in Francis MacManus (ed.), *The Years of the Great Test 1926-39* (Cork, 1978), p. 183.
160 Lee, *Ireland*, p. 224, quoting Seán O'Faoláin, *The Bell*, Vol. 7, No. 1, October 1943.
161 MA, OCC 7/58, Coyne to Moynihan, 5 July 1941.
162 Emmet O'Connor, *A Labour History of Ireland 1824-1960* (Dublin, 1992), p. 137.
163 Fisk, *In Time of War*, p. 438; *Seanad Debates*, Vol. 24, cols. 2568-602, 4 December 1940; *Dáil Debates*, Vol. 82, col. 1498, 3 April 1941. Walshe (Department of External Affairs) opposed the idea because there seemed to be 'many difficulties and not only of a social and religious character, connected with an uncontrolled scheme of this kind' (Fisk, *In Time of War,* p. 444).
164 *Seanad Debates*, vol. 24, cols. 2599-602.
165 ibid.
166 ibid., Vol. 25, col. 350, 30 January 1941.
167 O'Connor, *Labour History*, pp. 145-6; Kieran Allen, 'Forging the Links: Fianna Fáil, the Trade Unions and the Emergency', *Saothar*, Vol. 16, 1991, pp. 50 and 52; Charles McCarthy, *Trade Unions in Ireland, 1894-1960* (Dublin, 1977), p. 246.
168 Mike Milotte, *Communism in Modern Ireland: The Pursuit of the Workers' Republic Since 1916* (Dublin, 1984), p. 193.
169 McCarthy, *Trade Unions*, p. 208.
170 O'Connor, *Labour History*, p. 139; Keogh, *Twentieth-Century Ireland*, pp. 131-3.
171 O'Connor, *Labour History*, p. 142.
172 Francis Devine, 'Obituary Essay: "A Dangerous Agitator": John Swift, 1896-1990, Socialist, Trade Unionist, Secularist, Internationalist, Labour Historian', *Saothar*, Vol. 15, 1990, p. 11.
173 ibid.
174 Milotte, *Communism*, p. 192; McCarthy, *Trade Unions*, pp. 207-10; Allen, 'Forging the Links', p. 63; O'Connor, *Labour History*, p. 144. This was a typical example of Larkin's showmanship. When Owen Sheehy-Skeffington later enquired of him how he had had the confidence to pull this stunt off – what if the match went out or the paper didn't light? – Larkin revealed that he had ten matches tied together, sandpaper on the seat of his trousers and a copy of the Bill soaked in paraffin (Andrée Sheehy-Skeffington, *Skeff: The Life of Owen Sheehy-Skeffington, 1909-1970* (Dublin, 1991), p. 108).
175 Milotte, *Communism*, p. 192.
176 O'Connor, *Labour History*, p. 144.
177 ibid.
178 McCarthy, *Trade Unions*, pp. 229-46.
179 Keogh, *Twentieth-Century Ireland*, p. 133.
180 McCarthy, *Trade Unions*, pp. 229-46.
181 Roibeárd Ó Faracháin, 'Some Early Days in Radio', in Louis McRedmond (ed.), *'Written on the Wind': Personal Memories of Irish Radio, 1926-76* (Dublin, 1976), p. 46.
182 Milotte, *Communism*, p. 188.
183 John de Courcy Ireland, Letter in *Saothar*, Vol. 17, 1992, p. 12.
184 NA, D/J, No. 20, *Torch*, Coyne, 15 March 1941.
185 Milotte, *Communism*, pp. 182-9.
186 ibid., pp. 184-5. It was replaced in the North by *Red Hand* which was banned in October 1940.

187   MA, OCC 2/28, *Irish Workers' Weekly*.
188   NA, D/J, No. 20, Coyne to Roche, 25 March 1941.
189   MA, OCC 2/28, *Irish Workers' Weekly*. Goold (also known as Niall Gould Verschoyle) was also secretary of the Workers' Wartime Campaign Committee, whose meetings and activities were denied publicity and a member of the Dublin Unemployed Workers' Movement, which was the subject of a three-month ban on activities in June 1940 (NA, D/J, Press Censorship Monthly Reports, September 1940).
190   MA, OCC 7/58, 'Articles on Russia', Coyne, 27 June 1941.
191   Milotte, *Communism*, p. 191.
192   MA, OCC 2/28, *Irish Workers' Weekly*.
193   NA, D/J, No. 70, *Irish Workers' Weekly*, Coyne to Justice, 24 October 1941.
194   Milotte, *Communism*, p. 195; NA, D/FA (Sec.) A 55, 'Communist Activities in Ireland'.
195   Milotte, *Communism*, p. 196.
196   MA, OCC 2/122, 'Advertisements for Public Meetings and Lectures', CPI/Seán Nolan/New Books.
197   ibid.
198   MA, OCC 2/127, *Irish Freedom*.
199   de Courcy-Ireland, letter.
200   Sheehy-Skeffington, *Skeff*, pp. 104–5.
201   ibid., p. 105.
202   NA, D/J, No. 20, *The Torch*.
203   *The Torch*, 9 September 1939.
204   NA, D/J, No. 20, *The Torch*.
205   MA, OCC 2/30, Coyne to Industry and Commerce, 20 January 1941 (not issued).
206   NA, D/J, No. 20, *The Torch*.
207   ibid., Price to Connolly, 26 April 1941, Connolly to Price, 15 May 1941.
208   ibid., Coyne to O'Donoghue (Attorney General), 26 May 1941.
209   NA, D/J, No. 128, *Kimmage–Crumlin News*.
210   NA, D/J, No. 20, Coyne to Price, 28 May 1941.
211   ibid., Coyne to O'Donoghue, 26 May 1941.
212   ibid., O'Donoghue to Coyne, 26 May 1941.
213   *Dáil Debates*, Vol. 84, cols. 145 and 175, 24 June 1941.
214   MA, OCC 7/58, Coyne to Aiken, 30 June 1941.
215   *Dáil Debates*, Vol. 84, cols. 175–6, 25 April 1941.
216   MA, OCC 7/58, Coyne to Aiken, 30 June 1941.
217   MA, OCC 7/58, Coyne to Moynihan, 5 July 1941.
218   ibid.
219   NA, D/J, No. 20, *The Torch*.
220   Milotte, *Communism*, pp. 197–9; O'Connor, *Labour History*, pp. 150–1; Sheehy-Skeffington, *Skeff*, pp. 108–12; de Courcy-Ireland, Letter; Donal Nevin, 'Industry and Labour', in K.B. Nowlan and T.D. Williams (eds.), *Ireland in the War Years and After* 1939–51 (Dublin, 1969), pp. 101–2.
221   ibid.
222   O'Connor, *Labour History*, p. 151.
223   Devine, 'A Dangerous Agitator', p. 11.
224   NA, D/J, No. 130, *Bakery Trades Journal*.
225   A, D/J, Unnumbered, 'Dublin Dockers' Strike, 1944'.
226   *Dáil Debates*, Vol. 87, col. 2279, 2 July 1942.
227   *Dáil Debates*, Vol. 95, col. 363, October 1944.
228   *Dáil Debates*, Vol. 89, cols. 545–8, 4 February 19243; MA, OCC 2/42, Coyne to Chief Press Censor and Press Room, 21 October 1941.

229 NA, D/J, Unnumbered, 'Farmers' Strike'.
230 Allen, 'Forging the Links', p. 48.
231 Quoted by Nevin in Nowlan and Williams (eds.), *War Years and After*, p. 97.
232 MA, OCC 7/58, Coyne to Moynihan, 5 July 1941.
233 NA, D/J, 'Directions to the Press', 23 January 1941.
234 MA, OCC 7/58, Coyne to Moynihan, 5 July 1941.
235 Lee, *Ireland*, p. 224.
236 ibid., p. 227.
237 MA, OCC 2/42, Department of Local Government and Public Health to Chief Press Censor, 12 May 1942.
238 MA, OCC 7/58, Coyne to Moynihan, 5 July 1941.
239 Sheehy-Skeffington, *Skeff*, p. 105.
240 MA, OCC 7/58, Coyne to Moynihan, 5 July 1941.
241 See McMullen statement in ITGWU Conference Proceedings, 1942, p. 29 (quoted by Allen, 'Forging the Links', p. 54) and ITUC 1942 memo to government (quoted by Milotte, *Communism*, p. 193).
242 *Seanad Debates*, Vol. 25, col. 325, 30 January 1941.
243 Lee, *Ireland*, p. 237.
244 John A. Murphy, 'The Irish Party System, 1938–57', in Nowlan and Williams (eds.), *War Years and After*, p. 152.
245 ibid., p. 153.
246 *Seanad Debates*, Vol. 24, col. 2618, 4 December 1940.
247 ibid., col. 2619.
248 ibid., Vol. 29, cols. 1335–58, 21 February 1945.
249 *Dáil Debates*, Vol. 87, col. 2271, 2 July 1942.
250 *Seanad Debates*, Vol. 25, col. 315, 30 January 1941.
251 ibid., Vol. 29, col. 1414, 22 February 1945.
252 *Dáil Debates*, Vol. 87, col. 2294, 2 July 1942.
253 *Seanad Debates*, Vol. 28, col. 754, 27 January 1944.
254 MA, OCC 7/58, 'Notes for the Minister', January 1941.
255 *Seanad Debates*, Vol. 25, col. 315, 30 January 1941.
256 ibid., cols. 237–8.
257 ibid., Vol. 28, col. 867, 24 February 1944.
258 ibid.
259 ibid., Vol. 29, col. 1425, 22 February 1945.
260 ibid., cols. 1427–8.
261 ibid., Vol. 24, cols. 2599–600, 4 December 1940.
262 ibid., Vol. 29, col. 1441, 22 February 1945.
263 UCD Archives, Donal O'Sullivan Papers, P 20/5, 'Note to OUTIS', January 1944.
264 *Seanad Debates*, Vol. 24, col. 2626, 4 December 1940.
265 ibid., Vol. 29, col. 1428, 22 February 1945.
266 *Dáil Debates*, Vol. 95, cols. 1424–5 and 1449, 1 December 1944.
267 ibid., Vol. 77, cols. 232–9, 27 September 1939; Vol. 87, col. 2320, 2 July 1942.
268 Fisk, *In Time of War*, p. 161.
269 *Seanad Debates*, Vol. 25, col. 211, 29 January 1941.
270 NA, D/T, S 12381, OCC 'Note for the Minister' on Censorship Debate, March 1941. These extensive notes for the Taoiseach presented the case against the Censorship made by parliamentary critics and addressed the various charges made. The material for the rest of this section on criticism of the Censorship is taken from these notes and from the proceedings of the various debates on the Censorship in the Dáil and Seanad throughout the period.
271 *Seanad Debates*, Vol. 25, col. 233, MacDermot, 29 January 1941.
272 ibid., col. 321, Hayes, 30 January 1941.

273 NA, D/T, S 11586, 'Neutrality, Censorship and Democracy', Aiken memo, 23 January 1940.
274 NA, D/T, S 12381, OCC 'Note for the Minister', March 1941.
275 *Dáil Debates*, Vol. 86, col. 2283, 15 April 1942.
276 ibid., col. 2218.
277 See, for example, NA, D/J, R 44, 'James Dillon – Stops and Deletions'.
278 MA, OCC 7/58, 'Notes for Minister', January 1941.
279 NA, D/T, S 11586, Aiken/OCC memo for government, 15 January 1940.
280 ibid., 'Neutrality, Censorship and Democracy', 23 January 1940.
281 ibid., 'Memorandum regarding Censorship', 6 February 1940.
282 *Dáil Debates*, Vol. 82, col. 1506, 3 April 1941.
283 ibid., Vol. 81, col. 1524, 17 January 1941.
284 NA, D/J, R 37, 'Seán Piondar' (stopped and deleted proofs).
285 *Seanad Debates*, Vol. 25, col. 225, 29 January 1941.
286 *Dáil Debates*, Vol. 82, col. 1456, 3 April 1941.
287 For an account of Aiken's mission, see Joseph L. Rosenberg, 'The 1941 Mission of Frank Aiken to the United States: An American Perspective', *Irish Historical Studies*, Vol. XXII, No. 86, September 1980, pp. 162–77.
288 MA, OCC 2/85, Coyne to Traynor, 23 May 1941.
289 UCD Archives, Richard Mulcahy Papers, P7/C/113, Smyllie to Mulcahy, 21 May 1941.
290 NA, D/T, S 12043, Connolly to de Valera, 25 March 1941.
291 *Dáil Debates*, Vol. 84, col. 1501, 3 April 1941.
292 ibid., cols. 1481–2.
293 ibid., col. 1448.
294 Lee, *Ireland*, p. 238.
295 NA, D/J, No. 3, *Irish Times*, Smyllie to Censorship, 10 October 1941 and Censorship to Smyllie, 13 October 1941.
296 *Dáil Debates*, Vol. 86, cols. 609–15, Mulcahy, 15 April 1942; Vol. 87, cols. 2281–3, Dillon, 2 July 1942.
297 ibid., Vol. 87, col. 2257, Hannigan, 2 July 1942.
298 Carroll, *War Years*, p. 116.
299 NA, D/J, Press Censorship Reviews: 'Work of the Censorship'; Press Censorship Monthly Reports, February 1942.
300 *Dáil Debates*, Vol. 87, cols. 2271–2, 2 July 1942.
301 ibid., col. 2284.
302 ibid., Vol. 85, cols. 2217–18, 5 March 1942.
303 ibid., Vol. 87, col. 2313, 2 July 1942.
304 ibid.
305 MA, OCC 7/58, Aiken to Coyne, 11 April 1942.
306 *Dáil Debates*, Vol. 85, col. 1990, 18 February 1942.
307 NA, D/J, Press Censorship Reviews: 'Work of the Censorship'.
308 *Dáil Debates*, Vol. 85, cols. 1987–8, 18 February 1942.
309 Lee, *Ireland*, p. 239.
310 Murphy in Nowlan and Williams (eds.), *War Years and After*, p. 151.
331 ibid.
312 NA, D/J, No. 165, 'Neutrality'.
313 NA, D/J, R 37, 'General Election, 1942–43'.
314 NA, D/J, No. 165, 'Neutrality'.
315 ibid.
316 NA, D/J, R 37, 'General Election, 1942–43'.
317 NA, D/J, 'Controller's Correspondence', Smyllie to Censorship, 23 January 1943, Coyne to Smyllie, 27 January 1943 and Newman to Coyne, 29 January 1943.

318   *Dáil Debates*, Vol. 89, col. 503, 4 February 1943.

319   ibid., col. 504.

320   NA, D/J, Press Censorship Monthly Reports, February 1943.

321   *Dublin Opinion*, February 1943.

322   *Dáil Debates*, Vol. 89, col. 718, 18 February 1943.

323   NA, D/T, S 11306, 'Press Censorship of Election Speeches', Department of External Affairs memo and draft statement for de Valera, 15 February 1943.

324   Carroll, *War Years*, p. 170.

325   *Seanad Debates*, Vol. 27, col. 2242, 27 May 1943.

326   Keogh, *Twentieth-Century Ireland*, p. 136.

327   Lee, *Ireland*, p. 240.

328   An American intelligence report on the elections noted that the pro-Axis/fascist candidates of Ailtirí na hAiséirighe and Clann na Poblachta had all lost their deposits while the communist Larkins had both won in Dublin indicating that if the electorate had belligerent sympathies, they were more towards the Russians than the Axis (USNA, OSS, London Field Station Files, RG226, 'Significance of Irish Elections').

329   O'Sullivan pointed out that 'Fál' did not mean 'destiny' and that this was a popular error long discarded by scholars; according to him, Fál was probably a goddess in Celtic mythology.

330   UCD Archives, Donal O'Sullivan Papers, P 20/7, editor (*Times Pictorial*) to O'Sullivan, 26 October 1944, P 20/4 (proof of article), P 20/5 (letter by O'Sullivan, 22 January 1944); NA, D/J, R 23, *Times Pictorial* (stopped and deleted proofs).

331   Lee, *Ireland*, p. 240.

332   ibid., p. 241.

333   NA, D/J, R 38, 'General Election, 1944'.

334   NA, D/J, Press Censorship Monthly Reports, May 1944.

335   Lee, *Ireland*, p. 241.

336   *Dáil Debates*, Vol. 82, col. 1448, 3 April 1941.

337   Fisk, *In Time of War*, p. 162.

CONCLUSION

The end of the war in Europe led to the dismantling of the Emergency security apparatus.[1] The emergency censorship was lifted on 11 May 1945, the organisation was disbanded and the wartime censors returned to their peacetime duties. The ending of the open censorship led the post office to cease the telephone supervision it had been operating for G2 and the Department of Justice indicated its intention to stop issuing the warrants under which military intelligence had operated its covert wartime censorship. Dan Bryan, the director of G2, was not pleased with the proposed loss of such extraordinary powers and argued forcibly for their retention, pointing particularly to the dangers to the state posed by communist activities.[2] His efforts were unsuccessful, however, and the most intensive period of censorship in the history of the state came to an end.[3]

The extent of G2's activities had never been known, but the ending of the overt censorship was received with relief by the press, the cinema trade and the public who, as we have seen, packed the cinemas to view the many war features and newsreels which had been kept from Irish screens for the previous five and a half years. The *Irish Times* celebrated its new freedom with a series of photographs over the next two weeks under the heading 'They can be published now: pictures that were stopped by the censor during the war'. These mainly depicted scenes from the war, but included one photograph that featured P.J. Little, the Minister for Posts and Telegraphs, skating on a frozen pond in Dublin, which had been stopped because of the meteorological information it contained. Some of the excesses of the previous years were now coming to light, but, for the most part, the true extent of the censorship remained hidden, and even that which was revealed provoked little discussion or debate. Relief that the war and its dangers had passed, and a sense of pride in the successful prosecution of neutrality, enhanced by de Valera's famous broadcast reply to Churchill's attack on the policy at the war's end, contributed to a feeling that the ends justified the means. Added to this was the adverse effect of 'the thickened cobwebs of accumulated habitual suppression'[4] on the development of a critical analysis in the media, and in the broader social and political sphere.

We have seen how extensive and pervasive the Irish censorship was at all levels. In order that its activities can be judged in a comparative context it will be instructive to examine briefly wartime censorship in a number of other European neutral states and, firstly, because of the close ties which it had with Ireland, in belligerent Britain.

The powers of press censorship in wartime Britain were contained in the Emergency Powers (Defence) Act, upon which the Irish Emergency Powers Act was largely based. The British made two main claims about their press censorship which distinguished it from the Irish equivalent: that it was voluntary, and that it was purely a security censorship which did not interfere with the expression of opinion. Proper analysis has shown these claims to have little basis in reality.[5] The central point about the British system was that it involved an elaborate pre-censorship of information and that it achieved its aims by co-operation rather than confrontation with the press. In contrast to Ireland, relations with the press were very good; the newspapers were consulted on censorship policy, 'taken into the conspiracy' and given the impression that they were far freer than they actually were. In general, the censorship was handled with far more subtlety than it was in Ireland.

The total control over the information which reached the press ensured that nothing would be published which the authorities did not wish to be published; the decision not to censor opinion 'was made from the relative safety of knowing that all news released on which the media could form their opinions had already been censored at source while giving the impression of a voluntary system which provided an effective cover for official propaganda and a clearer conscience for a liberal democracy at war'.[6] When elements of the media did occasionally overstep the mark, such as the *Daily Mirror* criticisms of the manner in which the war was being run in 1942, a threat of suppression was sufficent to keep them in line; the publicity given to the *Mirror* incident actually suited the censors' purposes, reinforcing 'the illusion that censorship of opinion was not taking place'.[7] The control of radio and film in wartime Britain was similarly achieved primarily through pre-censorship, supplemented by ample powers of post-censorship for the occasional items which slipped through the net.

In Switzerland[8] the censorship was operated by the press and radio division of the army until early 1942 when it was put under the direct control of the federal council. (The army continued to be responsible for military censorship.) Following the formal change in control a number of newspaper editors were appointed as representatives of the press in a new consultative press commission which advised the censorship. The system had both preventative and punitive aspects, but mainly the latter. Press directives were issued, or certain matters were declared non-publishable; editors could ignore the

THEY CAN BE PUBLISHED NOW—8.

Pictures That Were Stopped by the Censor During the War

Mr. P. J. Little, Minister for Posts and Telegraphs, skating in Herbert Park, Dublin.

THEY CAN BE PUBLISHED NOW—5.
Pictures That Were Stopped by the Censor During the War

Allied motor vehicles move through a breach in the Siegfried Line defences on their way to Karlsruhe.

Three examples from the *Irish Times* series of 'Pictures that were stopped by the censor during the war', which ran for the two weeks following the lifting of censorship on 11 May 1945.

THEY CAN BE PUBLISHED NOW—13.
Pictures That Were Stopped by the Censor During the War

Twenty-year-old Laga Mandri Makildo, one of the fighting girl patriots of Yugo-Slavia, who alone destroyed many German trains.

censorship but at the risk of having their publications suppressed. A number of journals were suppressed entirely, while preventative censorship was imposed (as in Ireland, by means of submission before publication) on a number of periodicals by way of penalty when warnings were ignored. Particular issues of certain Swiss publications were confiscated, while a number of foreign papers were stopped at the frontiers.

For most of the war no Allied newspapers were sold in Switzerland and virtually all the external newspapers which circulated were German. In addition, Nazi propaganda papers like *Signal* were printed in French, German and Italian editions and were distributed freely, while Swiss newspapers were provided with material by the German legation. British propaganda was carried in a legation bulletin and by the BBC. The Swiss situation thus resembled that in Ireland, with one side – in the Irish case, the Allies – being in a dominant position with regard to propaganda. The major difference was that the Swiss had their own agencies and correspondents covering the war and were not reliant, as the Irish media were, on one side for an account and interpretation of events.

Besides military security, the censorship was directed principally against 'internal disruption' and particularly against the activities of communists and anarchists. Anybody who aided or carried out communist propaganda was liable to punishment; the Communist Party newspaper *Le Travail* was suppressed while a number of people were imprisoned or deprived of their civil rights for distributing communist tracts. The maintenance of morale, of course, was another primary objective, as was the case with all the wartime censorships.

While the Irish censorship set out to create 'a truly neutral outlook among newspaper readers', by preventing or confining expressions of partiality, treating neutrality as sacrosanct and prohibiting matter which was contrary to it, in Switzerland freedom of expression on the war, its participants and the issues at stake was not regarded as being incompatible with neutrality; hence, what an Irish official described as 'the shockingly pro and anti articles to be found in any Swiss paper'. The Swiss authorities originally took a line – in direct contrast to the Irish – that the press should be discouraged from influencing the creation of a state of public opinion described as 'neutralisation'; one paper was actually punished for advocating a policy of press reticence on the war with the object of making the Swiss 'neutral-minded'. At one point, Frederick Boland of the Department of External Affairs expressed surprise to Hempel at the anti-German sentiments sanctioned in the presses of countries bordering on the Reich – sentiments which, he assured the German minister, would never be permitted in Irish newspapers.[9]

Although they did not seek to create a 'moral neutrality' like the Irish, the Swiss authorities, as the war progressed, did begin to take some measures against partiality. In April 1942 the distribution and wearing of emblems indicating support for or opposition to any belligerent were banned and in the following month the paper *Weltwoche* received a public warning because of its 'one-sided judgements on war events'. In August 1942 a new federal council decree extended the existing provisions against internal disruption of the state to include persons who carried on propaganda for the abandonment of neutrality. It was also made an offence to insult the heads, government, diplomats, flags, etc. of foreign states. Despite these new restrictions, however, the press was still free to express views about the war of a character and to an extent which was never tolerated in Ireland.

The August decree was seen by the Irish authorities as demonstrating that the Swiss regarded pro-war propaganda as more harmful than anti-belligerent propaganda, and that mere unfriendliness towards a belligerent – in this case, Germany – on the part of a small group of Swiss newspapers entailed no risk of war, unless it actually created a body of opinion in favour of Switzerland going to war. The Irish Censorship did not make such fine distinctions and saw the exclusion of belligerent propaganda as a precondition for the maintenance of 'moral neutrality', the unity of the people behind the policy of neutrality and the handicapping of efforts to create a condition of 'warmindedness' among the population.

The operation of censorship in democratic Switzerland highlighted the excessiveness of the Irish censorship very clearly, yet even in non-democratic, fascistic Portugal the press enjoyed more freedom of expression on the war than its Irish counterpart. (Portugal's neutrality, like Ireland's, was made known to its people by the government and was not formally announced to the world, as was the case with Switzerland.) The Portuguese press had been censored since 1926 and the 1933 constitution gave the government the power to control the press; thus, no special legislation was required for the implementation of wartime censorship. While Salazar's authoritarian regime continued to use censorship to suppress political opposition and dissent, newspapers were given 'considerable latitude', particularly in comparison to Ireland, in relation to war news and views. The government organ *Diario da Mantia* had a pro-Axis bias, but most of the other papers leaned towards the Allies, particularly following the entry of Brazil to the war and the conclusion of the Azores agreement; once the Portuguese government had jumped on the Allied bandwagon, its own newspaper followed suit. Dispatches abroad by foreign correspondents had to be submitted while editors were summoned periodically for direction by the censorship officer; on the important occasion of the Azores agreement this was done by Salazar himself. Newspapers and periodicals from both sides continued to be sold; the Germans produced a special Portuguese edition of their war propaganda periodical *Signal* and subsidised the Nazi propaganda organ *Estera*. Foreign publications were scrutinised by the censorship and particular issues were occasionally suppressed. This occurred, as was the case in Ireland, when what was seen as derogatory or harmful reference was made to Portugal;

for example, the *Observer* of 10 October 1943 was suppressed because of a leading article on Salazar entitled 'Europe's Senior Dictator'.[10]

As with the other neutrals, the press in Sweden was relatively free in comparison to Ireland. Communists, again, were the principal victims of what was a mainly punitive censorship. In the first months of the war the communist paper *Ny Tagd* and the anti-Nazi *Trots Allt* had a number of issues confiscated and their editors imprisoned; in the case of the former, because of articles critical of the Finnish government, and the latter for attacks on Hitler. Swedish wartime legislation contained a provision for the prohibition of matter liable to cause offence to foreign governments and peoples and in April 1943 the authorities banned *Tyska Roster*, published by the German legation in Stockholm, because of an article on 'The Soviet Man', which was declared 'an uncomplimentary description of the Soviet people'. The British propagandist publication *News from Britain* was confiscated in April 1940.[11] In Ireland, as we have seen, official propagandist publications of this type were comparatively free from interference. In general, however, the Swedes, like the Swiss, had the advantage of having their own coverage of the war and did not regard the publication of pro-belligerent propaganda, the expression of pro-belligerent sentiments or general discussion and debate on the issues of the war as incompatible with neutrality.

Film censorship was applied with far less rigour in other neutrals also. German features and newsreels dominated the market in Switzerland, but British and American war films were also shown.[12] Portugal stopped screening German films because too few were produced to maintain the trade and the more numerous British and American products were shown instead. Newsreels were a prominent part of nearly all cinema performances, and the fear of disturbance, on the basis of which the Irish authorities justified the strictness of their censorship, was addressed by placing a notice on the screen before each performance calling on audiences not to demonstrate against the contents.[13] Swedes also had access to films which were never allowed to reach Irish screens.[14]

Postal and telegraph censorship was carried out by all neutrals, but while the overt Irish control was more limited because of resource deficiencies, some of its targets made it unusual. Although diplomatic communications were not generally interfered with, they were constantly monitored and their contents noted. Even representatives of the Irish government itself, specifically Leopold Kerney, the Irish minister in Spain, were not above suspicion and were targeted by the Censorship, in conjunction with G2. The Censorship 'Black List' included not only those suspected of being involved in subversion, but also anybody who was known to them or with whom they communicated. Dissenters of every political hue were targeted and even the most general criticisms of and observations on the situation in Ireland were removed from communications. Sexual morality also featured among the concerns of the Irish censors, as evidenced by the episode in which a Dutch

woman had a work visa withdrawn from her and her Irish lover was arrested on the basis of the sexually explicit nature of their correspondence,
which was first observed and subsequently stopped by the Censorship. Such
actions reveal a censorship mentality which did not differentiate between
a 'moral' and political agenda. The same mentality was behind the effective 'blacklisting' of Frank O'Connor in the war years.

Ireland's censorship culture, the low priority accorded to freedom of
information and expression, and the tradition of 'closed' government and
administration offer a part explanation for the relative extremism of its wartime system; there were a number of other contributory factors, arising
primarily from the particular nature of Irish neutrality. Ireland differed from
other neutrals in the emotional dimension which became attached to its
policy and the sense of moral superiority which became a corollary of it.
'The Irish', wrote Elizabeth Bowen at the time, 'have invested their self-respect
in it,'[15] and, as Lee has pointed out, the 'return on the investment of
self-respect' was safer,[16] and the self-righteous feeling strengthened, if information which revealed varieties of behaviour among the belligerents was
denied publicity. The Irish authorities wished the war to be seen as nothing
more than 'a conflict of materialism, a struggle between two opposing but
equally unspiritual sides'.[17] The entry of the Soviet Union made it even
more of an 'ungodly struggle', threw Irish spirituality into even sharper relief
and allowed Irish neutrality to become even more puritanical and self-
righteous. British claims to be fighting for freedom and democracy were
dismissed (arguably, with justification) by reference to its failure to take a
stand against fascist expansionism through the League of Nations and by
its own anti-democratic record in Ireland.[18] Writing after the war Gerald
Boland, the wartime Minister for Justice, referred to those responsible for
Katyn, Dresden, Hiroshima and Nagasaki 'having the cheek to try anyone
for war crimes'.[19] The point is a valid one, but it reveals a continuing wilful
refusal to acknowledge the nature of Nazism or the possibility that the
belligerents could have been 'unevenly matched in terms of savagery'.[20] To
have admitted a difference between them would have been to undermine
the basis of Irish moral superiority. This mind-set has been described by
one commentator as 'Emergencyitis': 'a curious compound of sanc-
timoniousness, pusillanimity, peasant self-interest and smugness . . . the
belief that our neutrality was a virtuous one, and that we piously looked
on while the bullies brawled, as if the outcome was of no interest to us'.[21]

Another factor was that Ireland, unlike Sweden or Switzerland, for example, could not defend its neutrality militarily. The successful prosecution
of Irish neutrality was the result of a number of factors, few of which lay
within Irish control. Yet, a need existed, for emotional and symbolic as well
as domestic political reasons, for the Irish to claim responsibility for its success, and the censorship was an obvious peg on which to hang such claims.
Aiken defined propaganda as 'one of the most important weapons of war'

and its expression in a neutral country, whether originating there or not, as, effectively, an act of war.[22] Such a framing not only justified the rigidity of the censorship but validated Ireland's claim to have been responsible for the success of its neutrality. De Valera's successful playing of the 'double game' was, of course, crucial and the censorship had an important role to play in this regard – in hiding the extent of Irish partiality and presenting a picture of correct neutrality to the Irish people and the outside world.

The lack of expenditure on defence generally also affected the defensive measure of censorship. The Irish organisation was less well-resourced than other wartime censorships, but what it lacked in resources (and, in some instances, legal power) it made up for in zeal and by the utilisation of existing censorship mechanisms, official and unofficial. The existing film censorship machinery and approach was extended so that neutrality became another article of faith to be defended with the same puritanical ardour normally applied to matters sexual. The 1908 Post Office Act was used to control internal post, not covered by the emergency legislation. Customs officials continued to act as the first line of defence against the outside world, while the co-operation of booksellers, newsagents, distributors and printers aided the Censorship enormously; indeed, Eason, the leading newspaper wholesaler and retailer, operated almost as if he was a part of the organisation. This reflected the general situation in Ireland whereby booksellers and newsagents, through their organisations, had a record of staunch support for the actions of the Censorship Board.[23] The emergency censorship shared other common features with the pre-existing censorship. The Censorship Board (established to enforce the Censorship of Publications Act), for example, often banned books in paperback, which were more widely accessible, while allowing the same titles to be sold in the more expensive hardback form. During the Emergency different standards were applied also; for example, 'cheap', mass market propaganda titles were subjected to stricter censorship than more expensive, 'higher quality' works; newspapers were more heavily censored than books; the cinema was more censored than the press or the theatre, etc. Such discrimination is common in all censorship and reveals much about its motivation and purpose.

The sense of threat contained in the potentially limitless powers of the Censorship ensured compliance in other areas, for example in the unofficial censorship of the theatre and the Irish Film Society. (In 1994, in a salutary reminder of how little the authorities have progressed in such matters, the Department of Justice forced the Irish Film Centre into withdrawing the banned film *Natural Born Killers* by threatening, in a manner which would have pleased Frank Aiken, to extend the powers of censorship over its private screenings and undermine its existence by changing the laws governing its operation.) The threat of forcing newspapers to submit each issue in full was generally sufficient to ensure their compliance with the demands of the Censorship. The fact that the *Irish Times* had to undergo this procedure for most of the war kept this potentially most troublesome paper 'in line', although it and other publications successfully bypassed the censorship on numerous occasions by the use of a variety of clever ruses.

The censorship was also strengthened by the importance that was laid upon it, as reflected in the fact that one of the most senior ministers of the government was the *de facto* minister for censorship. Frank Aiken's single-minded and dogged pursuit of his objectives in this area, and the direct role which he played, ensured that little, including papal and episcopal pronouncements and ministerial speeches, escaped the net; the Anglophobic instincts of the minister in charge were influential in some areas, for example in the censorship of obituary notices and the insistence on the use of Irish place-names. While Bertie Smyllie's guess that de Valera never realised the extent to which Aiken was using his powers may have been partly true, he never overruled the minister and was satisfied to leave the formulation and application of policy in this area to his trusted colleague.

Some general factors also aided the effectiveness of the censorship, for example: the state monopoly in broadcasting, the support of the Catholic Church hierarchy for the government's policy, the strength of localism and nationalism in Irish political culture, the tradition of secrecy in the operations of government, and, of course, the consensus about neutrality which existed. To what extent did the censorship itself contribute to that consensus?

It is generally accepted that the large majority of Irish people supported the policy of neutrality. Opposition did exist but it was small, divided and inconsistent, while the censorship was undoubtedly a major hindrance to its development. There were those like James Dillon who advocated Ireland joining the war against Nazism on moral and Christian grounds. Others could not conceive of pursuing a policy which was independent of British policy, while others again still saw Ireland's role as supporting Britain's enemy, no matter who that enemy happened to be. All sides regarded neutrality and, by extension, the Censorship, as operating against their viewpoint and in favour of those to whom they were opposed. (The organisation recorded accusations of bias by partisans on both sides, satisfied that it was 'doing its stuff' when the *Irish Times* was condemned by one of its readers as 'The Nazi Times'[24] and Dan Breen, TD denounced the *Irish Press* as being 'more red than Stalin' and 'more British than the British'.[25]) The argument that thousands voted with their feet against Irish neutrality by joining the British war effort[26] is problematic. In the first place, a large proportion were economic refugees, while all of those who joined up for ideological reasons did not necessarily believe that they should rather have been fighting the same fight as part of an Irish army. It should be noted also that there was not a direct correlation between partisans for both sides and those who opposed neutrality; many believed that Ireland should remain neutral, but sought the freedom to express their preferences. Some opponents pointed out that the international situation was fluid and changeable and that the freezing of a particular policy – backed up by the rigid application of censorship in protection of that policy – was not necessarily serving the best interests of the state or its people. They also argued that the 'unity' established by the actions of the Censorship was artificial and detrimental to morale and the 'mental equipment' necessary for meeting an invasion.[27]

Senator Frank MacDermot, a leading critic of neutrality and the Censorship, claimed that popular support for neutrality was due in great measure to the censorship as arguments against the policy, and news that would create anti-Nazi sentiment, were prohibited.[28] It is true that the censorship was used to prevent open discussion and debate on the subject of neutrality, on the basis that a public controversy about neutrality could lead to public disorder. Aiken envisaged a snowball effect if any moral judgements about the belligerents were allowed, eventuating in a civil war on the question of who Ireland should go to war against.[29]

Interestingly, John Maffey, the UK representative in Ireland, took the view that the effect of a censorship which ruled out attacks against belligerents was to the benefit of the British, as anti-British feeling, always there though often latent, was the dynamic of Irish public opinion.[30] Ultimately, however, the majority of people realised, just as the authorities did, that their interests were closely tied to those of the British and, especially following the entry of the US into the war, an Allied victory was what most people wanted to see. Yet, the ambivalent and ambiguous attitude to Britain, and the contradictory nature of the relationship between the two countries, confused and complicated the picture. Britain's historical record in Ireland was still a cause of resentment and it influenced the Irish world-view in a peculiar way; the notion that Irish suffering and British inequity were somehow unique dominated perspectives and hampered the development of a link between the Irish experience of imperialism and that of other countries and peoples and the development of a progressive, internationalist, anti-imperialist perspective on international relations and the war. The central symbolic function of neutrality was its assertion of independence from Britain, but, as Lee mischievously points out, 'an even fuller assertion of sovereignty would have been to actually go to war against Britain', as the Finns did against the Soviet Union. A symbolic war was preferable, and victory in it could be enjoyed so long, of course, as Britain won the real war.[31] While Ireland waged its 'phoney war' in public, using the censorship as a key weapon, it did as much as possible within the constraints of neutrality to help the 'old enemy' and its allies win the real one.

The most powerful symbol of British power in Ireland was its continuing presence in the North and the issue of partition was the basis for most of the anomalies which arose in the otherwise strict application of censorship. This was principally because (rhetorical) opposition to partition was regarded as having a unifying rather than a divisive affect. Anti-partitionist sentiment was, in fact, encouraged and the issue became progressively identified as the primary reason for neutrality; this was particularly so from the end of 1941 when the rationale of neutrality as a security policy waned, as the focus of the conflict shifted and the Americans entered the war and became a second occupying force in the North. Publicity was ensured by the Censorship for de Valera's hostile reaction to proposed conscription in Northern Ireland, his protests at the stationing of US troops there, and that state's repressive activities. At the same time, the benevolence of Irish neutrality towards the British and Americans and the existence of similar repression in the southern state was hidden, thus exaggerating the effect of publicity in relation to the North and further vindicating neutrality on the basis of continuing British oppression in Ireland. This linkage was copperfastened in public perception by de Valera's reply to Churchill at the war's end when he identified partition as the reason for neutrality more closely than ever before and ensured the binding of neutrality to the cause of Irish nationality in the postwar era.[32]

Technically, of course, anti-partitionist sentiment counted as propaganda against a belligerent; but, just as Germany was expected to show 'a certain consideration' for Ireland's close ties with Britain, so the latter would have to accept that partition was a legitimate cause for complaint during the war. It was regarded, furthermore, as an internal issue, unrelated to the war except insofar as Ireland felt it could identify itself with oppressed or divided nations.[33] However, in March 1945, as the war was nearing its end, the Censorship stopped the printing of posters for Ailtirí na hAiséirighe's anti-partition campaign. Coyne's view was that while no opportunity should have been lost to protest against 'the injustice of partition . . . it is even more important that nothing should be done at the present time to arouse ill-will against Great Britain and to cause bad blood between the British people and ourselves . . . let us use discretion until we are out of the wood'.[34] Ireland's postwar position was now the primary concern of the authorities and where there was a potential clash between rhetoric and reality, the practical demands of *realpolitik* were decisive. Reality also impinged in the form of the IRA whose violent expression of anti-partitionism was particularly unwelcome. The full weight of the state was brought to bear upon it, and the Censorship played its part by depriving it of the oxygen of publicity and attempting to deny this form of Republicanism any legitimacy. Ironically, it could be argued that the South's neutrality in contrast to the North's belligerence actually strengthened partition, as did the twenty-six county nationalism implicit in the state's wartime policy and appeals to the people. A further irony was that while the border was put forward as one of the reasons for neutrality, the existence of Northern Ireland was one of the factors which guaranteed the survival of that policy.

While anti-partitionism accounted for most of the anomalies in the strict application of censorship, others arose from another deep-seated feature of Irish political culture: anti-communism. Communiqués from the Soviet

Union were regarded with more suspicion than any others and were often prohibited on the basis of their source. In relation to film, Aiken noted 'the great difference between films displaying a Soviet defence of an "ism" and other types'.[35] Attacks on Soviet communism in the press, despite the fact that they constituted attacks on a belligerent after June 1941, were passed under the guise of 'theological and ethical' arguments and taking account of Ireland's 'natural . . . antipathy towards Communism'.[36] The various accusations made against the Censorship – that it was pro-British or pro-Axis – could not be sustained by the evidence. Only a charge of being anti-Soviet could have been held up, but this was never made; communists expected nothing else and others expected nothing less. However, Ireland's anti-communism was among the factors which influenced the Soviet Union in its blocking of Ireland's admission to the United Nations in the postwar period. Among the arguments used by a Moscow University expert on British and Commonwealth affairs was that attacks on the Soviet Union had been permitted in the Irish press during the war, while Hitler and Mussolini were protected and constantly referred to by their official titles. (This was presented as part of the evidence of Ireland's pro-fascist stance.) He also referred to the general situation whereby Marxist classics were banned.[37]

The censorship was also used against Irish communists and socialists, as well as against fascist and anti-Semitic groups, all of whom were viewed, like militant Republicans, as a threat to unity and public order. General matters of historical and political dispute were suppressed for the same reasons, while matter which highlighted the socio-economic inequities of the Emergency regime, whether emanating from radical groups or not, was suppressed because of the unwelcome light which it threw on material interests and the negative effect this would have had on the protection of 'national interests', the basis of government policy.

While the propagandist promotion of anti-partitionist sentiment was one of the tasks of the Censorship, it also performed other propagandist functions, direct and indirect.

It was suggested, in an internal review of its operations at the end of the war, that 'the most important work done by the Censorship was in calming a British press infuriated by lying stories' about Ireland.[38] As we have seen, the Censorship used its power over the external press to have 'friendly' articles published in a number of leading British newspapers. It also maintained close scrutiny over the contents of exported stories, particularly by Irish journalists, and heavily influenced the content of a number of dispatches by correspondents who had little choice but to comply in the interests of maintaining their livelihoods. Expediency was the guiding principle in dealing with visiting journalists who had the option of bypassing the censor by carrying stories out of the state and having them published once they were outside Irish control. Thus, articles which would ordinarily have been stopped were allowed if they contained some counterbalancing 'helpful' comments, denouncing partition, for example, or focusing attention on some 'positive' aspect of Irish neutrality. The control on information going abroad was extended to private communications for 'propaganda' as well as strictly 'security' reasons, and unless the opinions of individuals, particularly those of the 'West British' persuasion, about various aspects of wartime Ireland fitted the official picture, they were not forwarded. One of the Censorship's propaganda coups was its success in controlling the content of the influential 'March of Time' documentary/newsreel on Ireland and exploiting it to 'sell our story', as the Irish authorities wished to present it, on the world market. The use of the emergency censorship as a mechanism for presenting pro-government news and anti-partition propaganda to the outside world made it, in some ways, a forerunner of the (ultimately doomed) state-run Irish News Agency which was established in 1950 for this very purpose. (This 'experiment which aimed at punching a hole in the newspaper wall' lasted until 1958.)[39]

Propaganda and censorship are, of course, two sides of the same coin. The former attempts to achieve results by 'injecting content into communication', the latter by removing or limiting it.[40] Indeed, censorship which selectively suppresses certain views in favour of others is itself a form of propaganda. 'Propaganda by censorship', or 'negative propaganda' involves 'the selective control of information to favour a particular viewpoint';[41] this is precisely what the Irish Censorship was engaged in during the war, with the object, not of promoting one set of belligerents or the other, but of promoting that image of the war, Irish neutrality and Ireland in general which the government wished to present. Just as belligerent censorships sought to control information in a way that best served their respective war efforts, so the Irish Censorship sought to do so in a way that best served the 'limited war' against all sides in which, according to Aiken, Ireland was engaged.[42]

Both sides in the war carefully controlled coverage of the conflict to their own benefit and 'war news', as such, was difficult to disentangle from 'propaganda'. The perception of propaganda in the English language as something deceitful, dishonourable and undesirable was turned to their advantage by British and American propagandists in the Second World War by giving their enemies exclusive use of the word;[43] the British did not have a Ministry of Propaganda but a Ministry of Information, while the Americans had their Office of War Information. Furthermore, the Germans and the Japanese made no pretence about the role of their war correspondents; they were integrated into the state war machine and wrote nothing that did not aid the war effort, particularly morale. The British and Americans maintained the pretence of having independent war correspondents, linked to the idea that they also had a free press; they, in fact, had neither. Correspondents were never actually drafted into the armed forces, but they became increasingly integrated into the Allied war effort and were viewed by the authorities as a part of the war machine. Charles Lynch, who was accredited to the British army for Reuters, put it frankly: 'We were a propaganda arm of our governments. At the start the censors enforced that, but by the end we were our own censors. We were cheerleaders . . .'.[44] All the major media – news agencies, newspapers, radio stations, film companies – functioned likewise and, given the Anglo-American media domination of Ireland, the Irish Censorship was faced with a mammoth task.

Although the Censorship could be overzealous, illogical, irrational, inconsistent, absurd and pedantic, in general its approach, or at least the ideal which it strove to achieve, was quite defensible in relation to war news. The nature of the propaganda war was well understood and the notion that there was such a thing as objective, value-free 'news' in this context was rightly rejected. The British and Americans, it should be noted, were far better at disguising the 'slant', principally because they reported reverses and differences of opinion, and printed enemy communiqués; this was a propaganda ploy which gave the impression of a free press, thus boosting morale, while the true extent of the control was hidden.[45] In general, war news is expected to go beyond formal accounts of battles and offer 'hope, consolation or interpretation'.[46] It was the strict refusal of the Irish Censorship to allow such 'padding' and 'colour' which caused most dissatisfaction and which made the war coverage in the Irish press so anodyne. It should be noted that belligerent propaganda, in all its forms, was available in Ireland to those who wished to seek it out; it is impossible to state with certainty, but in general it is probably true to say that propaganda which was sought out usually 'preached' to the already 'converted'.

The Irish public was denied much information about the war because of the censorship; it should be noted, however, that no people received a 'full and honest' account because of the control exercised by the various governments and military authorities over information. The Irish control was merely the last of a number of censorship filters through which all coverage was passed. The war, in general, was not well reported by the Anglo-American media within whose sphere of influence Ireland lay. As we have seen, the decisive eastern front was the most poorly reported part of the whole conflict; the Battle of Kursk, for example, sandwiched in time between the Battle of Stalingrad and the Allied invasion of Sicily, is now acknowledged as having been one of the decisive military turning points of the war, yet it went unreported in the West.[47] The true nature of the disaster visited upon the Americans at Pearl Harbour remained concealed until after the war, early reports actually giving the impression that it had been an American victory![48] In general, there was an emphasis on battle, bravery and adventure and a failure to address the broader issues; for example, the US submarine offensive against Japanese oil tankers, which denied Japan its vital oil supplies and was largely responsible for its defeat, was not even reported upon because of a US Navy Department directive that nothing be written about submarines.[49]

The reality of Dresden was not reported in the Irish press at the time not because of the censorship but because Anglo-American news sources carried unquestioningly, in line with their general approach throughout the area-bombing campaign, the official line that this was an important military target. It was in fact a staging centre for refugees from the Soviet advance; 130,000 people are believed to have died in the horrific firestorm caused by the 750,000 incendiary bombs which were dropped on the city; bombers prevented fire engines and other emergency services from reaching Dresden while US planes machine-gunned survivors the next day as they struggled onto the banks of the Elbe. Some of these horrifying details began to appear in the press of other neutrals in the following weeks,[50] but not in the Irish press. This highlighted the major difference between Ireland and other neutrals in the area of media: the fact that the former had no war correspondents of its own and so could not even attempt an independent coverage of the war.

It is impossible to establish what difference a less rigid censorship would have made to the consensus about neutrality, especially in the second half of the war when the direct threat to Ireland had faded and the Allies were heading for victory. With regard to the role of the censorship in the survival of neutrality, it should be stated that if any of the belligerents had decided that the invasion of Ireland was a strategic necessity, they would not have needed the excuse of anti-neutral statements in the press to justify such action. Furthermore, the unpolluted hearts and minds of a united, resistant populace would hardly have counted for much in the absence of defensive firepower. Where the censorship was most effective was in influencing Irish self-perception about neutrality and in a support role in other areas of Fianna Fáil's domestic political and economic project.

It contributed, for example, to the temporary crushing of the IRA as a significant force and establishment of the 'rule of order' in the twenty-six counties. This was aided by the development of a specific twenty-six county nationalism whereby Irish public opinion was mobilised 'for the first time to consider the twenty-six-county state as the primary unit of national loyalty'.[51] (Fianna Fáil's Erskine Childers exemplified the synonymity of nation and state which developed when describing the Local Security Force as 'this volunteer army which, for the first time in history, brings the whole people of Ireland into the position of being responsible for the nation's security.'[52]) There was also the strengthening of the idea that the population of the state was 'a community' whose interests 'overrode the interests of any sectional groups'; this was a notion which was 'at the heart of Fianna Fáil's project'.[53] The censorship contributed to this development and also to the alliance which developed between Fianna Fáil and important sections of the trade union movement, just at the time when increasing state intervention in the economy required such good relations and anti-working class measures had the potential of provoking class conflict. (The Labour Party had long since accepted the notions of class harmony and national interest, and had failed to develop class consciousness or politics, allowing Fianna Fáil a clear field in establishing political hegemony over the Irish working class.[54]) The ITGWU claimed that the 'discipline and order' imposed by the unions during the war precluded a response on the part of workers which would have 'constituted a serious challenge to the economic policy of the Government'.[55] (This corporatist-type approach, in which organisations exercise control over their constituencies on behalf of the state, is itself a form of censorship.)

There was, in fact, no serious challenge to the government on any front. The Emergency Powers Act authorised the Censorship to do whatever was necessary or expedient for securing or maintaining public safety, the preservation of the state, public order and the provision or control of supplies and services. The generality of the principles that governed its operations allowed it to operate in a discriminatory manner which raised questions about the abuse of powers for party political purposes and, more fundamentally, about the class nature of the 'national interests' it set out to protect. Whatever potential opposition and dissent existed with regard to both domestic and international policy was smothered. The emphasis was on the preservation of the existing order. Neutrality, as interpreted and exercised by the government, was 'the only policy compatible with the security of the State' and thus became a *de facto* dogma. The democratic principle was reduced to its pragmatic simplification (the existing system and structures of parliamentary democracy); Aiken defined free speech as a 'liberalistic trimming' and presented the sovereignty of the state as the 'fundamental basis of democracy'.[56] This doctrine of 'sovereignty of the state' is ultimately guided by the principle of *salus rei publicae suprema lex* (the safety of the state is the supreme law)[57] and is more relevant to the tradition of absolute monarchy in which it is rooted than to the principles of democracy. Ireland was not alone among 'liberal democracies' in using the concept of national security as a justification for shutting off debate and stifling dissent; in adhering to the principle that secrecy and political censorship are intrinsic to the notion of security. The notion of a 'democratic concept of national security' whereby civil, political and even economic rights are 'major constituents of national security itself'[58] was unthinkable.

The system of parliamentary democracy that prevailed and which the government wished to protect was itself seriously compromised by the censorship of parliamentary opposition and particularly of election speeches. This did not raise too many problems within the system as the government and censorship had ensured a sufficient foreshortening of the political field to make dissenting contributions unlikely because of the electoral pitfalls they would create for their advocates. (Thus, while a significant number of Fine Gael members and representatives would have supported Irish entry into the war on the side of the Allies, only one – James Dillon – openly advocated such a course of action. His stand against the consensus led to his resignation from the party in 1942.) The extensive and arbitrary powers adopted by all democratic governments in wartime generally lead them, like totalitarian regimes, to suspect all who oppose them;[59] this tendency was given an added dimension in Ireland by the continuance of party politics and party government.

The information vacuum created by the censorship did help to create, to some extent at least, the 'moral neutrality' sought by the government, but in the process undermined the system of democratic decision-making, limiting people's options and denying them the opportunity of making informed choices about their individual and collective situation. This vacuum was often filled by rumours and scare stories, and could have been counterproductive if Irish neutrality had been put to the test.[60] In France, a flood of Nazi-inspired rumours released into a vacuum created by a censorship analogous to the Irish system is said to have hastened that country's demoralisation and collapse in 1940.[61]

Irish neutrality did survive, but the misinterpretation of the experience, facilitated by the censorship, deprived it of 'much of its potential value for the education of a people in genuine self-reliance'[62] and has subsequently distorted debate on the issue in a changing international context. In general, 'war conditions, even if they are experienced at one remove, can produce tremendous strains on society, rupture old relationships and provide the stimulus for new forms of rule';[63] Irish political culture, however, was particularly unreceptive to change and the emergency censorship was utilised in the protection of the political, social, economic and 'psychological' status quo. The structures and mentalities of Irish life were left largely unaffected;[64] in many respects, it was 'business as usual' in a rapidly changing world.

The excesses of cultural censorship had continued apace throughout the war years. The wartime restrictions on the outside markets that had sustained Irish writers did, however, force them to confront the censorship and the mentality which drove it more directly, principally through the pages of the new liberal journal *The Bell*.[65] A four-day debate in the Seanad in 1942 saw the first public appraisal of the Censorship Board; exposure and criticism led to the establishment of an appeals mechanism in 1946, but this made little practical difference and the postwar period saw the board continue to ban 'almost wholesale' most serious works of literature, culminating in a record number of bans in 1954.[66] The vast extension of censorship powers and the new levels of intrusiveness into private lives and control over what people could and could not read and see during the Emergency could not but have strengthened the censorship mentality in Irish life. A panoply of censorship regulations remained (and remain) on the statute books, symbolising the limitations of civic and democratic culture in Ireland, and contributing to the retardation of its development. The continuation of centralised and closed government, characterised by secrecy and clientelism, has had a similar effect.

Douglas Gageby, a distinguished postwar Irish journalist, claims that the strictness of the Emergency censorship 'probably had an effect on both the press and the public for some years after'.[67] The German ambassador to Ireland observed, a decade after the war, that Irish newspapers still lacked a perspective on world affairs. 'The Irish press', he wrote, 'in general only reaches the level of a provincial press'.[68] This situation gradually improved through the 1960s as increased education, prosperity and travel abroad, linked to economic modernisation and the advent of television, marked an emergence from the relative isolation in which the state had existed since its foundation. Despite this, however, the 'emergency mentality' persisted and the tentative moves towards openness received a serious setback because of the traditional 'national security reflex'[69] and concomitant censorious response of successive governments to the re-emergence of militant Republicanism in the context of the renewed Northern 'troubles'.

The official ending in 1994 of the state of emergency which had remained in place since 1939; the lifting of censorship restrictions in broadcasting; the increasing influence of more open European models of civic and political culture; the National Archives Act and freedom of information legislation – these developments have given cause for optimism about the future and the onset of a new era of 'openness, transparency and accountability'.[70] Such optimism must be tempered, however, by an acknowledgement of the frequent gap between rhetoric and reality; the fact that legislative change is but a small step on the road to changing a culture steeped in structural and self-censorship; the dangers of an increasing 'democratic deficit' accompanying European integration; the continuing existence of the Official Secrets Act and a wide range of censorship legislation; and the realisation that global developments (such as the replacement of state censorship with 'market censorship' and the concentration of control over global newsflow in the hands of a small number of countries and organisations) are increasingly important.

Much of the material contained in this study of censorship in Ireland during the Second World War has been brought to light for the first time. It adds a new dimension to the history of wartime Ireland and fills a gap in the history of Irish censorship, and in the history of wartime censorship on an international level. A number of issues which have been touched upon deserve more detailed research and analysis. For example, there is need for an evaluation of the impact of the Emergency on the state's administrative and political culture, and of its effect on the failure of the left in Irish politics. The development of twenty-six county nationalism during this period, and the longer-term implications of this phenomenon, deserves further attention. The brief examination of Irish censorship in a comparative context which was undertaken in this work could be usefully broadened to include more countries and extended beyond the time frame of this study. In general, a new history of wartime Ireland, based on the newly released archival material and the recent work on various aspects of the period, is overdue. Finally, while this book has filled a gap in the history of Irish censorship, that history needs to be rewritten, tracing the links in its development from the foundation of the state to the present day, placing it firmly in a comparative context and addressing, particularly, the role of censorship in weakening the development of a democratic and civic culture in Ireland.

NOTES AND REFERENCES

1   Eunan O'Halpin, 'Army, Politics and Society in Independent Ireland, 1923–1945', in T.G. Fraser and Keith Jeffery (eds.), *Men, Women and War* (Dublin, 1993), p. 171).

2   NA, D/FA (Sec.) A 8(1), memos and correspondence on Defence Security Intelligence, 16 May 1945 to 26 June 1945.

3   Telephone and postal supervision were continued under the civil authorities. In 1954 four temporary officials who had been employed for this task since 1939–40 were made permanent civil servants (O'Halpin in Fraser and Jeffery (eds.), *Men, Women and War*, p. 171).

4   Brian Farrell, *Irish Times*, 12 January 1994.

5   See, for example, Philip M. Taylor, 'Censorship in Britain in the Second World War: an overview', in A.C. Duke and C.A. Tamse (eds.), *Too Mighty to be Free: Censorship and the Press in Britain and the Netherlands* (Zutphen, 1987), pp. 157–77. Detailed accounts of British press censorship can be found in Francis Williams, *Press, Parliament and People* (London, 1946); Ian McLaine, *Ministry of Morale: Home Front Morale and the Ministry of Information in World War Two* (London, 1979); George P. Thompson, *Blue Pencil Admiral: The Inside Story of the Press Censorship* (London, 1947).

6   Taylor, 'Censorship in Britain', pp. 165–6.

7   ibid., p. 171.

8   The sources for this section are: MA, OCC 2/63, 'Press Censorship in Switzerland', including copies of Swiss Federal Council Decrees on censorship; NA, D/FA 205/8, reports from Cremins, Irish representative in Geneva; NA, D/FA 214/66, letter to Walshe on press censorship in Switzerland, 8 February 1943; NA, D/T, S 11306, Department of External Affairs (DEA) memo for de Valera on the press censorship of election speeches, 15 February 1943; *The Times* (London), 30 January 1943, 'Switzerland in War-time: resisting the assault of German propaganda'.

9   J.J. Lee, *Ireland 1912–1985: Politics and Society* (Cambridge, 1989), p. 265.

10 NA, D/T, S 11306, DEA memo, 15 February 1943; MA, OCC 7/1, DEA to Coyne on press censorship in Portugal, featuring the comments of the Irish chargés d'affaires in Lisbon, 15 February 1944.

11 NA, D/FA 214/66, Dulanty to DEA, January 1940; *Manchester Guardian*, 29 April 1940, *Irish Press*, stopped article, 12 April 1943.

12 MA, OCC 7/1, DEA to Coyne, 15 February 1944.

13 *Daily Express*, 10 February 1941.

14 MA, OCC 2/108, *Swedish News*, July 1942.

15 Robert Fisk, *In Time of War: Ireland, Ulster and the Price of Neutrality 1939–45* (London, 1985), p. 352.

16 Lee, *Ireland*, p. 262.

17 Fisk, *In Time of War*, p. 549.

18 See, for example, M.J. MacManus, 'Eire and the World Crisis', *Horizon*, Vol. V,

No. 25, January 1942, pp. 18–22.
19   Fisk, *In Time of War*, p. 549.
20   Lee, *Ireland*, p. 267.
21   Kevin Myers, 'An Irishman's Diary', *Irish Times*, 14 September 1990.
22   NA, D/T, S 11586A, 'Neutrality, Censorship and Democracy', Aiken memo, 23 January 1940.
23   Michael Adams, *Censorship: The Irish Experience* (Alabama, 1968), pp. 187–9.
24   NA, D/FA (Sec.) A9 (1), Coyne to Walshe, 6 May 1940.
25   NA, D/J, Press Censorship Reviews: 'Work of the Censorship', Dan Breen to the editor (*Irish Press*), 8 June 1942.
26   Trevor C. Salmon, *Unneutral Ireland: An Ambivalent and Unique Security Policy* (Oxford, 1989), p. 142.
27   See, for example, *Seanad Debates*, Vol. 25, censorship debate, January 1941.
28   NA, D/FA (Sec.) P 6, interview with MacDermot in the *New York Post*, 29 August 1941, quoted in a cablegram from the Washington Legation.
29   NA, D/T, S 11586A, 'Neutrality, Censorship and Democracy', Aiken memo, 23 January 1940.
30   T. Ryle Dwyer, *Strained Relations: Ireland at Peace and the USA at War, 1941–45* (Dublin, 1988), p. 56 (quoting Maffey memo on a conversation with de Valera, 24 December 1941).
31   Lee, *Ireland*, p. 262.
32   Ronan Fanning, 'Irish Neutrality – An Historical Review', *Irish Studies in International Affairs*, Vol. 1, No. 3, 1982, pp. 32–3.
33   Fisk, *In Time of War*, p. 170.
34   NA, D/J, No. 135, 'Ailtirí na hAiséirighe', Coyne, 1 March 1945.
35   MA, OCC 7/55, Aiken note, February 1944.
36   NA, D/J, Press Censorship Reviews: *The Standard*; D/J, Press Censorship Monthly Reports, September 1939.
37   Dermot Keogh, *Ireland and Europe 1919–1948* (Dublin, 1988), p. 203.
38   NA, D/J, Press Censorship Reviews: 'Work of the Censorship'.
39   Douglas Gageby, 'The Media, 1945–70' in J.J. Lee (ed.), *Ireland 1945–70* (Dublin, 1979), p. 130.
40   Terence H. Qualter, *Opinion Control in the Democracies* (New York, 1985), p. 148.
41   J.A.C. Brown, *Techniques of Persuasion: From Propaganda to Brainwashing* (Middlesex, 1983), p. 16.
42   NA, D/T, S 11586A, 'Neutrality, Censorship and Democracy', Aiken memo, 23 January 1940.
43   Michael Balfour, *Propaganda in War 1939–45: Organisations, Policies and Publics in Britain and Germany* (London, 1979), p. 429.
44   Phillip Knightley, *The First Casualty: The War Correspondent as Hero, Propagandist and Myth Maker from Crimea to Vietnam* (London, 1975), pp. 332–3.
45   See Taylor, 'Censorship in Britain', pp. 173–5
46   Qualter, *Opinion Control*, p. 139
47   Knightley, *First Casualty*, p. 262
48   ibid., p. 272
49   ibid., p. 299
50   ibid., pp. 313–14
51   Terence Brown, *Ireland: A Social and Cultural History, 1922–1985* (London, 1985), pp. 215–16
52   Quoted in Jim Dukes, 'The Emergency Services', *The Irish Sword*, Vol. XIX, Nos. 75 and 76, 1993–4, p. 68
53   Kieran Allen, 'Forging the Links: Fianna Fáil, the Trade Unions and the Emergency', *Saothar*, Vol. 16, 1991, p. 54.

54 See Paul Bew, Ellen Hazelkorn and Henry Patterson, *The Dynamics of Irish Politics* (London, 1989), p. 145.
55 Allen, 'Forging the Links', quoting *ITGWU Conference Proceedings*, 1942, p. 29.
56 NA, D/T, S 11586A, 'Neutrality, Censorship and Democracy', Aiken memo, 23 January 1940.
57 John Keane, *The Media and Democracy* (Cambridge, 1991), p. 113.
58 Richard Norton-Taylor, 'Secrecy that makes enemies of us all', *The Guardian*, 22 August 1995, quoting from Laurence Lustgarten and Ian Leigh, *In From the Cold: National Security and Parliamentary Democracy* (Oxford, 1994).
59 Qualter, *Opinion Control*, p. 147.
60 Among the rumours which circulated in the early months of the war was one that de Valera had been shot and another that Aiken had been interned in Arbour Hill jail. The government exploited the information vacuum in 1944 when it leaked rumours about an imminent American invasion around the time of the American Note episode, whipping up a feeling of threat and panic which suited its political purposes.
61 Qualter, *Opinion Control*, p. 160; Thompson, *Blue Pencil Admiral*, p. 42.
62 Lee, *Ireland*, p. 269.
63 Allen, 'Forging the Links', p. 48.
64 Lee, *Ireland*, p. 262.
65 Brown, *Ireland*, p. 174; Kieran Woodman, *Media Control in Ireland 1923–1983* (Southern Illinois, 1985), pp. 78–9.
66 Brown, *Ireland*, p. 198. The literary censorship is treated in detail in Woodman, *Media Control*; Michael Adams, *Censorship: The Irish Experience* (Alabama, 1968); and Julia Carlson (ed.), *Banned in Ireland: Censorship and the Irish Writer* (London, 1990).
67 Gageby, 'The Media', p. 125.
68 Lee, *Ireland*, p. 607.
69 Dermot Keogh, 'Ireland and "Emergency" Culture, Between Civil War and Normalcy, 1922–1961', Dermot Keogh (ed.), *Ireland: A Journal of History and Society*, Vol. 1, No. 1: 'Irish Democracy and the Right to Freedom of Information', 1995, p. 35.
70 For example, ibid., pp. 35–6.

APPENDIX 1

Memorandum for government from Frank Aiken, 23 January 1940

NEUTRALITY, CENSORSHIP AND DEMOCRACY

In view of the fact that statements made by certain Members of the Oireachtas were censored recently, and that action was taken against the *Irish Times* for ignoring the Press Censor's orders, it is likely that the question of censorship will arise for discussion when the Dáil meets. Certain of the statements which were prohibited publication were to the effect: (a) that one of the belligerents was a moral outlaw and deserving of destruction. This statement was embellished with the most vituperate epithets; (b) that we should declare our sympathy with its opponent; and (c) that we should abandon neutrality and actively participate in the war.

The line likely to be taken by certain Members in the Dáil is that censorship is neither necessary nor democratic; that according to international law people in a neutral state can think and say what they please about belligerents, and that if democracy is to survive they must be allowed to do so. It will probably be argued that this is a democratic country; that all citizens, and particularly representatives of the people and newspapers are entitled to express their opinion as to whether we should or should not continue neutral in view of changing circumstances, and that it is not only a gross violation of the personal rights guaranteed in Article 40 of the Constitution to prevent them from doing so, but dangerous from the point of view that this power might be used by an Executive to suppress the organisation of public opinion in favour of war, when war would be the best policy to safeguard the vital interests of the nation and to defend the moral principles which are vital to the well-being of the human race.

In view of the arguments which are likely to be used, certain points are set out hereunder in order to prove that it is both legitimate and necessary, in the present circumstances, for the survival of both neutrality and democracy, to maintain a censorship, and under that censorship to suppress the publication of matter which might be calculated to endanger the neutrality of the State and, in particular to suppress matter of the following type:-

307

(a)   statements or suggestions casting doubt on the reality of such neutrality or the wisdom and practicability of maintaining neutrality;

(b)   epithets or statements or terms of a nature likely to cause offence to the Governments of friendly States or to the members thereof;

(c)   expressions likely to cause offence to the peoples of friendly States whether applied to individuals or to the method or system of Government or to the culture of the people of such State.

Long before the present war the Government announced that it was its policy in the event of war to prevent any Power using this country as a base for an attack against England.

At the beginning of the war the Government announced that it was its policy to remain neutral and that it required extraordinary powers in order to make effective provision 'for securing the public safety and preservation of the State in time of war'. As there was some doubt that the expression 'time of war' might be held by legalistic minds not to include 'the time when there is taking place an armed conflict in which the State is not a participant but in respect of which each of the Houses of the Oireachtas shall have resolved that arising out of such conflict a national emergency exists effecting the vital interests of the State', the Oireachtas proceeded to pass unanimously an amendment of the Constitution which extended the definition 'time of war' to include the time in which the State was neutral. Very few, or no other Acts of Parliament, were passed with the same unanimity in the Oireachtas, or accepted with such unanimity by the people as a whole.

One of the extraordinary powers which the Government sought and obtained was that whenever the Government was of opinion that it was 'necessary or expedient for securing the public safety or the preservation of the State', or for the maintenance of public order in 'time of war' (as amended), it should have the power to make an order 'for prohibiting the publication or spreading of subversive statement and propaganda and authorise and provide for the control and censorship of newspapers and periodicals'. No amendment was suggested that this power should preclude the Government from suppressing the publication of statements likely to endanger our neutrality although the whole Act was discussed in relation to the declaration of neutrality made by the Taoiseach on behalf of the Government.

Apart altogether from the specific power given to the Government, in time of war or neutrality, to impose a censorship, we have the fact that the Government under Article 28 of the Constitution is given complete executive power, subject to the provisions of the Constitution. A specific exception to the executive power vested in the Government is made in relation to acts of war and it is declared that 'the State shall not participate in any war save with the consent of Dáil Eireann' unless in the case of actual invasion.

The Government is, therefore, specifically precluded from declaring war, and it is clearly to be inferred that it must not provoke war, and that it must use its executive authority to prevent any of its citizens provoking war. It must, in fact, do all in its power to keep the peace with other States until the Dáil decides that it is in the national interest to declare war.

In these days one of the most important weapons of war is propaganda. Indeed it would not be surprising to find that the Germans were using more man and brain power in spreading their own propaganda and stopping that of the Allies, than in their submarine campaign. In these days, therefore, no matter what the old and very much out of date international conventions contain, it behoves neutrals who want to remain at peace to walk warily in the zone of the propaganda war.

So well was this realised that following upon the declaration of war by England and France on Germany the Government set up a Censorship Branch. This Branch immediately proceeded to ban the publication of statements which might endanger our neutrality. Since then the Dáil has met on several occasions but no Member tabled a motion that the Government should allow a public discussion to take place on the question as to whether we should continue to be neutral or to participate in the war. Thus the legality of the Government's action in suppressing statements which might endanger our neutrality is reinforced not only by the great mass of public opinion but also, it can be fairly claimed, by the active consent of the Members of the Oireachtas.

Notwithstanding the fact that few would be found to question the legality of the Government's action in regard to censorship and neutrality, there may be some who will say that individual citizens and public representatives should be allowed to talk offensively about the belligerents and advocate the declaration of war on one or other of them. Freedom of this kind might have had certain usefulness in other countries in olden times in providing an outlet for a certain type of people who like blowing off steam, but in our country and in our circumstances it would be positively dangerous. As a nation we have a definite grievance against the nearest belligerent, but the Government have declared with general consent that we would be unwise, in the interest of the nation, to engage in war against this belligerent. Not all of our people approve of this policy, and if a certain section were allowed to talk offensively about the morals of Germany in relation to its aggression in Poland and elsewhere, we can be quite sure that others would try to express in even more offensive terms their detestation of British morality. If we were a nation of Dillons words would only lead to words. But we are not. And if a competition of this sort were allowed to start between gentlemen who would confine themselves to words, they would very quickly get supporters who would wish to use stronger arguments, and it might very well be that we would have a civil war to decide the question as to which of the European belligerents we should declare war upon.

Consequently, it would be the Government's duty, if it had not legal power to repress such activity, to seek that power immediately; and, as it has the power, it is its duty to use it.

Apart from the question of internal trouble arising through the expression of belligerent opinion, there is the question of international law and courtesy to friendly nations. There is nothing in the old Hague Convention which precludes neutrals from expressing sympathy with one belligerent and antipathy to the other as long as these feelings do not find expression in acts of war violating impartiality.

Nowadays, however, as has already been pointed out, propaganda is an important weapon of war, and the use of that weapon against a belligerent even by a neutral is coming more and more to be regarded as an act of war. But apart from the new status of propaganda, if a nation in its own interests prohibits the expression of antipathy to one belligerent and does not prohibit it in relation to the other, there is no doubt that the belligerent offended against will regard it as a departure from the impartial conduct which neutrality imposes. In our own interests and according to our declared policy we must suppress propaganda against the nearest belligerent and are thus naturally led to prevent propaganda against the other.

So much for the question as to whether censorship is legitimate and necessary to secure the continuance of neutrality. But what about democracy?

There are some self-styled democrats who would hold on to the peace time liberalistic trimmings of democracy while the fundamental basis of democracy was being swept from under their feet by the foreign or domestic enemies of their democratic State. Wise men, however, discard these trimmings when necessary in order successfully to maintain the fundamental right of the citizens freely to choose by whom they shall be governed. Wise Constitutions provide for such emergencies. Our own Constitution does so in Article 28. Under this Article the Dáil wisely gave the Government the power to legislate, when necessary during the emergency, by Decree. Thus the much loved trimming of discussion before legislation went by the board. Thus was the Government given the power to do away with a lot of other trimmings if and when necessary 'for the purpose of securing the public safety and the preservation of the State'. But the Government must summon the people's representatives to meet from time to time, and the Dáil has the power to ask all questions and to discuss all the affairs of Government and to change the Government if they think it wise. Between the meetings of the Dáil no representative has any more right than has an ordinary citizen to do or say anything that might embroil our people in war or render it more difficult for them to stay out of war.

The right of declaring war is a corporative right of the Dáil and no member of the Oireachtas or ordinary citizen has any reasonable grounds for complaint if he is prevented in time of war, in the interests of the preservation of the State, from expressing his opinion on the question of war and peace outside a meeting of the Dáil, in a manner which might endanger peace, and, more particularly when the majority of the Members of the Dáil have agreed to give the Government the right to suppress the publication of such opinions outside the Dáil.

Any argument that 'time of war' is different from 'time of neutrality' has no basis in our constitutional law and little or none in fact. The Constitution makes no legal difference but rather emphasises the identical gravity of the two emergencies. Neutrality is not like a simple mathematical formula which has only to be announced and demonstrated in order to be believed and respected. Instead of earning the respect and goodwill of both belligerents, it is regarded by both with hatred and contempt, 'He who is not with me is against me'. In the modern total warfare it is not a condition of peace with both belligerents, but rather a condition of limited warfare with both, a warfare whose limits, under the terrific and all prevailing force of modern total warfare, tend to expand to coincide with those of total warfare. In cold economic and military fact it is becoming more and more difficult to distinguish between the seriousness of the two emergencies called war and neutrality, indeed in terms of expenditure of man power and resources, and the general upset of normal life, the difference is rather one of geographical location than of legal status as a belligerent or a neutral. In the last war the belligerent Japan spent less than neutral Switzerland. Neutral Belgium is already spending from £60 to £80 millions a year in this trouble. A neutral perilously located in regard to the main belligerents may have to make more extensive use of censorship and other emergency powers than a belligerent situated a long way from the main theatre of war.

If the Dáil wishes, it can withdraw the right of censorship it gave the Government, but until it so decides the Government must use that power and all its other powers to maintain the neutrality of this democratic State.

When the Dáil is not in session and a situation arises which, in the opinion of one or more members of the Dáil necessitates a declaration of war, the proper constitutional democratic course for them to pursue is to ask the President, in pursuance of his powers under Article 13,2,3° of the Constitution to summon the Dáil for that purpose, if the Government refuses to do so.

If newspapers or ordinary citizens feel aggrieved they can make representation to their elected representatives.

Whoever says he is not satisfied with such a system of democracy in 'time of war' is either a very foolish democrat or an agent provocateur for those who want to overthrow democracy or to embroil us in civil or foreign war.

(National Archives, Dublin, Department of an Taoiseach, S 11586A)

APPENDIX 2

I.   DEFENCE FORCES.

Information of practically any kind relating to or affecting Defence Forces. Originals to be submitted in all except very trivial cases.

II.   DEROGATORY REFERENCES TO DEFENCE FORCES AND IRISH DEFENSIVE SITUATION.

Originals to be submitted in exceptional or glaring cases for present.

III. FOREIGN DEFENCE FORCES IN OR NEAR ÉIRE.

Rumours dealing with activities or alleged activities of the Forces (Ships, submarines, aircraft, etc.) of foreign States in or near Irish territory. (N.B. These should be submitted at once when not similar versions of stories already known to authorities.)

IV.   FOREIGN DEFENCE FORCES.

(a)   Foreign Defence Forces

(b)   Foreign Countries relating to war generally.

Interesting or important information relative to the Defence Forces, War Effort, Military Situation or Economic and Political Situation of Belligerent States, etc.

V.   ALIENS AND PERSONS OF ALIEN ORIGIN AND ASSOCIATIONS OR SYMPATHIES.

Duplicates of the notes kept by examiners in the Foreign

312

Correspondence Section on foreign correspondents in certain sections would be of assistance. Lists of aliens will be provided and Censorship can assist by adding ones not on lists or persons of alien origin and sympathies not already listed.

VI. EVASION OF CENSORSHIP AND OTHER EMERGENCY REGULATIONS.

   (a)   Evasion of Irish Censorship. (Particulars to be noted in all cases.)

   (b)   Evasion of Foreign Censorship.

   (c)   Particulars of evasion of other Emergency Regulations directly affecting Defence.

   (d)   Use of Ireland or Irish Post as means of evading War Regulations of other countries.

VII. FOREIGN ACTIVITIES IN IRELAND OR RELATING TO IRELAND.

   Information on persons or organisations conducting activities of any kind affecting Ireland on behalf of foreign Governments, organisations or persons either in Ireland or abroad.

   Activities might be: (a) Political, (b) Propaganda, (c) Espionage, etc.

VIII. INFORMATION RELATIVE TO:

   (1)   Irish position in relation to war (when not covered by I).

   (2)   Irish Political and Diplomatic Relations arising out of the War.

   (3)   References to Irish Neutrality and War Policy (when references, writers or addresses are of any importance).

   (4)   Possible invasion of Ireland (when not covered by III).

   (N.B. When important originals in those cases are sent to Controller a copy should be sent to Military Intelligence.)

IX. Supply from Ireland of Stores, Equipment, etc., for other Defence Forces and Related Services.

X.   ASSISTANCE BY IRISH RESIDENTS TO WAR EFFORTS OF OTHER COUNTRIES.

Information to be segregated by countries and to cover:-

(a)   Recruiting to British and Other Forces, General de Gaulle's etc.

(b)   Financial Aid, Loans, Subscriptions, Interest Free Loans, Gifts for specific purposes such as purchase of aircraft etc.

(c)   Subscriptions and Aid to Voluntary Organisations of various kinds such as Foreign Red Cross and similar Organisations.

(d)   Propaganda on behalf of belligerents.

N.B. The data collected under these heads would be with a view to indicating the general nature and extent of such activities and not to cover isolated individual acts.

XI.   ORGANISATIONS AND ACTIVITIES OF FOREIGN GROUPS IN IRELAND.

Data relative to activities, organisational, cultural and social of above.

XII.   INTERNATIONAL POLITICAL ORGANISATIONS or POLITICAL ACTIVITIES OF INTERNATIONAL BODIES SUCH AS:

(a)   Communism

(b)   Political activities of International Jewish Organisations

(*National Archives, Dublin, Department of Justice, Postal Censorship: 'Organisation and Administration', Appendix I*)

APPENDIX 3

DIRECTIONS TO THE PRESS

EMERGENCY POWERS (No. 5) ORDER, 1939

To the Proprietor of
the . . . .

      I, MICHAEL KNIGHTLY, CHIEF PRESS CENSOR, an authorised person, in exercise of the powers conferred upon me by the Emergency Powers (No. 5) Order, 1939, hereby direct that there shall not be published (save and except at the request of or with the permission of the Government or of an authorised person) in the . . . . or in any poster or placard issued in connection therewith any matter of the following classes, that is to say

DEFENCE FORCES.

(1)   Matter relating to the Defence Forces or to aircraft or vessels belonging to the State and, in particular, matter relating to

    (a)   the number, description, armament, equipment, disposition, movement or condition of the said Defence Forces, aircraft or vessels or their operations or intended operations;

    (b)   the manufacture or storage or place of manufacture or storage of war material, or works or measures connected with the fortification or defence of any place on behalf of the State.

(2)   Matter calculated to prejudice recruiting for, or to cause disaffection in, any of the Defence Forces.

FOREIGN AIR, NAVAL OR MILITARY FORCES.

(3)   Matter related to the presence or supposed presence within the State or in the vicinity of the State or its territorial waters any air, naval or military forces of any foreign state.

SAFEGUARDING NEUTRALITY.

(4)   Matter which would or might be calculated to endanger the policy of strict neutrality of the State and in particular:

   (a)   Statements or suggestions casting doubt on the reality of such neutrality or on the wisdom or practicability of maintaining neutrality,

   (b)   Epithets or terms of a nature liable to cause offence to governments of friendly states or members thereof,

   (c)   Expressions likely to cause offence to the peoples of friendly states whether applied to individuals or to the method or system of governments or to the culture of the people of such states.

WEATHER REPORTS.

(5)   Matter relating to weather reports and forecasts and any reference to meteorological conditions.

COMMERCIAL SHIPPING AND AIRCRAFT.

(6)   Matter relating to the whereabouts of commercial ships or aircraft within the State or the territorial waters thereof or to the movements of such ships and aircraft to or from the State.

SUPPLIES.

(7)   Unauthorised statements relating to the existence or dangers of shortage of essential supplies whether of a general nature or in respect of particular commodities.

FINANCIAL.

(8)   Matter which would or might be calculated to impair the financial stability of the State and in particular:

   (a)   Matter reflecting adversely on the solvency of the Exchequer and other public financial institutions or bodies, the standing of State securities or credit and the value or security behind the national currency,

(b)   Statements or suggestions tending to or likely to cause uneasiness or panic among depositors in banks including the Post Office Savings Bank or amongst holders of State securities,

(c)   Reports or rumours of the intended imposition of new taxation or Customs and Excise duties or the intended revision of existing taxation or duties.

CIVIL SERVICE.

(9) Matter likely to provoke discontent amongst servants of the State or that would be liable to cause a withdrawal of labour by any branch of the Civil Service.

Dated this 16th day of September, 1939.
Michael Knightly

. . . .

Chief Press Censor

SECRET — NOT FOR PUBLICATION.

EMERGENCY POWERS (No. 5) ORDER, 1939.
DIRECTION TO THE PRESS (NEW SERIES) No. 1.

To the Proprietor of the

. . . .

I, MICHAEL KNIGHTLY, Chief Press Censor, an authorised person, in exercise of the powers conferred on me by the Emergency Powers (No. 5) Order, 1939, and of every and any other power me in this behalf enabling, hereby prohibit the publication in the above-mentioned newspaper, or in any poster or placard in connection therewith, of any matter of the classes specified in the Schedule to this direction unless such matter has been submitted for censorship to an authorised person and the publication thereof has been permitted by an authorised person. For the purpose of this direction the expression "the war" or "war" wherever they occur in the said

Schedule mean any war or wars now in progress or lately terminated in any part of the world, and the expression "belligerent" means a belligerent in the war as thus defined.

Every direction heretofore given by an authorised person pursuant to Article 5 of the said Emergency Powers (No. 5) Order, 1939, is hereby revoked.

SCHEDULE.

NATIONAL DEFENCE.

1. **Defence Forces.** Matter relating to the Defence Forces (including the Local Defence Force) or to aircraft or vessels belonging to the State, their numbers, description, armament, equipment, location, disposition, movement or condition and, in particular, matter relating to personnel and appointments or matter indicating the designation or location of any garrison, unit or post, or disclosing any information concerning the operations or intended operations of said Defence Forces, aircraft or vessels.

2. **Military stores.** Matter relating to the manufacture, description, disposal, or storage or place of manufacture or storage of war material.

3. **Fortified positions.** Matter relating to works or measures connected with the defence or fortification of any place in the State.

4. **Air and sea ports.** Matter relating to the topography or equipment of or facilities available at any air or sea port in the State.

5. **Causing disaffection.** Matter calculated to prejudice recruiting for or to cause disaffection in the Defence Forces (including the Local Defence Force) or the Garda Siochana (including the Local Security Force).

6. **Civilian defence.** Matter relating to passive defence measures for the protection of the civil population, including air raid precautions, evacuation arrangements, etc.

7. **Photographs, maps and plans.** Matter consisting of photographs, maps, plans, sketches or other representations of a topographical nature likely to be prejudicial to the defence and security of the State.

8. **Defence Conference.** Matter relating to the meetings or proceedings of the Defence Conference and, in particular, any account or

forecast of the matters discussed or to be discussed or of action taken or to be taken by or on the recommendation of the said Defence Conference.

INTERNATIONAL RELATIONS.

9. **Neutrality of the State.**

Matter likely to be prejudicial to the neutrality of the State and, in particular, statements or suggestions casting doubt on the reality of or the practicability of maintaining or continuing to maintain such neutrality.

10. **Offensive comment on friendly states.**

Matter consisting of comment (including expressions, epithets or terms) likely to cause offence to the governments or peoples of friendly states, whether relating to individual persons or to the method or system of governments or to the culture, customs or habits of the people of such states.

11. **External relations and diplomatic activities.**

Matter likely to affect the relations of the State with other states and, without prejudice to the generality of the foregoing, matter relating to diplomatic activities by which the State would or might be affected irrespective of whether or not the State is or has been a party to such activities.

12. **Foreign comment on the State.**

Matter consisting of references to the government, the institutions of government or to the people of the State by members of the government or parliament of any other state, and foreign press or radio comment of every description relating to the government, the institutions of government or the people of the State.

13. **Book reviews.**

Matter consisting of a review or notice of any publication in any case where such publication contains matter likely to cause offence to the governments or peoples of friendly states.

FOREIGN AIR, NAVAL, OR MILITARY FORCES AND PERSONNEL.

14. **Recruiting.**

Matter relating to recruitment for the forces of any foreign state.

15. **Irishmen in foreign forces.**   Matter consisting of references to, letters from, or statements made by or purporting to have been made by any person of Irish nationality serving in the forces of any of the belligerents.

16. **Obituary and other notices.**   Matter relating to persons serving or who have served in the forces of any foreign state and consisting of notices or advertisements concerning births, deaths, or marriages, or of social announcements, in which mention is made of the military or other ranks, titles, appointments, or place of service of such persons.

17. **Decorations.**   Matter relating to the award of decorations or honours or to the mention in despatches of persons serving or lately serving in the forces of any of the belligerents.

18. **Internees.**   Matter relating to the internment by the State of naval, military, or air personnel of any of the belligerents.

19. **Deaths or burials.**   Matter relating to the death or burial in the State of naval, military or air personnel of any of the belligerents.

WARLIKE ACTS.

20. **Hostilities directly affecting the State.**   Matter relating to hostilities or acts of war directed or which appear to have been directed against the State.

21. **Hostilities indirectly affecting the state.**   Matter relating to hostilities between the forces of any of the belligerents which have taken place or are alleged to have taken place in or over the territory of Ireland (including the Six Counties) or the surrounding seas.

22. **Presence of foreign troops.**   Matter relating to the presence or supposed presence in, over or in the vicinity of the State or its territorial waters of any air, naval, or military forces or personnel of any of the belligerents.

23. **Bombs, mines, etc.**   Matter relating to the falling of bombs or the washing up of mines on the territory of the State.

24. Ships or aircraft in transit to or from Ireland or Irish-owned. Matter relating to attacks on or war damage sustained by or to the following
(*a*) any ship or aircraft in transit to or from any port in Ireland (including the Six Counties);
(*b*) any Irish ship or Irish aircraft anywhere.

25. Landing of survivors from ships or aircraft. Matter relating to the landing in the State of sick or injured persons or survivors from ships or aircraft attacked, damaged or lost as a result of warlike action in any part of the world, as well as accounts of the experiences of such sick or injured persons or survivors.

26. Wreckage, etc. Matter relating to the washing up on the coasts of the State of bodies or wreckage or to the finding or disposal thereof.

WAR NEWS, ETC.

27. War news or comment. Matter consisting of news or comment relating to the war which might reasonably give offence to the government or people of any foreign state.

28. War pictures. Matter consisting of pictorial representations (other than maps unaccompanied by propagandist comment) which relate directly or indirectly to the war.

29. Posters and the war. Matter relating directly or indirectly to the war which is intended for publication in any poster or placard.

30. Advertisements and the war. Matter consisting of commercial advertisements or notices which refer directly or indirectly to the war.

31. War charities. Matter relating to collections, appeals, or other activities whether by a single person or by a group of persons, or by any organisation for the purpose of
(*a*) providing for the supply of munitions of war for any of the belligerents, or
(*b*) for providing financial or other aid for persons affected adversely or injured as a result of the war.

32. Propaganda. Propaganda on behalf of or against any of the belligerents.

PUBLIC ORDER AND SECURITY.

33. Political or public offences. (*a*) Matter relating to outrages of a public or political character.

(*b*) Matter relating to the arrest, detention, trial, imprisonment or punishment of any person or persons in connection with any offence of a political or public character or under the provisions of the Offences Against the State Act, 1939, or the Emergency Powers Act, 1939, or any Orders made thereunder.

34. Non-compliance with the law. Matter advising, advocating or urging non-compliance with any Act of the Oireachtas or any Order made thereunder for the time being in force.

35. Public alarm. Matter likely to cause public alarm and, in particular, matter relating to attacks on members of the Defence Forces (including the Local Defence Force) or the Garda Siochana (including the Local Security Force) or on military or police posts or Government or public buildings.

36. Disparagement of State Forces. Matter tending to bring into ridicule the Defence Forces (including the Local Defence Force) or the Garda Siochana (including the Local Security Force).

37. Disaffection amongst State employees. Matter relating to the existence or alleged existence of discontent or disaffection amongst State employees or bearing on any actual or alleged or suggested withdrawal of labour or acts of sabotage by any person or persons in the employment of the State.

38. Inquests, etc. Matter relating to the death or burial of any person who has died while in lawful custody.

FINANCE.

39. Financial stability of the State. Matter which would or might impair the financial stability of the State and, in particular, matter reflecting adversely on the solvency of the Exchequer and other public financial institutions or bodies, the standing of State securities or credit or the value of or security behind the national currency.

40. Bank deposits and State securities. Matter tending to or likely to cause uneasiness or panic among depositors in banks (including Post Office Savings Banks) or amongst holders of State securities.

41. Taxation forecasts. Matter consisting of reports and rumours of the intended imposition of new taxation, Customs and Excise duties, or the intended revision of existing taxation or duties.

TRADE AND SUPPLIES.

42. Shortage of supplies. Matter relating to the existence or likelihood of shortages of supplies whether of a general nature or in respect of particular commodities.

43. Cargoes. Matter relating to the arrival, departure, or disposal of cargoes or part cargoes (including particular goods or commodities) at any port in the State.

44. Livestock. Matter relating to: -
(a) cattle, horses or other livestock sold or purchased for shipment abroad or to the movement, consignment, shipment, or disposal of any such cattle, horses or livestock; or
(b) cattle, horses, or other livestock purchased abroad for shipment to the State.

45. Disease in livestock. Matter relating to occurrence of disease in livestock within the State.

46. Bread. Matter in which use is made of the expression "black bread" or of the word "black" in relation to bread.

COMMERCIAL SHIPPING AND AIRCRAFT.

47. Commercial shipping and aircraft Matter relating to the whereabouts of commercial ships or aircraft within the State or the territorial waters thereof or to the movements of such ships or aircraft to or from the State.

MISCELLANEOUS.

48. Weather. Matter consisting of weather reports and forecasts and any reference to meteorological conditions.

49. Wireless. Matter consisting of communications or messages (other than matter broadcast for general public reception) received or intercepted by means of a wireless receiving apparatus.

50. Official statements. Matter relating to any matter which has been the subject of an official statement by the Government Information Bureau, other than the text of such statement.

51. Advertise-ments   *(a)* Matter consisting of advertisements (other than advertisements expressed to be issued by or on behalf of any business firm) relating to the purchase, sale or exchange of any commodity which is the subject of a rationing order or a maximum prices order for the time being in force.

(b) Matter consisting of advertisements issued by or on behalf of any person or persons or business firm outside the State offering to buy or sell gold, silver, plate or precious stones.

52. Carrier pigeons.   Matter relating to the finding of carrier or homing pigeons to which there is attached any article which appears to be a means of identification or a message.

53. Omissions in news-papers.   Matter consisting of any reference to or purported explanation of the omission of any matter from any issue of a newspaper.

54. Censorship.   Matter relating, either generally or with reference to specific instances, to the policy, administration, operation or activities of the censorship in general or of any of its branches.

55. General.   Matter not included in any of the foregoing classes the publication of which would be likely to be prejudicial to the public safety or the preservation of the State, or to the maintenance of public order, or to the provision and control of supplies and services essential to the life of the community.

Dated this 15th day of August, 1941.

MICHAEL KNIGHTLY,
Chief Press Censor.

(National Archives, Dublin, Department of Justice, 'Directions to the Press')

BIBLIOGRAPHY

PRIMARY SOURCES

Office of the Controller of Censorship
(*Military Archives, Cathal Brugha Barracks, Dublin*)

Files of the Office of the Controller of Censorship, 1939–45. The files are indexed and organised under the following headings: 1. Office of the Controller of Censorship, 2. Press Censorship, 3. Postal Censorship, 4. Telegraph Censorship, 5. Emergency Powers Orders, 6. Immunities and Exemptions, etc., 7. Miscellaneous Questions Relating to Censorship, and 8. Parliamentary Questions. A small number of files are 'closed' but the vast majority are available for examination.

Department of Justice
(*National Archives, Dublin*)

Although the Department of Justice had no direct responsibility for the emergency censorship (except for the role played by the official film censor) it became the repository for the majority of the files relating to it after the war. They include hundreds of numbered folders containing correspondence with editors, cuttings and general matters covering the treatment of most of the publications with which the Censorship had dealings; a series of 'R' folders containing stopped and deleted proofs from the principal publications and in relation to specific subjects; a series of un-numbered folders relating to various other matters with which the Press Censorship had to deal; reviews of relations with the national newspapers, the provincial press, some other Irish publications, the 'extern' press and of the work of the Press Censorship in general; directions to the press; instructions to press censors on how to deal with specific items and subjects; and the monthly reports of the Press Censorship branch.

The Justice files also contain the monthly reports of the Postal and Telegraph divisions, an extensive memorandum on the organisation and administration of the Postal Censorship, and miscellaneous other folders relating to the operations of these two branches. There are also a small number of files relating to the film censorship.

Department of Foreign Affairs
(*National Archives, Dublin*)

A number of files from this department relate directly to the press, postal, telegraph and film censorship, consisting primarily of matter touching upon the state's international relations, such as: postal and telegraph censorship in relation to the various missions of foreign governments in Ireland; complaints and representations from foreign representatives with regard to the press and film censorship; reports on censorship in other countries, etc. There is also a separate collection of files from the secretary's office, divided into 'A' and 'P' files, which contains extensive material relating to all aspects of the censorship. Of special interest are those which contain correspondence with the Office of the Controller of Censorship and with G2 (Military Intelligence), which liaised closely with the Department of External Affairs throughout the war. Many of this department's general files were also consulted for information on matters not directly related to the censorship. (A number of files remain 'closed', particularly those relating to postal censorship.)

Department of the Taoiseach
(*National Archives, Dublin*)

This department's 'S' files contain useful material relating to all aspects of the censorship. Of particular value are the files relating to planning and organisation and an extensive report by the controller, Thomas J. Coyne, prepared at the war's end, in which he surveys the wartime censorship, analyses its strengths and weaknesses from his perspective, and makes suggestions on how the system could be improved in any future emergency.

Cabinet Minutes
(*National Archives, Dublin*)

Books of minutes of cabinet meetings, containing occasional references to the censorship.

G2, Military Intelligence
(*Military Archives, Dublin*)

A number of the G2 files are available at the discretion of the military archivist.

OSS and US State Department Reports
(*National Archives, Washington DC*)

Files and reports relating to Ireland, 1939–45. (Thanks to Aengus Nolan.)

Parliamentary papers

The Dáil and Seanad were important as the only public fora where the censorship could be discussed and criticised, have its activities exposed and where it could be made somewhat accountable. There were a number of debates on the issue in both houses throughout the period, as well as a series of Dáil questions. The Dáil and Seanad Debates thus provided a useful and easily accessible source of information.

Other government publications

Bunreacht na hÉireann (Constitution of Ireland), 1937
Acts of the Oireachtas, 1923–45 (Government Publications, Stationery Office, Dublin)
Statutory Rules and Orders, 1939–45 (Government Publications, Stationery Office, Dublin)

Personal papers

Frederic H. Boland papers (Trinity College, Dublin)
Dan Bryan papers (Archives Department, University College Dublin)
Éamon de Valera papers (Franciscan Archives, Killiney)
Frank Gallagher papers (National Library of Ireland)
David Gray papers (F.D. Roosevelt Library, Hyde Park, New York)
Richard Hayes papers (National Library of Ireland)
Frank MacDermot papers (National Archives, Dublin)
Richard Mulcahy papers (Archives Department, University College Dublin)
Donal O'Sullivan papers (Archives Department, University College Dublin)

Note: Unfortunately, the Frank Aiken papers (Archives Department, University College Dublin) were not yet open to researchers at the time of completion of this work.

Newspapers and periodicals

The Bell, 1940–45
The Cork Examiner, 1939–45
Dublin Opinion, 1939–45
The Irish Independent, 1939–45
The Irish Press, 1939–45
The Irish Times, 1939–45
The Irish Workers' Weekly, 1939–41
The Leader, 1939–45
The Standard, 1939–45
The Sunday Independent, 1939–45
The Torch, 1939–44
Workers' Action, 1941–2

The Daily Express, 10 February 1941, article on censorship in Portugal
The Irish Times, 28 October 1972, article on the release in London of John Betjeman's wartime dispatches from Dublin
The Irish Times, 3 September 1979, 'The Days of Emergency' (anniversary supplement)
The Manchester Guardian, 29 April 1940, article on censorship in Sweden
The Manchester Guardian, 16 May 1945, leading article on the Irish censorship
The Times (London), 30 January 1943, 'Switzerland in War-time – Resisting the assault of German propaganda'
The Wolfe Tone Annual (1944 banned edition, published in 1945)

Television

'The Emergency', RTE September 1989

Interviews

Unfortunately, all of the major actors in the drama of the Emergency censorship are deceased. Interviews with a number of the leading figures were obtainable from a range of secondary sources, and are referred to in the relevant places. Discussions with many 'ordinary' people who lived through the Emergency years were very helpful to a better understanding of the period in general and the impact of the censorship in particular. (My thanks to all of them.)

SECONDARY SOURCES

Books and articles

Adams, Michael, *Censorship: The Irish Experience,* University of Alabama Press, 1968

Allen, Kieran, 'Forging the Links: Fianna Fáil, the Trade Unions and the Emergency', *Saothar*, Vol. 16, 1991, pp. 48–56

Andrews, C.S., *Man of No Property: An Autobiography (Vol. Two)*, Mercier Press, Cork and Dublin, 1982

Article 19, *Information, Freedom and Censorship: World Report, 1991*, Library Association Publishing, London, 1991

Article 19, *No Comment: Censorship, Secrecy and the Irish Troubles*, Article 19, London, 1989

Balfour, Michael, *Propaganda in War 1939–1945: Organisations, Policies and Publics in Britain and Germany*, Routledge and Kegan Paul, London, 1979

Bell, J. Bowyer, *The Secret Army: The IRA 1916–1979*, The Academy Press, Dublin, 1979

Bew, Paul, Ellen Hazelkorn and Henry Patterson, *The Dynamics of Irish Politics*, Lawrence and Wishart, London, 1989

Boland, Kevin, *The Rise and Decline of Fianna Fáil*, Mercier Press, Cork, 1982

Bourdieu, Pierre, *Language and Symbolic Power*, Polity Press, Cambridge, 1991

Bowman, John, *De Valera and the Ulster Question 1917–1973*, Clarendon Press, Oxford, 1982

Boylan, Henry, *A Dictionary of Irish Biography,* 2nd edn, Gill and Macmillan, Dublin, 1988

Brady, Conor, *Guardians of the Peace*, Gill and Macmillan, Dublin, 1974

Bridgman, Jon, *The End of the Holocaust: The Liberation of the Camps*, Batsford, London, 1990

Brown, J.A.C., *Techniques of Persuasion: From Propaganda to Brainwashing*, Penguin Books, Middlesex, 1983

Brown, Terence, *Ireland: A Social and Cultural History, 1922–1985*, Fontana Press, London, 1985

Browne, Vincent (ed.), *The Magill Book of Irish Politics*, Magill Publications, Dublin, 1981

Brunicardi, Daire, 'The Marine Service', *The Irish Sword*, Vol. XIX, Nos. 75 and 76, 1993–4, pp. 77–85

Butler, Hubert, *Escape from the Anthill*, The Lilliput Press, Mullingar, 1986

Butler, Hubert, Letter on Irish reactions to the Holocaust, *Irish Times*, 14 December 1978

Carlson, Julia (ed. for Article 19), *Banned in Ireland: Censorship and the Irish Writer*, Routledge, London, 1990

Carroll, Joseph T., 'A Tale of Old Ireland', articles on the censorship, *Irish Times*, 7 August 1993 to 13 August 1993

Carroll, Joseph T., 'US – Irish Relations, 1939–45', *The Irish Sword*, Vol. XIX, Nos. 75 and 76, 1993–4, pp. 99–105

Carroll, Joseph T., *Ireland in the War Years, 1939–1945*, David and Charles, Newton Abbot, 1975

Carter, Carolle J., 'Ireland: America's Neutral Ally, 1939–41', *Éire–Ireland*, Vol. 12, No. 2, 1977, pp. 5–13

Carter, Carolle J., *The Shamrock and the Swastika: German Espionage in Ireland in World War II*, Pacific Books, Palo Alto, California, 1977

Chadwick, Owen, *Britain and the Vatican during the Second World War*, Cambridge University Press, 1986

Chomsky, Noam, *Necessary Illusions: Thought Control in Democratic Societies*, South End Press, Boston, 1989

Chubb, Basil, *The Government and Politics of Ireland*, 3rd edn, Longman, London and New York, 1992

Clarke, Desmond M., 'Emergency Legislation, Fundamental Rights and Article 28. 3. 3° of the Irish Constitution', *The Irish Jurist*, Vol. 12, Part 2, 1977, pp. 217–33

Cole, Robert, 'The Other "Phoney War": British Propaganda in Neutral Europe, September–December 1939', *Journal of Contemporary History*, Vol. 22, 1987, pp. 455–79

Connolly, Cyril, 'Comment', *Horizon*, Vol. V, No. 25, January 1942, pp. 3–11

Coogan, Tim Pat, *De Valera: Long Fellow, Long Shadow*, Hutchinson, London, 1993

Coogan, Tim Pat, *The IRA*, Fontana, London, 1971

Coultass, Clive, 'British Feature Films and the Second World War', *Journal of Contemporary History*, Vol. 19, 1984, pp. 7–22

Cronin, Seán, *Washington's Irish Policy 1916–1986: Independence, Partition, Neutrality*, Anvil Books, Dublin, 1987

Cullen, L.M., 'Aiken and Censorship', letter to the *Irish Times*, 17 May 1995

Cullen, L.M., *Eason and Son: A History*, Eason and Son, Dublin, 1989

de Courcy-Ireland, John, Letter in *Saothar*, Vol. 17, 1992, pp. 11–12

Desmond, Robert W., *Tides of War: World News Reporting 1931–1945*, University of Iowa Press, 1984

Devine, Francis, 'Obituary Essay: "A Dangerous Agitator": John Swift, 1896–1990, Socialist, Trade Unionist, Secularist, Internationalist, Labour Historian', *Saothar* Vol. 15, 1990, pp. 7–19

Doherty, Richard, *Irish Generals: Irish Generals in the British Army in the Second World War*, Appletree Press, Belfast, 1993

Driscoll, Dennis, 'Is Ireland Really "Neutral"?', *Irish Studies in International Affairs*, Vol. 1, No. 3, 1982, pp. 55–61

Dudley Edwards, Owen, *Éamon de Valera*, GPC Books, Cardiff, 1987

Duggan, John P., 'The German Threat – Myth or Reality?', *An Cosantóir*, September 1989, pp. 6–12

Duggan, John P., *A History of the Irish Army*, Gill and Macmillan, Dublin, 1991

Duggan, John P., *Neutral Ireland and the Third Reich*, The Lilliput Press, Dublin, 1989

Dukes, Jim, 'The Emergency Services', *The Irish Sword*, Vol. XIX, Nos. 75 and 76, 1993-4, pp. 66-71

Dwyer, T. Ryle, *De Valera's Finest Hour: In Search of National Independence, 1932-1959*, Mercier Press, Cork, 1982

Dwyer, T. Ryle, *De Valera: The Man and the Myths*, Poolbeg, Dublin, 1991

Dwyer, T. Ryle, *Irish Neutrality and the USA 1939-1947*, Gill and Macmillan, Dublin, 1977

Dwyer, T. Ryle, *Strained Relations: Ireland at Peace and the USA at War 1941-45*, Gill and Macmillan, Dublin, 1988

Fanning, Ronan, 'Irish Neutrality - An Historical Review', *Irish Studies in International Affairs*, Vol. 1, No. 3, 1982, pp. 27-38

Fanning, Ronan, 'Neutral Ireland?', *An Cosantóir*, September 1989, pp. 45-8

Fanning, Ronan, 'Open file on censorship days' ('1940-1961, the National Archives'), *Sunday Independent*, 5 January 1992

Fanning, Ronan, ' "The Rule of Order": Eamon de Valera and the IRA, 1923-1940', in John P. O'Carroll and John A. Murphy (eds.), *De Valera and his Times*, Cork University Press, 1983

Fanning, Ronan, *Independent Ireland*, Helicon, Dublin, 1983

Fanning, Ronan, *The Irish Department of Finance, 1922-58*, Institute of Public Administration, Dublin, 1978

Fielding, Raymond, *The American Newsreel 1911-1967*, Oklahoma Press, 1972

Fisk, Robert, ' "But What About Democracy?" ', *An Cosantóir*, September 1989, pp. 2-5

Fisk, Robert, *In Time of War: Ireland, Ulster and the Price of Neutrality 1939-45*, Paladin, London, 1985

FitzGerald, Garret, 'Neutrality came from fear of ourselves, not Germany', *Irish Times*, 6 May 1995

Forde, Frank, *The Long Watch: The History of the Irish Mercantile Marine in World War Two*, Gill and Macmillan, Dublin, 1981

Foster, R.F., *Modern Ireland 1600-1972*, Penguin, London, 1988

Foster, R.F., *Paddy and Mr Punch: Connections in Irish and English History*, Penguin, London, 1993

Gageby, Douglas, 'The Media, 1945-70', in J.J. Lee (ed.), *Ireland, 1945-70*, Gill and Macmillan, Dublin, 1979

Gaughan, J. Anthony, *Alfred J. ORahilly, Vol. 2: Public Figure*, Kingdom Books, Dublin, 1989

Gorham, Maurice, *Forty Years of Irish Broadcasting*, Talbot Press, Dublin, 1967

Gray, Tony, *Mr Smyllie, Sir*, Gill and Macmillan, Dublin, 1991

Green, Candida Lycett, *John Betjeman Letters, Volume One: 1926-1951*, Methuen, London, 1994

Healy, Michael P., Letter on the censorship, *Irish Times*, 26 September 1991

Inglis, Brian, *West Briton*, Faber and Faber, London, 1962

Keane, John, *The Media and Democracy*, Polity Press, Cambridge, 1991

Keatinge, Patrick, *A Place Among the Nations: Issues of Irish Foreign Policy*, Institute of Public Administration, Dublin, 1978

Keogh, Dermot, 'De Valera, the Catholic Church and the "Red Scare", 1931-2', in John P. O'Carroll and John A. Murphy (eds.), *De Valera and his Times*, Cork University Press, 1983

Keogh, Dermot, 'Eamon de Valera and Hitler: An Analysis of the International Reaction to the Visit to the German Minister, May 1945', *Irish Studies in International Affairs*, Vol. 3, No. 1, 1989, pp. 69–92

Keogh, Dermot, 'Ireland and "Emergency" Culture, Between Civil War and Normalcy, 1922–1961', Dermot Keogh (ed.), *Ireland: A Journal of History and Society*, Vol. 1, No. 1: 'Irish Democracy and the Right to Freedom of Information', 1995, pp. 4–43

Keogh, Dermot, 'Profile of Joseph Walshe, Secretary, Department of Foreign Affairs, 1922–46', *Irish Studies in International Affairs*, Vol. 3, No. 2, 1990, pp. 59–80

Keogh, Dermot, *Ireland and Europe 1919–1948,* Gill and Macmillan, Dublin, 1988

Keogh, Dermot, *Ireland and Europe 1919–1989: A Diplomatic and Political History*, Hibernian University Press, Cork and Dublin, 1989

Keogh, Dermot, *The Vatican, the Bishops and Irish Politics, 1919–1939*, Cambridge University Press, 1986

Keogh, Dermot, *Twentieth-Century Ireland: Nation and State,* Gill and Macmillan, Dublin, 1994

Keogh, Dermot, *Ireland and the Vatican: The Politics and Diplomacy of Church-State Relations 1922–1960*, Cork University Press, 1995

Keogh, Dermot and Aengus Nolan, 'Anglo-Irish Diplomatic Relations and World War II', *The Irish Sword*, Vol. XIX, Nos. 75 and 76, 1993–4, pp. 106–30

Knightley, Phillip, *The First Casualty: The War Correspondent as Hero, Propagandist, and Myth Maker from Crimea to Vietnam*, André Deutsch, London, 1975

Lee, J.J., 'Aspects of Corporatist Thought in Ireland: The Commission on Vocational Organisation, 1939–43', in Art Cosgrove and Donal MacCartney (eds.), *Studies in Irish History presented to R. Dudley Edwards*, University College Dublin, 1979

Lee, J.J., *Ireland 1912–1985: Politics and Society*, Cambridge University Press, 1989

Liddel Hart, B.H., *History of the Second World War*, Cassel, London, 1970

Longford, The Earl of, and Thomas P. O'Neill, *Eamon de Valera,* Gill and Macmillan, Dublin, 1970

Lyons, F.S.L., *Culture and Anarchy in Ireland, 1890–1939*, Oxford University Press, 1982

Lyons, F.S.L., *Ireland Since the Famine*, Fontana, London, 1973

Mac Aonghusa, Proinsias (ed.), *Quotations from Eamon de Valera*, Mercier Press, Cork, 1983

McCarthy, Charles, *Trade Unions in Ireland, 1894–1960*, Institute of Public Administration, Dublin, 1977

McIlroy, Brian, *Irish Cinema: An Illustrated History*, Anna Livia Press, Dublin, 1988

McLaine, Ian, *Ministry of Morale: Home Front Morale and the Ministry of Information in World War Two*, George Allen and Unwin, London, 1979

McMahon, Deirdre, *Republicans and Imperialists: Anglo-Irish Relations in the 1930s*, Yale University Press, New Haven and London, 1984

MacManus, Francis (ed.), *The Years of the Great Test 1926–39*, Mercier Press, Cork, 1978

MacManus, M.J., 'Eire and the World Crisis', *Horizon*, Vol. V, No. 25, January 1942, pp. 18–22

McRedmond, Louis (ed.), '*Written on the Wind': Personal Memories of Irish Radio, 1926-76,* Gill and Macmillan/RTE, Dublin, 1976

Mandel, Ernest, *The Meaning of the Second World War,* Verso, London, 1986

Manning, Maurice, *Irish Political Parties: An Introduction* ('Studies in Irish Political Culture, 3'), Gill and Macmillan, Dublin, 1973

Matthews, James, *Voices: A Life of Frank O'Connor,* Gill and Macmillan, Dublin, 1983

Milotte, Mike, *Communism in Modern Ireland: The Pursuit of the Workers' Republic Since 1916,* Gill and Macmillan, Dublin, 1984

Milward, Alan S., *War, Economy and Society 1939-1945,* University of California Press, 1979

Moynihan, Maurice (ed.), *Speeches and Statements by Eamon de Valera, 1917-73,* Gill and Macmillan, Dublin, 1980

Murphy, John A., 'The Achievement of Eamon de Valera', in John P. O'Carroll and John A. Murphy (eds.), *De Valera and his Times,* Cork University Press, 1983

Murphy, John A., *Ireland in the Twentieth Century,* Gill and Macmillan, Dublin, 1975

Myers, Kevin, 'An Irishman's Diary', *Irish Times,* 14 September 1990, 13 April 1995 and 9 May 1995

Neuhold, Hanspeter, 'Permanent Neutrality in Contemporary International Relations: A Comparative Perspective', *Irish Studies in International Affairs,* Vol. 1, No. 3, 1982, pp. 13-26

Norton-Taylor, Richard, 'Secrecy that makes enemies of us all', *The Guardian,* 22 August 1995

Nowlan, Kevin B. and T. Desmond Williams (eds.), *Ireland in the War Years and After 1939-51,* Gill and Macmillan, Dublin, 1969

Ó Broin, León, *Just Like Yesterday, An Autobiography,* Gill and Macmillan, Dublin, 1985

O'Carroll, Donal, 'The Emergency Army', *The Irish Sword,* Vol. XIX, Nos. 75 and 76, 1993-4, pp. 19-46.

O'Carroll, John P. and John A. Murphy (eds.), *De Valera and his Times,* Cork University Press, 1983.

Ó Ceallaigh, Daltún (ed.), *Reconsiderations of Irish History and Culture: Selected Papers from the Desmond Greaves Summer School, 1989-93,* Léirmheas, Dublin, 1994

O'Connor, Emmet, *A Labour History of Ireland 1824-1960,* Gill and Macmillan, Dublin, 1992

Ó Corcora, Micheál and Ronald J. Hill, 'The Soviet Union in Irish Foreign Policy', *International Affairs,* Vol. 58, No. 2, Spring 1982, pp. 254-70

Ó Duinn, Tomás, 'An Irishman's Diary', *Irish Times,* 16 January 1992

O'Faoláin, Seán, *Vive Moi!,* Sinclair-Stevenson, London, 1993

O'Halpin, Eunan, 'Army, Politics and Society in Independent Ireland, 1923-1945', in T.G. Fraser and Keith Jeffery (eds.), *Men, Women and War,* The Lilliput Press, Dublin, 1993

O'Halpin, Eunan, 'Aspects of Intelligence', *The Irish Sword,* Vol. XIX, Nos. 75 and 76, 1993-4, pp. 57-65

O'Halpin, Eunan, 'Intelligence and Security in Ireland, 1922-45', *Intelligence and National Security,* Vol. 5, No. 1, January 1990, pp. 50-83

O'Shea, Finbarr, 'Government and Trade Unions in Ireland, 1939-1946: The Formulation of Labour Legislation', MA thesis, UCC, 1988

O'Toole, Fintan, 'Our second World War finally comes to an end', *Irish Times*, 10 February 1995

Oram, Hugh, *The Newspaper Book: A History of Newspapers in Ireland, 1649–1983*, MO Books, Dublin, 1983

Orr, Charles, Letter on the censorship, *Irish Times*, 21 August 1993

Pronay, Nicholas and D.W. Spring (eds.), *Propaganda, Politics and Film, 1918–45*, Macmillan, London, 1982

Qualter, Terence H., *Opinion Control in the Democracies*, St Martin's Press, New York, 1985

Quigley, Martin S., *Peace Without Hiroshima: Secret Action at the Vatican in the Spring of 1945*, Madison Books, Maryland, 1991

Raymond, Raymond J., 'American Public Opinion and Irish Neutrality, 1939–1945', *Éire–Ireland*, Vol. 18, No. 1, 1983, pp. 20–45

Raymond, Raymond J., 'David Gray, the Aiken Mission and Irish Neutrality, 1940–41', *Diplomatic History*, Vol. 9, Winter 1985, pp. 55–71

Rhode, Eric, *A History of the Cinema from its Origins to 1970*, Allen Lane, London, 1976

Rhodes, Anthony, *The Vatican in the Age of the Dictators 1922–45*, Hodder and Stoughton, London, 1973

Robertson, James C., *The British Board of Film Censors: Film Censorship in Britain, 1896–1950*, Croom Helm, London, 1985

Robins, Kevin and Frank Webster, 'The Media, the Military and Censorship', *Screen*, Vol. 27, No. 2, March–April 1986, pp. 57–63

Rockett, Kevin, Luke Gibbons and John Hill, *Cinema and Ireland*, Croom Helm, London and Sydney, 1987

Rosenberg, Joseph L., 'The 1941 Mission of Frank Aiken to the United States: An American Perspective, *Irish Historical Studies*, Vol. XXII, 1980, pp. 162–77

Ryan, John, *Remembering How We Stood: Bohemian Dublin at Mid-Century*, Taplinger Publishing, New York, 1975

Salmon, Trevor C., *Unneutral Ireland: An Ambivalent and Unique Security Policy*, Clarendon Press, Oxford, 1989

Schmitt, David E., *The Irony of Irish Democracy: The Impact of Political Culture on Administrative and Political Development in Ireland*, Lexington Books, Massachusetts, 1973

Share, Bernard, *The Emergency: Neutral Ireland 1939–45*, Gill and Macmillan, Dublin, 1978

Sheehy-Skeffington, Andrée, *Skeff: The Life of Owen Sheehy-Skeffington, 1909–1970*, The Lilliput Press, Dublin, 1991

Shipman, David, *The Story of the Cinema: An Illustrated History, Volume One: From the Beginnings to Gone With the Wind*, Hodder and Stoughton, London, 1982

Short, K.R.M. (ed.), *Film and Radio Propaganda in World War II*, Croom Helm, London and Canberra, 1983

Smyllie, R.M., 'Unneutral Neutral Éire', *Foreign Affairs*, Vol. 24, No. 2, January 1946, pp. 316–26

Smyth, Patrick and Ellen Hazelkorn (eds.), *Let in the Light: Censorship, Secrecy and Democracy*, Brandon, Dingle, Co. Kerry, 1993

Stephan, Enno, *Spies in Ireland*, Four Square Books, London, 1965

Strydom, Piet, 'Challenging the Boundaries: On Freedom of Speech, Protest and Irish Political Culture', unpublished paper, 1987

Swift, John P., *John Swift: An Irish Dissident*, Gill and Macmillan, Dublin, 1991

Taylor, Philip M., 'Censorship in Britain in the Second World War: an Overview', in A.C. Duke and C.A. Tamse (eds.), *Too Mighty to be Free: Censorship and the Press in Britain and the Netherlands*, De Walburg Pers, Zutphen, 1987

Taylor, Philip M. (ed.), *Britain and the Cinema in the Second World War*, Macmillan Press, London, 1988

Taylor, Richard, *Film Propaganda: Soviet Russia and Nazi Germany*, Croom Helm, London, 1979

Thompson, George P., *Blue Pencil Admiral: The Inside Story of the Press Censorship*, Sampson Low, Marston & Co., London, 1947

Van Hoek, Kees, *Diplomats in Dublin*, Talbot Press, Dublin, 1944

Wakeman, John (ed.), *World Film Directors, Volume One, 1890–1945*, The H.W. Wilson Company, New York, 1987

Wheal, Elizabeth-Anne, Stephan Pope and James Taylor, *A Dictionary of the Second World War*, Grafton Books, London, 1989

Whyte, J.H., *Church and State in Modern Ireland, 1923–1970*, Gill and Macmillan, Dublin, 1971

Williams, Francis, *Press, Parliament and People*, William Heinemann, London, 1946

Williams, T., Desmond, 'A Study in Neutrality', *The Leader*, January to April 1953

Woodman, Kieran, *Media Control in Ireland 1923-1983*, Southern Illinois University Press, 1985

Young, Peter, 'The Way We Were', *An Cosantóir*, September 1989, pp. 33–8

INDEX